# SYSTEMATIC THEOLOGY

## Volume I

# SYSTEMATIC THEOLOGY

## ROMAN CATHOLIC PERSPECTIVES

## Volume I

*Francis Schüssler Fiorenza*
*and*
*John P. Galvin, Editors*

**FORTRESS PRESS**    Minneapolis

*Dedicated to the memory of*
*John A. Hollar*

SYSTEMATIC THEOLOGY
Roman Catholic Perspectives, volume I

Scripture quotations unless otherwise noted are either from the Revised Standard Version of the Bible, copyright © 1946, 1952, and 1971 by the Division of Christian Education of the National Council of Churches, or from the New Revised Standard Version of the Bible, copyright © 1989 by the Division of Christian Education of the National Council of Churches.

Book design and typesetting by ediType
Cover and jacket design by Jim Gerhard

**Library of Congress Cataloging-in-Publication Data**

Systematic theology : Roman Catholic perspectives / Francis Schüssler
  Fiorenza and John P. Galvin, editors.
      p.  cm.
    Includes bibliographical references and indexes.
    ISBN 0-8006-2460-2 (v. 1 : alk. paper)—ISBN
  0-8006-2461-0 (v. 2 : alk. paper)
      1. Catholic Church—Doctrines.   2. Theology, Doctrinal.
  I. Fiorenza, Francis Schüssler.   II. Galvin, John P., 1944–
  BX1751.2.S888   1991
  230'.2—dc20                                                     91-678
                                                                  CIP

The paper used in this publication meets the minimum requirements of American National Standard for Information Sciences—Permanence of Paper for Printed Library Materials, ANSI Z329.48-1984 ∞™

Manufactured in the U.S.A.                                        AF 1-2460

95   94   93   92   91   1   2   3   4   5   6   7   8   9   10

# CONTENTS

## Volume II

# CONTRIBUTORS

---

**Anne M. Clifford, C.S.J.,** is Assistant Professor of Theology at Duquesne University. Her publications include "Creation Science: Religion and Science in North American Culture," in William Shea, ed., *The Struggle over the Past: Fundamentalism in the Modern World*.

**Regis A. Duffy, O.F.M.,** is Associate Professor of Theology at the University of Notre Dame. His publications include *Real Presence* (1982), *On Becoming Catholic* (1984), and *The American Emmaus* (1992).

**Avery Dulles, S.J.,** is the Laurence J. McGinley Professor of Religion and Society at Fordham University. He is the author of fifteen books, including *Models of the Church* (1974), *Models of Revelation* (1983), and *The Reshaping of Catholicism* (1988).

**Michael A. Fahey, S.J.,** is Dean and Professor of Ecclesiology and Ecumenism at the Faculty of Theology, St. Michael's College, University of Toronto. His most recent major publication is *Baptism, Eucharist, and Ministry: A Roman Catholic Perspective*.

**Francis Schüssler Fiorenza** is Charles Chauncey Stillman Professor of Roman Catholic Theological Studies at Harvard University. He is the author of *Foundational Theology: Jesus and the Church* (1984) and over eighty articles in the areas of systematic and foundational theology; he also co-edited and translated Friedrich Schleiermacher's *On the Glaubenslehre* (1981).

**John P. Galvin** is Associate Professor of Systematic Theology and Chair of the Department of Theology at The Catholic University of America. He has contributed to numerous theological journals, to *A World of Grace: An Introduction to the Themes and Foundations of Karl Rahner's Theology*, and to *The Praxis of Christian Experience: An Introduction to the Theology of Edward Schillebeeckx*.

**Roger Haight, S.J.,** is Professor of Systematic Theology at Weston School of Theology. His latest book is *Dynamics of Theology* (1990).

**Monika K. Hellwig** is Landegger Distinguished University Professor of Theology at Georgetown University. Among her recent publications are *Jesus, the Compassion of God* and *Gladness Their Escort: Homiletic Reflections for Sundays and Feastdays, Years A, B, and C.*

**Elizabeth A. Johnson, C.S.J.,** is Associate Professor of Theology at The Catholic University of America. She has published numerous journal articles and *Consider Jesus: Waves of Renewal in Christology* (1990).

**Catherine Mowry LaCugna** is Associate Professor of Theology at the University of Notre Dame. She has published numerous journal articles, and her book, *God for Us: The Trinity and Christian Life,* will be published in 1992.

**David N. Power, O.M.I.,** is Professor in the Department of Theology at The Catholic University of America. His publications include *Worship: Culture and Theology* (1991), *The Sacrifice We Offer: The Tridentine Dogma and Its Reinterpretation* (1987), and *Unsearchable Riches: The Symbolic Nature of Liturgy* (1984).

**David Tracy** is the Andrew Thomas Greeley and Grace McNichols Greeley Distinguished Service Professor of Catholic Studies at the Divinity School, the University of Chicago; Professor in the Committee on the Analysis of Ideas and Study of Methods; and Professor in the Committee on Social Thought. A member of the American Academy of Arts and Sciences, his most recent works include *Plurality and Ambiguity* and *Paradigm Change in Theology* (with Hans Küng).

# ABBREVIATIONS

---

AG   *Ad Gentes* (Vatican II's Decree on the Church's Missionary
      Activity)

DF   *Dei Filius* (Vatican I's Constitution on the Catholic Faith)

DS   H. Denzinger and A. Schönmetzer, eds., *Enchiridion Symbolorum*

DV   *Dei Verbum* (Vatican II's Constitution on Divine Revelation)

EM   *Eucharisticum Mysterium* (instruction of the Sacred Congregation
      of Rites)

GS   *Gaudium et Spes* (Vatican II's Pastoral Constitution on the Church
      in the Modern World)

LG   *Lumen Gentium* (Vatican II's Constitution on the Church)

NA   *Nostra Aetate* (Vatican II's Declaration on Non-Christian
      Religions)

PG   *Patrologia Graeca*, ed. J. B. Migne

PL   *Patrologia Latina*, ed. J. B. Migne

SC   *Sacrosanctum Concilium* (Vatican II's Constitution on the Sacred
      Liturgy)

UR   *Unitatis Redintegratio* (Vatican II's Decree on Ecumenism)

# PREFACE

---

Preceding and following the Second Vatican Council, Roman Catholic theology experienced profound growth and development. These volumes seek to explain the major elements of Roman Catholic theology as it has developed in the wake of Vatican II. They are intended to present postconciliar theology as faithful to the Roman Catholic tradition, influenced by historical and ecumenical studies, open to new philosophical currents, and sensitive to diverse historical and cultural situations.

Planning for these volumes began a few years ago when John A. Hollar of Fortress Press and the editors agreed that a brief exposition of systematic theology from a Roman Catholic perspective would be a useful addition to current theological literature. Karl Rahner's *Foundations of Christian Faith* is an exemplary introduction to major areas of Roman Catholic theology. Yet its philosophical categories often pose a difficult challenge for the student of theology. Moreover, it does not cover several topics important to systematic theology. The need for a less advanced but more comprehensive treatment was obvious. Some classic treatments existed. Yet, preexisting Vatican II, they were somewhat dated. Several excellent catechetical and popular volumes existed. But they often presented the basics of Christian faith without reference to contemporary developments in theological method and categories. We therefore envisioned a collaborative work that would be comprehensive in its coverage, understandable to students, and centered around the current state of the question and the diverse developments in Roman Catholic theology since Vatican II.

In asking individual contributors to offer brief expositions of specific theological treatises, we requested that each contributor keep five specific goals in mind. First, the work was to be rooted in Roman Catholic theology. This goal did not mean that the authors should follow either the manualist deductive method or a one-sided apologetical approach that seeks to prove certain theses. Rather, it meant that individual authors had a double task: to present the teaching of the Roman Catholic church and to discuss significant contemporary Roman Catholic theological reflection. They should integrate into their exposition the relevant Roman Catholic teachings from, for example, Nicaea, Chalcedon, Trent, Vatican I and II, and papal documents, as applicable to the specific topic under discussion. They should make clear what the Roman Catholic teaching is in regard to specific topics. In addition, they should refer to the most significant contemporary theological proposals from leading Roman Catholic theologians (such as, Karl Rahner, Edward Schillebeeckx, Yves Congar, Henri de Lubac, Hans Urs von Balthasar, Joseph Ratzinger, Gustavo Gutiérrez, and others).

The authors, of course, would write from their own specific perspectives as theologians and as Roman Catholics. This goal explains the choice of the title and subtitle. The volumes deal primarily with systematic theology, hence the title; yet in dealing with the specific topics, they represent diverse Roman Catholic theological viewpoints, as the subtitle indicates. We did not intend a handbook of Roman Catholic faith, in the sense that a catechism or a collection of official church doctrines might be. Instead we wanted a work that would explain the diverse theological perspectives within Roman Catholic systematic theology in the post–Vatican II historical situation.

Second, a major impetus to Roman Catholic theology within the twentieth century has come from historical studies. These historical studies have enormously influenced diverse areas of Roman Catholic thought and life. The historical-critical study of the Scriptures has led not only to a much more nuanced understanding of the origins of Christianity, but has also made possible a great degree of ecumenical consensus, as is evident, for example, in the bilateral accords between Roman Catholic and Lutheran scholars about justification, Petrine ministry, and Mary. Historical studies of Christian writers of the ancient church have also influenced liturgical renewal and sacramental practices. Other historical studies have shown that dominant interpretations of Thomas often reflected the rationalistic spirit of the age in which they were written rather than the theology of Thomas. Studies of the Council of Trent and of Vatican I have shown that their decisions were much more nuanced and much more sensitive to historical complexities than scholars had previously thought.

In the light of such influences, the contributors were especially asked to highlight how historical studies have uncovered traditions that have been neglected—-traditions that had become, in Karl Rahner's words, "the forgotten truths" of Catholicism. It is the achievement of Vatican II that its renewal of Roman Catholicism took place by means of a genuine struggle to reappropriate the tradition and wisdom of Catholicism.

Third, the contributors should take into account current hermeneutical theories and philosophical reflections. Many modern thinkers, from philosophy, sociology, history, and science, have influenced contemporary Roman Catholic thought. Philosophers such as Kant and Heidegger or Gadamer and Ricoeur have deeply affected contemporary theologians. Phenomenology as well as critical theory, literary theory as well as neopragmatism, have all had their impact. Individual authors will obviously have distinct philosophical and theological perspectives. Consequently, one or two perspectives might dominate in one contribution, whereas other perspectives will influence other contributors. In any event, the contributors were asked to spell out some of these influences in their contributions.

Fourth, contributors were asked to take into account the ecumenical dimension of theology, especially recent consensus and bilateral statements where relevant. They were to explain Roman Catholic theological statements in a way that is sensitive to other Christian churches, especially where the views of other Christians should lead Roman Catholic theologians to be more self-critical. The ecumenical context also requires that Roman Catholic theology not neglect its identity, and so the contributors were asked to make clear, where appropriate, the distinctive Roman Catholic theological position on various topics.

Fifth, the contributors were asked to be attentive to the current emphasis on practice, which has been especially highlighted in recent theologies of liberation. Roman Catholics and all Christians should be sensitive to the social and practical dimensions of their beliefs and reflections. The relation between theory and practice should not be seen simply as a concern of liberation theology in general or Latin American liberation theology in particular. Instead, it affects all aspects of theology. Many readers of the book will be engaged in diverse forms of ministry and come to theology with an ecclesial commitment. Thus the volumes should, where appropriate, address these concerns.

Of course, each contributor has addressed these five tasks in a distinct way. As individual contributors they reflect the diversity of contemporary Roman Catholic theology. Nevertheless, the above goals do provide the parameters for each contribution. Beyond these parameters, the editors did not intend to give the volume a specific theological orientation; nor did they seek to place the contributions within a uniform mold. Realizing that a collection of texts differs from the treatment of a single author and wanting to display the diversity within Roman Catholic theology, we decided that the volumes should follow the classic order of modern theological treatments. We sought to take into account the instructional order of many theological schools, especially in Master of Arts or Master of Divinity programs. Therefore, the order of the various treatises accords with the instructional order in many of these programs. The subject matter of the first volume is usually taught in the first or second year of studies, while the material in the second volume is usually covered in the second or third year.

In addition, it was our intention that the expositions would treat all of the major treatises within systematic theology, though not exhaustively. We did not intend that these two volumes should present the detail that a manual or textbook on an individual subject will provide. The volumes are not textbooks for individual courses in one or another locus. The size of individual treatises prohibits the required comprehensiveness. It is, however, hoped that the volumes serve as a survey and summary of many major topics covered in courses. They can also serve as review volumes for theological students seeking to survey the vast material that they have covered in their systematic theology courses. The volumes can perhaps also serve with some instructional guidance as introductory volumes that can present students with a view of the whole before they delve into the individual treatises. The volumes can also help those who have completed their formal theological education, but now seek some updating into the contemporary theological scene.

The editors wish to thank those who have helped us in various stages of the work's publication. We are especially thankful to J. Michael West of Fortress Press, who guided the manuscript to the final stages of its publication. We are especially grateful to Lucie Ferranti, John Gutierrez, Charles Kletzsch, David Lamberth, Frank Matera, Katherine Messina, and Elizabeth Pritchard for editorial and proofreading assistance.

The volumes are dedicated to the memory of John A. Hollar, the late Editorial Director of Fortress Press. The idea for the work came from discussions with him. Without his inspiration and vision, without his continued support and encouragement at the very early stages, these volumes might not have seen the light of day. He was attracted to the idea that a volume on systematic theology written by Roman Catholic theologians and published by a Lutheran-sponsored press would help make Roman Catholic theology available not only to Roman Catholics but also to a broader Protestant audience. It would also demonstrate to Roman Catholics the ecumenical character of the Fortress Press publishing program. His sudden and unexpected death brought sadness to all. If these volumes contribute to further understanding of Roman Catholic theology among Lutherans and Roman Catholics, it is in no small measure due to the ecumenical vision that he brought to publishing. For this reason, these volumes are dedicated to the memory of Dr. John A. Hollar, our editor and friend.

*Francis Schüssler Fiorenza*                                        *John P. Galvin*
Harvard Divinity School            The Catholic University of America

# 1

## SYSTEMATIC THEOLOGY: TASK AND METHODS

# 1

# SYSTEMATIC THEOLOGY: TASK AND METHODS

## *Francis Schüssler Fiorenza*

———————

This essay seeks to present a historical, descriptive, and systematic introduction to Roman Catholic conceptions of theology and theological method. After some introductory observations on the historical use of the term *theology* and on the Christian Scriptures as theological writings, the first section will profile three classic conceptions of theology, namely, those of Augustine, Aquinas, and Neo-Scholasticism. The second section will then analyze five contemporary approaches to theology, indicating the strengths and weaknesses of each. A third section will assess the diverse challenges that Roman Catholic theology faces today. It will propose as an adequate method of theology one that seeks to integrate diverse elements and criteria. Since discussions of method are usually more abstract than treatments of particular beliefs, a reader less familiar with or less interested in theological method might prefer to read the other chapters first and to return later to this analysis of theological method.

## FRAGILITY OF THEOLOGY

Theology is a fragile discipline in that it is both academic and related to faith. As an academic discipline, theology shares all the scholarly goals of other academic disciplines: it strives for historical exactitude, conceptual rigor, systematic consistency, and interpretive clarity. In its relation to faith, theology shares the fragility of faith itself. It is much more a hope than a science. It is much more like a raft bobbing upon the waves of the sea than a pyramid based on solid ground.

Throughout its history, Christian theology has endured this ambiguity. The relation of theology to faith has always reminded Christian theologians of its fragility, yet they have constantly argued for its disciplinary character and its scientific rigor. For example, Origen and Augustine sought to relate Christian theology to the philosophical knowledge and disciplines of late antiquity. In the medieval university setting, Thomas Aquinas began his *Summa Theologiae* by asking whether sacred doctrine as a discipline makes a distinctive contribution to knowledge beyond the philosophical discipline about God. In the nineteenth century, both Friedrich Schleiermacher and Johann von Drey argued for theology's rightful status within the modern university against challenges to that status. In the twentieth century, Christian theologians face the challenge to theology's rightful academic place both by the dominance of the natural sciences and by the emergence of religious studies, which sometimes relegates theology to a confessional discipline not based in the university.

The term *theology* is ambiguous etymologically, historically, and systematically. Etymologically, *theology* means the "word," "discourse," "account," or "language" (*logos*) of God (*theos*). The question, however, remains: Does it mean the Word of God as a subjective genitive, namely, God's own discourse? Or is it an objective genitive, meaning discourse about God? The former refers to the divine discourse itself, whereas the second refers to the human effort to understand the divine.[1] Within the early Christian tradition, both usages are present. Saint Augustine uses the term *theologia* in the *City of God* in its objective sense to refer to discourse about the divine (*de divinitate ratio sive sermo*).[2] Among the Greek writers, Dionysius the

---

1. Ferdinand Kattenbusch, "Die Entstehung einer christlichen Theologie: Zur Geschichte der Ausdrücke *theologia, theologein, theologos*," *Zeitschrift für Theologie und Kirche* 11 (1930): 161–205 (reprinted as *Die Entstehung einer christlichen Theologie* [Darmstadt: Wissenschaftliche Buchgesellschaft, 1962]). See also Gerhard Ebeling, "Theologie I. Begriffsgeschichtlich," *Religion in Geschichte und Gegenwart*, col. 754–70; J. Stiglmayr, "Mannigfache Bedeutungen von 'Theologie' und 'Theologen,'" *Theologie und Glaube* 11 (1919): 296–309.

2. Augustine *City of God* 8.1.

Areopagite (ca. sixth century), for example, uses *theologia* not to designate a human science, but the divine discourse itself, particularly the divine discourse of the Holy Scriptures. The Holy Scriptures do not just speak of God but are God's speech. Today this usage no longer prevails, and theology refers primarily to the human study of God.[3]

Historically, the term *theology* emerged as a common and comprehensive term for Christian theology only after the thirteenth century. Among the early Christian writers, the term primarily referred to the pagan philosophical speculation about God rather than to Christian discourse about God, for the latter focused on the divine plan or economy of salvation. Christian discourse, called Christian doctrine, was not simply theo-logy; it was not just another philosophical doctrine about God alone. Instead Christian discourse explicated God's "economy." It spoke of God's saving plan and action in Jesus Christ and in the Christian community. In the early medieval period, *sacra doctrina*, *sacra scriptura*, and *sacra* or *divina pagina* were the customary terms for the discipline. They expressed the primacy of the Christian Scriptures in Christian doctrine. As the medieval teaching evolved from a commentary on the Scriptures or from an exposition of questions appended to scriptural texts to a full-fledged systematic discussion of controversial issues, the term *theology* emerged as the umbrella expression for Christian doctrine. It was in the thirteenth century that the term *theology* came to have the comprehensive meaning that it has for us today.[4]

Considered systematically, the present usage of the term is also ambiguous. *Theology* is often used as an umbrella term to cover all the theological disciplines. Yet the term also denotes a specific discipline known as systematic theology. The division of the theological disciplines is the result of a long process within modern times.[5] *Theology* is also often used in contradistinction from religious studies, the former referring to a confessional approach, the latter prescinding from such commitments.[6] Yet "religious studies" and "theological studies" are sometimes used interchangeably.

---

3. See Joseph Ratzinger, *Principles of Catholic Theology: Building Stones for a Fundamental Theology* (San Francisco: Ignatius Press, 1987), 320–22.

4. J. Riviére, "Theologia," *Revue des sciences religieuses* 16 (1936): 47–57.

5. Edward Farley, *Theologia: The Fragmentation and Unity of Theological Education* (Philadelphia: Fortress Press, 1983).

6. Francis Schüssler Fiorenza, "Theological and Religious Studies: The Contest of the Faculties," in Barbara Wheeler and Edward Farley, eds., *Shifting Boundaries: Contextual Approaches to the Structure of Theological Education* (Atlanta: Westminster Press, 1991).

The nature and method of theology are issues about which much diversity exists in the history of Christian thought, a diversity of schools, methods, and approaches.[7] Nevertheless, amid all this diversity there are several constants. In examining the tasks and methods of theology, we must recognize both the diversity and the constancy.

One constant is the Scriptures, a primary element of Christian communities' tradition and identity.[8] Yet the meaning of the Scriptures depends upon their interpretation. Augustine's interpretation of the Scriptures relied heavily on his background theory of Neo-Platonic hermeneutics. In the nineteenth century, the historical-critical method came into use as an interpretive tool. Today a multiplicity of hermeneutical theories affect our practices of interpretation. The constant of Scripture remains, yet the means of interpretation vary. The same is true of a community's tradition and creedal statements.

The experience of the community is another constant within theology. Yet that constant has also functioned diversely. Not only do different communities have different experiences, but different theologies have weighted communities' experience differently and have employed quite diverse categories to interpret that experience. The appeal to a community's experience is a constant, but its function differs considerably throughout the history of Christian theology.

Another constant is the reliance on some basic approach, procedure, or method to interpret the Scriptures, tradition, and experience. Such a procedure may be a general, implicit approach or an explicit, specific method. Such procedures constitute what could be called background theories, for they affect how the community interprets its discourse, its tradition, and its experience. Therefore, analyses of the nature of Christian theology, its task and method, should attend to the interplay between the constants of tradition, experience, and background theories that interpret tradition and experience.[9]

## CHRISTIAN SCRIPTURES:
## TESTIMONY AND THEOLOGICAL REFLECTION

Modern theology has become acutely aware that theological reflection is at the center of the Scriptures. The Scriptures are not simply

---

7. Yves Congar, *A History of Theology* (Garden City, N.Y.: Doubleday, 1968).

8. Francis Schüssler Fiorenza, "The Crisis of Scriptural Authority: Interpretation and Reception," *Interpretation* 44 (1990): 353–68.

9. The systematic nature of the task of attending to tradition, experience, background theory, and community is developed in the final section of this essay.

sources for theological reflection but themselves are examples of theological reflection. The Christian Scriptures do not simply witness to Jesus as the Christ; nor do they merely testify to the faith of the early Christian communities. Their witness takes place in the midst of an attempt to interpret Jesus theologically and is the testimony of a reflective faith. The Christian Scriptures, therefore, are constituted not only by the symbols and testimonies of faith, but also by that theological reflection emerging within those symbols and testimonies.

Such a view of the Christian Scriptures contrasts with previous views. Formerly, the Scriptures were seen primarily as a source providing principles for theology or as the object of theological reflection. In the nineteenth century, some scholars acknowledged only certain writings of the Scriptures as embodiments of theological reflection. They viewed, for example, Paul and John as great theologians, but the authors of the Synoptics only as collectors or editors of source materials. Today, it is commonly agreed that all the writings are theological. There is no part of the Christian Scriptures that is not at the same time an expression of a reflective witness and a believing theology.

This conviction was strongly affirmed in the Second Vatican Council. The Dogmatic Constitution on Divine Revelation (*Dei Verbum*) accented the extent to which theological reflection permeates the New Testament writings. Section 19 in chapter 5 affirms: "The sacred authors wrote the four Gospels, selecting some things from the many which had been handed on by word of mouth or in writing, reducing some of them to a synthesis, explicating [*explanantes*] some things in view of the situation of their churches, and preserving the form of proclamation but always in such a fashion that they told us the honest truth about Jesus."[10] This text refers to the selection of materials, the interpretation of traditions, explanations related to specific situations, theological synthesis, and pastoral applications. All of these elements make up the writing of the Gospels. The four Gospels give witness to Jesus in reflecting theologically on his meaning and significance for their particular pastoral situations.

This recognition of the relation between theological reflection and the New Testament writings has entered into the contempo-

---

10. Second Vatican Council, Dogmatic Constitution on Divine Revelation (*Dei Verbum*), in Walter M. Abbott, ed., *The Documents of Vatican II* (Chicago: Follet Publishing Co., 1966). See also the commentary by Joseph Fitzmyer in *Theological Studies* 25 (1964): 386–408. See the extended commentary on the constitution in vol. 3 of Herbert Vorgrimler, ed., *Commentary on the Documents of Vatican II* (New York: Herder, 1969).

rary conceptions of the nature of the Scriptures and their origin.[11] Recent theories of inspiration have related inspiration to the very formation of the Scriptures.[12] The complex elements that led to the formation of the Scriptures—originating events and their interpretation, new situations, and new reflection—are integrated within the theory of inspiration. Inspiration belongs to the whole process of the community's reflection and interpretation of its originating events. This whole process of the formation of the Scriptures provides, some argue, paradigms for our theological reflection.[13]

Today we are aware that the Scriptures are theological. They do not only contain the subject matter of theology. They also embody specific and differing theological visions. This awareness corresponds to a consensus among Christian theologians and church documents.[14] Moreover, our awareness of the historicity of Christian theology and the Christian Scriptures is one of the specific characteristics of modern theology. Yet before we survey modern and contemporary conceptions of theology, we will examine three classic and influential conceptions of theology.

## THREE CLASSIC PARADIGMS OF THEOLOGY

The Augustinian, Thomistic, and Neo-Scholastic approaches to theology represent the three most influential traditions within Western Roman Catholic theology as an academic discipline. In addition to these approaches, the Roman Catholic tradition contains many other schools of theology. A rich diversity of ascetic, spiritual, and liturgical theologies exists in the West. Monastic as well as academic traditions exist. Eastern Christianity contains other rich traditions. My focus on just the Augustinian, Thomistic, and Neo-Scholastic approaches is not meant to slight these other traditions; it is meant to provide a somewhat more detailed examination of those traditions most influential in Western academic theology. Such a focus, moreover, enables one to grasp much more clearly the major changes and transitions

11. Karl Rahner, "Theology of the New Testament" and "Exegesis and Dogmatic Theology," in *Theological Investigations* (New York: Crossroad, 1966), 5:23–41. See also Rahner's *Inspiration in the Bible*, 2d rev. ed (New York: Herder, 1964).

12. See Paul Achtemeier, *The Inspiration of Scripture: Problems and Proposals* (Philadelphia: Westminster Press, 1980).

13. See James P. Sanders, *Canon and Community: A Guide to Canonical Criticism* (Philadelphia: Fortress Press, 1984).

14. See the collection of essays illustrating this point: Roland Murphy, ed., *Theology, Exegesis, and Proclamation* (New York: Herder and Herder, 1971). See also Bruce Vawter, *Biblical Inspiration* (Philadelphia: Westminster Press, 1971).

that have occurred in the academic study and teaching of Roman Catholic theology.[15]

## AUGUSTINE: CHRISTIAN DOCTRINE AS WISDOM

During the early church period, the plurality and diversity of theological conceptions are unmistakable. In the second century, the apostolic fathers (Clement of Rome, Hermas, Ignatius, Polycarp) continually wrestled with the relation between Christianity and Judaism. The Apologists (Justin, Aristides, Athenagoras) sought to relate Christianity to the educated and philosophical culture of the Greco-Roman empire. Of the anti-Gnostic writers, Irenaeus especially contributed to theological method not only through his understanding of tradition and of the rule of faith, but also through his exposition "hypothesis" or system of truth.[16] In the third century, the schools of Antioch and Alexandria developed distinctive exegetical approaches and the beginnings of systematic theology sprouted their roots in the work of Origen.

### Beginning of Systematic Theology in the Greek Church

Origen's *On First Principles (Peri Archon)* makes a threefold contribution to a systematic presentation of the Christian faith. First, Origen attempted to give a foundation for the scientific exegesis of the Scriptures.[17] Second, he developed a systematic theory of religious knowledge. Third, he gave a systematic presentation of theology that indeed has earned him the label of the first systematic theologian.[18] Origen's *On First Principles* (published in 220) has been traditionally seen as a first attempt to bring the truths of the Christian faith into a theological synthesis. The traditional edition of this work, however, distorts its actual genre, which has been brought to light by a recent critical edition.[19] The book is neither a *summa* nor a systematic

---

15. For a complete survey of the history of Christian theology and doctrine, see the five-volume work by Jaroslav Pelikan, *The Christian Tradition* (Chicago: University of Chicago Press, 1971–88). Earlier and somewhat dated presentations are: Reinhold Seeberg, *The History of Doctrines* (Grand Rapids, Mich.: Baker House, 1977; German edition, 1895); Adolf von Harnack, *History of Dogma*, 7 vols. (New York: Dover, 1961; German edition, 1900).

16. See Philip Hefner, "Theological Methodology and St. Irenaeus," *Journal of Religion* 44 (1964): 294–309.

17. See Joseph Wilson Trigg, *Origen: The Bible and Philosophy in the Third-Century Church* (Atlanta: John Knox, 1983).

18. Marguerite Harl, *Origène et la fonction révélatrice du Verbe Incarnè* (Paris: Éditions du Seuil, 1958), 346–59.

19. See Marguerite Harl's essays "Recherches sur le *Peri archon* d'Origène vue d'une nouvelle édition: La division en chapitres," in F. L. Cross, ed., *Studia Patris-*

theology, but rather a systematic exposition of God's relation to the world.

In his preface, Origen explains that the church's tradition contains the canon of faith, and the theologian has the responsibility to explicate its inner rationale and implications. In seeking to accomplish this task, Origen adopted a specific genre of philosophical literature—one that dealt with questions of physics as the foundation of philosophy. This genre sought for a first principle or the first principles of the universe. As a Christian, Origen considered God to be the beginning or first principle of the world. Therefore he sought to synthesize the issues of physics, philosophy, and theology. The first part of *On First Principles* is a general treatise. It deals with God the Father, Christ, the Holy Spirit, and the Trinity, then with the four types of rational creatures, and finally with the created world and its return to God. The second part, following the same order, deals with special topics under each of these headings. Finally, there is a recapitulation of the topics. The overall effect is to show that all comes from the divine unity and returns to the divine unity. Through such an arrangement Origen explicated his Christian faith in relation to the philosophical categories and literature of his time.

### Augustine's Scientific Conception: Knowledge and Wisdom

Although Origen's originality has led many to consider him the first systematic theologian, it is Saint Augustine who has had the major impact upon the development of Christian systematic theology in the West. Augustine's contribution to the development of Western theological method lies in his conception of theology as wisdom, his hermeneutical rules for the interpretation of Scripture, and his influence upon the structure of the medieval *summa*.

Significant for Augustine's understanding of theology, or more properly, Christian doctrine, is his distinction between wisdom (*sapientia*) and knowledge (*scientia*). Whereas wisdom has as its object the eternal and unchangeable reality, knowledge is the rational insight into visible, perceptible, changeable, and temporal things.[20] Augustine does not equate knowledge with an empirical rationality, as our modern view does. Instead Augustine views wisdom and human hap-

---

*tica* III, Texte und Untersuchungen zur Geschichte der altchristlichen Literatur 78 (Berlin: Akademie-Verlag, 1961): 57ff., and "Structure et cohérence du *Peri archon*," in Henri Crouzel, ed., *Origeniana* (Bari, Italy: Istituto di letteratura cristiana antica, 1975), 11–32. The critical edition is in Henri Crouzel and Manlio Simonetti, eds. and trans., *Sources chrétiennes* (Paris: Éditions du Cerf, 1978 and 1980).

20. Augustine *On the Trinity* 12.15.25. See also 12.14.22–23.

piness as the goal of knowledge—a knowledge stemming from three sources: experience, authority, and signs.[21]

Knowledge from *experience* is not, as in modern experimental science, gained from experimentation characterized by confirmation and verification of hypotheses. Instead this knowledge starts with the world of appearances in order to arrive at the intelligible and the first cause of things. Knowledge proceeds from the visible to the invisible, from appearances to reality. Knowledge from experience is, therefore, a knowledge of the intelligible.

Knowledge from *authority* is knowledge based not on what one experiences oneself, but rather on testimony. Although Augustine maintains that knowledge from direct experience is preferable to knowledge based on human authority, he argues that the situation is different in regard to the authority of divine wisdom. The invisible has become visible in Christ. Through his miracles, life, and teaching, Christ is the mediator and revealer of truth; he is the divine authority.[22] Moreover, the Scriptures contain the testimony to his authority as the revealer of the divine truth. This testimony calls for a faith in Christ and provides for a knowledge based on his authority.[23]

In addition, there is knowledge from *signs*, which also enables one to go beyond the knowledge of immediate experience.[24] The external form of a perceptible sign refers to something else, hidden from the senses, in the way, for example, smoke refers to a fire. Signs are of two kinds: either natural or "given" (*signa data*). Natural signs make us aware of something without the intention of signifying, as smoke makes us aware of fire. "Given" signs are signs that occur when someone wills they occur.[25] They are given by humans or by God. The most important of them is the Word. As a sign the Word is a source of knowledge and learning. The words of Scripture are signs that refer to the transcendent. The key task of the interpreter of the Scriptures, therefore, is to interpret their transcendent reference. A

21. For an analysis of Augustine's method, see Rudolf Lorenz, "Die Wissenschaftslehre Augustinus," *Zeitschrift für Kirchengeschichte* 67 (1955/1956): 29–60 and 213–51.

22. See Augustine *On the Trinity* 13.19.24 (*Patrologia Latina*, 42, col. 1034).

23. See Augustine's "Letter 120" to Consentius 120.2.9.1–3 (*Corpus Scriptorum Ecclesiasticorum Latinorum* 63, 182, 16–19). See Karl-Heinrich Lütcke, *"Auctoritas" bei Augustinus* (Stuttgart: Kohlhammer, 1968).

24. For Augustine's conception of sign, see R. A. Markus, "St. Augustine on Signs," and B. Darrell Jackson, "The Theory of Signs in St. Augustine's *De Doctrina Christiana*," in R. A. Markus, ed., *Augustine: A Collection of Critical Essays* (Garden City, N.Y.: Doubleday, 1972), respectively, 61–91 and 92–137.

25. J. Engels, "La doctrine du signe chez saint Augustin," in F. L. Cross, ed., *Studia Patristica* VI, Texte und Untersuchungen zur Geschichte der altchristlichen Literatur 81 (Berlin: Akademie-Verlag, 1962), 366–73, argues that "signa data" should not be translated as "conventional signs" because of their intentional character.

genuine interpretation of the Scriptures yields a knowledge of the verbal signs of the invisible God. Consequently, a correspondence exists between Augustine's interpretation of the Scriptures and his theory of knowledge.

## Augustine's Hermeneutical Rules

In *On Christian Doctrine*, Augustine developed principles and rules for the interpretation of the Scriptures.[26] In so doing, Augustine provided important and influential contributions to rhetoric, education, theology, and hermeneutics. Augustine's hermeneutical theory should be understood in relation to his Neo-Platonic background and his attempt to come to grips with the incarnation of the divine wisdom. The Platonic *chorismos* schema, namely, the distinction between the changeable and unchangeable, the temporal and eternal, provides the background theory to his rules of interpretation.[27] The changeable should be interpreted in relation to the unchangeable, the temporal to the eternal, the world to the transcendent, historical events to the divine plan of salvation, and the human Christ to the Divine Word. Augustine's hermeneutical theory bases signification upon the ontological priority of the unchangeable eternal to the changeable and material.

This conviction (concerning the ontological priority of the transcendent reality over the material sign) leads Augustine to his basic principle of hermeneutics: What is of primary importance is not so much our knowledge of the material sign that enables us to interpret the eternal reality, but rather it is our knowledge of the eternal reality that enables us to interpret the material sign. This hermeneutical principle applies not only to allegorical and typological but also to literal interpretation. To understand the words of the Bible properly as signs of eternal reality, one must acknowledge that reality.

In order to know the eternal reality, a spiritual ascent and purification are necessary. Such a spiritual purification is, therefore, a presupposition for interpreting Scripture. "A real understanding of Scripture—one that does not stop at the external words—demands a

---

26. See Peter Brunner, "Charismatische und methodische Schriftauslegung nach Augustins Prolog zu De doctrina christiana," *Kerygma und Dogma* 1 (1955): 59–69, 85–103; C. P. Mayer, " 'Res per signa'—Der Grundgedanke des Prologs in Augustins Schrift De doctrina christiana und das Problem der Datierung," *Revue des études Augustiniennes* 20 (1974): 100–112; Hermann-Josef Sieben, "Die 'res' der Bibel: Eine Analyse von Augustinus, *De doctr. chris.* I–III," *Revue des études Augustiniennes* 21 (1975): 72–90.

27. See Cornelius Petrus Mayer, *Die Zeichen in der geistigen Entwicklung und in der Theologie des jungen Augustinus* (Würzburg: Augustinus Verlag, 1974), vols. 1 and 2.

moral purification and Augustine proposes a scheme of seven stages leading to it."[28] The seven stages are: first, the *fear* of God that leads toward a recognition of God's will; second, *piety* so in meekness we attend to the Scriptures; third, a knowledge that grasps that *charity*, the love of God and of neighbor, is the sum of the Scriptures; fourth, the gift of *fortitude* in hungering and thirsting for justice; fifth, the counsel of *mercy* by which one exercises the love of neighbor and perfects oneself in it; sixth, the *purification* of the heart from its attachments to the world; and seventh, *wisdom* of divine contemplation.[29]

The interrelation between spiritual purification and the interpretation of the Scriptures points to what in Augustine's view is the major problem of hermeneutics. This problem is not the distance between the horizon of past times and the horizon of present times. Nor is it the problem of grasping the literal meaning in its literalness, as in modern biblical fundamentalism. Though Augustine is aware of historical differences and of linguistic problems in ascertaining the correct literal meaning, for him the central problem of hermeneutics is much more basic. It is the problem of understanding the transcendent referent. The person who interprets the words only in their literal or historical sense and not in their reference to the transcendent has failed to grasp the meaning of the Scriptures.

In cases of doubt, Augustine proposes some basic principles. One principle asks whether the interpretation in question leads to a greater love of God and neighbor. Indeed, he writes that if someone "is deceived in an interpretation which builds up charity, which is the end of the commandments, he is deceived in the same way as a man who leaves a road by mistake but passes through a field to the same place toward which the road itself leads."[30] The knowledge of Scripture entails for Augustine not new information but the discovery of God's will leading to the contemplation of the eternal truths, the object of wisdom, and of the blessed life. Another principle underscores the communal context of interpretation, namely, the faith of the church as an interpreting community. This faith is most clearly manifest in the church's rule of faith as expressed in the creed.[31]

Today we face two contrasting tendencies. On the one hand, exegetical practice stresses a scientific objectivity and neutrality that aim to be free from subjective presuppositions. On the other hand,

---

28. See Ragnar Holte, *Béatitude et Sagesse: Saint Augustin et le problème de la fin de l'homme dans la philosophie ancienne* (Paris: Études Augustiniennes, 1962), 342.

29. Augustine *On Christian Doctrine*, bk. 2.7.9–11.

30. Augustine *On Christian Doctrine*, bk. 1.36.41.

31. See Howard J. Loewen, "The Use of Scripture in Augustine's Theology," *Scottish Journal of Theology* 34 (1981): 201–24.

contemporary hermeneutical theory underscores the significance that one's pre-understanding and application have for interpretation. It is contemporary hermeneutical theory that seeks to retrieve and reappropriate (though with a contrasting horizon and different categories) the classic relation between life-practice and interpretation that Augustine expressed with his combination of Christian beliefs and Neo-Platonic categories. Hermeneutical theory today affirms that a life-relation to the subject matter to be interpreted is essential to understanding. This hermeneutical affirmation raises the question of the proper life-relation to the subject matter of the Christian Scriptures.

This question (implied in the hermeneutical theories of Martin Heidegger and Hans-Georg Gadamer) has been raised within theological hermeneutics. Yet it has been raised quite diversely by existential hermeneutics and by liberation theology.[32] The existential approach (represented by Rudolf Bultmann's classic essay on hermeneutics) asks: Since the Scriptures are about God's revelation, how then do humans have a pre-understanding of God's revelation?[33] Bultmann's answer refers to Augustine, for it asserts that the issue guiding our approach to the Scriptures is the quest for God that is implied in the question of the meaning of human life. Liberation theology, in contrast, understands this life-relation and pre-understanding as the self-transcendence of solidarity with the poor and oppressed. The existential question of Bultmann's hermeneutics and the solidarity affirmed by liberation theology both stand in a continuity—yet with considerable modifications—with Augustine's stress on self-transcendence and spiritual purification as a condition for the proper understanding of Scriptures. As such, they contrast sharply with the objectivism of much modern historicism.

## Augustine's Influence on the West

Augustine strongly and directly influenced the method, content, and arrangement of medieval theology. His specification of the

---

32. Martin Heidegger, *Being and Time* (New York: Harper and Row, 1962), sections 31 and 32; Hans-Georg Gadamer, *Truth and Method*, 2d rev. ed. (New York: Crossroad, 1989), 265–307.

33. See Rudolf Bultmann, "The Problem of Hermeneutics" and "Is Exegesis without Presuppositions Possible?" in his *New Testament Mythology and Other Basic Writings*, ed. Schubert M. Ogden (Philadelphia: Fortress Press, 1984). Bultmann relates his notion of pre-understanding and question to Augustine: "Unless our existence were moved (consciously or unconsciously) by the question about God in the sense of Augustine's 'Thou hast made us for thyself, and our heart is restless until its rests in thee,' we would not be able to recognize God in any revelation" (p. 87).

relation between faith and understanding was decisive for medieval theology and theological method. Augustine quoted an early Latin translation of Isaiah 7:9 ("Unless you believe, you will not understand") in order to suggest not only that faith seeks and understanding finds, but also that one seeks understanding on the basis of faith.[34] This verse and idea find their classic formulation in Anselm's prologue to his *Proslogion*: "I do not seek to understand in order to believe, but I believe in order to understand. For I believe even this: that I shall not understand unless I believe."[35] For Anselm, the attempt to gain understanding and rational insight into the truths was an obligatory task and the key to his theological method. Anselm's explication of this Augustinian starting point provided the basis for the Scholastic theological method.

Augustine's view of faith's relation to understanding relates to his understanding of the role of authority in knowledge and the role of the church within theology. Augustine declared that it is the authority of the apostolic sees that determines which Gospels are canonical; that is, the decisions of the apostolic sees are decisive for determining which texts are acknowledged as Scripture. In addition, the creeds as explications of the rule of faith provide a standard for the interpretation of Scripture. Moreover, Augustine's treatment of the articles of faith in the creed as the reality of faith, and especially the order of his exposition in the *Enchiridion* and *On Christian Doctrine*, influenced the structure and arrangement of topics in the medieval *summas*.[36] *On Christian Doctrine* divides the content of Christian doctrine into reality (*res*) and signs (*signa*). The signs are the words of Scripture and the reality is the triune God. In *On Christian Doctrine* Augustine discusses the Apostles' Creed (see book 1, chaps. 5–21), and in so doing he sketches the following outline of Christian doctrine: First is the reality, the triune God, the goal of all human striving. Second is the divine wisdom that has become human and who heals the sick. His teachings and gifts are given to the church, his bride, for the forgiveness of sins. This outline influenced two authors, Gennadius of Marseilles and Fulgentius of Ruspe, who in turn influenced

---

34. Augustine *On the Trinity* 15.2.2. The translation of the Latin Vulgate differed, for it had "not abide" instead of "not understand."

35. See chapter 1 of *Proslogion*. For the context and role of Anselm in medieval theology, see Gillian Rosemary Evans, *Anselm and a New Generation* (Oxford: Clarendon Press, 1980); Richard Campbell, "Anselm's Theological Method," *Scottish Journal of Theology* 32 (1979): 541–62.

36. See Alois Grillmeier, "Vom Symbolum zur Summa," in *Mit ihm und in ihm: Christologische Forschungen und Perspektiven* (Freiburg: Herder, 1975), 585–636.

the arrangement of the medieval *Summa Sententiarum*.[37] Their treatment of the material is Augustinian and Western, especially insofar as they do not follow the Eastern stress on the economy of salvation, a stress that underscored the soteriological significance of the Christ event and the unity between creation and salvation history. Instead they follow Augustine's order and discuss first faith and then the objects of faith: God and Christ. They thereby pave the way for Peter Lombard.

After 1215 Peter Lombard's *Four Books of Sentences* was for all practical purposes the medieval textbook. Lombard follows the Augustinian outline and he distinguishes between reality and signs. Books 1 to 3 treat the *res* (reality): book 1 treats the triune God; book 2 discusses creation; and book 3 discusses Christ (including the virtues). Book 4 is about the signs, the sacraments. Lombard's outline was taken over by many medieval theologians and strongly influenced the order of the presentation of their material.[38]

In addition to Augustine's influence on the systematic arrangement of medieval *summas*, his influence on concrete doctrines is inestimable. It is impossible for Christian theologians to discuss the doctrine of the Trinity, the nature of sin, the theory of original sin, the role of grace, the efficacy of the sacraments, the nature of ministry, or the relation between church and state without reference to the contributions of Augustine. His influence extends not just to medieval theology, but also to the Reformation and to key theological movements within modern theology. Many of the views of Luther and Calvin were attempts to retrieve Augustine's understanding of grace and human nature. Within the twentieth century this constructive influence remains: Reinhold Niebuhr's *The Nature and Destiny of Man* provided a brilliant reformulation of Augustine's understanding of human nature and sin and then applied that reformulation to political life.[39] Henri de Lubac sought to recover Augustine's understanding of nature and grace over against Neo-Scholasticism.[40] Karl Rahner sought to counter popular misconceptions of the Trinity by

37. The outlines of Gennadius of Marseilles's *Liber sive definitio ecclesiasticorum dogmatum* and Fulgentius of Ruspe's *Liber de fide ad Petrum* show their indebtedness to Augustine and their contrast with Eastern theological treatises. See Alois Grillmeier, "Patristische Vorbilder frühscholastischer Systematik: Zugleich ein Beitrag zur Geschichte des Augustinismus," in Cross, ed., *Studia Patristica* VI.

38. The outline influenced Thomas in the *Summa Theologiae*, with some modifications. Thomas locates the virtues not in his treatment of Christ, but in his anthropology.

39. Reinhold Niebuhr, *The Nature and Destiny of Man* (New York: Charles Scribners, 1941).

40. Henri de Lubac, *The Mystery of the Supernatural* (New York: Herder, 1967); idem, *Augustinianism and Modern Theology* (New York: Herder, 1968).

retrieving and developing some aspects of Augustine's theology of the Trinity.[41]

## AQUINAS: SCHOLASTIC METHOD AND THOMAS'S *SACRA DOCTRINA*

In 1879 Leo XIII's encyclical *Aeterni Patris* declared Thomas to be the leading Scholastic theologian, the "Angelic Doctor," "omnium princeps et magister."[42] Thomas's influence upon Roman Catholic systematic theology is indeed unsurpassed. One cannot conceive of Roman Catholic theology without his influence. Yet much of theology that claims to be Thomist represents in reality theological presuppositions, views, and conclusions that are distinct from his. This difference is of such importance that within German theological literature, the terms *Thomanism* and *Thomism* are commonly employed to differentiate Thomas from Thomists.[43]

I shall examine Thomas's understanding of theology in three steps. First, I shall consider the development of the Scholastic theological method as the context for his theological method. Second, I shall analyze Thomas's definition of theology and the specific meaning of the title *sacra doctrina*. Finally, I shall address the criteria of theology. What constitutes for Thomas good theology or what counts as a considered theological judgment? The answers to these questions display some of the considerable differences between medieval theology and contemporary theology.

### Background to Scholastic Method and Theology

The maturation of theology as an academic discipline coincided with the gradual development of the twelfth-century schools into universities. The growth of the universities and the advancement of the liberal arts had a decisive impact on the development of theology, particularly systematic theology.[44] At the beginning of the twelfth century, several kinds of schools existed in Europe: the monastic school, the cathedral school, schools attached to individual scholars, and in Italy the urban schools that taught liberal arts.

---

41. Karl Rahner, *The Trinity* (New York: Crossroad, 1970).

42. On the authority of Thomas, see Heinrich Stirnimann, "Non-'tutum'–tuto tutius? Zur Lehrautorität des hl. Thomas," *Freiburger Zeitschrift für Theologie* 1 (1954): 420–33.

43. Gottlieb Söhngen, *Der Weg der abendländischen Theologie* (Munich: Pustet, 1959).

44. Gillian Rosemary Evans, *Old Arts and New Theology: The Beginnings of Theology as an Academic Discipline* (Oxford: Clarendon Press, 1980).

Instruction at the medieval university developed from the reading (*lectio*) to the practice of the disputation (*disputatio*) of questions. This development provided the context for the emergence of the theological *summas* with their diverse "articles."[45] Medieval university lectures first focused on the reading and learning of texts. Since the primary text was sacred Scripture, the discipline was called *sacra doctrina*.[46] The lectures on the text at first amounted to verbal glosses. The lecturer explained the words of the texts, the sense of the passages, and finally the *sententia* or diverse opinions about the more profound meaning and significance of the texts. The questions and opinions that arose in relation to the meaning of the scriptural text increased in number and length. These questions, however, gradually detached themselves from the text in which they had originated. In becoming separated from the text, they were then collected, giving rise to florilegia, compilations, and *summas* in which diverse opinions regarding various questions were collected.[47]

The development from the *lectio* to the *disputatio* entailed an important shift not only in teaching, but also in method. The *lectio* was primarily interpretive, for it consisted of a reading, exposition, and gloss of the text of some recognized authority. The *disputatio* consisted in a lively academic debate. It assumed divergence of opinion and differences among authorities. The method of disputation started out not from an authoritative text, but from a set of questions that pointed to a set of propositions that could be doubted. "From this starting point, the pro and con are brought into play, not with the intention of finding an immediate answer, but in order that under the action of *dubitatio* [doubt], research be pushed to its limit. A satisfactory explanation will be given only on the condition that one continue the search to the discovery of what caused the doubt."[48] The "on the contrary" of the *quaestio* is not the author's thesis, but rather the alternate position. The response of the master follows both positions and resolves the doubts that the question raises.[49]

45. M. D. Chenu, *Toward Understanding Saint Thomas* (Chicago: Henry Regency, 1964). See also his *Théologie comme science* (Paris: J. Vrin, 1943).

46. See Beryl Smalley, *The Study of the Bible in the Middle Ages* (Oxford: Blackwell, 1952); Gillian Rosemary Evans, *The Language and Logic of the Bible* (New York: Cambridge University Press, 1984).

47. For the background to the development of the medieval *summas*, see Johannes Beumer, "Zwischen Patristik und Scholastik: Gedanken zum Wesen der Theologie an Hand des Liber de fide ad Petrum des hl. Fulgentius von Ruspe," *Gregorianum* 23 (1942): 326–47.

48. Chenu, *Toward Understanding*, 94.

49. See F. A. Blanche, "Le vocabulaire de l'argumentation et la structure de l'article dans les ouvrages de Saint Thomas," *Revue des sciences philosophiques et théologiques* 14 (1925): 167–87.

For this method of instruction the contribution of Peter Abelard and his student Peter Lombard was decisive. Peter Abelard compiled a set of passages from the patristic writings on issues of Christian doctrine and practice. He called this compilation *Yes and No (Sic et Non)*.[50] As its title suggests, the compilation uncovered the disagreements, contradictions, and differences of opinion in theology. Abelard's approach was innovative insofar as he applied a method common in canon law to issues of doctrine. Medieval canon lawyers, familiar with diverse interpretations of law and practice, sought to educate and to resolve disputes through such collections of conflicting opinions.

Abelard's introduction to *Yes and No* offered several rules for overcoming conflicts of opinion: (1) examine the authenticity of the text or passages; (2) look for later emendations, retractions, or corrections; (3) attend to diversity of intention, for example, the difference between a precept and a counsel; (4) note the distinction of historical times and circumstances; (5) attend to differences in the meaning of terms and their references; and (6) if unable to reconcile the diversity, give greater weight to the stronger witness or greater authority. In this endeavor the Scriptures retained prime authority. Abelard sought to demonstrate the difference of opinion among Christian authors.[51] It was they, rather than the Scriptures, that disagreed and it was their differences of opinion that needed resolution. Abelard's attention to the problem of the disagreements within the tradition came to characterize medieval theological instruction. His student Peter Lombard compiled a collection of diverse opinion that served as a text of medieval education.

### *Thomas's Understanding of* Sacra Doctrina

In the twelfth century, the issue was not yet whether theology is a science, but rather whether faith is a knowledge. A common answer was that faith is more than opinion but less than knowledge. Faith has more certitude than opinion but less than knowledge. Faith is neither a *scientia opinativa* nor a *scientia necessaria*, but a *scientia probabilis*. Faith is, therefore, a form of knowledge that is a grounded opinion with probable certitude.[52] In the twelfth century, *sacra doctrina* was

---

50. D. E. Luscombe, *The Influence of Abelard's Thought in the Early Scholastic Period* (Cambridge: Cambridge University Press, 1969).

51. See the careful analysis of Abelard's intention and the correction of von Harnack's widespread view, in Martin Grabmann, *Geschichte der scholastischen Methode* (Freiburg: Herder, 1911), 2:168–229.

52. See Richard Heinzmann, "Die Theologie auf dem Weg zur Wissenschaft: Zur Entwicklung der theologischen Systematik in der Scholastik," *Münchener Theologische Zeitschrift* 25 (1974): 1–17.

not yet distinct from the interpretation of Scripture. "Yet the idea of a scientific theology, which apodictically derived its conclusions from evident principles, led to a notion of theology as an independent question and consequently led to the question of its relation to the other disciplines."[53]

This question of the relation between *sacra doctrina* and the other disciplines was discussed within the Franciscan schools. Edward Kilwardby had asked what the relation was between theology, metaphysics, and other sciences. The *Summa Halensis* answers that both theology and metaphysics are wisdom because they relate to the first causes. When medieval theologians first called theology a "science" (*scientia*), they often used the notion of *scientia* in a general sense.[54] William of Auxerre and Alexander of Hales sought to specify theology as a science by employing Aristotle's notion of science. Thomas, however, went a step further in that he took over Aristotle's division of the sciences and applied the notion of "subalternate science" to describe sacred doctrine as a science.[55]

Thomas's understanding of the nature of *sacra doctrina*, the subject matter of the first article of his *Summa Theologiae*, has been and remains an object of considerable controversy. The first commentator on Thomas's *Summa*, Cardinal Thomas de Vio Cajetan (1469–1534), argues that in the first article *sacra doctrina* refers neither to faith nor to theology, but rather to the knowledge revealed by God. In the second article, it refers to knowledge as an intellectual habit concerning the conclusions drawn from that knowledge.[56] The Louvain theologian Francis Sylvius (1581–1649) argues that *sacra doctrina* is the habit of Scholastic theology derived from the principles of faith.[57] In recent times, Yves Congar interprets *sacra doctrina* as the process of Christian instruction. It is, however, not just the academic theological discipline or simply a collection of theological truths, but rather the whole process of teaching and instruction. Congar interprets the notion of Christian instruction in a broad sense

---

53. Charles H. Lohr, "Theologie und/als Wissenschaft im frühen 13. Jahrhundert," *Internationale katholische Zeitschrift* 10 (1981): 327 (my translation). For a comparison of Augustinian and modern conceptions of science, see Charles H. Lohr, "Mittelalterlicher Augustinismus und neuzeitliche Wissenschaftslehre," in Cornelius Petrus Mayer, ed., *Scientia Augustiniana* (Würzburg: Augustinus Verlag, 1975), 157–69.

54. See Peter Lombard *Sententiae* lib. 3, dist. 35, cap 1.

55. For a survey of the diverse medieval positions, see Ulrich Körpf, *Die Anfänge der theologischen Wissenschaftstheorie im 13. Jahrhundert* (Tübingen: J. C. B. Mohr, 1974).

56. Cajetan *In I Summa* q. 1, a. 1 and 2.

57. Sylvius *Opera Omnia* I, q. 1, a. 1.

to include both Scripture and theology.[58] Gerald van Ackeran, following Congar, argues that sacred Scripture, sacred doctrine, and theology proper are distinct realities in a causal context. Scripture relates to *sacra doctrina* as an external instrument, as its efficient cause. God, however, is the principal cause.[59] Criticizing these approaches, James Weisheipl, a recent biographer of Thomas, argues that *sacra doctrina* primarily refers to faith,[60] whereas Thomas O'Brien argues that it refers to a distinct academic discipline.[61]

If one locates Thomas within the medieval discussions about academic disciplines, then it becomes clear that by *sacra doctrina* Thomas meant an academic discipline alongside philosophy. Thomas uses the Aristotelian distinction of sciences to illumine his conception of "sacred doctrine" as distinct from the philosophical understanding of "theology" as the philosophical doctrine of God. Aristotle had distinguished two kinds of sciences: One proceeds from principles of natural reason, such as arithmetic and geometry. Another proceeds from principles that are from a superior knowledge. For example, optics proceeds from principles of geometry; music from principles of arithmetic. Thomas suggest that *sacra doctrina* is a science of the second type (a subalternate science) because it proceeds from principles known in a superior science, namely, the knowledge that God possesses. Therefore, the knowledge proper to *sacra doctrina* comes to us only through God's revelation. Its principles are based on the revelation of divine knowledge and divine wisdom.

Thomas's understanding of *sacra doctrina* as a science involves the reduction or resolution (*resolutio*) of theological statements to the articles of faith. Yet such a procedure should not be understood as a purely axiomatic and deductive procedure, as if *sacra doctrina* were just another type of classical geometry. The personal faith in the articles of faith is important to his theological method in the sense that theology is anchored within the prescientific faith, both in regard to its content and certainty. Through the virtue of faith the

---

58. Yves Congar, "*Traditio und Sacra Doctrina* bei Thomas von Aquin," in *Kirche und Überlieferung: Festschrift J. R. Geiselmann* (Freiburg: Herder, 1960), 170–210. French text in *Église et tradition* (Le Puy-Lyon: Mappus, 1963), 157–94.

59. Gerald van Ackeran, *Sacra Doctrina: The Subject of the First Question of the Summa Theologica of St. Thomas Aquinas* (Rome: Catholic Book Agency, 1952).

60. See James Weisheipl, "The Meaning of *Sacra Doctrina* in *Summa Theologiae* I, q. 1," *Thomist* 38 (1974): 49–80. See his important biography of Thomas, *Friar Thomas d'Aquino* (New York: Doubleday, 1974) and his essay "The Evolution of Scientific Method," in V. E. Smith, ed., *The Logic of Science* (New York: St. John's University, 1964), 58–86.

61. Thomas O'Brien, "'*Sacra Doctrina*' Revisited: The Context of Medieval Education," *Thomist* 41 (1977): 475–509.

Christian theologian participates in the divine knowledge.[62] Therefore, it could be stated that in addition to its axiomatic character, *sacra doctrina* has a hermeneutical character. Its task is to interpret the prescientific faith.[63]

### Basis and Subject Matter of Sacra Doctrina

Having argued that *sacra doctrina* is a distinct discipline, Thomas then raises the issue of the mode of argument or authority within the discipline. How does *sacra doctrina* make judgments and how does it argue? Thomas distinguishes carefully between making judgments according to inclination and making judgments according to knowledge. The second way of judging (*per modum cognitionis*) characterizes *sacra doctrina* as an academic discipline. For as Thomas notes, this second way of making judgments is "in keeping with the fact that it [*sacra doctrina*] is acquired through study."[64]

**Basis of *Sacra Doctrina*.** The discipline of *sacra doctrina* is based upon the Scriptures in two ways. First, since *sacra doctrina* has its origin in divine revelation, its authority is founded on the Scriptures of this revelation. Second, *sacra doctrina* is a distinctive discipline because it has its specific authoritative text, the sacred Scriptures. As a distinct discipline, *sacra doctrina* has its own authorities. Its arguments proceed from the authority of divine revelation in the Scriptures. In Scholastic theology, the term *authority* has diverse meanings, most associated with a practice of teaching and arguing.[65] Instruction, even in nontheological subjects, was based on the texts of writers who constituted the authority in question. Authority referred to the quality of a person who was qualified and whose writings were thereby trustworthy. The text itself, as a quotation from a writer, became a *dictum auctoritatis*. Authority and quotation thus became interchanged. In the disciplines, this respect for authority meant that academic work was often commentary or interpretation of an authoritative text.[66] Since *sacra doctrina* consisted primarily in

---

62. Thomas Aquinas *Summa Theologiae* I-II, q. 110, a. 4: "homo participat cognitionem divinam per virtutem fidei."

63. See Ludger Oeing-Hanhof, "Thomas von Aquin und die Gegenwärtige Katholische Theologie," in Willehad Paul Eckert, ed., *Thomas von Aquino: Interpretation und Rezeption* (Mainz: Matthias-Grünewald, 1974), 243–306, esp. 260–70.

64. Thomas Aquinas *Summa Theologiae* I, q. 1, a. 6, ad 3.

65. M. D. Chenu, "'Authentica' et 'Magistralia'," *Divus Thomas (Piacenza)* 28 (1925): 3–31.

66. See Edward Schillebeeckx, *Revelation and Theology* (New York: Sheed and Ward, 1967), 1:223–58.

a commentary on the Scriptures, it was also called *sacra scriptura* or *sacra pagina* and its authoritative text was the Scriptures. As the disputation of individual questions increased and became independent of the interpretation of the text, the term *theology* came to replace these terms.

The authority that Thomas attributes to Scripture is evident in his division of authorities, where he distinguishes between proper or intrinsic authority and necessary and probable argument.[67] *Sacra doctrina* makes use of sacred Scripture *properly*, and its arguments from Scripture carry the weight of necessity. Since Christian faith rests on the revelation given to the apostles and prophets, the canonical Scriptures have, for Thomas, a primal significance and authority. *Sacra doctrina* also uses the authority of the doctors of the church properly, but only with probable effect. *Sacra doctrina* relies on philosophers only as extrinsic and probable. It makes use of them only in those questions in which one can know the truth by natural reason.

This point is significant for understanding the relations between Roman Catholic and Lutheran and Reformed traditions of theology. Martin Luther sharply criticized Scholastic theology for excessive reliance on Aristotle's philosophy. Contrasting his theology of the cross with a Scholastic theology of glory, he identified the latter with the natural theology of Scholasticism.[68] In the twentieth century, Karl Barth likewise sharply criticized the defense of natural theology in Thomist philosophy and theology. Such criticisms often overlook the authority and primacy of Scripture within medieval theology and for Thomas Aquinas. A Scandinavian Lutheran theologian, Per Erik Persson, has done a great service in arguing that Thomas attributes an authority to Scripture that is overlooked in the traditional Reformation and Protestant neo-orthodox polemic against Scholasticism.[69]

The primacy that Thomas attributes to Scripture limits the role of philosophy. Philosophy cannot demonstrate the truth of *sacra doctrina*, since the latter's principles are based on revelation. Philosophy can only demonstrate that the truths of revelation do not contradict reason. Furthermore, philosophy can also illumine the meaning of these truths by the use of metaphors and examples. Through logical

---

67. Thomas Aquinas *Summa Theologiae* I, q. 1, a. 8.

68. See Martin Luther, "Heidelberg Disputation: Theological Theses," in Timothy F. Lull, ed., *Martin Luther's Basic Theological Writings* (Minneapolis: Fortress Press, 1989), 30–32.

69. Per Erik Persson, *Sacra Doctrina: Reason and Revelation in Aquinas* (Philadelphia: Fortress Press, 1970).

explication philosophy elaborates the implications of the articles of faith.[70]

**Subject Matter of *Sacra Doctrina*.** *Sacra doctrina* as a discipline has not only distinct principles but also a distinct object: God as the source and goal of all things insofar as they refer to God. Within an Aristotelian conception of science, the subject matter of a discipline is determined by the object or end that provides the unity of that discipline. For Thomas, God is the end that provides the unity of *sacra doctrina*. Only to the extent that created things relate to God as their origin and goal are they the proper subject matter of theology.

This principle determines the theocentric structure of the *Summa Theologiae*, which uses the Aristotelian causal schema as well as the Neo-Platonic *exitus-reditus* schema to express the relation of all created reality to God. Thomas's arrangement differs from other Scholastic authors.[71] Some followed a more systematic or conceptual order. Peter Abelard's arrangement was faith, love, and the sacraments. Peter Lombard referred to *res* and their signs. Others followed a salvation-historical order. Hugo of Saint Victor, Alexander of Hales, and Bonaventure referred to the Christ and his redemptive work and benefits. In the decades immediately preceding Thomas, Peter Lombard's arrangement was modified through salvation-historical considerations, not in the sense of a chronological salvation history, but rather as the explication of God's work of creation and re-creation, the invisible re-creation of grace and the visible re-creation in Christ and the sacraments. This outline, evident in Magister Hubertus's *Colligite Fragmenta* (1194–1200), is the pattern that Thomas followed.[72] However, Thomas stands in the context of the rediscovery of Aristotle within the West. He uses the Aristotelian conception of science (namely, the appeal to diverse causes: efficient, final, exemplary, and material) to refer all to God's creative activity. He thereby elaborates God's work of salvation history, namely, creation and re-creation, into the Neo-Platonic *exitus-reditus* schema.

---

70. Thomas Aquinas *Summa Theologiae* q. 1, a. 5, ad 2.

71. For a survey of interpretations, see Otto Hermann Pesch, "Um den Plan der Summa Theologiae des hl. Thomas von Aquin. Zu Max Seckler's neuem Deutungsversuch," *Münchener theologische Zeitschrift* 16 (1965): 128–37 and his more recent book, *Thomas von Aquin* (Mainz: Matthias-Grünewald, 1988), 381–400.

72. See Richard Heinzmann, "Der Plan der 'Summa Theologiae' des Thomas von Aquin in der Tradition der frühscholastischen Systembildung," in Eckert, ed., *Thomas von Aquino*, 455–69.

**Thomas Aquinas and Magisteria.** The issues of the foundation and authorities underlying theology raise for us the question of the relation between theology and magisterial authority. At the time of Aquinas an understanding of magisterium prevailed that differs considerably from ours. Today it has become customary to refer to a magisterium, in a singular sense. This contemporary use of *magisterium* is the result of a long historical development and has diverse backgrounds.[73] Thomas employed the plural term *magisteria* and distinguished between a pastoral magisterium and a teaching magisterium.

Thomas distinguished between two functions, prelacy and magisterium, and two kinds of teaching, preaching and doctrinal teaching. The function of prelacy (*praelatio*) belongs to the bishops, and their teaching involves preaching (*doctrina praedicationis*). Theologians have the function of magisterium, and their teaching involves Scholastic doctrine (*doctrina scholastica*). Whereas Thomas ascribes the title of magisterium primarily to the theologian in the forum of teaching magisterium, he attributes to bishops a magisterium of prelacy and preaching. To quote Thomas's own terminology, bishops have a "pastoral magisterium" (*magisterium cathedrae pastoralis*), whereas the theologians have a "magisterial magisterium" (*magisterium cathedrae magistralis*).[74]

Concerning what today is called the papal magisterium, Thomas attributes to the pope both judicial and doctrinal competence. Defining matters of faith is a judgment made by the pope because the more important and difficult questions are referred to him. However, as Yves Congar points out: "It is fact that St. Thomas has not spoken of the infallibility of the papal magisterium. Moreover, he was unaware of the use of magisterium in its modern sense."[75]

---

73. Yves Congar, "Pour une histoire sémantique du terme 'Magisterium'" and "Bref histoire des formes du 'Magistère' et des ses relations avec les docteurs," *Revue des sciences philosophiques et théologiques* 60 (1976): 85–98, 99–112. For the development of the concept of ordinary magisterium, see John P. Boyle, "The 'Ordinary Magisterium': Towards a History of the Concept," *Heythrop Journal* 20 (1979): 380–98 and 21 (1980): 14–29.

74. For the distinction between pastoral and teaching magisterium, see Thomas Aquinas *Quodl.* 3.4.1, ad 3 (Parma ed., 9:490–91). See also *Contra Impugn.* cap. 2 (Parma ed., 15:3–8). For the theological implications see Avery Dulles's two essays "The Magisterium in History: Theological Considerations" and "The Two Magisteria: An Interim Report," in his collection *A Church to Believe In* (New York: Crossroad, 1983), 103–33. See also the special issue of *Chicago Studies* 17, no. 2 (Summer 1978) entitled *The Magisterium, the Theologian, and the Educator.*

75. Yves Congar, "Saint Thomas Aquinas and the Infallibility of the Papal Magisterium (Summa Theol., II-II, q. I, a. 10)," *Thomist* 38 (1974): 102; Ulrich Horst, "Das Wesen der 'potestas clavium' nach Thomas von Aquin," *Münchener theologische Zeitschrift* 11 (1960): 191–201.

## NEO-SCHOLASTICISM:
## ITS DISTINCTIVE CHARACTERISTICS

In the medieval period of Scholastic theology, diverse schools and traditions flourished. Bonaventure, Duns Scotus, William of Ockham, and many others contributed significantly to theology. Yet in the modern period, Thomism dominates. Thomas's *Summa* replaced Peter Lombard's *Sentences* as the basic textbook of classroom instruction. Although the Neo-Scholasticism that developed in the period following the Renaissance and the Reformation swore its allegiance to Thomas, it manifests decisive differences from Thomas's own thought and categories—differences that twentieth-century historical studies have brought to light.

### From Scholasticism to Post-Tridentine Catholicism

The transformations and shifts from medieval Scholasticism to Neo-Scholasticism were in large part occasioned by the controversies surrounding the Protestant Reformation and by the influence of the Renaissance. Some of the changes in theological method, however, had already begun within late medieval Scholasticism itself. These changes can be traced back to the development of theological censures. It was the issue of theological errors and the awareness of a distinction between theological and philosophical errors that led to a new development in theological method. They led to an increasing emphasis on authority and to a growing number of theological sources.

A comparison between the thirteenth and sixteenth centuries makes this transformation obvious. In the thirteenth century, following Aristotle's notion of science from the *Posterior Analytics*, Thomas considered the articles of faith as the principles of an understanding and presentation of Christian doctrine. Thomas assumed that a basic harmony existed between natural reason and supernatural revelation. Disharmonies resulted from errors in philosophy, and one could correct them through the teaching of Scripture and the doctors of the church.

Certain developments within the fourteenth and fifteenth centuries made it no longer feasible to refer to Scripture and tradition as the basic authorities in the same way that Thomas did. The controversy about the papacy as well as the conflict between councils, the papacy, and the universities concerning the authority to watch over doctrine necessitated a more complex theological method. Such a method, initiated by John of Torquemada and used by Johann Eck in his debate with Martin Luther during the Leipzig Disputations in 1519,[76] was further developed by Albert Pigge and Bartolomé Carranza in the polemic of the Counter Reformation.[77] This theological method sought to determine Catholic truths (*veritates catholicae*) by appealing to Scripture, tradition, the councils, the teaching of the papacy, etc. Such a method signaled a situation far different from that of Aquinas. In the sixteenth century, the theological method became the search for the evident principles within the diverse sources. This question of the authorities within diverse sources faced Melchior Cano, a Spanish Dominican theologian. His proposals, influencing Baroque Scholasticism, initiated the beginning of the development from Baroque Scholasticism to Neo-Scholasticism.[78]

*Baroque Scholasticism*

Melchior Cano wrote *De locis theologicis* (literally "concerning theological places"), a book about the sources of theological authority. This book, published posthumously in 1563, represented a new and distinctive theological approach. In the Renaissance, various loci were assembled for different disciplines and Cano extended this practice to theology. He developed a list of places where theology could look for the sources of its arguments and reasoning.

In adapting the practice of collecting various loci to the discipline of theology, Cano followed not the Aristotelian but rather the humanist concept of locus. This concept, developed by Rudolph Agricola, a humanist, followed Cicero and viewed the loci as *sedes argumenti*.[79] Cano's difference from Aristotle is important. For Cano, the term *locus* did not refer to either the premises of a syllogism or the principles of theology, as within medieval theology. Instead the term referred to the place where theology finds its authorities.[80]

---

76. See the two works by P. Polman, *Die polemische Methode der ersten Gegner der Reformation* (Münster: Aschendorf, 1931) and *L'élément historique dans la controverse religieuse du XVIe siècle* (Gembloux: J. Duculot, 1932).

77. Albert Pigge, *Hierarchiae ecclesiasticae assertio* (1538) and Bartolomé Carranza, *De necessaria residentia personali episcoparorum* (1547). See Charles H. Lohr, "Modelle für die Überlieferung theologischer Doktrin: Von Thomas von Aquin bis Melchior Cano," in Werner Löser, et al., eds., *Dogmengeschichte und katholische Theologie* (Würzburg: Echter Verlag, 1985), 148–67, esp. 164–67.

78. For a corrective to many presentations of the significance and contribution of Scholastic schools of theology in Spain, see Melquiades Andres, *La teología española en el siglo xvi* (Madrid: Biblioteca de autores cristianos, 1976), vol. 2. For theological method and Cano, see esp. pp. 386–424.

79. Cano differed not only from Aristotle but also from the Lutheran Scholastic Melanchthon, who used locus as a *locus communis*.

80. Whereas Ambroise Gardeil originally interpreted Cano as understanding loci in the Aristotelian sense, Albert Lang argues that Cano follows Cicero and has a

Cano thereby sought to establish the foundations of Roman Catholic theology with reference to the weight of the authorities that underlie that theology. He listed ten sources of authority from which one could argue theologically: (1) Scripture, (2) oral tradition, (3) the Catholic church, (4) the general councils, (5) the Roman church, (6) the fathers of the church, (7) the Scholastic theologians, (8) human reason, (9) philosophers, and (10) history. The first seven were, according to Cano, properly speaking theological authorities, whereas the last three were extrinsic to theology.[81]

A further development took place from the Baroque Scholasticism of the sixteenth century to the Neo-Scholasticism of the nineteenth and twentieth centuries. For this development, the writings of the Parisian theologian Denis Petau (Dionysius Petavius) were decisive. Today one commonly thinks of Robert Bellarmine and Francis Suarez as the leading theological figures of the sixteenth and seventeenth centuries. At the beginning of the twentieth century, however, Neo-Scholastic theologians considered Denis Petau most significant, so much so that the Neo-Scholastic theologians Carlo Passaglia and Clemens Schrader labeled him "theologorum facile princeps."[82] Petau's influence consisted not only in his development of the theological use of historical sources, but also in his understanding of the nature of theology.[83]

Petau developed a conception of theology as a deductive science—a decisive shift from the medieval conception. Petau argued that theology achieves the status of scientific discipline to the degree that it employs a deductive method. Theology advances in knowledge by deducing conclusions from premises of faith by means of premises of reason. Philosophy is the intermediate link within a syllogistic process of theology. Petau's conception presumed as an implicit background theory that a deductive syllogism constitutes the scientific nature of a discipline. Therefore, theology is a strict science, he

---

different understanding of loci. See A. Lang, *Die theologische Prinzipienlehre der mittelalterlichen Scholastik* (Freiburg: Herder, 1964). The general interpretation today follows the direction establish by Albert Lang. See also Elmer Klinger, *Ekklesiologie der Neuzeit* (Freiburg: Herder, 1978) and M. Jacquin, "Melchior Cano et la théologie moderne," *Revue des sciences philosophiques et théologiques* 9 (1920): 121–41.

81. Lohr, "Modelle für die Überlieferung theologischer Doktrin: Von Thomas von Aquin bis Melchior Cano," 148–67.

82. See Walter Kasper, *Die Lehre von der Tradition in der Römischen Schule* (Freiburg: Herder, 1962), 379.

83. See Michael Hoffmann, *Theologie, Dogma und Dogmenentwicklung im theologischen Werk Denis Petaus* (Munich: Herbert Lang, 1976); Ignace-Marcel Tshiamalenga Ntumba-Mulemba, "La méthode théologique chez Denys Petau," *Ephemerides Theologicae Lovanienses* 48 (1972): 427–78; and Leo Karrer, *Die historisch-positive Methode des Theologen Dionysius Petavius* (Munich: M. Hueber, 1970).

argued, only insofar as it uses a deductive process to arrive at theological conclusions. This notion of the deductive, syllogistic theological conclusions became the distinctive Neo-Scholastic conception of theology as a scientific discipline. This understanding of the scientific character formed the structure and procedure of the Neo-Scholastic handbooks of theology.

## Neo-Scholastic Theology

Characteristic of the Neo-Scholastic approach is the development of the theological manual, which became the major instrument of theological instruction. Whereas Baroque Scholasticism had produced several significant commentaries on Thomas's *Summa Theologiae*, Neo-Scholasticism's distinctive contribution was the theological school manual. These manuals followed a set approach. They sought first to clarify the Catholic position on a particular topic, then to demonstrate its veracity with arguments drawn from the Bible and early church writers, and finally to refute the errors of Protestantism. This approach and the methodology of the manuals display the influence of Petau's conception of theological method. Influenced by the Cartesian emphasis on clear and distinct ideas, Neo-Scholasticism sought to incorporate these scientific ideals into its theological approach.[84] The three elements of Neo-Scholastic theological method display a starting point and approach that differed considerably from medieval Scholastic disputation and from the Baroque Scholastic commentary.

**Starting Point: Church Teaching.** The Neo-Scholastic manuals began their treatment of theological topics with theses explicating church teaching. The first text that adopted this practice was the 1771 *Theologie Wirceburgensis*—a widely used and distributed manual of theological instruction. The treatment began with a thesis about church teaching because Neo-Scholastic theology considered church teaching to be the immediate rule of faith (*regula fidei proxima*). It was this teaching that provided a clear rule and definite standard enabling believers to ascertain those truths contained in Scriptures and traditions. The Scriptures and traditions themselves were considered to be the remote rule of faith.[85] This distinction between immediate and remote rule of faith expressed the post-Tridentine and

---

84. Alexandre Ganoczy, *Einführung in die Dogmatik* (Darmstadt: Wissenschaftliche Buchgesellschaft, 1983). For an analysis of the three-step method, see B. Durst, "Zur theologischen Methode," *Theologische Revue* 26 (1927): 297–313 and 361–72.

85. See Kasper, *Die Lehre von der Tradition*, 40–47.

apologetical concern of Neo-Scholasticism to elucidate the content of the Roman Catholic faith in the most precise and shortest formulas. The exactitude and brevity facilitated the preaching, teaching, and learning of the formulas of faith.[86]

Such an approach constituted two decisive changes from traditional Scholasticism: one affecting the form of presentation, the other, the role of Scripture. The manner of presentation changed from the *quaestio* to the thesis. It was the *quaestio* in high Scholasticism and the *disputatio* in late Scholasticism that provided a framework for teaching. Traditional Scholastic teaching began with disputed questions, whereas modern Scholastics began with theses about church teaching. This contrast between modern and medieval Scholasticism has been well described by Chenu, a noted historian: "For an article is a *quaestio*, not a *thesis*, the word that was to be used in the manuals. The change in terms is in itself a denunciation of the heinous reversal to which have been subjected the exalted pedagogical methods set up in the XIIth century universities: 'active methods,' mindful to keep open, even under the dead-weight of school work, the curiosity of both the student and the master."[87]

The second change concerned the role of Scripture. Medieval Scholasticism had given a priority to the Scriptures and much of the instruction was basically a commentary on Scripture. Disputed questions were resolved by an appeal to authority, the most proper and intrinsic being Scripture, for, as Thomas had maintained, an argument based on the authority of the Scriptures bore intrinsic and necessary probity. For Neo-Scholasticism, the situation was radically different. In reaction to the Reformation's appeal to the Scriptures, Neo-Scholastic theologians began to argue that the Scriptures are often misinterpreted. Therefore, they argued that the church's official teaching is the primary and proximate rule of faith.

This specification of official church teaching as the proximate rule of faith led to a distinctive characteristic of the Neo-Scholastic approach, namely, the careful delineation of the binding or obligatory character of church teaching.[88] Theological propositions were classified regarding their centrality to faith, their degree of certitude, and their corresponding censure. Theological propositions, for example, could express truths that were formally revealed. These were classified as "of divine faith" (*de fide divina*) and their denial consisted of

---

86. Ganoczy, *Einführung*, 130–43.

87. Chenu, *Toward Understanding*, 96.

88. For the distinctiveness of the Neo-Scholastic understanding of magisterium, see T. Howland Sanks, *Authority in the Church: A Study in Changing Paradigms* (Missoula, Mont.: Scholars Press, 1974).

heresy. Propositions that were not only formally revealed but also defined as such by the magisterium were considered of "defined divine
faith," whereas what the ordinary magisterium taught as revealed
truth was labeled simply *de fide*. The next rank were statements that
indirectly flowed from the teaching office of the church. They were
defined as belonging to ecclesiastical faith as such or they were simply and generally acknowledged as belonging to ecclesiastical faith.
Other theological positions were classified with corresponding lesser
notes: such as, proximate to faith, theologically certain, of common
opinion, and of probable opinion.

The attempt at clear and distinct classifications of theological
propositions corresponded in part to a philosophical attitude prevalent at the time. Neo-Scholasticism had a Cartesian scientific ideal
of clear and distinct ideas. Through its distinct classifications, this
approach of Neo-Scholasticism set the parameters of theological debates and discussions. Dissent and disagreements were possible but
only within the framework of a graded hierarchy of propositions.
Although in reaction to the Neo-Scholastic approach many theologians have criticized such distinctions, today a balanced reassessment
is taking place. Such classifications are not without value, for they
had the advantage of identifying areas for disagreement and dissent.
They prevent one from indiscriminately viewing all elements of the
tradition as central and essential to the Roman Catholic faith.

**Proof from the Sources: Scripture and Tradition.** The second
step sought to demonstrate the truth of the thesis in its relation to
the sources of faith, namely, Scripture and tradition.[89] The demonstration from the sources, however, followed a definite procedure.
The demonstration took place not independent from the magisterial teaching, but precisely from the perspective of that teaching.
It was not an attempt to provide a historical-critical analysis of the
sources within their own historical context and questions. Instead
the selection and reading of the sources were determined by the
proposition that one sought to demonstrate. In practice, the passages
from the Scriptures and from early Christian writers were reduced
to proof-texts for a particular proposition. They were often cited
independently of their context and were interpreted primarily as
demonstrations of the truth of a particular doctrinal thesis.

Such a procedure was explicitly justified by the distinction between the proximate and remote rule of faith. The proximate rule

---

89. For an analysis of the Roman School's understanding of tradition, see Kasper,
*Die Lehre von der Tradition.*

of faith provided the interpretive key for understanding the meaning and proof-value of the remote source of faith. As one Neo-Scholastic theologian explicitly advocated: "The demonstrative power of the Sacred Scripture, as inspired, as well as that of the documents of the tradition depend upon the church's teaching office because those sources have value for us in the order of knowledge only as a result of the help of the teaching office."[90]

**Speculative Exposition.** The third step sought to give a systematic explication of the thesis and thereby lead to a more profound understanding of its truth. The teaching of the church, affirmed in the thesis and demonstrated in the appeals to Scripture and tradition, was then in this final step further illumined through philosophical reflection. This reflection drew upon examples, analogies, and comparisons from natural experience. These examples illustrated the thesis and elaborated its meaning. In this step, the systematic reflection sought to relate the particular thesis to other beliefs and sought thereby to present the coherence of the thesis with the other beliefs.

At the same time this step sought a certain "actualization" of the thesis. Insofar as it addressed questions of the day, it applied the thesis to concrete issues. In other words, it sought to demonstrate how traditional truths could be correlated with modern questions and contained answers to them. A further element present in this third part was the attempt to resolve the debates among the diverse Scholastic schools (for example, between the Thomists or Scotists or between diverse Thomistic opinions) in order to provide a greater conceptual clarification. Within the framework of Neo-Scholasticism, philosophical reflection served as an instrument or tool of theological reflection rather than as a challenge or critique. The purpose of philosophy was to bring a deeper understanding of theological truths.

### Crisis of Neo-Scholastic Theology

Today Neo-Scholastic theology is often criticized by those seeking to bring theology up-to-date. Such criticisms often overlook the achievements of Neo-Scholastic theology. It sought to deal with problems of its time just as theologians do today. In the face of rationalist criticisms of revelation and concrete forms of religion, Neo-Scholastic theology sought to develop an apologetic for revelation and for institutional religion. In the face of the rationalist

---

90. Durst, "Zur theologischen Methode," 310 (my translation).

advocacy of clear and distinct ideas, it sought to define as clearly as possible what constituted Christian revelation. Its rationalistic understanding of truth in terms of definite propositions and distinct ideas was in part due to the rationalism against which it fought. In a period of ecumenical controversy, it sought to delineate carefully—though defensively—the distinctiveness of Roman Catholic identity. Neo-Scholastic theology sought to defend its faith against the challenges of its age. What today often appears as its failure can be in part traced to its indebtedness to the currents and categories of its own day.

Nevertheless, two basic problems led to a crisis within Neo-Scholastic theology.[91] These problems occasioned the shift from classical to contemporary approaches to theology. The first was the increased awareness of the historical character of human thought in general, which when applied to theology led to the recognition of the historical character of theological affirmations. The second was the development of a new relationship between theology and philosophy. The development of transcendental, phenomenological, hermeneutical, and existential philosophy affected a shift in the role of philosophy within theological method. Philosophy was no longer limited to an auxiliary or instrumental role within the theological task.

## SUMMARY

The three classic theological approaches (Augustinian, Thomist, and Neo-Scholastic) display common elements as well as significant differences. All emphasize the tradition (especially the Scriptures), the scientific character of the discipline of theology, the importance of the community of the church, and the role of experience. Yet, how these four elements are interrelated and combined differs considerably. There is a shift from Augustine's emphasis upon the relation between personal purification and the correct interpretation of Scripture, to Thomas's emphasis on *sacra doctrina* as an academic discipline with its authorities and rules, to the Neo-Scholastic emphasis on the church's teaching as the proximate rule to interpret Scripture and tradition as the remote rule of faith.

Yet each of these shifts cannot be understood without taking into consideration the background theories informing each approach's conception of what it meant to be "scientific" and what it meant to interpret the tradition. Augustine is incomprehensible without Neo-Platonism, Thomas without Aristotelianism, and Neo-Scholasticism

---

91. Walter Kasper, *The Methods of Dogmatic Theology* (Shannon, Ireland: Ecclesia Press, 1969).

without its rationalistic and Cartesian reception of Scholasticism. The attempt to think critically and theologically about the objects of the Christian faith is present in these three classic types of Roman Catholic theology, yet all three are intricately linked with specific philosophical and theoretical background theories.

# FIVE CONTEMPORARY APPROACHES TO THEOLOGY

Within contemporary Roman Catholic theology many distinctive methods and approaches are employed. To give some idea of this diversity, several "ideal types" will be described: transcendental, hermeneutical, analytical, correlational, and liberational. These approaches represent "ideal types" to the extent that they are theoretically distinct. However, in practice these approaches are not mutually exclusive and are indeed often combined. A specific theologian may predominantly follow one approach while at the same time borrowing insights, categories, and methods from other approaches. For example, a liberation theologian may, within a particular argument, employ a transcendental analysis or a recent hermeneutical theory, even though liberation theology as a theological movement is quite distinct from a transcendental or hermeneutical theology.

## TRANSCENDENTAL THEOLOGY

The description "the turn to the subject" (that is, the focus on human subjectivity and its role within human knowledge and religious belief) best characterizes much of modern Roman Catholic theology that attends to the challenges of modern philosophy initiated by Descartes and Kant. Such a turn was particularly prevalent in the eighteenth and nineteenth centuries, when many theological schools sought to take up the challenges of modern philosophy. These attempts, however, were rebuffed during the pontificates of Pope Pius IX and Pope Leo XIII. The latter sanctioned Thomism as the official philosophy of the Roman Catholic church. Consequently, in the beginning of the twentieth century, Thomism became the dominant Roman Catholic direction within philosophy and theology. However, in the 1940s and 1950s a new beginning was made. This time theology sought to integrate modern philosophy and Thomistic philosophy. This endeavor of engagement with modern philosophy, from its initial attempts, to its rebuff, and to its renewed attempts, needs to be examined in more detail.

*The Turn to the Subject in Modern Theology*

The efforts at incorporating modern philosophy came to fruition within the early nineteenth century. Georg Hermes, professor at the University of Münster and Bonn, sought to explicate a starting point for theology that incorporated the Cartesian principle of doubt. Anton Günther, though a private scholar and theological author in Vienna, was the most influential German-speaking Roman Catholic theologian of the nineteenth century. He sought to develop theology on the basis of an anthropology and categories that were strongly influenced by Descartes. Theologians of the Tübingen School (von Drey, Möhler, Staudenmeier, Kuhn, and Schell) were in dialogue with German Idealism, especially with such major figures as Hegel, Jacobi, Schleiermacher, and Schelling.[92] They sought to develop Roman Catholic theology by drawing upon the insights and categories—though with considerable modifications—from these thinkers in order to relate the content and history of faith to human subjectivity.

The Neo-Scholastic movement reacted against these attempts to reconcile modern philosophy and Roman Catholic theology. Ecclesiastical and political influences were brought to bear on Catholic educational institutions. As a result, several significant theologians lost their teaching positions. The papacy promulgated Thomism as the "official philosophy" of Roman Catholic theology. Yet this Thomism, today called Neo-Thomism, was a special brand of Thomism. It reacted against modern philosophy and the Enlightenment, and yet it was as much a child of modernity as it was a foe of modernity. This Neo-Thomism sharply separated nature and grace; it expanded the preamble of faith into a full-blown natural theology; and it developed a fundamental theology and apologetics in distinction from systematic theology. These developments were deeply indebted to the very modernity that Neo-Thomism opposed.[93]

The dialogue with modern philosophy, however, did not end with the imposition of Neo-Thomism. In time the antimodernist polemic waned and Neo-Thomists moved away from their polemic against modern philosophy. Instead genuine historical studies flourished.[94] Within this context, attempts emerged among the heirs of the Thomist revival to relate Thomas's theology to modern philosophy. Those Roman Catholic theologians most influential at the Second

---

92. For a comprehensive survey, see Donald J. Dietrich, *The Goethezeit and the Metamorphosis of Catholic Theology in the Age of Idealism* (Frankfurt: Peter D. Lang, 1979).

93. For the historical development of fundamental theology, see Francis Schüssler Fiorenza, *Foundational Theology: Jesus and the Church* (New York: Crossroad, 1984).

94. The works of Grabmann, Glorieux, Chenu, etc. are just a few examples.

Vatican Council and in postconciliar times were all trained in the Neo-Scholastic tradition and, with the exception of Hans Küng and Joseph Ratzinger, wrote their dissertations or first major works on Thomas. They sought to reinterpret Thomas Aquinas independently from the presuppositions and views of Neo-Scholasticism. They brought to the fore the theological dimensions of Thomas's thought. They recovered the Augustinian elements within Thomas's theology. They demonstrated that the abstract contrast between nature and supernature in Neo-Scholasticism was not authentically Thomist. As a theological movement, this effort was powerful and effective because it neither jettisoned the past out of fascination with the modern nor rejected the modern out of nostalgia for the past. Rather it opened a way to bring Thomas's theology in contact with modern philosophy.

The results of this movement are indeed impressive. Karl Rahner's study of the epistemology of Aquinas incorporates both Kantian and Heideggerian categories.[95] Bernard Lonergan's two dissertations (on operative grace and on the relation between inner word and ideas) relate Thomas to modern cognitional theory.[96] Edward Schillebeeckx's dissertation on Thomas's understanding of the sacraments relates the sacraments to a phenomenology of encounter.[97] Both Henri Bouillard's study on the relation between grace and nature[98] and Henri de Lubac's historical studies on the development of the notion of the supernatural show the importance of Augustinian elements—which Neo-Thomism had neglected—in Thomas's theology.[99] Even the following generation of theologians (most notably, Johann Baptist Metz, Max Seckler, and Otto Hermann Pesch) continued this dialogue with Thomas Aquinas.[100]

95. Karl Rahner, *Spirit and the World* (New York: Herder and Herder, 1968). See the introduction by F. Fiorenza, "Karl Rahner and the Kantian Problematic," xix–xl.

96. Bernard Lonergan, *Verbum: Word and Idea in Aquinas*, ed. David Burrell (Notre Dame, Ind.: University of Notre Dame Press, 1967); idem, *Grace and Freedom: Operative Grace in the Thought of St. Thomas Aquinas*, ed. J. P. Burns (New York: Herder and Herder, 1971), 1224–30

97. Edward Schillebeeckx, *De sacramentele heilseconomie: Theologische bezinning op St. Thomas' sacramentenleer in het licht van de traditie en van de hedendaagse* (Antwerp: Nelissen, 1952). A volume summarizing the systematic results appeared as *Christ, the Sacrament of Encounter with God* (New York: Sheed and Ward, 1963).

98. Henri Bouillard, *Conversion et grâce* (Paris: Éditions du Cerf, 1944).

99. Henri de Lubac, *The Mystery of Salvation* (New York: Herder and Herder, 1967); idem, *Augustinianism and Modern Theology* (New York: Herder and Herder, 1969).

100. Johann Baptist Metz, *Christliche Anthropozentrik* (Munich: Kösel Verlag, 1962). See also Max Seckler, *Instinkt und Glaubenswille* (Mainz: Matthias-Grünewald, 1961); idem, *Das Heil in der Geschichte: Geschichtstheologisches Denken bei Thomas von Aquin* (Munich: Kösel, 1964); Otto H. Pesch, *Theologie der Rechtfertigung bei Martin Luther und*

*Karl Rahner's Transcendental Phenomenology*

The development of the transcendental method in Roman Catholic theology is particularly significant.[101] The term *transcendental* is a technical philosophical term with diverse historical meanings. In Scholastic philosophy *transcendental* referred to what was applicable to all being. For example, "goodness" is transcendental because it applies to everything that exists (e.g., God, angels, human persons, objects of nature), whereas quantity applies only to material reality. In modern philosophy, Kant used the term *transcendental* to refer to the a priori conditions of possible experience. A transcendental analysis, in this sense, investigates the conditions and possibility of knowledge through an analysis of human cognition.

Within contemporary transcendental Roman Catholic Thomism, the term *transcendental* carries a third meaning that combines the previous two. It includes the Kantian meaning to the extent that it refers to the subjective conditions of possible knowledge. In this sense, the term *transcendental* is given a theological twist insofar as it refers to the conditions of our knowledge of revelation. Systematic theology is transcendental when it investigates the "a priori conditions in the believer for the knowledge of important truths of faith."[102] The term *transcendental* also retains an element of its Scholastic sense to the degree that it refers to the infinite horizon of human knowledge. In this sense, the word *transcendental* refers to the unlimited dynamism of the human intellect striving to grasp not just specific objects of experience but the meaning of the totality of reality.

The origin of transcendental Thomism lies with Joseph Maréchal, a professor of philosophy at the Belgian Jesuit Scholasticate. He related the metaphysics of Thomas Aquinas to modern philosophy, particularly that of Kant and Fichte. Through his teaching and his five-volume work, *Le point de départ de la métaphysique*,[103] Maréchal had an enormous influence upon continental Roman Catholic philosophers and theologians. Of the theologians influenced by Maréchal who have come to represent the direction of the transcendental approach within theology, Karl Rahner is by far the most

*Thomas von Aquin* (Mainz: Matthias-Grünewald, 1967); and idem, *Thomas von Aquin: Grenze und Grösse mittelalterlicher Theologie* (Mainz: Matthias-Grünewald, 1988).

101. Otto Muck, *The Transcendental Method* (New York: Crossroad, 1968); and Harold Holz, *Transzendentalphilosophie und Metaphysik* (Mainz: Matthias-Grünewald, 1966).

102. Karl Rahner, "Transcendental Theology," in *Sacramentum Mundi* (New York: Herder and Herder, 1970), 6:287.

103. Joseph Maréchal, *Le point de départ de la métaphysique*, 5 vols., 3d ed. (Brussels: Museum Lessianum, 1944–49).

influential and renowned. Influenced not only by Maréchal but also by Martin Heidegger (especially his earlier work), Karl Rahner has written about the whole range of Christian theological topics. His editorial work is also extensive and influential. For years he edited the Denzinger collection of church documents. As editor, he also published several major encyclopedias and dictionaries of theology, *Lexikon für Theologie und Kirche*, *Sacramentum Mundi*, *Dictionary of Theology*, and an important series on controversial questions, *Quaestiones Disputatae*. He was also influential in establishing the international journal *Concilium*.

**Rahner's Starting Point.**   Central to Rahner's approach is his analysis of human experience of knowledge and freedom as an experience of an "absolute and limitless transcendentality."[104] This experience both constitutes and expresses the historical nature of human persons as radically open toward the transcendent, as oriented to the absolute mystery called God. In Rahner's view, this radical orientation toward the absolute is not only constitutive of human nature, but also results from God's full historical self-communication and presence to humanity—a self-communication that has at the same time a history, namely, the history of God's saving presence to the world.

**Rahner's Method.**   Rahner outlines his method in several points.[105] First, through acts of knowledge and freedom, human persons transcend themselves. The act of knowing an individual object or the act of willing an individual action has a dimension of unlimited openness. Knowledge and volition are not limited to one object or to one act but are unlimited. The first step is this experience of the limitlessness of our knowing and willing as an experience of the openness of our subjectivity toward the transcending infinite. The unlimitedness of the horizon of our knowing and willing comes to the fore in our questioning and searching for the meaning of the horizon of our existence. We look beyond objects of experience for meaning and we are confronted with incomprehensible mystery.

Second, in this search for meaning, we experience ourselves as radically finite and yet with unlimited questions. We experience reality as an incomprehensible mystery, but at the same time we hope that there is a fulfillment of the highest possibility of human exis-

104. Karl Rahner, "Reflections on Methodology in Theology," in *Theological Investigations* (New York: Crossroad, 1974), 11:94.

105. Here I follow Rahner's exposition in *Foundations of Christian Faith* (New York: Seabury, 1978), 208–12. The exposition differs somewhat in enumeration, but not content, from his essay on method quoted in the previous footnote.

tence. We hope that ultimately reality is meaningful. Though finite and limited, we have the hope for an absolute fullness of meaning. We hope and trust that the absolute mystery of our being is a Thou who is absolutely trustworthy.

Third, Rahner argues for unity between historical existence and subjective human existence. This unity means that God's self-communication (revelation) as well as the human hope for it are historically mediated. They "appear" together in concrete human history. Consequently, the historical and contingent at the same time announces and awakens hope in the presence of the infinite and absolute. In short, the human hope for meaning is historical hope that emerges in history as a result of God's presence in human history. In Rahner's interpretation, the historical mediation of the infinite within the finite means that God is first of all present in the historical and contingent as promise and as hope in the face of human finitude and death.[106]

Fourth, since human persons exist in history and time, they search history for God's self-promise as final and irreversible. They search history for an answer to their quest for meaning. They search for what could be considered an absolute fulfillment in itself of the meaning of history. They search for a historical event that brings an irrevocable promise to the world.

Fifth, Rahner's final point is the development of the notion of "absolute savior," which he explicates with the argument that the historical mediation of God's irreversible presence to the world can be expressed only in a free subject. Only such a free subject can be the "exemplar" of God's presence. For God's presence to be freely offered and accepted, it must be made and accepted in a free human subject. Such an individual accepts human finitude and as such is accepted by God and thus has exemplary significance for the world.

### Comparison between Aquinas and Rahner

A comparison between the *Summa Theologiae* of Aquinas and Rahner's *Foundations of Christian Faith* illustrates important shifts in theological presuppositions and method. Thomas wrote the *Summa* as a handbook for students. Rahner wrote his book as a "basic course" (the original German title was *Grundkurs*) that aimed to introduce beginning theological students to Christian theology and faith. Although such a comparison is not entirely appropriate—for the former is a *summa* of theology, whereas the later is a text of

---

106. Rahner, *Foundations*, 210.

fundamental theology—the comparison is helpful in showing their distinct theological presuppositions.

Rahner begins with an analysis of human persons, their acts of knowing and willing and their basic existential quest for meaning. The quest for meaning and experience of absolute mystery coupled with the experience of sin and grace constitute the beginning chapters. His starting point is anthropological not only insofar as he begins with this anthropological analysis, but also insofar as the content of the basic Christian beliefs is related to the anthropological question. God's revelation, salvation history, christology, the church and sacraments, and eschatology are interpreted in relation to their significance for human nature.

Thomas's starting point and structure are theocentric. After the first question on the nature of *sacra doctrina*, Thomas begins part 1 of the *Summa Theologiae* by addressing the issue of the existence and nature of God as one and triune; this is followed by a discussion of what God has created. Part 2 treats human nature and its virtues. Part 3 deals with christology, the sacraments, and eschatology. This structure has been interpreted as following Aristotelian as well as Neo-Platonic patterns. Neo-Scholastic interpretations of Thomas underscored that the three parts fit Aristotelian categories of causality: part 1, God as the efficient cause; part 2, God as the final cause; and part 3, God as the exemplary cause of all. Medieval historians pointed to the Neo-Platonic pattern that emphasizes the origin off all things from God and the return of all things to God (*exitus-reditus*).[107] Part 1 is the *exitus:* God and the creation proceeding from God; part 2 is the *reditus:* the return to God; part 3 treats the model as well as the means of the return. These interpretations of the structure of the *Summa* convey its theocentric structure.

The difference between *Foundations* and the *Summa* is most conspicuous in regard to the locus and role of anthropology. Whereas Thomas located anthropology in part 2 of the *Summa*, Rahner locates anthropology in the beginning of *Foundations*. Anthropology constitutes for Rahner the starting point as well as constant reference point of theological reflection. The starting point is the human quest for ultimate meaning that raises the question of God and looks to history, specifically to God's revelation in Christ, for a response. The individual contents of faith are all related to the structures of human existence and to the human quest for ultimate meaning. In

---

107. M. D. Chenu, "Le plan de las Somme théologique de S. Thomas," *Revue Thomiste* 45 (1939): 93–107. For an interpretation that suggests a salvation-historical outline, see Ulrich Horst, "Über die Frage einer heilsökonomischen Theologie bei Thomas von Aquin," *Münchener theologische Zeitschrift* 12 (1961): 97–111.

this way, Rahner's theology seeks to relate anthropocentricism and theocentrism. They are not opposed, but proportionately correlated.

### Beyond Transcendental Theology

The turn to the subject not only represents an important movement of modern theology. It also underscores the theological task of relating the content and subject matter of theology to human subjectivity. Nevertheless, the turn to the subject is not without its criticisms. Hans Urs von Balthasar especially has argued that the anthropological turn in modern theology, particularly as developed by Karl Rahner, reduces religious truth to the perspective of anthropology and thereby does less justice to other perspectives. Von Balthasar has developed his major systematic work as a triptych: The first part outlines a theological aesthetics that approaches revelation from the standpoint of the beautiful. The second part treats revelation as a dramatic interplay. The third part considers revelation as idea and word. The code words for the three parts are: theo-phany = aesthetics; theo-praxy = dramatic theory; and theo-logy = logic.[108] Von Balthasar has influenced Walter Kasper and Joseph Ratzinger in their respective criticisms of Rahner's transcendental approach. Kasper's own theological approach seeks to complement a transcendental approach with a systematic incorporation of history, the latter being indebted to the nineteenth-century tradition of the Tübingen School.[109]

In addition to such criticism of a transcendental method, other contemporary theological approaches attempt to go beyond a transcendental method insofar as they incorporate into the theological task other dimensions that relocate the role of human subjectivity.[110] Contemporary linguistic philosophy and hermeneutical theory underscore that the human subject exists within a world of language

---

108. For a criticism of Karl Rahner, see Hans Urs von Balthasar, _Cordula oder der Ernstfall_, 3d ed. (Einsiedeln: Johannes Verlag, 1987). For an introduction to von Balthasar's own position, see Medard Kehl and Werner Löser, eds., _The von Balthasar Reader_ (New York: Crossroad, 1982). His own systematic system is developed in three sets of volumes: _The Glory of the Lord: A Theological Aesthetics_, 3 vols. (San Francisco: Ignatius Press, 1983–88); _Theodramatik_ (Einsiedeln: Johannes-Verlag, 1973–83), of which volume 1 has been translated, _Theo-drama: Theological Dramatic Theory: Prolegomena_ (San Francisco: Ignatius Press, 1989); and _Theologik_ (Einsiedeln: Johannes-Verlag, 1985).

109. Walter Kasper, _Jesus the Christ_ (New York: Paulist, 1976); idem, _The God of Jesus Christ_ (New York: Crossroad, 1984); and idem, _Theology and Church_ (New York: Crossroad, 1989).

110. Francis Schüssler Fiorenza, "Theology: Transcendental or Hermeneutical," _Horizons_ 16 (1989): 329–41.

and a tradition of cultural meaning. Political and liberation theologies underscore that the socio-political arena is the broader context in which to view the human person. They emphasize the significance of the social and political for the formation and dignity of the human person. The differences from the transcendental approach will become clearer in analysis of these other approaches.

## HERMENEUTICAL THEOLOGY

Hermeneutics deals with theories of interpretation.[111] All approaches to theology are hermeneutical insofar as they include interpretation, be it the interpretation of the Scriptures, creeds, traditions, or experience. Moreover, some theologians attempt to combine transcendental analysis and hermeneutical theory within their approaches. Nevertheless, recent hermeneutical theory underscores the transcendence of language to human subjectivity in a way that brings to the fore the differences between a transcendental and a hermeneutical approach to theology. At the same time the emphasis within hermeneutical theory on the transcendence of language and on the universal scope of hermeneutics opens hermeneutical theory to the criticisms raised by liberation and political theologies as well as critical theory.[112]

### Experience and Language

A major distinction between a hermeneutical and a transcendental approach rests on their different interpretations of the relationship between experience and language. Transcendental theology appeals to religious experience that underlies creedal and doctrinal formulations. Such a transcendental approach views language as expressive: Doctrinal formulations are propositional statements that express a basic religious experience. At the turn of the twentieth century, modernist theologians viewed religious experience as much more basic than religious doctrine because they considered doctrines as mere linguistic expressions of religious experience. Therefore, they thought that doctrinal formulations could be exchanged for different but equivalent formulations.

---

111. For a history of hermeneutics, see Richard Palmer, *Hermeneutics* (Evanston, Ill.: Northwestern University Press, 1969), and Kurt Mueller-Vollmer, ed., *The Hermeneutic Reader* (New York: Crossroad, 1985).

112. See Jürgen Habermas's critique of hermeneutical idealism in Justus George Lawler and Francis Fiorenza, eds., *Cultural Hermeneutics* (entire issue of *Continuum* [1970]: 7).

Hermeneutical theory criticizes this view on the following grounds: Such an expressive view of language and doctrine overlooks the degree to which language does not just express but also constitutes experience. Therefore, religious language is not only expressive, but also constitutive of religious experience. Thus some hermeneutical theorists argue that one should understand religion not merely as an expressive phenomenon but rather as a cultural linguistic phenomenon.[113] Others argue, on the contrary, that the cultural linguistic view of language is basically a further development that includes transcendental philosophy but goes beyond it.[114] The hermeneutical view of the relation between language and experience has had significant influence on theological reflection. In this regard, the philosophers Hans-Georg Gadamer and Paul Ricoeur have been especially influential.

*Classics: The Authority of a Tradition*

Gadamer's major point is that "understanding is to be thought of less as a subjective act than as participating in an event of tradition, a process of transmission in which past and present are constantly mediated."[115] Employing several key ideas, Gadamer explicates this notion of understanding as a participation in tradition. The notion of the classic is central to Gadamer's hermeneutics. Classics are significant as outstanding exemplifications of human understanding. Moreover, classics have an "effective-history" to the extent they influence our horizon and specify our self-understanding. Opposing the Enlightenment's prejudice against tradition, Gadamer argues for a "pre-judgment" in favor of the classics. The endurance of the classic through history demonstrates its value and significance. A classic encounters us with a certain authority and claim.

The interpretation of classics is further explicated with the idea of the "fusion of horizons." Understanding takes place not insofar as one abstracts from one's horizon and places oneself in the shoes of the author, but rather insofar as one merges one's own horizon with that of the text and its author. The "fusion of horizons" is

---

113. This is the important argument made by George Lindbeck, *The Nature of Doctrine* (Philadelphia: Westminster Press, 1985). His criticisms of Karl Rahner and of David Tracy tend to minimize the role of hermeneutical reflection within their theologies.

114. Charles Taylor, *Human Agency and Language: Philosophical Papers* (New York: Cambridge University Press, 1985), 1:213–92.

115. Hans-Georg Gadamer, *Truth and Method*, rev. ed. (New York: Crossroad, 1989), 290.

achieved when the classic is so interpreted that its claim upon one's own present is acknowledged.[116]

Gadamer's hermeneutical theory has been further developed and in part modified by Paul Ricoeur's explication of the significance of metaphor and narrative structure as well as by his stress on the importance of interrelating the modes of explanation and understanding.[117] Commenting on Aristotle's definition of a metaphor in terms of similarity,[118] Ricoeur suggests that a metaphor does not merely further explicate a similarity between images and ideas that is already present. Instead a metaphor produces a resulting similarity. Meanings, previously dissimilar, are brought together. The resulting "semantic shock" creates new meaning. A metaphor, therefore, forges a new meaning by bringing together opposing meanings. Ricoeur extends his analysis from the use of metaphor in sentences to the narrative structure of the whole text. The emplotment of a narrative creates new meaning by bringing together a plot and the characters, occasions, episodes, and events of the story.

Paul Ricoeur modifies Gadamer's hermeneutical approach by introducing "explanation" as complementary to "understanding." The hermeneutical focus on "understanding" takes into account the role of pre-understanding and life-relation vis-à-vis the subject matter of a text. Yet there are also methods of "explanation"—for example, historical-critical, social-critical, and literary-critical analysis, and, especially for Ricoeur, the structuralist analysis of sentences and texts. A full interpretation of the subject matter of the text must include not only the attention to our pre-understanding and life-relation, but also structural and analytical analyses.

Using the hermeneutical theories of both Gadamer and Ricoeur, David Tracy explores the nature of religious and Christian classics. In addition, he defines systematic theology primarily as hermeneutical and proposes that the task of Christian systematic theology is the interpretive retrieval of the meaning and truth claims of

---

116. Gadamer, *Truth and Method*, 369–79. For two good expositions of Gadamer, see Joel C. Weishammer, *Gadamer's Hermeneutics: A Reading of Truth and Method* (New Haven, Conn.: Yale University Press, 1986), and Georgia Warnke, *Gadamer: Hermeneutics, Tradition and Reason* (Stanford, Calif.: Stanford University Press, 1987).

117. Paul Ricoeur, *The Rule of Metaphor: Multidisciplinary Studies of the Creation of Meaning in Language* (Toronto: University of Toronto, 1977); idem, *Time and Narrative*, 3 vols. (Chicago: University of Chicago Press, 1984, 1985, 1988). See also the important collection of Ricoeur's essays, *Hermeneutics and the Human Sciences*, ed. Josiah Thompson (New York: Cambridge University Press, 1981).

118. Aristotle *Poetics* 1459a.4–8.

the Christian classic.[119] In explicating his conception of systematic theology as hermeneutical, Tracy accepts Gadamer's notion of understanding as participating in a tradition. However, he accepts Ricoeur's modifications of Gadamer and appropriates some of Ricoeur's categories. Therefore, Tracy underscores the importance of the explanatory modes of historical-critical, literary-critical, and social-critical analysis as complementary to interpretive modes of understanding.

### Beyond Hermeneutics

The development of hermeneutical theology coincides with the emergence of several crises. These crises affect not only our understanding of tradition and the sources of theology, but also our understanding of present-day experience. The first crisis involves the meaning and significance of tradition. The importance of hermeneutics increases the degree to which the meaning, significance, and validity of the religious tradition become remote and obscure to the present. The more the meaning and the authority of the traditional sources of theology become remote and obscure, the more it becomes necessary to interpret them so as to explicate their meaning and significance.[120] To the extent that the historical, cultural, and social distance between the past and the present increases so as to make the past more obscure, irrelevant, or even oppressive, to that extent the need for an interpretation of past traditions increases.

A second crisis affects personal experience. The more personal experience is no longer viewed as transparent, the more the need increases for a hermeneutics of experience. Today one often gives psychological, social, and behavioristic interpretations of human intentions and actions. The meaning of human action is no longer simply identified with the agent's self-interpretation of that action. The result is a conflict of interpretations of human action: one based on conscious intention, explicit motives, and self-interpretation, another based on unreflective causes, social factors, and hidden reasons. The interpretation of experience and action becomes necessary insofar as the meaning of experience and action is no longer assumed to be manifest and evident.

---

119. David Tracy, *The Analogical Imagination* (New York: Crossroad, 1981), 99–153; idem, *Plurality and Ambiguity: Hermeneutics, Religion, Hope* (New York: Harper and Row, 1987).

120. See Odo Marquard, *Farewell to Matters of Principle* (New York: Oxford University Press, 1989).

These two crises lead to a third crisis, the crisis of hermeneutics itself, which emerges when interpretation alone does not suffice to resolve the other two crises.[121] This crisis occurs when not merely the application of a tradition's meaning and significance is at issue, but rather when the tradition itself is radically challenged or when the conflicts within the tradition are incapable of ready reconciliation. This crisis also occurs when an experience itself is challenged. Then it is no longer a question of the interpretation of that experience, but rather of the adequacy of the experience itself. In Claude Geffré's words: "The crisis of hermeneutics is not simply a crisis of language—it is a crisis of thought."[122] It is then necessary to go beyond interpretation to a reconstruction of either tradition or experience. What is at stake is not just the meaning of a tradition or experience, but its truth. As Joseph Cardinal Ratzinger notes, "Christian theology does not just interpret texts: it asks about truth itself."[123]

## ANALYTICAL APPROACHES TO THEOLOGY

Some approaches are analytical insofar as they provide analytical tools that help one to carry out the theological task and to clarify theological issues. Two analytical approaches have become especially influential within contemporary Roman Catholic theology. These approaches attempt to underscore either (1) the significance of a metatheory, specifically epistemology for method in general and theological method, (2) or the significant role (often implicit) of models and paradigms in theological reflection.

### Metatheory: Method in Theology

Bernard Lonergan has contributed to contemporary Roman Catholic theology by showing that it is important for theology to address some basic questions of epistemology: What is the nature of human knowledge? What are the basic procedures of human cognition? Lonergan argues that such questions are much more basic than specific theological controversies and that they even underlie particular methodological issues. For epistemological assumptions, often implicit and unexamined, determine the outcome of these theolog-

121. Claude Geffré, *The Risk of Interpretation: On Being Faithful to the Christian Tradition in a Non-Christian Age* (New York: Paulist Press, 1987), 21–45.

122. Geffré, *Risk of Interpretation*, 32.

123. Joseph Ratzinger, *Church, Ecumenism and Politics* (New York: Crossroad, 1988), 154.

ical controversies and methodological issues. Such epistemological assumptions need to be examined, for they are fundamental not just to theology, but to every discipline and to every form of inquiry.

Lonergan has examined such basic questions and assumptions. He has developed an epistemological "metatheory" of human cognition and demonstrated its relevance for theological method. As a metatheory, his analysis of human cognition entails a high degree of abstraction. It analyzes those cognitional structures and procedures that are often presupposed but not explicated in concrete theological debates. By examining the issues of epistemological metatheory involved in theological controversies, Lonergan has thereby related concrete theological issues to more general classic and perennial philosophical debates (for example, idealism versus materialism, subjectivism versus objectivism). He often resolves the theological issues with reference to philosophical solutions. He shows that his philosophical advocacy of a critical realism over and against idealism and materialism is significant not only for epistemology, but also for concrete theological issues.[124]

Lonergan develops his understanding of critical realism in relation to the transition from the classical Aristotelian understanding of scientific method to a modern empirical method.[125] He affirms that the result of every scientific method is open to further correction and revision. Thereby he emphasizes that genuine objectivity is not simply a naive realism that equates knowledge with simply taking a look. Objective knowledge is not simply a passive reception; it entails a critical realism in which the subjectivity of the knower also actively orders the world of meaning. This activity of human subjectivity needs to be taken into account in theological method. Lonergan's account of theology does this in two ways: (1) it explicates the structures of human cognition; and (2) it develops the relation between the horizon of subjectivity and the structure of cognition.

**Structure of Knowing and Theological Method.** Lonergan argues that knowing involves a fourfold structure: the experience of data, the understanding of their meaning, the assessment of their value,

---

124. For example, Lonergan makes the cognitional issues relevant to christology. See his *The Way to Nicea: The Dialectical Development of Trinitarian Theology* (Philadelphia: Westminster Press, 1976). The development of trinitarian theology is sketched in relation to epistemology: Tertullian represents a materialist approach, Origen, an idealist, and Athanasius, a critical realist.

125. See Bernard Lonergan, *Insight* (New York: Philosophical Library, 1957); idem, *A Third Collection* (Philadelphia: Westminster Press, 1985). See the commentary in Vernon Gregson, *The Desires of the Human Heart* (New York and Mahwah, N.J.: Paulist Press, 1989).

and finally an evaluative decision. Since this pattern of knowing takes place in all acts of knowledge, its structure is relevant to all disciplines and sciences, not just philosophy or theology. To illustrate its relevance for theological method, Lonergan proposes that the methods and tasks of theology are rooted in the more basic invariant structure of human consciousness with its movement from experience to understanding, to judgment, and finally to decision.

This structure provides a basis for classifying the diverse tasks of theology as diverse functional specialities. Lonergan relates the fourfold structure of knowing to specific intentional objects and to specialties of theology so as to divide the theological task into two phases. The first phase of theology corresponds to the fourfold cognitional structure. It involves research (assembling data), interpretation (understanding its meaning), history (judging the implied assertions and data), and dialectic (clarifying the issues and making a decision or taking a stand). These four procedures are transcendental in that they form the structure of all human knowledge. Everyone (believers, nonbelievers, scientists, philosophers) follows the same basic procedure. If someone wanted to criticize this cognitional scheme, Lonergan argues, that person would in fact prove its validity because he or she would need to assemble data, interpret and evaluate the data, and, finally, make a decision.

The second phase of the theological task begins after one has made a decision and taken a stance. This phase, involving the subjective horizon of the theologian, encompasses foundations, doctrinal theology and systematic theology, and communications. It again follows the cognitional structure but in reverse. One moves from the foundation of a decision (foundational theology), to judgments of truth (doctrinal theology), to understanding (systematic theology), and, finally, to experience (communications—practical theology).

**Conversion and Theological Method.**   Crucial to the second phase of the theological task is the foundational role of the decision that is explicated by the category of conversion.[126] The notion of conversion brings out the significance of the intentionality of the knowing and believing subject for the constructive task of theology. Moreover, Lonergan's concrete explication of conversion expands his treatment from the realm of metatheory to a transcendental theology. Lon-

---

126. For contemporary expositions and further developments of Lonergan's notion of conversion, see Walter Conn, *Conscience: Development and Self-transcendence* (Birmingham, Ala.: Religious Education Press, 1981); Stephen Happel and James J. Walter, *Conversion and Discipleship: A Christian Foundation for Ethics and Doctrine* (Philadelphia: Fortress Press, 1986).

ergan incorporates the intentionality of the knowing and believing subject into theological method through an analysis of conversion. He explicates the intentionality of conversion as intellectual, moral, and religious. Intellectual conversion involves deciding that knowing is not the same as simply taking a good look at the data or forming concepts. Intellectual conversion entails a decision and a movement of self-transcendence, for knowing entails a complex and reflective human operation of continued questioning for evidence, reasons, and comprehensive viewpoints.

Moral conversion changes the criteria for moral decisions from satisfaction to value.[127] Moral conversion entails opting for what one judges to be truly of value and good, even when value and satisfaction conflict. Such judgments of value comprise a knowledge of reality and an intentional response to value. Therefore, moral conversion presupposes intellectual conversion. Moreover, to the degree that value is placed above satisfaction, moral conversion is a form of self-transcendence and can be related to cognitive, moral, and affective development.[128]

Religious conversion, like intellectual and moral conversion, entails self-transcendence. Religious conversion, however, goes beyond the self-transcendence of intellectual and moral conversion insofar as it is constituted by that self-transcendence entailed in the shift to ultimate meaning and value. Lonergan characterizes religious conversion with the following set of terms: "being grasped by ultimate concern," "other-worldly falling in love," and "unrestricted love."[129] Religious conversion is not simply a matter of becoming religious, but is rather a total reorientation of one's life.

Lonergan's synthesis is not without its critics. Likening Lonergan to Schleiermacher, Langdon Gilkey has argued that the foundational role given to conversion lessens the public dimension of the theological tasks and opens Lonergan's method to the charge of subjectivism.[130] Although such a charge raises an important issue, it overlooks the hermeneutical dimension of all experience. Understanding presupposes a life-relation to the subject matter to be understood. Therefore, religious knowledge and the interpretation

---

127. Lonergan, *Method in Theology* (New York: Crossroad, 1972), 241.

128. See Walter Conn, *Christian Conversion: A Developmental Interpretation of Autonomy and Surrender* (Mahwah, N.J.: Paulist, 1986), for the relation of Lonergan's understanding of conversion to moral and psychological theories of development.

129. Ibid., 241–44.

130. See Langdon Gilkey, "Empirical Science and Theological Knowing," in Philip McShane, ed., *Foundations of Theology* (Notre Dame, Ind.: University of Notre Dame Press, 1972), 76–101. In the same volume David Tracy raises a similar criticism: see "Lonergan's Foundational Theology: An Interpretation and a Critique," 197–222.

of religious texts presuppose a life-relation to the subject matter of the text. The interpretation of religion involves a double hermeneutic, for that interpretation should be based not only upon the model or category that the interpreter uses to understand or to explain a religious event, action, or symbol, but also upon the meaning that the religious agents themselves attribute to that religious event, action, or symbol.[131] Lonergan's notion of conversion, coupled with his critical realism, seeks to hold in balance the tension between objectivity and subjectivity in a way that undercuts the criticism.

In addition, the critical question emerges whether major authors and positions in the history of philosophy (Hume, Kant, or Hegel) or in the history of theology (Tertullian, Origen, Athanasius) can be reduced to abstract epistemological categories such as materialistic empiricism, idealism, or critical realism, as Lonergan has often done. Nevertheless, Lonergan has provided an invaluable service. In applying his cognitional metatheory to specific historical theological controversies, he has highlighted the significance of epistemology for concrete theological positions.

## Models and Category Analysis

The use of the term *model* has become widespread in a variety of disciplines. In the natural sciences, a model is a way of representing a phenomenon so as to illustrate some of its basic properties and their interconnections.[132] A model highlights certain features and neglects others. In so doing, it provides an arrangement of concepts that delineates a specific vision of a phenomenon from a particular perspective. An analogous use of models has become current within systematic theology to illumine the perspectival nature of theological categories.

**Avery Dulles and Models in Theology.** Avery Dulles, one of the leading contemporary Roman Catholic theologians in North America, has consistently made use of models within theology. He has used models to understand the church, revelation, the ecumenical movement, christology, and Catholicism. His most influential application of models concerns the understanding of the church.[133] In *Models of*

131. See my *Foundational Theology* (285–301) for arguments for the hermeneutical dimension of experience and the double hermeneutic that seeks to show that appeals to a neutral public or common experience overlook the conditioned nature of all experience.

132. Marx W. Wartofsky, *Models: Representation and the Scientific Understanding* (Boston: D. Reidel Company, 1979).

133. Avery Dulles, *Models of the Church* (New York: Doubleday, 1974).

*the Church*, Dulles argues not only that various ecclesiologies differ in their understandings of the church, but also that this difference is in part due to the employment of different models of the church. He identifies institution, mystical communion, sacrament, herald, and servant as different models prevalent in contemporary theology. In later writings, he adds the model of discipleship as another comprehensive model.[134]

The importance of this method (and, in part, a reason for the influence of Dulles's book) is that it enabled Roman Catholics of diverse theological persuasions to understand one another and to engage in a cooperative conversation. Theologians and ministers with an outlook based on the model of the church as institution did not understand the horizon of theologians and ministers influenced by a vision of the church based on the model of *communio*. The awareness of diverse models implies that each perspective grasps, in a particular way, a significant and indispensable dimension of the church, while at the same time showing that other perspectives are equally valid. In the era following the Second Vatican Council, when diverse ecclesiologies often clashed with one another in theory and practice, such an approach contributed greatly to recognition and acceptance of diverse positions.

In his study of revelation Avery Dulles proposes the following diverse models for interpreting different theologies of revelation: doctrine, history, inner experience, dialectical presence, and new awareness.[135] He proposes that an understanding of revelation as symbolic can best incorporate the perspectives of each of these models. These diverse models of revelation, moreover, often affect and underlie diverse conceptions of theological method as well as ecumenism.

**Category Analysis.** In addition to analyzing implicit epistemologies and models, contemporary theology has become sensitive to the use of diverse categories within theology. There is, thus, an increasing awareness of the significance and diversity of categories that underlie theological affirmations. The Congregation for the Doctrine of the Faith has taken up this problem in its document *Mysterium Ecclesiae*, which deals with the historicity of Christian doctrine.[136] This document affirmed several points: (1) the incompleteness of every

─────────────────────────

134. Avery Dulles, *A Church to Believe In* (New York: Crossroad, 1982).

135. Avery Dulles, *Models of Revelation* (New York: Doubleday, 1983).

136. The official English translation is: "In Defense of Catholic Doctrine," *Origins* 32 (July 19, 1973): 97, 99–100, 110–23. See Ratzinger's commentary in *Principles*, 228–30.

doctrinal affirmation, (2) the contextuality of doctrinal affirmations insofar as they are responses to particular questions, (3) the linguisticality of all doctrines, and (4) the distinction between the truth affirmed in a particular doctrinal formulation and the philosophical categories and worldviews used to express that truth.

*Mysterium Ecclesiae,* written in response to Hans Küng's criticism of papal infallibility,[137] asserts that while doctrinal statements are historically and linguistically conditioned they still are determinate affirmations of the truth. It maintains that doctrinal statements not only approximate the truth, but express some determinate aspect of truth, albeit in a historical, contextual, linguistic, and categorically specific manner. This affirmation of the historicity of the expressions and categories contained in doctrinal expression poses an important challenge for the understanding and assessment not only of the content of the doctrinal statements, but also of the categories central to theological method.

Traditional doctrines have been formulated with categories borrowed from particular philosophical traditions. Today, the adequacy of such categories is often challenged and questioned. Does "transubstantiation" or "transignification" best express the Roman Catholic beliefs about the eucharist? Is the formula "two natures and one person" adequate to express what traditional christological dogmas affirm? Is the reality expressed by the concept of "hypostatic union" better stated by the concept of "hypostatic identification"? Should the efficacy of the sacraments be expressed with the categories of Aristotelian causality or with categories drawn from a phenomenology of encounter? Hence within theology there is debate over whether the new categories or formulations are more or less adequate than the traditional ones. The philosophical debate underlying the theological debate is just as complex. The distinction between content and category or conceptual scheme is as much challenged as it is advocated.[138]

The analysis of basic categories is important for an understanding not only of doctrinal formulations, but also of theological method. Much of contemporary theology cannot be understood unless one takes into account certain shifts in basic categories. One example of such a shift is the result of Martin Heidegger's influence on Roman Catholic theology. In *Being and Time,* Heidegger argued that the ontological categories used from Greek philosophy

---

137. Hans Küng, *Infallible: An Inquiry* (New York: Doubleday, 1971).

138. See Donald Davidson's classic essay "On the Very Idea of a Conceptual Scheme," now in his collection, *Inquiries into Truth and Interpretation* (Oxford: Clarendon, 1984), 183–98.

to Descartes are inadequate to describe the temporality, historicity, and facticity of human existence in the world. Therefore, he sought to replace these categories with categories drawn from an analysis of human existence in its temporality.[139] These categories, which he called "existentials," characterize what is specific to human existence: being-toward-death, care, self-interpretation.[140] Much of Rahner's theology can be adequately understood only when one realizes that beyond traditional Scholastic categories, he has appropriated Heidegger's "existentials." In a similar fashion, Lonergan has shifted "from a faculty psychology to intentionality analysis" with the result "that the basic terms and relations of systematic theology will not be metaphysical, as in medieval theology, but psychological."[141] Similar examples could be drawn from other theologians (Edward Schillebeeckx, Piet Schoonenberg, Charles Curran) or from theological movements (e.g., liberation theology). Consequently, contemporary theology needs to engage in metatheoretical reflection upon the basic categories employed in theological affirmations.

### Beyond Metatheory

An important point in considering all metatheories, be they epistemological theories or analyses of models and categories, is that such metatheories are in themselves not theological methods, despite all their utility for theology and theological method. This point has been forcefully raised by Karl Rahner. In his comments on Lonergan's notion of functional specialties in theology, Rahner questions whether Lonergan's method is sufficiently and specifically theological.[142] In his view, Lonergan is not so much developing a theological method as he is describing the cognitional structures involved in every act of human inquiry from searching the skies for clues to the origin of the universe to searching a cookbook for data on how to bake a cake. The very title of Lonergan's book indicates this fact, for the work is not entitled "theological method" but rather *Method in Theology*.[143] A similar criticism can be raised against the use of models in theology. They provide helpful analyses, but theological reflection needs

---

139. Heidegger, *Being and Time*, 41–49.
140. Ibid., division 2, 277–487.
141. Lonergan, *Method in Theology*, 343.
142. "Lonergan's theological methodology seems to me to be *so generic that it really fits every science*, and hence is not the methodology of theology as such, but only a very general methodology of science in general, illustrated with examples taken from theology" (Karl Rahner, "Some Critical Thoughts on 'Functional Specialties in Theology,'" in McShane, ed., *Foundations of Theology*, 194).
143. Lonergan, *Method in Theology*.

to go beyond merely analyzing the advantages and disadvantages of each model; it needs to take up theology's constructive and systematic task. In this regard the following approach, employing a method of correlation, provides a more comprehensive view of theological method.

## THE METHOD OF CORRELATION

The method of correlation emerged in the nineteenth century as an explicit theological method. In the twentieth century it has become widely accepted, particularly due to the influence of Paul Tillich. Some modified form of the method of correlation has been taken over by many major Roman Catholic theologians. A sketch of Paul Tillich's use of the method of correlation will provide background to its use in contemporary Roman Catholic theology.

### Background

**Nineteenth-century Reaction to Schleiermacher.** The method of correlation has its origins in the "mediation theology" (*Vermittlungstheologie*) of mid–nineteenth-century German Protestant theology.[144] This theological movement sought to mediate between the traditional theological starting point of Scripture and Schleiermacher's starting point of religious experience. It advocated a method of correlation as a means to mediate science and faith as well as Scripture and reason.

**Paul Tillich's Conception of Correlation.** Paul Tillich developed the method of correlation with a specific understanding of correlation.[145] The three possible types of correlation are: statistical, as in the correlation of data; logical, as in the interdependence of concepts (for example, whole and part); and real, as in the interdependence of things and events. These three types are also present in theology. The statistical correlation between religious symbols and what they symbolize constitutes the problem of religious knowledge. The logical correlation between concepts of the divine and those of the human determines the meaning of language about God and the world. And the correlation of the real interdependence of things

---

144. Ragnar Holte, *Die Vermittlungstheologie* (Uppsala: University of Uppsala Press, 1965).

145. Paul Tillich, *Systematic Theology* (Chicago: University of Chicago Press, 1951–63), 1:59–66; see also 2:14. See John P. Clayton, *The Concept of Correlation: Paul Tillich and the Possibility of a Mediating Theology* (New York: De Gruyters, 1980).

and events is found in the correlation between one's ultimate concern and that about which one is ultimately concerned. This third correlation is specific to the relationship between the divine and the human within religious experience. This correlation in the divine-human relation expresses a real correlation between the divine and the human on the real and ontological level.

Tillich's definition and application of the method of correlation are diverse. He elaborates the method of correlation in terms of the correlation between question and answer as well as in terms of the correlation between form and content. Concerning the former correlation, he writes: "Theology formulates the questions implied in human existence, and theology formulates the answers implied in divine self-manifestation under the guidance of the questions implied in human existence."[146] His concrete application of the method of correlation is very complex, for he uses correlation not only to express the correlation between question and answer. He also uses the method to express the correlation between the form and content of human experience of finitude and human religious symbolization.[147] Tillich analyzes reason, being, existence, and history to underscore the emergence of a basic question that can then be correlated with the symbols of revelation, God, Christ, Spirit, and the kingdom of God.

### Correlation in Contemporary Roman Catholic Theology

Today many Roman Catholic theologians maintain that a method of correlation best expresses the theological task. As Hans Küng notes, a widespread consensus exists that theology deals with two poles and that these two poles must be correlated. Despite this consensus, important differences exist regarding how each of these poles should be understood and how they should be correlated. A brief description of four particular examples of the method will illustrate significant similarities and differences. These four are: Edward Schillebeeckx's critical correlation and structural principles, Hans Küng's use of a critical confrontation between the historical Jesus and the present, Rosemary Radford Ruether's correlation with the prophetic principle, and David Tracy's mutually critical correlation.

**Critical Correlation and Principles of Identity: Schillebeeckx.** Schillebeeckx formulates the method of correlation as a "critical

146. Tillich, *Systematic Theology*, 1:61.
147. See Langdon Gilkey, *Gilkey on Tillich* (New York: Crossroad, 1990), 56–78, 171–96.

correlation between the two sources of theology . . . on the one hand the tradition of Christian experiences and on the other present-day experiences."[148] This formulation of correlation differs from Paul Tillich's conception. Tillich distinguishes between the medium and source of revelation in order to affirm that experience' is a medium but not a source of revelation. In distinction, Schillebeeckx's correlation is between "two sources" of theology that he labels the two poles of theology: the experiences of the tradition and present-day experiences. He calls for a "critical correlation and on occasion the critical confrontation of these two 'sources.' "[149] Schillebeeckx further delineates these two poles.

In analyzing the tradition of Christian experience (the first pole), Schillebeeckx maintains that despite their diverse theologies the New Testament writings have an underlying unity in a basic experience of salvation from God in Jesus. It is "this basic experience that is interpreted in diverse ways but nevertheless the same."[150] That experience is composed of four formative principles: the belief that God wills the salvation of all (theological-anthropological principle); the belief that Jesus is the definitive disclosure of God's starting point (christological mediation); the belief that God's story in Jesus continues in the message and life style of the church (ecclesial mediation); and the belief that the story of salvation cannot be fulfilled on earth (the eschatological dimension).

In analyzing contemporary experience (the other pole), Schillebeeckx proposes that it is characterized by two contrasting elements: its hopeful orientation to the future and its confrontation with an excess of suffering and senseless injustice. The utilitarian individualism of Western modernity is a major reason and cause for this contrast. This utilitarian individualism leads both to the hope for the future and to suffering and injustice. While its central value is freedom, this freedom is permeated with utilitarian individualism, which, linked with science and technology, often becomes a means of maximizing self-interest.

Schillebeeckx argues that a critical correlation should take place between the story of Jesus and modern utilitarian individuals. The story of Jesus evokes and calls us to conversion. The evoking of this metanoia is the goal of a critical correlation. Therefore, for Schillebeeckx, critical correlation primarily means the confrontation with the story of Jesus that elicits conversion. Underlying Schillebeeckx's

---

148. Edward Schillebeeckx, *Interim Report on the Books "Jesus" and "Christ"* (New York: Crossroad, 1981), 50.

149. Ibid, 51.

150. Ibid.

understanding of the method of correlation is a distinction between ephemeral, conjunctural, and structural history. Ephemeral history is the fact-constituted history of the events of every day that come and go. Conjunctural history is much more expansive and includes the long cultural axes of history. Structural history is invariable, serving as the axis around which the ephemeral and conjunctural revolve.[151] The aim of a critical correlation is to ascertain the structural identity of Christian experience expressed in the diverse categories of conjunctural epochs, for example, Palestinian or Hellenistic. The purpose of ascertaining the structural identity within the conjunctural is to enable the identity of the Christian story to impact upon the present Christian experience and thereby to allow the story of Christ's salvation to become for us an offer of salvation that confronts modern experience and critically corrects modern attitudes of individualism and possessiveness.

**Critical Confrontation and the Living Jesus: Küng.** Preferring the term _critical confrontation_ over _critical correlation_, Hans Küng has developed the method of correlation as a method of critical confrontation between the living Jesus and the present situation.[152] Küng changes the term _correlation_ to _confrontation;_ he prefers to speak of "two poles" rather than "two sources"; and he describes the two poles quite differently than Schillebeeckx does.

The task of theology is to bring about a critical confrontation between the living Jesus and the present situation. The first pole is the living Jesus rather than the biblical symbol or the Christ of faith. Although in the course of his writings Küng has modified his position to include the Christian tradition, his emphasis is on the earthly Jesus. The earthly Jesus—the early Jesus as known through historical-critical research—is the norm and criterion for the Christian faith. In Küng's words, historical-critical research on Jesus can help us see that "the Christ of faith in whom we believe is really the man Jesus of Nazareth and not someone else nor, by some chance, no one at all."[153] Historical-critical research helps us to avoid constructing or adhering to false images of the Christ of faith. It brings us into contact with the Jesus of history, the norm and criterion of the Christ of faith.

---

151. See Edward Schillebeeckx, _Jesus: An Experiment in Christology_ (New York: Crossroad, 1979).

152. Küng's basic essay on the method of correlation appeared in Leonard Swidler, ed., _Consensus in Theology? A Dialogue with Hans Küng and Edward Schillebeeckx_ (Philadelphia: Westminster Press, 1980), then with modifications in Hans Küng, _Theology for the Third Millennium_ (New York: Doubleday, 1988).

153. Küng, _Theology for the Third Millennium_, 111.

In critically confronting the first pole with the second one, Küng also disagrees with Schillebeeckx's description of the pole of contemporary experience. Küng does not follow Schillebeeckx's view of modernity. It is not so much a utilitarian individualism that characterizes modernity and leads to the excessive suffering of modernity. Instead modernity is characterized by the proliferation of bureaucracies and a lack of individual freedom. The freedom of Jesus' critique of the law stands in critical confrontation with the law of this bureaucratic modernity.

**Correlation and the Prophetic Principle: Ruether.** Rosemary Radford Ruether develops the method of correlation from a feminist theological perspective and with an emphasis upon the prophetic principle. She does not propose the method of correlation as a method of general consensus, as Hans Küng does, for she argues that the method of correlation can be diversely applied.[154] She understands the prophetic principle as a dynamic critical principle.[155] It is a principle insofar as it does not refer to a specific tradition or set of texts; rather it is a principle within diverse traditions and texts. As a dynamic principle it is not static but changes and is transformed. As a critical principle it criticizes oppression in the forms of classism, racism, and sexism. In her words, "Feminist theology that draws on Biblical principles is possible only if the prophetic principles, more fully understood, imply a rejection of every elevation of one social group against others as image and agent of God, every use of God to justify social domination and subjugation."[156]

**Mutually Critical Correlation: Tracy.** David Tracy suggests that a "widely accepted definition" of the theological task is "to establish mutually critical correlations between an interpretation of the Christian tradition and an interpretation of the contemporary situation"; it is "a revised correlation method" that is "in fact nothing other than a hermeneutically self-conscious clarification and correction of traditional theology."[157] It is hermeneutically self-conscious because it

---

154. Rosemary Radford Ruether, "Is a New Christian Consensus Possible?" in Swidler, ed., *Consensus in Theology?* 33–39.

155. See Rosemary Radford Ruether, "Feminist Interpretation of the Method of Correlation," in Letty M. Russell, ed., *Feminist Interpretation of the Bible* (Philadelphia: Westminster Press, 1985), 111–24.

156. Rosemary Radford Ruether, *Sexism and God-Talk: Toward a Feminist Theology* (Boston: Beacon, 1983).

157. Robert M. Grant with David Tracy, *A Short History of the Interpretation of the Bible*, rev. ed. (Philadelphia: Fortress Press, 1984), 170.

does not so much appeal to the Christian fact as it appeals to mutually critical correlations between two sets of interpretations.[158]

In elaborating his conception of the method of correlation, David Tracy takes over and develops the distinction that Schubert Ogden has proposed between criteria of appropriateness to the tradition and criteria of intelligibility to the situation.[159] Taking over the analytical distinction between truth and meaning, Ogden argues that the criteria of appropriateness, drawn from the apostolic witness, determine the meaning or identity of Christianity. The criteria of intelligibility to the situation provide criteria for the truth of the Christian faith.

Tracy carefully distinguishes and defines these criteria in developing his conception of the method of correlation. The criteria of appropriateness, understood as theological criteria, imply that it is "theologically crucial to judge every later theological statement in terms of its appropriateness to the apostolic witness expressed normatively in the Scriptures."[160] Such an interpretation of appropriateness differs considerably from Ruether's emphasis on the prophetic principle or Küng's emphasis on the living Jesus. In distinction to Küng, it is "not the 'historical Jesus' but the confessed witnessed Christ that is theologically relevant."[161]

The criteria of intelligibility address or correlate the message to the present situation. The criteria of intelligibility concern the issue of "relative adequacy" to contemporary experience and situation. It is important that the criteria of relative adequacy to the contemporary be such that they allow the classic event to have a disclosing and transformative impact upon the situation. Tracy develops the nature of correlation with the help of the dialectic of event and response, the dialectic of explanatory and interpretive modes, and a model of conversation. The correlation between the two poles is understood as a conversation and a critical correlation. This corre-

---

158. David Tracy, "What Is Fundamental Theology?" *Journal of Religion* 54 (1974): 13–34. Revised as chapter 2 of *Blessed Rage for Order* (New York: Crossroad, 1975).

159. See Schubert Ogden, *On Theology* (New York: Harper and Row, 1986), 1–22. In addition to *Blessed Rage for Order*, see Tracy, *The Analogical Imagination*, and *Plurality and Ambiguity*.

160. Grant and Tracy, *Short History*, 175. Tracy is aware that such a criterion can be taken to imply identity and exclude criticism from later development. Therefore, he nuances his statement: "Criteria of appropriateness insist that all later theologies in *Christian* theology are obliged to show why they are not in radical disharmony with the central Christian witness expressed in the Scriptures. In that restricted sense, Scripture, as the original apostolic witness to Jesus Christ, norms but is not normed (*norma normans sed not normata*) by later witnesses" (p. 176).

161. Tracy, *The Analogical Imagination*, 301–2 n. 97. See Elizabeth A. Johnson, "The Theological Relevance of the Historical Jesus: A Debate and a Thesis," *The Thomist* 48 (1984): 1–43.

lation can differ insofar as the correlation can be one of identity, similarity-in-difference, or even confrontation.[162]

The diversity of approaches advocating that the proper method of theology is a method of correlation indicates how widespread is its acceptance. The method of correlation has much in common with classic conceptions of theology, yet also differs from these conceptions. On the one hand, it assumes the authority and validity of the past religious tradition, correctly interpreted, and seeks to apply it to the present. On the other hand, it perceives a greater distance between past message and present situation than did traditional theology. Therefore, correlation is not simply a fact, but rather the result and the goal of the theological task. In working toward this goal, the theological method of correlation is often combined with other methods, for example, a transcendental analysis of the religious dimension of human subjectivity or a hermeneutical retrieval of the significance of religious traditions.

### Beyond Correlation

Several reservations can be advanced regarding the method of correlation. However, in view of the diverse conceptions of correlation, these reservations are not equally applicable to all. First, the method of correlation often rests on a distinction between language and the reality expressed in language. Such a distinction downplays the historicity of language and culture, for it assumes that different cultural expressions, categories, and language can change while the reality expressed in and through these categories remains the same and, therefore, can be correlated.

Second, the method of correlation emphasizes continuity and identity. It does not sufficiently take into account change and non-identity in the development of faith and theology. Unless one excessively formalizes the tradition to an abstract formula, it is necessary to understand the tradition in categories that go beyond correlation and include development, transformation, and change.

Third, the method of correlation does not sufficiently take into account the need for a critique of tradition. The critique I refer to is not simply a matter of criticizing the formulations of tradition in order that the underlying experience or affirmations of the tradition might more readily shine forth. Rather this critique is one that reexamines the experiences and affirmations themselves.

---

162. David Tracy, "The Uneasy Alliance Reconceived: Catholic Theological Method, Modernity and Postmodernity," *Theological Studies* 56 (1989): 548–70.

## LIBERATION THEOLOGIES

The term *liberation theology* does not refer to a single theological method but rather to diverse theological movements. In a narrow sense, liberation theology is a contemporary theological movement within Latin America. According to this restricted definition, liberation theology is a movement that focuses on the political, economic, and ideological causes of social inequality within Latin American countries and between Latin America and North America. Strongly influenced by Johann B. Metz's development of a political theology,[163] Latin American theologians offer a distinctive interpretation of modern society, eschatology, and political change. They advocate liberation rather than development as the central theological, economic, and political category. Even within this narrow sense, there is, however, a broad diversity of theological positions and method among Latin American liberation theologians.

In a broad sense, the term *liberation theology* refers to any theological movement that criticizes a specific form of oppression and views liberation as integral to the theological task. Feminist theologies, African-American theologies, and certain Asian theologies are major types of liberation theology. The term has also been appropriated by American Indians, ethnic groups, and other minority groups to express a mode of theological reflection. Despite significant differences among diverse liberation theologians, several common features characterize their methods. These characteristics allow one to speak of a shared method with four distinctive steps in common.

### Starting Point

Liberation theologies take an analysis of their concrete socio-political situation as their starting point. Their analysis seeks to uncover oppression, exploitation, alienation, and discrimination. The interpretation of experience as an experience of oppression is common to all liberation theologies. For example, the stark contrast between the rich and poor within individual countries as well as between the advanced and developing nations leads Latin American liberation theologians to single out the relations of dependency and exploitation between nations as decisive contributing factors to this inequality.[164] African-American liberation theology focuses upon the

---

163. See Johann Baptist Metz, *Theology of the World* (New York: Crossroad, 1969).

164. See Gustavo Gutiérrez, *A Theology of Liberation*, rev. ed. (Maryknoll, N.Y.: Orbis Books, 1988). On the relation between political and liberation theology, see Francis Fiorenza, "Political Theology and Liberation Theology: An Inquiry into Their Fun-

discrimination against Africans and African-Americans in the history of Christianity. Feminist theologians focus upon the oppression of women in patriarchally structured societies.

## Critique of Ideology

The second common step is to read the tradition from the perspective of the experience of the oppressed. This reading involves a "hermeneutics of suspicion" or a critique of ideology. It looks for ideological distortions in the tradition that lead to oppression, and it critiques those elements. The degree and extent of suspicion in this hermeneutic vary from theologian to theologian. Quite often, Latin American liberation theologians seem to indicate that only the tradition subsequent to the New Testament or subsequent to the historical Jesus evidences ideological distortions. Many will, for example, critique this interpretive tradition in order to return to the original intention of the New Testament writings or to the historical Jesus, who was clearly on the side of the poor.[165]

Within feminist liberation theology the reading of the situation is much more complex.[166] First of all the New Testament traditions are diverse. Whereas some traditions and texts are permeated with ideas and attitudes discriminatory toward women, other traditions proclaim the equality of male and female in Christ. An example of the former is the household codes of the New Testament that refer to the subordination of women to men and that incorporate an Aristotelian patriarchal order. They originated in an attempt to respond to charges that Christianity was antifamily or against Roman social order. Insofar as Christianity allowed women and slaves to convert to Christianity independently of their "head" or "owner" (the paterfamilias), Romans viewed and criticized Christianity for being antifamily and subversive of the social order. The house codes are in part explainable by this charge.[167] Consequently, the critique of ideology is in some feminist theologies applied not only to the

damental Meaning," in Thomas McFadden, ed., *Liberation, Revolution and Freedom: Theological Perspectives* (New York: Seabury, 1975), 3–29.

165. Juan Luis Segundo, *The Historical Jesus of the Synoptics* (Maryknoll, N.Y.: Orbis Books, 1985); Jon Sobrino, *Jesus in Latin America* (Maryknoll, N.Y.: Orbis Books, 1987).

166. For the difference between the approach of Juan Luis Segundo and a feminist critical theory of liberation, see Elisabeth Schüssler Fiorenza, *Bread not Stone* (Boston: Beacon Press, 1984), 43–63.

167. Elisabeth Schüssler Fiorenza, *In Memory of Her* (New York: Crossroad, 1983), 251–84. See also idem, *Bread not Stone*, 65–92.

interpretation of the New Testament, but to the New Testament itself.

Standpoints for the critique of ideology differ within liberation theologies. Some liberation theologians relate the current experience of oppression to other standards, such as the historical Jesus or the prophetic principle. The critique of ideology rests then on the correlation between the two standards. For others, such a correlation is often advanced with insufficient historical discernment. For them, the experience of oppression becomes a standard by which the Scriptures are read. It is not just the tradition of interpreting the New Testament that is "reread" in light of experiences of oppression; the New Testament itself is also reread in light of those experiences. Therefore, the criterion of the critique becomes the experience of oppression; that experience serves as the basic criterion by which other criteria are evaluated.

### Subjugated Knowledge

In addition to criticizing ideological distortions of past and current cultural traditions, liberation theology understands the retrieval of subjugated knowledge as a part of its constructive theological task. The theological task thus includes retrieving forgotten religious symbols, neglected ecclesial practices, and ignored experiences. While history often records the memory and interpretation of the victors, it often silences the voices and interpretations of the victims.[168] A task within liberation theology, therefore, is to bring to light the knowledge and experiences of those whose voices have been silenced.[169] Liberation theology uncovers in the past not archetypes, but prototypes of liberation.[170]

### Praxis as Criterion

Praxis is, within liberation theologies, not just a goal but also a criterion of theological method.[171] The Greek term _praxis_ is

---

168. See especially Johann Baptist Metz, _Faith in History and Society_ (New York: Crossroad, 1980); idem, _The Emergent Church_ (New York: Crossroad, 1986); and Matthew Lamb, _Solidarity with Victims_ (New York: Crossroad, 1982).

169. Sharon Welch, _Communities of Resistance and Solidarity_ (Maryknoll, N.Y.: Orbis Books, 1985).

170. Rebecca Chopp, _The Power to Speak_ (New York: Crossroad, 1989). See her systematic appropriation of Elisabeth Schüssler Fiorenza's notion of prototype in chapter 2.

171. Clodovis Boff, _Theology and Praxis_ (Maryknoll, N.Y.: Orbis Books, 1987); Rebecca Chopp, _The Praxis of Suffering_ (Maryknoll, N.Y.: Orbis Books, 1986).

deliberately used by liberation theologians to accentuate an important distinction that in fact goes back to Aristotle. In the *Nicomachean Ethics* Aristotle distinguished practice (*poiesis*) as a technical skill, involved in making something, from practice (*praxis*) as a way of life. Whereas the former is a matter of technical skill (*techne*), the latter expresses a basic way of living life.[172] Adopting this Aristotelian notion of praxis, critical theorists and revisionist Marxists have sought to take up Karl Marx's emphasis on social and political praxis while avoiding Marx's technocratic and economic reduction of the notion.[173] Liberation theologians have followed this direction insofar as when they affirm that praxis is both the goal and criterion of their theologies, they are affirming that their goal is not some technocratic organization, some social structure, or some economic plan, but rather a way of life. The term *praxis* specifies that the liberation they seek is more than a mere technocratic or economic development— it is a liberation that has religious, social, political, and personal dimensions.

Present life experiences and praxis provide liberation theologians not only sources from which they criticize tradition and the present situation, but also criteria for the assessment of theological affirmations. At the same time a liberated praxis is also the goal of liberation theology. As such, praxis is the other side of the coin of a hermeneutics of suspicion or the critique of ideology. This emphasis upon praxis within liberation theology can be seen as a sort of consequentialism within theology. As a key concept, however, it is in need of clarification. The appeal to praxis is often an appeal to the immediacy of experiences of oppression. Yet at the same time such appeals to praxis as a normative source and an anticipated goal raise the question of the assessment of praxis itself. If judgments are to be made about praxis, then certain legitimate and necessary questions emerge: What is the interpretive framework of such judgments? What background theories are implied or assumed in such judgments? How is praxis itself interpreted and assessed? Such questions move one to a theological method that includes praxis as a central theological and political element, but is a method necessarily broader in scope.

---

172. Aristotle *Nicomachean Ethics* 6.2.1139a.19–20; 6.4.1140a.1–23; 6.7.1141b.16.
173. See especially Jürgen Habermas, *Theory and Practice* (Boston: Beacon Press, 1973).

# TOWARD A MORE COMPREHENSIVE
# THEOLOGICAL METHOD

Contemporary theology faces challenges that make the ever-complex task of theology even more complex. Such challenges are cultural, religious, economic, scientific, and political. Moreover, how theologians interpret these challenges often determines how they understand the theological task. If theologians assess the present situation as secularized, as being characterized by the absence of past moral values and the demise of traditional religious meanings, then they view the retrieval of these values and the reactualization of these meanings as the paramount theological task. If they place the political, social, and racial oppressions in the forefront, then overcoming these oppressions is a major goal of theology. If they take human alienation or personal inauthenticity to be the basic problem, then the attainment of authenticity and the overcoming of alienation are their primary goals.

## CHARACTERISTICS OF THE MODERN SITUATION

This section discusses three characteristics of the modern situation constituting a challenge for the theological task. These characteristics are not external challenges to theology, but are internal to theology and affect the very nature of theological reflection. These challenges are basic ambiguities that characterize our present situation. They are pluralism and unity, rationality and its critique, and, finally, power and its oppressiveness.

### Ambiguity of Pluralism and Unity

The impact of cultural pluralism on theology is obvious. Pluralism has philosophical, religious, and political implications for theology. In a widely noted essay, Karl Rahner has argued that previously one could assume a particular philosophy or worldview as a standard to which one could appeal to link theology and culture.[174] This philosophy, whether Thomist, transcendental, phenomenological, existential, or analytical, served as an accepted philosophical standard. Today, however, no single philosophy or philosophical view exists as such a standard or cultural medium for theological reflection. If one expresses Christian belief in particular philosophical

---

174. Karl Rahner, "Pluralism in Theology and the Unity of the Creed in the Church," *Theological Investigations* (New York: Crossroad, 1974), 11:3–23.

categories, then one has not *eo ipso* made that belief more public or more warranted. Philosophical views are often no less particularistic than the religious beliefs themselves.

For theology the consequences of such pluralism are twofold. First, one can no longer expect a synthesis between theology and culture. Some hold a romantic ideal that such a synthesis occurred in medieval times, and they long for its return, but that is a mere pipe dream. The pluralism of the culture itself hinders such syntheses. Second, this pluralism also implies that theology does not appeal to a particular philosophy as a link between faith and rationality. Instead theology itself takes up the task of mediation in full awareness of the historicity of philosophy and the pluralism of theology.[175] Theology then seeks to articulate the Christian faith as existing within a pluralistic culture.[176]

In addition to philosophical pluralism, the theological task must confront religious pluralism. The presence of other world religions and the reality of other faiths increasingly make their imprint upon Christian theology. The question of Lessing's "Parable of Nathan the Wise" has become paradigmatic for contemporary theology. In this parable, each son (representing Judaism, Islam, and Christianity) maintains that he alone has received the true ring (divine revelation) from their father. The sons go before a court judge with their contesting claims. The judge observes that the ring is alleged to have a magic power affecting the life-practice of each bearer. Yet not one of them lives such an exemplary life of love that would prove possession of the true ring. The judge concludes that perhaps no one has the ring or maybe only in the future will the ring's power be manifest in one of them. The question remains unresolved and is left to some future and infinitely more capable judge to decide.

Lessing's position is somewhat enigmatic.[177] Is he affirming that no religion possesses the true ring or is he, more likely, pointing to the importance of life-practice? Lessing's parable challenges us ever more today. We are more than ever aware that Christianity is one religion among many. Not just Islam and Judaism, but also Buddhism, Confucianism, and many other religions display the vitality and claims of their paradigmatic religious visions. When viewed to-

---

175. For a contemporary account of rationality, see Hilary Putnam, *Reason, Truth and History* (New York: Cambridge University Press, 1981), esp. 103–218.

176. See Claude Geffré, "Pluralité des théologies et unité de la foi," in Bernard Lauret and François Refoulé, eds., *Initiation à la pratique de la théologie* (Paris: Éditions du Cerf, 1982), 117–42; Yves Congar, *Diversity and Communion* (Mystic, Conn.: Twenty-Third Publications, 1985), 9–43.

177. See Henry E. Allison, *Lessing and the Enlightenment* (Ann Arbor: University of Michigan Press, 1966).

gether, they display the plurality of religious visions. They thereby challenge Christian theology to articulate the significance, meaning, and unconditionality of the Christian vision not in isolation from other religious visions, but in relation to them.

Yet modernity is characterized not only by the growing awareness of philosophical and religious pluralism, but also by the increasing realization of the unity of the world. Economic systems increasingly link nations and groups of nations with each other. Population growth and technological development take place in all nations within a natural ecosystem. Interdependency among all nations is not only economic, but also environmental. All humans depend upon the ecosystem. In addition, the increased awareness of human rights (along with their violation) and democratic ideals as extending to all races, nations, and genders points to an increasing awareness of a "common humanity" of all peoples of the earth—an earth increasingly smaller through the growth in communications technology.

The task for theology is both to take pluralism seriously and to explore the particularity and significance of the Christian vision without reducing religious language to an isolated language-game that neglects other religious visions and the global situation of humanity.

### Ambiguity of Rationality and Its Critique

The task of theology relates to conceptions of rationality. The nature of rationality within the modern world faces a double challenge. It faces the challenge of the modern Enlightenment, and it faces the growing critique of the Enlightenment.[178] Both the Enlightenment and its critique challenge theology. The Enlightenment and its modern conception of rationality have been significant for Roman Catholic theology, for in the Roman Catholic tradition theology has always sought a unity between faith and reason. As Cardinal Joseph Ratzinger has recently argued: "Faith is not to be placed in opposition to reason, but neither must it fall under the absolute power of enlightened reason and its methods. . . . It has always been clear from its very structure that Christian faith is not to be divorced from reason."[179]

However, the Enlightenment had a very specific conception of rationality and knowledge. It believed that science had developed

---

178. Max Horkheimer and Theodor W. Adorno, _Dialectic of Enlightenment_ (New York: Seabury, 1972).

179. Ratzinger, _Principles_, 325.

correct and cumulative methods of acquiring knowledge. By replacing ancient superstitions, traditional religions, and unexamined
authorities, these methods gave promise for eliminating poverty and
ignorance, for decreasing disease and hunger, and for providing an
increase in material goods and happiness.[180] Today we are aware of
the limitations of science and scientific rationality. Though we are
aware that scientific rationality has led to great advances in technology and to significant material advantages, we are also aware of
its limitations and dangers. The result is that we face a crisis of rationality. This crisis of rationality was articulated forcefully in the
critical theory of the 1940s,[181] and the crisis is at the center of
the current postmodern critique of technocratic as well as scientific
rationality.[182] The modernist belief in the progress of science and
reason is intensely criticized for overlooking the negative side of this
progress and for a "substitutional universalism," that is, for claiming
as universal what is in reality a specifically Eurocentric viewpoint.[183]

This ambiguity of rationality and its critique presents a particularly acute challenge to theology. On the one hand, theological
reflection cannot neglect the growth of methodology that has so affected the humanities. The theological analysis of religious classics
and even the Scriptures cannot neglect the application of contemporary methods to these texts. In addition, many religious beliefs
presuppose particular scientific worldviews and they have at least
been expressed in them. For theology to overlook the growth in scientific knowledge and rationality is to withdraw into a ghetto. At the
same time, theological reflection needs to avoid scientific positivism
that apes the scientism of technocratic rationality. Moreover, since
theology articulates the religious belief in transcendence, it has as
its task to underscore what transcends scientific rationality. Thereby,
theology offers a challenge to positivist and reductionist conceptions
of human reason.

---

180. See Langdon Gilkey, *Society and the Sacred* (New York: Crossroad, 1988), 3–14,
73–105. See also his earlier work, *Religion and the Scientific Future* (New York: Harper
and Row, 1970).
181. Max Horkheimer, *Critique of Instrumental Reason* (New York: Seabury, 1967).
See also from a different perspective, Alvin Gouldner, *The Dialectics of Ideology and
Technology* (New York: Basic Books, 1976).
182. See Jean-François Lyotard, *The Postmodern Condition: A Report on Knowledge*
(Minneapolis: University of Minnesota Press, 1984); idem, *The Differend* (Minneapolis: University of Minnesota Press, 1988). For a general survey, see Steven Connor,
*Postmodernist Culture: An Introduction to Theories of the Contemporary* (Oxford: Black-
well, 1989). For a critical view, see Jürgen Habermas, *The Philosophical Discourse of
Modernity: Twelve Lectures* (Boston: Beacon, 1987).
183. Francis Schüssler Fiorenza, "The Impact of Feminist Theory on My Work,"
*Journal of Feminist Studies in Religion* (Spring 1991).

*Ambiguity of Power and Its Oppressiveness*

The modern world has witnessed an impressive growth of scientific, technological, and political power. The domination of nature and the structural organization of society have led to an increase in material well-being. Yet at the same time this increase in wealth and health has gone hand in hand with an increase in poverty and hunger. The domination of nature has gone hand in hand with exploitation and devastation of large segments of the globe. Growth in the standard of living has been limited to some people, nations, and continents. Alongside of increased prosperity is increased poverty. These exist not only in separate parts of the world, but side by side in the very same cities and towns. The growth in political power, freedom, and equality for some has been accompanied by racial genocide, gender discrimination, and national oppression. Power is two-edged: It not only enables positive control, but it also makes possible exploitative domination.

This ambiguity of power challenges a reflective faith in two ways. First, the ambiguity presents a challenge that affects the mission and structure of faith. It calls for a faith that does justice, for a faith sensitive to the imbalances of power and wealth, for a faith with eyes turned toward the downtrodden and poor. Second, the poor and oppressed bring a view of society and history that is otherwise often neglected.[184] The sociology of knowledge has exposed the degree to which the material conditions of life impact culture and influence thought. The categories with which individuals understand reality or interpret their past develop within structures of power and domination. We stand in a life-relation and a power-relation that influence how we understand ourselves, our world, and others.

Consequently, as liberation theologians emphasize, the task of theology involves not only the critique of nonreligious ideologies that dominate the consciousness of societies, but also the critique of those very ideologies permeating and fostered by religious traditions. The ambiguity of power challenges theology to be self-critical in its service to God, to humanity, and to nature.

## FOUR ELEMENTS OF THEOLOGICAL METHOD

The task of Christian theology is the elaboration of the Christian vision and identity in the face of the above challenges. This vision encompasses not only discourse about God and about Christ, but

---

184. Gustavo Gutiérrez, *The Power of the Poor in History* (Maryknoll, N.Y.: Orbis Books, 1983).

also discourse about the Christian community in its relation to other communities. Such a complex task is not arbitrary, but entails diverse criteria.

### Reconstructive Hermeneutics: The Integrity of the Tradition

The task of elaborating the Christian vision and identity encompasses many elements, including an interpretation of the Christian community's tradition, Scriptures, creeds, councils, practices, and past reflection. It also encompasses the attempt to bring the Christian community's tradition into relation with philosophical and scientific discourse, with the ongoing experience and practice of faith in the world, and with other communities of discourse with which the Christian community interacts.

**Scripture and Tradition.** The interpretation of the Christian community's past involves an interpretation of the authority of its tradition. Within the context of the authority of the tradition, the role of Scripture and its relation to tradition are important issues that have become controverted since the Reformation. They received new significance through the Second Vatican Council. The major impetus for the renewal of these issues came from intense historical research on the early Christian writers and the early church's liturgy and from the application of historical-critical studies to the Bible. The emergence of the biblical movement within the Roman Catholic church has shown the importance of the Scriptures for Catholic spirituality, church life, and doctrine. This movement has led to a reexamination of the Council of Trent's teaching in relation to the Reformation's *sola scriptura.*

Two basic views of tradition have emerged, as can be illustrated by the debate between Joseph Geiselmann and Joseph Ratzinger. Geiselmann maintains that tradition is the living presence of Scripture. Tradition does not so much add to Scripture as it has translated Scripture into the living presence of the church. Geiselmann seeks to underscore his argument through a careful interpretation of the Council of Trent's position on the relation between Scripture and tradition and maintains that every age relates to Scriptures.[185]

Ratzinger makes a twofold argument that is important for our understanding of tradition. First, Geiselmann's position minimizes

---

185. Joseph Rupert Geiselmann, "Das Konzil von Trient über das Verhältnis der Heiligen Schrift und der nicht geschriebenen Traditionen," in Michael Schmaus, ed., *Die mündliche Überlieferung* (Munich: Kösel, 1957); idem, *The Meaning of Tradition* (New York: Herder and Herder, 1966).

the role of the early Christian writers in the post–New Testament times and, thereby, dehistoricizes tradition. It overlooks that lacunae in the historical foundation do not speak against tradition. The dogmas of 1854 and 1950 affected the Roman Catholic understanding of tradition, for they presupposed that a historical demonstration did not mean that one had to demonstrate that a dogma was explicitly believed in at the beginning of the church, but only that a cross section of the church at times believed in it. Ratzinger in fact maintains that "whatever the whole Church holds to have been revealed *has* been revealed and belongs to the authentic tradition of the Church."[186] There is a significance of the post–New Testament church that has been eliminated by a historical-critical method that reduces faith to the Scriptures.

Second, Ratzinger shows that the understanding of tradition that the Council of Trent worked out was indeed quite nuanced and complex. Trent combined pneumatological, liturgical, and doctrinal views to emphasize diverse strata within the concept of tradition. Revelation is inscribed not simply in the Bible but in the hearts of Christians. Consequently the Spirit speaks through the whole life of the church, including its conciliar and liturgical activity. Trent's teaching on tradition sought to affirm that the revelation of God in Christ "was accomplished in historical facts, but has also its perpetual reality today, because what was once accomplished remains perpetually living and effective in the faith of the Church, and Christian faith never simply refers to what is past but equally to what is present and to what is to come."[187]

**Hermeneutics of the Tradition.**   The importance of tradition and its presence within the Christian church raise the issue of an adequate approach to the interpretation of tradition in regard to both its ongoing development and the continual reconstruction of its integrity. The Congregation for the Doctrine of the Faith's *Mysterium Ecclesiae* points out the importance of linguistic categories, historical contextualization, incompleteness, and worldviews in a way that acknowledges the historicity of tradition. It criticizes a position that in a Neo-Platonic fashion views tradition primarily as approximations to the truth rather than as historically and linguistically conditioned

---

186. Ratzinger, *Principles*, 139. See also Albert Lang, *Der Auftrag der Kirche* (Munich: Max Hueber, 1962), 2:290–92; Joseph Ratzinger, "Revelation and Tradition," in Karl Rahner and Joseph Ratzinger, *Revelation and Tradition* (New York: Herder and Herder, 1966).

187. Joseph Ratzinger, "On the Interpretation of the Tridentine Decree on Tradition," in Rahner and Ratzinger, *Revelation and Tradition*, 65.

affirmations of faith. An interpretation of tradition must seek to take into account the historicity of tradition as well as the significance of its affirmations.

It is important to avoid some basic misreadings of the nature of tradition. These are views of tradition as: static identity, decay, or progressive development. Each of these views captures some aspect of tradition, but erroneously extrapolates this aspect into a total view of tradition. One view affirms a *static identity*. In this view, neither decay nor development, neither change nor growth takes places. Instead tradition appears as the affirmation of what always was, is, and will be. This view attempts to crystalize the value of tradition through an affirmation of a lack of change and development. Another extreme views tradition as *decay* away from pristine origins. This view is more common within a direction of liberal theology influenced by Albrecht Ritschl's critique of metaphysics rather than within Roman Catholic theological circles—though one does encounter it there also. It views the postbiblical period as a period of decay. The development of doctrine or the institutional growth and development of the church consist of a falling away from the pristine biblical charism. Today, some even locate this decay within the New Testament itself. They seek to distinguish sharply between the historical Jesus or the early Christian community's explication of its faith in the Christ and the later development of organized structures representing early Catholicism. This view correctly grasps the primal significance of the early New Testament witnesses to Jesus. However, it overlooks the significance of later development, be it the first centuries of Christian community or the medieval and modern development of Christianity. The essence of Christianity should not be reduced to an archaeology of beginnings.[188]

The third view considers tradition as a *progressive development* or evolution. Such a view often presupposes an organic model of tradition. All development is looked upon as a progressive improvement. Such a view neglects the possibility of distortions. Moreover, it is important to acknowledge that previous ages of Christianity do not relate to the present as childhood or adolescence to maturity, for the noncontemporaneity of a previous stage can be a genuine challenge to the prejudices of modern developments.

**Integrity of the Tradition.** It is important in the interpretation of tradition to distinguish between the idea of a principle of Christian

---

188. Joseph Ratzinger, *Das Problem der Dogmengeschichte in der Sicht der katholischen Theologie* (Cologne: Opladen, 1966).

faith and the idea of the foundation of Christian faith. This distinction between principles and foundation is often used in moral philosophy and in epistemology.[189] One can illustrate this distinction in regard to the Christian tradition with the example of slavery. Today as Christians we affirm that slavery is wrong and that one cannot be a Christian and advocate slavery. Yet we cannot trace to the foundational origins of Christianity a prohibition against slavery. Quite the contrary. Yet today the incompatibility of slavery and Christianity is a principle of Christian faith and morals.

The tradition develops and changes in a way that constantly reconstructs what it considers to be paradigmatic, what it considers to be its vision or "essence." How it does so cannot be adequately addressed in terms of categories of static identity, decay, or development. Instead there is a constant reconstruction of its understanding of what is paradigmatic to its vision. In this reconstruction, background theories, retroductive warrants, and the community of discourse play important roles. Each of these will be further elucidated in detail in one of the following sections. In brief, background theories are implicit assumptions, philosophical or scientific, about the world and science; the notion of retroductive warrants refers to the way contemporary practices and experiences work backwardly to affect interpretations or hypotheses and their validation; and finally, the concept of communities of discourse refers to the fact that meaning and assessment take place in the context not of an abstract human reason, but in a specific historical tradition and linguistic community.

*Background Theories*

The term *background theory* is currently used in the philosophy of science and in ethical theory to designate those implied theories that impact upon considered hypotheses and judgments. The term has its origin in the philosophy of science. Henri Poincaré coined the term *auxiliary hypotheses* to describe the presupposed hypotheses about physical phenomena that are necessarily assumed in a given practical application of geometry. If the hypothesis does not agree with the observation, then one achieves coherence by either adopting different axioms or by modifying relevant auxiliary hypotheses. Within ethical theory, the application of ethical principles to practice entails relevant background notions about human nature or human society. In general, everyone makes use of some sort of background

---

189. See Alan Donagan, *The Theory of Morality* (Chicago: University of Chicago Press, 1977).

theories, but specific theories vary from person to person and from age to age.

**Historically Considered.**  Since background theories are implicit, they are often presupposed or assumed without explicit reflection. It is therefore important in reflecting about theological method to attend to the presence of implicit background theories. Judgments about Christian identity or Roman Catholic identity as judgments about the meaning of a religious tradition often rely on implicit background theories not only about the self, society, and the world, but also about the means and methods of interpreting past tradition and present experience. These background theories affect one's judgments about one's Christian or Catholic identity just as one's judgments about identity affect one's assessment of the nature and appropriateness of various background theories.

The preceding discussion of the history of theological method referred to certain background theories: Augustine's understanding of Christian doctrine presupposed the Neo-Platonic theory of signs, the notion of interior light, and self-transcendence. Aquinas's understanding of *sacra doctrina* presupposed Aristotle's division of sciences, his notion of subalternate science, and the explanatory role of Aristotelian causality. Karl Rahner presupposed in part a transcendental understanding of experience and language as well as Heidegger's analysis of the existentials of human *Dasein* (being-there). Contemporary hermeneutical theory with its exposition of the classic, metaphor, and narrative presupposed an understanding of the relation between language and experience that differed from that of the transcendental approach.

**Systematically Considered.**  The contemporary shift in philosophical background theory has been described by Bernard Lonergan as a shift from logic to method, from essences to systems, from a division of sciences according to formal and material objects to one according to fields and methods, from necessary deduction to probable inferences, and from faculty psychology to intentionality analysis. This shift from logic to method entails for Lonergan a conception of theology as an ongoing process of revision and correction.[190]

---

190. Nevertheless, insofar as my proposal suggests a method of broad reflective equilibrium, it places less emphasis than Lonergan does on intentionality analysis and the transcendental analysis of structures of cognition. Instead it suggests that such analyses of human subjectivity and its structures of cognition provide one of several background theories.

My description of theology as encompassing diverse elements—
the reconstructive hermeneutic of the tradition, relevant background
theories, retroductive warrants, and the community as a community
of discourse—concurs with Lonergan's basic description of the shift
from logic to method. It suggests that one essential element of the
systematic task of theology is the explication of theological reflection
in relation to diverse background theories. Such theories are quite
diverse. They include philosophical theories about human nature,
ethical theories about social justice, psychological theories about personal development, scientific theories about the beginnings of the
universe, epistemological theories about human cognition, and literary theories about interpretation—to name a few of the relevant
background theories. Each can play a role in the development of a
theology.

The notion of reflective equilibrium suggests that theological reflection advances in part through a critical interaction between one's
interpretation of the Christian tradition and one's interpretation of
relevant background theories. The correction is mutual. It may very
well be that a background theory influences the interpretation of the
tradition. Scientific theories of evolution and literary theories about
genre have influenced the interpretation of the Genesis accounts of
creation. The Christian tradition's understanding of the dignity of
the human person has influenced the assessment and adoption of
psychological theories of human development. Sometimes the mutual influence is reciprocal: The biblical notion of solidarity with the
poor and disadvantaged related to theories of social justice and the
notion of a "difference principle" whereby the least advantaged in
society are accorded rights.[191]

Any consideration of the relation between background theories and the interpretation of the Christian tradition needs to take
into account the historicity of culture and the pluralism of society so that no one background theory is uncritically accepted as
an infallible norm, even if it be the latest phenomenological theory
about human intentionality, the most recent epistemological theory
about the structures of human cognition, or the latest anthropological and psychological account of gender differences. Scientific and
philosophical viewpoints of our culture are indeed also historically
conditioned and subject to revision. A modernist theology that takes
these background theories as infallible standards—be the theory an
Aristotelian account of virtue, or a Husserlian account of subjectiv-

---

191. Francis Schüssler Fiorenza, "Politische Theologie und liberale Gerechtigkeits-
Konzeption," in Edward Schillebeeckx, ed., *Mystik und Politik: Johann Baptist Metz zu
Ehren* (Mainz: Matthias Grünewald, 1988), 105–17.

ity, or the latest philosophical theory espousing particularism and relativism—fails to recognize the historicity of culture.

### Retroductive Warrants

The terms *retroductive* and *retroductive warrants* are not commonplace. However, the terms have a specific meaning in current methodological discussion within contemporary philosophy of science, epistemology, and ethics, and a specific relevance to theological method. The meaning of the term *retroductive warrant* and its use within theological reflection can be illuminated in various strata: by its use within contemporary philosophy of science, by Newman's illative sense, by liberation theology's appeal to the hermeneutical role of the oppressed, and by Rahner's indirect method of theology.

**Theoretical and Practical Fruitfulness.** A retroductive warrant within the philosophy of science or epistemology refers to the fertility of a hypothesis, idea, or theory.[192] It refers to the ability of the hypothesis or theory to carry forward the scientific enterprise. Retroductive warrants differ from experimental justifications. A retroductive warrant is not so much an inductive confirmation as it is the theoretical and practical fruitfulness that flows from the imaginative construal of all the available evidence. A warrant is retroductive to the extent that it offers the most feasible and comprehensive explanation of the phenomenon, accounts for unexpected and unanticipated phenomena, and enables the scientific endeavor to move on in practice.

This theoretical and practical fruitfulness is both prospective and retrospective. It is prospective in that a good theory anticipates novel phenomena, that is, phenomena not belonging to the data to be explained. The more novel and unexpected phenomena are predicted and explained, the more adequate the theory. Such fruitfulness prevents a theory from being merely an ad hoc explanation. Such fruitfulness is also retrospective to the extent that it is better able to help organize, integrate, and explain the past data and phenomena.

Recently Ernan McMullin, a philosopher of science, has compared a scientist's development of a theory to a poet's development of a metaphor.[193] The poet develops the metaphor not by impli-

---

192. See Ernan McMullin, "The Fertility of Theory and the Unit for Appraisal in Science," *Boston Studies in the Philosophy of Science* 39 (1976): 395–432.

193. Ernan McMullin, "The Motive for Metaphor," *Proceedings of the American Catholic Philosophical Association* 55 (1982): 27–39; idem, "A Case for Scientific Realism,"

cation but by suggestions. The metaphor explores what is not well understood in advance, and through creative suggestion it illumines past, present, and future experience. In my opinion, the situation is analogous for theology. Theological theory advances not simply by implication or correlation, but rather through the creative suggestion by which the experience of the community's past, present, and future is illuminated. Theological reflection advances when it offers creative metaphors that enable the community to carry forth and reconstruct its tradition in relation to its ongoing experience.

**Illative Sense.** The idea of retroductive warrants from experience can also be illustrated by John Henry Newman's notion of an illative sense.[194] This notion of the illative sense has in particular influenced twentieth-century Roman Catholic fundamental theology (especially Rahner and Lonergan).[195] With his notion of the illative sense Newman anticipated much of the contemporary neopragmatic and hermeneutic critique of an abstract conception of reason or of a strictly formal conception of method and rational argumentation. Modern pragmatic philosophers have criticized a Cartesian type of foundationalism that starts from absolute doubt. The illative sense represented Newman's attempt to criticize abstract starting points and to steer a middle path between reducing religion to a matter of emotion or sentiment and reducing argumentation to a formal logical or deductive reasoning. He drew on Aristotle's notion of prudent practical judgment (*phronesis*) to illustrate a type of knowledge that he called the illative sense. This illative sense, however, has a theoretical dimension that goes beyond Aristotle's limitation of prudential knowledge to practical knowledge.[196] The detective, the farmer, and the scholar make judgments based upon their reflective intuitions. These judgments are related to their experience and character.

Religious judgments are similar to moral judgments. They are not simply the outcome of abstract logic, but result from practical reasoning. Just as practical reason is based upon a learned experience, so too does a link exist between moral knowledge and ethical experience. The illative sense is therefore linked to the character

in Jarrett Leplin, ed., *Scientific Realism* (Berkeley: University of California Press, 1984), 8–40, esp. 26–35.

194. John Henry Newman, *An Essay in Aid of a Grammar of Assent* (Oxford: Clarendon Press, 1985), esp. chaps. 8 to 10.

195. See Thomas J. Norris, *Newman and His Theological Method* (Leiden: E. J. Brill, 1977).

196. Gerard Verbeecke, "Aristotelian Roots of Newman's Illative Sense," in James D. Bastable, ed., *Newman and Gladstone Centennial Essays* (Dublin: Veritas, 1978), 177–95.

and experience of individuals that affect the beginning, process, and conclusion of reasoned and considered judgments. In short, practical experience determines what persons become; it affects not only who they are but also their whole process of reasoning, ranging from the selection of principles, to the mode of argumentation, to the construction of conclusions.

**Hermeneutical Role of the Oppressed.** The determinations of reasoning by character and experience—determinations illustrative of the illative sense—receive a concrete specification in the various theologies of liberation. Liberation theology attributes a hermeneutical significance to the experience of the oppressed. This experience of oppression affects how the tradition is read, interpreted, and applied. The experience of oppression serves as a retroductive warrant in that it challenges that which is often taken as a matter of course; it provides a view of history from the underside of history; and it suggests new readings and applications of the tradition.[197]

Two examples can illustrate the retroductive and retrospective character of the experience of oppression. The first example has been brought to the fore by feminist theology. Classical theology always emphasized the transcendence of God to all human categories and it developed theories of analogy that relativized the application of human categories of God, as, for example, when the Fourth Lateran Council affirmed that in every similarity between God and creature, the dissimilarity is even greater.[198] Nevertheless, in popular Christian religious imagery male language and metaphors outweighed female metaphors to express God. This popular practice was philosophically justified by linking male paternity with God's creativity insofar as male paternity was viewed as the principle of creativity. Today due to the impact of feminist theology, we are beginning to retrieve nonmale and nonpatriarchal images of God from the Scriptures and from classical attributions.[199] The experience of women is thereby serving as a retroductive warrant for the retrieval, reconstruction, and construction of myriad images of the incomprehensible God. Another significant event for Christianity has been the

197. See Lee Cormie, "The Hermeneutical Privilege of the Oppressed," *Catholic Theological Society of America, Proceedings* 33 (1978): 155–81.

198. Denzinger-Schönmetzer, *Enchiridion Symbolorum*, 806: "because it is not possible to affirm a similarity between creator and creature without affirming an even greater dissimilarity" (my translation).

199. Elizabeth Johnson, "The Incomprehensibility of God and the Image of God Male and Female," *Theological Studies* 45 (1984): 441–65. For a systematic retrieval of the images of God as mother, lover, and friend, see Sallie McFague, *Models of God: Theology for an Ecological, Nuclear Age* (Philadelphia: Fortress Press, 1987).

Holocaust.[200] For centuries, the Christian tradition distinguished its Christian identity from Jewish identity with language, metaphors, and arguments that were often negative and often fed into an anti-Judaism or anti-Semitism. The experience of the Holocaust serves as a retroductive warrant propelling Christians to understand their identity in a way that is neither hostile nor degrading to Jews.

**Indirect Method.** With reference to Newman's illative sense, Karl Rahner has introduced in fundamental theology the notion of an "indirect method."[201] While acknowledging the importance of historical arguments, Rahner argues that historical arguments need to be supplemented by an indirect method. Such an indirect method appeals in part to formal transcendental considerations and in part to practical experience. A Christian moves from what he or she experiences as a Christian back to a consideration of particular historical beliefs. The indirect method presupposes that the criteria of theological argument are not simply historical or inductive or deductive, but also have a practical experiential dimension. Though more elusive than induction or historical arguments, such an approach moves from Christian experience and practice to an interpretation of one's community and tradition. This indirect method is for Rahner a decision of practical reason directed toward the presence of God in the contingencies of history.[202]

### Theology and the Community of the Church

All the above diverse dimensions of retroductive warrants show that theology is a theoretical-practical discipline. It entails prudential and considered judgments. These prudential judgments have a basis not only in tradition, but also in an ongoing experience. The plurality of criteria, the practical dimension of experience, and the prudential character of judgments lead to a final consideration: Whose judgments? The question of theological method is not simply a question of academic expertise or individual opinion. Theology relates to a community: a community of discourse and of faith.[203]

Roman Catholicism has a long tradition that points out the relation between the discipline of theology and the community of the

---

200. See Johann Baptist Metz, *The Emergent Church*, 17–33.

201. Rahner, *Foundations*, 8–10, 346–68.

202. Rahner seeks to bring Newman's illative sense in relation to Ignatius of Loyola's theology of decision. See "Reflections on a New Task for Fundamental Theology," in *Theological Investigations* (New York: Crossroad, 1979), 16:156–66.

203. See Francis Schüssler Fiorenza, "Foundations of Theology: A Community's Tradition of Discourse and Practice," *Proceedings of the CTSA* 41 (1986): 107–34.

church. This venerable tradition affirms that Roman Catholic theology to be genuinely Roman Catholic should be "catholic" (that is universal) and should stand in accord with the bishop of Rome. Roman Catholic identity has been defined in terms of "catholicity" and in terms of unity with the bishop of Rome. This tradition indeed affirms both as intertwined. For an individual, community, theologian, or theological school to separate from communion with the bishop of Rome means detachment from the Roman Catholic church and thereby loss of the individual's or group's catholicity.

The importance of communion with the bishop of Rome is often translated into the affirmation of obedience to the Roman magisterium. Though such an affirmation expresses a central affirmation of Roman Catholicism, it does not, if taken by itself, totally encompass the relation between the discipline of theology and the community of church or the nature of theology itself. Such a view needs to be complemented by other considerations: the nature of the magisterium within the church; the possibility of dissent and free speech within the church; and the methodological question of how the magisterium itself does theology.[204] Since the first and second issues are treated below in Avery Dulles's chapter on faith and revelation and in Michael Fahey's chapter on the church, the focus here will be on the third issue.

As regards theological method, the issue of the relation to the magisterium involves the complementary and indeed basic methodological question: How does the magisterium do theology? To the extent that the tradition is challenged by new background theories, by new experiences, and by the emergence of conflicts within the tradition itself, a fundamental methodological question is: How should the magisterium itself meet these challenges and how does it meet them? For example, in the nineteenth century the growing acceptance of theories of evolution and the increasing influence of Darwinian views appeared to challenge traditional beliefs about the divine creation of humans. Theories of evolution appeared, at first glance, to discredit the biblical accounts of the creation of the first human couple. They also appeared to invalidate the Aristotelian teleological accounts of human nature and to challenge the specific "dignity" of human nature. Over the past half-century, except in certain biblicist or fundamentalist circles, Roman Catholic teaching has shifted away from rejecting theories of evolution. It has acknowledged the diverse literary genres and traditions in the composition of

---

204. For a helpful treatment of the magisterium, see Francis Sullivan, *Magisterium: Teaching Authority in the Catholic Church* (New York: Paulist, 1983).

Genesis, and it has sought to integrate Christian belief in divine creation with a theory of evolution and with a historical-critical analysis of the biblical texts.

The shift took place across several fronts: an increasing influence of scientific theories about the evolution of the human race, the increasing acceptance of the applicability of literary forms to an understanding of the Genesis accounts, and the increasing replacement of Aristotelian biology and its notion of teleology by other philosophical and biological conceptions of human nature. Within Roman Catholic theology, the influence of Teilhard de Chardin and of Karl Rahner enabled Roman Catholics to understand evolution in a way that was not reductionistic, but ennobling. It enabled them to combine a belief in divine creation with a conviction about evolution. At first some of these attempts were resisted. The Vatican's Pontifical Biblical Commission moved from a cautious, if not negative, stance toward the historical-critical method toward a more positive acceptance. This shift contributed in part to a reinterpretation of the tradition that enabled bringing together new scientific background theories about human origin with the Christian faith in creation. Such an example shows that any account of theology and theological method should include and explain how changes (entailing discontinuity along with continuity) take place within the church, both within official magisterial statements and within the church in general. This broader problem underlies the sensitive and difficult ecclesiological question of the role of a teaching office within the church. It is a distinct, even if not completely separate, issue from that of the nature of authority within the church.

One of the best known Roman Catholic church historians of the twentieth century, Hubert Jedin, an expert on the Council of Trent, offers a helpful survey and typology of models of how the exercise of theology and the exercise of the teaching office or magisterium de facto existed throughout the history of Roman Catholicism. By describing five historically different models of the exercise of the teaching office within the history of the Roman Catholic church, Jedin highlights historical facts often neglected, and he suggests that the Roman Catholic community should strive to avoid the one-sidedness and possible weaknesses within each of these historical models.[205]

1. During the classical period of early Christianity the leading theologians were bishops, with few major exceptions (Tertullian, Ori-

_____

205. Hubert Jedin, "Theologie und Lehramt," in Remigus Bäumer, ed., _Lehramt und Theologie im 16. Jahrhundert_ (Münster: Aschendorff, 1976), 7–21.

gen, and Clement of Alexandria). In the West, the bishop-theologians were Ambrose and Augustine; in the East, Basil the Great, Gregory of Nazianzus, Gregory of Nyssa, John Chrysostom, and Cyril of Alexandria. The teaching authority was exercised individually and through episcopal synods and ecumenical councils.

2. In the early Middle Ages, the controversy about transubstantiation in the case of Berengar of Tours provided a typical example of the magisterial judgment and decision-making in regard to doctrinal issues. First, local synods in Paris (1051) and Tours (1054) evaluated and rejected Berengar's understanding of the eucharist. Then the case was referred to the bishop of Rome, and the case was discussed by the Roman synod. Finally, the case was referred to the Fourth Lateran Council, as the largest and most universal synod. There were three stages: local synod, Roman synod, and the council as universal synod called and directed by the pope.

3. In the fourteenth and fifteenth centuries, the significant role of university faculties of theology is evident. As Jedin notes, "In the late middle ages, the theological faculties of the universities exercise quite clearly magisterial functions, especially the faculty of the Sorbonne. They condemn theological errors that are known to them or brought before them."[206] Since Pope Innocent III, canons of general councils obtained the power of law only when they were given to the faculties of law and made the subject matter of instruction.[207] Not only did the university theology faculties exercise a teaching office within the church, but they were corporatively invited to councils along with bishops and abbots. At the Council of Constance, doctors of theology and of canon law were incorporated with voting rights. A concrete illustration of the significance of their right to vote is the Council of Basel. In the vote of December 1436, cardinals and bishops represented less than one-tenth of the voting members.

4. The practice of the Council of Trent provides another model. Theologians were invited to the council by the pope, by the bishops, by superior generals of the religious orders, or by civil rulers (the emperor and the kings of Spain and France). As a general council, Trent had to have representatives of the Christian laity, hence the invitations by the "Christian Princes." In the third session (1561), the earlier medieval practice was followed in that the universities (Louvain, Cologne, and Ingolstadt) were invited as official representatives to Trent. Yet at Trent many of the bishops, especially the Italian and

---

206. Ibid, 12.
207. Knut Wolfgang Nörr, "Päpstliche Dekretalen und römisch-kanonischer Zivilprozess," Walter Wilhelm, ed., *Studien zur europäischen Rechtsgeschichte* (Frankfurt: Klostermann, 1972), 53–65.

Spanish bishops, were educated theologians and were influenced by the humanist movement. This was especially true of those Italian and Spanish bishops who were members of religious orders.

5. A final model is illustrated by the First and Second Vatican Councils. Here no university faculty of theology was corporatively invited as in the medieval period or as at Trent. The bishops were the voting members, and theologians were present primarily as advisers to the bishops.

Jedin's brief survey shows how the tradition and practice of the Catholic church throughout its history have varied. Today, one often encounters one-sided views: Only bishops are teachers within the church. Or: Only academic theologians have expertise. The tradition of the Roman Catholic church has been much broader and more varied. Today when the task of theology has become so complex, the questions so varied, the problems so pressing, it is important that the voices of diverse faithful within the church be heard and have a rightful impact upon the decision-making within the church.

## CONCLUSION

The task of theology entails a constant challenge to the church as a community of faith and discourse. The challenge is to reconstruct the integrity of the church's tradition in light of relevant background theories and warrants from contemporary experience. Such a task is extremely complex. As Bernard Lonergan has noted, it entails a shift from logic to method, and such a shift entails a profound change in consciousness.[208] This change in consciousness requires an openness to discourse within the community, not only to its past, but also to the future. Such a discourse becomes open to the integrity of the past and future when it takes the voices of other communities into account and listens to voices that have been previously not heard.

The emphasis on combining retroductive warrants, background theories, the integrity of the tradition, and the catholicity of the church as a community of discourse heightens the requirement of comprehensiveness for theological method. An adequate theological method embraces diverse sources and a plurality of criteria. Theological method does not consist simply in correlating contemporary questions with traditional answers or symbols. Instead theological method consists of making judgments about what constitutes the integrity of the tradition and what is paradigmatic about the tradition. It consists of reflecting upon the relevant background theories (both

---

208. Lonergan, *A Third Collection*, 3–22.

of the tradition and of one's own situation) and taking into account the ongoing practice and experience of the community, as expressed in diverse voices, so that it can be a truly catholic theology.

# FOR FURTHER READING

## HISTORY OF THEOLOGY

Congar, Yves. *A History of Theology*. Garden City, N.Y.: Doubleday, 1968.

A somewhat dated but still valuable introduction to the history of the understanding of theology. It originally appeared as an article in the classic French encyclopedia *Dictionnaire de Théologie*.

Cunliffe-Jones, Hubert, ed. *A History of Christian Doctrine*. Philadelphia: Fortress Press, 1978.

Diverse contributors make the volume somewhat uneven. Some excellent individual sections. More attention is given to the classical than to the modern period.

Evans, Gillian R., et al. *The Science of Theology*. Vol. 1 of *The History of Christian Theology*. Grand Rapids, Mich.: Eerdmans, 1986.

A popular introduction to theology written by one of England's most prolific contemporary writers on medieval theology.

Harnack, Adolf von. *History of Dogma*. 7 vols. New York: Dover, 1961; German edition, 1900.

A classic and still informative treatment, though dated. Von Harnack's view of doctrine as a postbiblical, Hellenistic development has been modified by recent work on the Hellenistic period of Judaism.

Pelikan, Jaroslav. *The Christian Tradition*. 5 vols. Chicago: University of Chicago Press, 1971–88.

A complete and masterful survey. Written as a counterpoint to von Harnack, the volumes take into account the role of liturgy and piety as sources of theology. The annotated bibliography in volume 1, 358–76, provides an important guide.

## THEOLOGICAL METHOD

Braaten, Carl E., and Robert W. Jensen. *Lutheran Dogmatics*. 2 vols. Philadelphia: Fortress Press, 1984.

A contemporary statement of Lutheran systematic theology, the work was written by individual Lutheran theologians in accordance with the classic loci of theology.

Fiorenza, Francis Schüssler. *Foundational Theology: Jesus and the Church*. New York: Crossroad, 1984.

Discusses the major problems of fundamental theology, the resurrection of Jesus, the foundation of the church, and the nature of fundamental theology with reference to Neo-Scholastic, transcendental, hermeneutical, and contemporary approaches to theology.

Kasper, Walter. *The Methods of Dogmatic Theology.* Shannon, Ireland: Ecclesia Press, 1969.

A booklet that outlines the shift from a Neo-Scholastic approach to theology to contemporary and more historically oriented approaches.

Kaufmann, Gordon D. *An Essay on Theological Method*. AAR Studies in Religion, no. 11. Rev. ed. Missoula, Mont.: Scholars Press, 1979.

A contemporary reformulation of a liberal Protestant understanding of the theological method and the constructive task of theology.

Küng, Hans. *Theology for the Third Millennium*. New York: Doubleday, 1988.

A collection of Küng's essays that deal with the nature of theology and theological method.

Latourelle, René. *Theology and Salvation*. New York: Alba House, 1970.

Latourelle seeks to relate the contemporary emphasis on salvation history to traditional topics on the nature of theology and fundamental theology.

Lauret, Bernard, and François Refoulé. *Initiation à la pratique de la théologie*. 6 vols. Paris: Éditions du Cerf, 1982.

A French series that is sensitive to current historical, philosophical, and practical developments and seeks to relate theory and practice. The volumes represent the best of current French Roman Catholic theology.

Lindbeck, George. *The Nature of Doctrine*. Philadelphia: Westminster Press, 1985.

This monograph is much more than its title indicates. It suggests a cultural linguistic approach to theology over against propositional and expressive approaches.

Pannenberg, Wolfhart. *Theology and Philosophy of Science*. Philadelphia: Westminster Press, 1976.

Pannenberg, a German Lutheran theologian, presents various conceptions of science and history, a history of conceptions of theology, and his own conception of theology as the history of religion.

Rahner, Karl. *Foundations of Christian Faith*. New York: Seabury, 1978.

This book exemplifies Rahner's transcendental fundamental theology as developed in relation to the basic idea of Christianity and the contents of the Christian faith.

Ratzinger, Joseph. *Principles of Catholic Theology: Building Stones for a Fundamental Theology*. San Francisco: Ignatius Press, 1987.

A collection of Cardinal Ratzinger's essays on Scripture and tradition, church and theology, faith and theology.

Tracy, David. *Blessed Rage for Order*. New York: Seabury, 1975. Idem. *The Analogical Imagination*. New York: Crossroad, 1981.

Two important volumes on the nature of theology and theological method. Especially important is the development of the method of correlation and the understanding of theology as hermeneutical.

## DIVISIONS OF THEOLOGY

Ebeling, Gerhard. *The Study of Theology*. Philadelphia: Fortress Press, 1978.

Ebeling, a German Lutheran theologian, proposes a conception of theology with attention to the distinct disciplines of theology.

Farley, Edward. *Theologia: The Fragmentation and Unity of Theological Education*. Philadelphia: Fortress Press, 1983.

Historical presentation of the origin of the division of theology into the fourfold pattern: biblical, historical, systematic, and practical.

Lonergan, Bernard. *Method in Theology*. New York: Crossroad, 1972.

Lonergan explains the significance of human cognitional structures for the use of method within theology and for an eightfold division of disciplines within theology.

# 2

## FAITH AND REVELATION

# 2

## FAITH AND REVELATION

### *Avery Dulles*

It is fundamental to Catholic belief that any salutary relationship to God depends on God's free and gracious manifestation accepted in faith. Described as "the beginning and root of all justification,"[1] faith is seen as an affirmative intellectual response to revelation. Without a prior revelation on God's part faith would be impossible, for it would have no basis and no object. And without faith, the whole edifice of Christian existence would collapse.

Not only for the Christian life but for theology too, revelation and faith are of constitutive importance. Theology is a disciplined reflection on faith and thus also on revelation. It seeks to serve the church by accurately establishing the contents of revelation, by spelling out the theoretical and practical consequences of revelation, by critically examining current doctrine and practice in the light of revelation, by exhibiting the coherence and credibility of revelation, by vindicating the beliefs and practices of the church on the basis of revelation, and by refuting views at odds with revelation. Karl Rahner, a representative contemporary theologian, has declared: "Theology is the *science* of faith. It is the conscious and methodical explanation and explication of the divine revelation received and grasped in faith."[2] Still more recently, Walter Kasper has described revelation as "the final presupposition, basis, means, and norm of everything that purports to be Christian."[3] The importance of the theme of this chapter should therefore be evident.

# REVELATION

## THE CONCEPT OF REVELATION

The word *revelation* (Latin, *revelatio*; Greek, *apocalypsis*) means etymologically the removal of a veil (Latin, *velum*; Greek, *kalymma*), hence, dis-closure. The idea that God reveals is pervasive in the Bible and was taken for granted from the dawn of Christianity. Only in the seventeenth century, when rationalists began to deny or minimize revelation, did Christian theologians attempt to define and defend the concept in a systematic way. Vatican Council I (1869–70) included

---

1. Council of Trent, Decree on Justification, chap. 8, quoted in H. Denzinger and A. Schönmetzer, eds., *Enchiridion Symbolorum, Definitionum et Declarationum de Rebus Fidei et Morum*, 36th ed. (Freiburg: Herder, 1976), no. 1532. This work will hereafter be cited in the text by the initials DS, followed by the paragraph number.

2. Karl Rahner, "Theology. I. Nature," in K. Rahner, ed., *Encyclopedia of Theology: The Concise "Sacramentum Mundi"* (New York: Seabury-Crossroad, 1975), 1687.

3. Walter Kasper, "Offenbarung Gottes in der Geschichte. Gotteswort in Menschenwort," in B. Dreher et al., eds., *Handbuch der Verkündigung* (Freiburg: Herder, 1970), 1:53–96, here 53.

a chapter on revelation in its Constitution on the Catholic Faith (*Dei Filius* [hereafter DF]). Here it described revelation as a supernatural manifestation by God "of himself and the eternal decrees of his will"; this manifestation is objectively contained in traditions that come from Christ through the apostles and in Scriptures inspired by the Holy Spirit (DS 3004–6).

Vatican Council II (1962–65), building on the theological prob-ings of several generations since Vatican I, was able to produce a substantial Constitution on Divine Revelation (*Dei Verbum* [hereafter DV]). Without proposing a strict definition of revelation the coun-cil described it as the action by which God freely makes known the hidden purpose (*sacramentum*) of the divine will and lovingly speaks to human beings as friends, inviting them "into fellowship with him-self" (DV 2). In its chapter on the nature of revelation (chap. 1) *Dei Verbum* emphasized the dynamic and interpersonal dimensions. In comparison with Vatican Council I, *Dei Verbum* is more personalistic, trinitarian, and christocentric.[4]

The theological concept of revelation, set forth in official church teaching, differs in some respects from current popular usage. In common speech the word is often applied to a sudden, unexpected disclosure that comes to an individual with exceptional power, depth, and clarity. The Greek word *apocalypsis*, which is the closest equiv-alent to "revelation" in the Greek Bible, generally refers to an extraordinary psychological experience in which the recipient feels removed from the circumstances of mundane life and transported into a higher world. Theologically, however, revelation does not nec-essarily involve any such disruption. As we shall see, it can come in a non-ecstatic manner through nature, historical records, current events, and living proclamation. Thus many biblical terms other than *apocalypsis* may be taken in specific contexts as referring to what modern theology would call revelation. Among them are *logos theou* (Word of God), *phanerosis* (manifestation), *epiphaneia* (appear-ance), *gnosis* (knowledge), and *aletheia* (truth). We should be on guard against attributing to revelation in the theological sense all the qualities associated with the word in popular usage.

## TYPES OF REVELATION

To avoid confusion, it is well at the outset to make certain funda-mental distinctions. In an *active* or dynamic sense, revelation is the

---

4. These and other characteristics of Vatican II's theology of revelation are noted by René Latourelle in his *Theology of Revelation* (Staten Island, N.Y.: Alba House, 1966), 486–87.

process of God's self-disclosure—a gradual process that extends, as we shall see, over long periods of history. In an *objective* sense, revelation denotes the fund or "deposit" of knowledge, insights, and wisdom resulting from the process just referred to. The fruits of the process, "objectively" contained in Scripture and tradition, are transmitted to believers by education in the church, the living community of faith.

Revelation is said to be *immediate* in the case of persons who receive it directly from God, rather than from other persons who have previously received it. It is *mediate* when passed on from the first recipient to other believers. This distinction should not be made too rigid, since new revelation is normally accorded only to persons who have been prepared for it by the reception of revelation already given, and since the transmission of past revelation may be accompanied by God's present self-manifestation.

A further distinction is between *natural* and *historical* revelation. "Natural" revelation normally means the self-manifestation of God through the regular order of nature as described, for instance, in Paul's sermon at Lystra (Acts 14:15-17). God's self-disclosure through the inner voice of conscience may also be called natural, inasmuch as the law of God is held to be inscribed upon the human heart so that those who have no positive law from God "do by nature what the law requires" (Rom. 2:14; see Vatican II, Pastoral Constitution on the Church in the Modern World [*Gaudium et Spes* (hereafter GS)], 16). "Historical" revelation, by contrast, is made to particular individuals and groups through particular events that occur, or have occurred, at special times and places.

The natural revelation described in the last paragraph ought to be distinguished, at least conceptually, from the natural knowledge of God obtained by rational inference from created things.[5] Revelation, even when given through nature, is a free and personal self-manifestation of God, calling for the free and personal response of faith. Natural knowledge, on the other hand, is an achievement of human reason, which assents necessarily to demonstrative arguments. As we shall see, all revelation, properly so called, is supernatural. Thus the meaning of *natural* as opposed to *historical* should not be confused with the meaning of *natural* as opposed to *supernatural*.

---

5. Vatican II in *Dei Verbum*, no. 3, refers, as we shall see, to revelation through nature. In *Dei Verbum*, no. 6, Vatican II takes up the contrast made by Vatican I in *Dei Filius* (DS 3004) between revelation and the natural knowledge of God from created things. Thus Vatican II seems to make a distinction between the natural knowledge of God and revelation through nature.

It should also be noted that I am concerned, in this article, with *public* revelation, given by God to the whole human race, to an entire people, or to the church as the people of God of the new covenant. I am not concerned with *private* revelation, which may on occasion be given to one or several individuals for some special reason. Public revelation must be communicable to all members of a society and must be certified by signs that make it generally credible. I shall discuss the question of credibility in the second part of this article, dealing with faith.

## THE MODES OF COMMUNICATION

I have already distinguished between natural and historical revelation. Natural revelation is directed in principle to all human beings, and may also be called "general." Stating the Catholic position on this point, Vatican Council II asserted: "God, who through the Word creates all things (cf. Jn. 1:3) and keeps them in existence, gives human beings an enduring witness to himself in created realities (see Rom. 1:19-20)" (DV 3). Again, in its Pastoral Constitution on the Church in the Modern World, it declared: "All believers of whatever religion have always heard his [God's] revealing voice [*vocem et manifestationem Eius*] in the discourse of creatures" (GS 36).

Natural revelation is only preliminary. Jews, Christians, and Muslims, among others, hold that God's self-disclosure has occurred more fully and intimately through special events at particular times and places. Historical revelation unfolds in a meaningful sequence of deeds and words, as indicated by Vatican Council II: "This plan of revelation is realized by deeds and words having an inner unity: the deeds wrought by God in the history of salvation manifest and confirm the teaching and realities signified by the words, whereas the words proclaim the deeds and clarify the mystery contained in them" (DV 2).

This sentence needs to be unpacked. On the one hand the council asserts that revelation is given in historical deeds or facts. The Old and New Testaments are primarily concerned with recounting the great deeds that marked God's self-manifestation to ancient Israel and to the apostles. Central to this history are the events of the exodus (including the Sinai covenant), the conquest of the Holy Land, the exile and return, and, in the New Testament, the life, death, and resurrection of Jesus, together with the founding of the Christian church. During the 1940s and 1950s many Protestant and Catholic scholars, especially biblical theologians, argued for the primacy of deeds or acts over words and concepts as carriers of revelation.

Vatican II, seeking a balanced approach, wisely avoided any dichotomy between deeds and words. Throughout the Bible the events of salvation history are identified and interpreted by inspired prophets, priests, apostles, and evangelists. Without these highly selective and interpreted accounts it might not be possible to perceive the revelatory quality of the events themselves. Taken as naked, objective occurrences, the events do not disclose their own divine significance, at least to us, who are unable to reconstruct them in detail. Even to the ancient Israelites, much of their history seemed scarcely reconcilable with the promises made to the patriarchs and kings of old. Only the prophetic interpretation of current events, together with new promises of national restoration, sustained the faith of a pious remnant under conditions of adversity.

We may conclude, then, that "words," in the sense of human language, play an essential role in the process of revelation. The words serve to identify the revelatory events, to interpret them, to preserve their memory, and to transmit them together with their saving significance. It may be objected, of course, that the words presuppose that the revelation has already been given and received, for it would not be possible to proclaim what was as yet unknown. The objection rests on a theory according to which thought precedes verbal formulation and expression. In reality, however, thought and formulation develop concurrently, so that our ideas are not mature until we have expressed them, at least to ourselves. Even if, by exception, a revelation were completely imparted before being put into words, it would not at that point be public; it would not have been given to a people as such. I conclude, therefore, that public revelation, even when it first occurs, includes some measure of verbal expression. The original recipients verbalize the revelation to themselves and their community, and this initial verbalization is constitutive of the revelation itself. I shall return to the verbal component in the third part of this chapter, when I consider the transmission of revelation through Scripture and tradition.

External events and spoken or written words, though integral to the process of revelation, are not revelation until their divinely intended meaning is perceived and accepted. For this to happen, they must be apprehended not simply as intramundane phenomena but as self-manifestations of God. They must be seen as communicating God's thoughts and intentions. The primary content of revelation is not some new information about humanity or nature; rather the primary content is precisely God. To indicate this, Vatican Council I, as quoted above, spoke of revelation as a manifestation by God "of himself and the eternal decrees of his will" (DS 3004), and Vatican

Council II stated that by revelation God makes known "himself and the hidden purpose [*sacramentum*] of his will" (DV 2).

Because God "dwells in unapproachable light" (1 Tim. 6:16), revelation is necessarily somewhat mysterious. Vatican Council I stated that the primary contents of revelation, divine mysteries, "so far excel the created intellect that even after they have been given in revelation and accepted in faith, they still remain covered by the veil of faith and wrapped in a kind of darkness as long as, in this mortal life, 'we are away from the Lord, for we walk by faith, not by sight' (2 Cor. 5:6-7)" (DS 3016). Vatican Council II called attention to the interpersonal character of the loving action by which God takes human beings "into fellowship with himself" (DV 2).

Because it is a call to personal union with God, revelation presupposes in the human recipient a certain affinity with the infinite, the divine. Revelation is a grace, an anticipation of the blessed union to be consummated in heaven. God's word, which comes externally through visible and tangible signs, resounds also within, in the depths of the human consciousness.

Involving as it does these two dimensions, revelation normally takes on a symbolic structure.[6] A symbol is a sign pregnant with a plenitude of meaning that must be evoked, because it eludes direct statement. The revelatory events and words of Scripture exemplify this structure. In the Old Testament, the miracles of the exodus, the theophanies of Sinai, and the visions of the prophets and seers are highly symbolic, as are, in the New Testament, events such as the baptism, transfiguration, crucifixion, and resurrection of Jesus. The very events of revelation history are symbols fraught with a meaning deeper than clear concepts or propositional language can convey. Each symbol, taken in its historical and literary context, contains a whole range of interlocking meanings that cannot be spelled out adequately in objective conceptual discourse.

Symbol, as Paul Ricoeur has said, "gives rise to thought"[7] and, indeed, shapes the very thought to which it gives rise. A revelation that begins with symbolic communication gradually generates a whole series of reflections and interpretations that explicate its meaning. Thus the metaphor "Jesus is the Good Shepherd" can be reexpressed to say: Jesus takes care of his followers as a faithful shepherd takes care of his sheep. The propositions clarify the metaphor up to a point, but are abstract and incomplete. By fragmenting the density of the original symbol, they blunt its power. Yet proposi-

---

6. For a fuller discussion of the symbolic structure of revelation see Avery Dulles, *Models of Revelation* (Garden City, N.Y.: Doubleday, 1983), chap. 9, 131–54.

7. Paul Ricoeur, *The Symbolism of Evil* (Boston: Beacon, 1967), 347–57, esp. 348.

tional commentary pertains to revelation insofar as it elucidates the meaning of the symbols, preventing certain misinterpretations. The Christian doctrines set limits to the kinds of significance that can be found in the Christian symbols. The doctrines, however, are not independent revelation; they live off the power of the symbols.

The revelatory modes of communication, then, include the order of nature, historical events, symbolic words, interior illuminations, and propositional statements. All of these are integral to the process of revelation. But it is better not to speak of "revealed events," "revealed words," or "revealed propositions," as though these media were the contents of revelation itself. The true content of revelation—revelation in the objective sense—is the divinely intended and humanly perceived significance of the events and words. By participation in the community of faith the individual believer can have reliable access to the revelatory meaning of the signs and symbols through which God's self-disclosure has taken place and through which God's salvific designs have been made known. Through these signs and symbols believers can more fully grasp God's revelation than they could through the use of unaided reason.

## SPECIAL REVELATION IN SALVATION HISTORY

As contrasted with the "general" revelation given through the order of nature, the revelation given through particular historical events may be called "special." Christianity rests on a series of such events as presented and interpreted in Holy Scripture. Modern theologians have found meaningful patterns in this history. The Anglican biblical theologian Alan Richardson persuasively presented the opinion that "the distinctive character of Israel's history was that it was built around a series of disclosure situations, which through the activity of prophetic minds became interpretative of Israel's historic destiny and ultimately of the history of all mankind."[8] The events are not self-interpreting, but they lend themselves to the interpretations given to them by the prophets, apostles, and biblical authors. Seen in this light, the events manifest God as personal, free, loving, merciful, just, patient, and powerful. At the same time, salvation history exhibits humanity and the world as objects of God's powerful mercies and as destined by God for redemption and glory. The exceptional events of salvation history, as narrated in the Bible, serve as interpretative keys to illuminate the riddles of life.

---

8. Alan Richardson, *History Sacred and Profane* (Philadelphia: Westminster Press, 1964), 224.

According to Christian faith the history of revelation comes to a climax and focus in the life, teaching, sufferings, death, and resurrection of Jesus Christ, together with the sending forth of the Holy Spirit from the risen Christ. Jesus, as the incarnate Word of God, may in some sense be called revelation itself. Vatican Council II asserts: "The deepest truth about God and the salvation of human beings [the essential content of revelation] is made clear to us in Christ, who is the Mediator and at the same time the fullness of all revelation" (DV 2).

If revelation is understood as symbolic communication, the primacy of Christ is not difficult to grasp. The divine Son, the Word of God, is symbolically present and active in Christ's human nature, which becomes a medium through which the divine manifests itself. For us who do not immediately encounter Christ in his incarnate life, his character and meaning have to be mediated by proclamation, Scriptures, liturgy, and sacraments, and only to the extent that this mediation is successful does Christ become for us the fullness of revelation. But if the mediation is successful, Christ does appear as a uniquely powerful and unsurpassable revelation of God. His life in the flesh, together with his message of forgiveness, supremely manifests what God chooses to be in free grace toward humankind. In Christ's wonderful deeds, especially his miracles, God's kingdom may be seen breaking into the history of the world. The crucifixion, as a symbolic event, expresses the sacrificial character of God's redemptive love. The resurrection symbolizes, by its very reality, the victory of that redemptive love over all that could oppose it, even hatred and death. Without Christ we could not come to know and respond to God as the one who "so loved the world that he gave his only Son" (John 3:16).

Vatican Council II, in its Pastoral Constitution on the Church in the Modern World, concisely stated the revelatory meaning of Christ:

> The Church believes that Christ, who died and was raised up for all, can through his Spirit offer human beings the light and the strength to measure up to their lofty vocation. Nor has any other name under heaven been given them by which they can be saved. The Church likewise holds that in its Lord and Master can be found the key, the center, and the goal of all human history [GS 10; see also GS 44].

## REVELATION AND THE RELIGIONS

Some authors, notably the Swiss Protestant Karl Barth, have sharply contrasted revelation and religion. Revelation they regard as God's word, coming wholly from above, whereas religion is in their view an effort of sinful human beings to lay hold of the divine. This contrast is overdrawn. Revelation itself demands a human response; it achieves a human and public presence when taken up into religion. Religion, insofar as it is rooted in revelation, is holy and divine.

Judaism and Christianity are the religions directly corresponding to biblical revelation. In them we can study the dialectical relationship between a specific revelation and the human response. The question then arises whether the nonbiblical religions owe their existence to some kind of revelation, either general or historical, rather than being due simply to human reasoning and initiative. A number of Catholic theologians hold that revelation is reserved to the biblical religions, but official Catholic teaching, as we have seen, admits that revelation is accessible, in some measure, to people of all cultures and religions.

Vatican Council II, in its Declaration on Non-Christian Religions (*Nostra Aetate* [hereafter NA]), cautiously hinted that revelation lies at the root of nonbiblical religions. It spoke of them as being based on "a certain perception of that hidden power which hovers over the course of things and over the events of human life" and, in many cases, on a "recognition" of a supreme divinity and even of God as Father. The teachings of these religions, said the declaration, "often reflect a ray of that Truth which enlightens all human beings." Although "the Catholic Church rejects nothing that is true and holy in these religions," it must never cease to "proclaim Christ as 'the way, and the truth, and the life' (Jn. 14:6)" in whom the fullness of the religious life is to be found (NA 2).

Some theologians, including Karl Rahner,[9] argue to the revelatory character of non-Christian religions from the universal salvific will of God. If God seriously wills that every human person achieve eternal life, it seems altogether probable that grace must be at work in the hearts of the unevangelized. If so, it be may supposed that the myths, rituals, and beliefs of the religions bear traces, at least, of a grace-given awareness of God, and hence of revelation. Although the mutual contradictions among the religions prevent us from holding that all of them are simply revealed, the common themes that underlie many of these religions may well be the effect of God's revealing presence working on the human consciousness.

Even if one denies revelation in nonbiblical religions, one must acknowledge much good in them. Through dialogue it may be possible for all the religions, including Christianity, to be enriched and

---

9. Karl Rahner, *Foundations of Christian Faith* (New York: Crossroad, 1982), 311–21. This theme is recurrent in Rahner's work.

in some ways corrected. In entering such a dialogue Christians will have no reason to conceal or doubt their own positions regarding Christ as the summit of revelation. Reflections of divine truth are to be sought in all religions.

## REVELATION: PAST, PRESENT, AND FUTURE

Thus far I have concentrated on the revelation given in the past, especially the special revelation given in biblical times, with its culmination in Jesus Christ. The New Testament writers were convinced that in Christ God had surpassingly fulfilled the hopes and expectations of Israel and that the mission of the church was to preserve and proclaim God's final self-revelation in Christ. Increasingly in later books of the New Testament the term *faith* is used in an objective sense to designate the deposit of revelation committed to the church (Jude 3; 1 Tim. 6:20; 2 Tim. 1:12, 14).

The modern mind, deeply impressed by the limitations imposed by the particularities of time and culture, has difficulty in admitting that there can be any absolute or unsurpassable disclosure within history. Even thinkers who reject the inevitability of progress and deny that "later is better" consider that each age may be able to surpass its predecessors in some respects and that to equate revelation with an ancient deposit would condemn the church to a continual loss of vitality and actuality.

Vatican Council II, conscious of these concerns, avoided repeating the formula sometimes used that revelation "ceased with the death of the last apostle."[10] Instead, after describing Jesus as the perfecter and fulfillment of revelation, it stated: "The Christian dispensation, therefore, as the new and definitive covenant, will never pass away, and we await no further public revelation before the glorious manifestation of our Lord Jesus Christ (see 1 Tim. 6:14 and Tit. 2:13)" (DV 4). In the Constitution on the Church (*Lumen Gentium* [hereafter LG]) Vatican II depicted the church as capable of showing forth "in the world the mystery of the Lord in a faithful though shadowed way, until at the last it will be revealed in total splendor" (LG 8). These two statements avoid giving the impression that the church already possesses a total grasp of revelation in

---

10. On at least two occasions the Theological Commission or its subcommissions rejected several *modi* requesting that *Dei Verbum*, no. 4, be amended to state explicitly that revelation was closed (*clausam*) with the death of the apostles. See the *relationes* of July 3, 1964, and November 20, 1964. These are found respectively in the *Acta Synodalia Sacrosancti Concilii Oecumenici Vaticani II*, Periodus 3, vol. 3 (1974), and Periodus 4, vol. 1 (1976), p. 345.

its fullness, but at the same time they emphasize the church's obligation to adhere faithfully to "the mystery of the Lord," the "Christian dispensation," the "new and definitive covenant."

In the New Testament the fullness of revelation in Christ is not presented as excluding subsequent revelation. The Gospel of John ascribes this function to the Paraclete, the Spirit of truth, who will declare to the apostles many things that Jesus himself was not able to say in his earthly ministry (John 15:26; 16:12-15). In Acts and the Pauline letters the apostles are portrayed as receiving revelations to guide them as they shape the doctrine, mission, worship, and structures of the early church. In the Apocalypse (Book of Revelation) the seer of Patmos receives visions and locutions that are normative for the churches for which the book is intended (Rev. 22:18-19).

In early patristic times living prophets continued to play a central role in the direction of the church. Following in the footsteps of Saint Augustine, Saint Bonaventure and many medieval theologians used the term *revelation* to mean the interior illumination and attraction needed for any act of faith.[11] Throughout the Middle Ages it was held that God's self-disclosure continued through the fathers and doctors of the church and likewise through councils. At the Council of Trent a prominent theologian declared: "In the general councils the Holy Spirit has revealed to the Church, according to the needs of the time, numerous truths which were not explicitly contained in the canonical books [of Scripture]."[12] Yet it was taken as axiomatic that no postbiblical revelation could essentially change the content of Christian faith.

The theme of ongoing revelation fell into oblivion from the sixteenth through the nineteenth centuries, when revelation was understood almost exclusively as an objective deposit of truth. Some modernist theologians such as Alfred Loisy, influenced by Hegelian evolutionism, revived the theme at the beginning of the twentieth century, but they gave the impression that God's revelation in Jesus Christ was only a provisional stage on humanity's forward march to an ever deeper unity with the divine. Vatican Council II, while

---

11. Latourelle, in his *Theology of Revelation*, briefly summarizes the theme of interior revelation in Augustine (pp. 139–40) and Bonaventure (pp. 155–56). The same theme, he points out, recurs in the sixteenth-century Dominicans Melchior Cano and Domingo Bañez (ibid., 180–83). To the contrary, the Jesuits Francisco Suárez and Juan de Lugo equated revelation with the external proposal of God's word (ibid., 183–87).

12. From a written submission "de traditionibus ecclesiae" attributed, with some uncertainty, to Claude Le Jay; text in Görres-Gesellschaft, ed., *Concilium Tridentinum Diariorum, Actorum, Epistolarum, Tractatuum Nova Collectio* (Freiburg: Herder, 1930), 12:523. The English translation of Yves Congar's *Tradition and Traditions* (New York: Macmillan, 1966), 122, gives a faulty page reference.

insisting on the permanence of the covenant established in Christ, recognized that God is not silent in our time. Several quotations will illustrate this point.

The Constitution on Divine Revelation asserts that "in the sacred books, the Father who is in heaven meets his children with great love and speaks with them" (DV 21). Not only Scripture but also tradition is seen as a locus of continuing revelation. Through tradition "God, who spoke of old, uninterruptedly converses with the Bride of his beloved Son; and the Holy Spirit, through whom the living voice of the gospel resounds in the Church, and through it in the world, leads believers to all truth and makes the word of Christ dwell in them abundantly (see Col. 3:16)" (DV 8). The Constitution on the Liturgy (*Sacrosanctum Concilium* [hereafter SC]) emphasizes the multiple presence of Christ in his church, especially in its liturgical celebrations, when the minister performs sacred actions, when the Scriptures are read, and when the congregation prays and sings (SC 7). Finally, the Pastoral Constitution on the Church in the Modern World speaks of the signs of the times as indications of "God's presence and purpose in the happenings, needs, and desires in which this people [the church] has a part along with other people of our age" (GS 11; see also GS 4).

A comprehensive doctrine of revelation, then, cannot limit itself to God's self-disclosure in biblical times; it must deal with God's active presence to the church and the world today, without which the good news of the gospel, which is admittedly normative, might easily be dismissed as a piece of inconsequential historical information.

The Constitution on Divine Revelation, as I have noted, speaks of "the glorious manifestation of our Lord Jesus Christ" as the consummation of revelation (DV 4). In so doing it revives the biblical theme of eschatological revelation. Saint Paul addresses the Corinthians as believers who "wait for the revealing of our Lord Jesus Christ" (1 Cor. 1:7). In 2 Thessalonians Paul speaks of the day "when the Lord Jesus is revealed from heaven with his mighty angels in flaming fire" (2 Thess. 1:7). Elsewhere in the Pauline corpus we read of the promised time when "Christ who is our life appears" (Col. 3:4). The Letter to the Hebrews speaks of Christ appearing a "second time...to save those who are eagerly waiting for him" (Heb. 9:28). The pastoral letters have numerous references to Christ's future coming in glory (e.g., 1 Tim. 6:14; Titus 2:13).

This eschatological dimension of revelation is important not only for the sake of fidelity to the Scriptures but also because of the attunement of our age to progress and to the future. As Joseph Ratzinger notes in his commentary on *Dei Verbum*, article 4, the eschatological reference "now shows from within faith the provisional nature of Christianity and hence its relatedness to the future, which exists together with the connection with the Christ event that has taken place once and for all, so that it is impossible to state the one without the other."[13] Christ and his revelation have finality precisely because he is "the one who is to come," bearing in himself the promise of the ultimate future.

The splendor of the risen Christ mediates to the saints in heaven the immediate vision of God. With transformed minds they gaze upon the splendor of God reflected in the face of the glorious Christ (see 2 Cor. 4:6). The blessed who live with Christ know and will eternally know God through an interior grace that is called, in theological terminology, the light of glory. The light of faith, in the present life, provides a faint anticipation of the face-to-face vision that will then be given. The Constitution on the Church eloquently describes the final manifestation of God:

> When Christ shall appear and the glorious resurrection of the dead takes place, the splendor of God will brighten the heavenly city and the Lamb will be the lamp thereof (see Apoc. 21:23). Then in the supreme happiness of charity the whole church of the saints will adore God and "the Lamb who was slain" (Apoc. 5:12), proclaiming with one voice: "To him who sits upon the throne, and to the Lamb, blessing and honor and glory and might, forever and ever" (Apoc. 5:13-14) [LG 51].

# FAITH

## THE CONCEPT OF FAITH

In Catholic systematic theology the term *faith* is generally used to designate the provisional knowledge or awareness of the divine that is given in this life to believers who adhere to revelation. Vatican Council I described faith as "the full homage of intellect and will to God who reveals" (DS 3008). Then, in a sentence that sums up the fruits of a long theological development, the council declared:

> The Catholic Church professes that this faith, which is the "beginning of human salvation" (see Trent, DS 1532), is the supernatural virtue whereby, inspired and assisted by the grace of God, we believe that what he has revealed is true, not because the intrinsic truth of the contents

---

13. Joseph Ratzinger, Commentary on *Dei Verbum*, chap. 1, in Herbert Vorgrimler, ed., *Commentary on the Documents of Vatican II* (New York: Herder and Herder, 1969), 3:177.

is seen by the natural light of reason but because of the authority of God himself, the revealer, who can neither be deceived nor deceive [DS 3008].

Building on this authoritative statement, Vatican Council II restated the same doctrine with a slight shift of emphasis:

The "obedience of faith" (Rom. 16:26; see 1:5; 2 Cor. 10:5-6) must be given to God who reveals, an obedience by which one entrusts [*committit*] one's whole self freely to God, offering "the full submission of intellect and will to God who reveals" (Vatican I, DS 3008), and freely assenting to the revelation given by him [DV 5].

Before we proceed to a more detailed analysis of these lapidary statements of the two Vatican councils, it may be helpful to situate this conciliar teaching within the range of meanings conveyed by the Greek word *pistis*, the Latin *fides*, and the English word *faith* in other contexts. Faith in the broader sense is not only assent to what a person says. More fundamentally it is trust in the person, as appears from statements such as, "I have faith in you," "I put my faith in you." Then again, faith or *pistis* can be used to signify faithfulness, for example in the statements "I have kept faith with you" and "You broke faith with me." Vatican Council I, while emphasizing assent to God's word as true, did not adopt an exclusively intellectualist perspective. It spoke of the homage of both will and intellect to the authority or majesty of God the revealer. Vatican II made a particular effort to build into its statement the dimensions of trust, commitment, obedience, and submission. But it did not minimize the intellectual element of assent to the content of God's revelation. The intellectualist emphasis, already prominent in the Gospel of John, has been strong in the Catholic tradition, especially in the Scholastic theology of the Middle Ages and the Counter Reformation.

## THE VIRTUE AND THE ACT OF FAITH

Building on certain texts from Saint Paul, such as 1 Corinthians 13:13, medieval theologians distinguished sharply between faith, hope, and charity, which they described as the three theological virtues—virtues because they were stable dispositions of the human spirit oriented toward good acts; theological because they had God as their object. Thomas Aquinas explained how the theological virtues order human beings toward the beatific vision. Through faith we assent to God as our last end and to the way of salvation prescribed by God; through hope we tend toward the vision of God as something that we can, through grace, attain; through charity, the highest form of love, we enter into an affective union with God, the source of our eternal blessedness.[14]

Charity, as the virtue that makes one a sharer in the divine nature, is the form or soul of all other virtues, including faith. In a person who lacks charity faith cannot achieve its true purpose. Such a faith is called "dead" or "formless" faith (see James 2:17). According to the Council of Trent faith without the addition of hope and charity does not unite one to Christ or make one a living member of Christ's body (DS 1531). The faith that offers eternal life is a living faith that "works through charity" (see Gal. 5:6). But a believer who loses charity by willfully turning away from God may still retain the gift of faith. The faith that remains in such a person is still the theological habit of faith, and is a gift of God. It may serve as a basis for repentance and for a return to God's grace and favor.

Virtues are specified and defined by their acts. The principal act of faith, as distinct from other virtues such as hope and charity, is to believe. Belief, however, is not the only act of faith. As Thomas Aquinas explains, faith has a secondary act, which is external: namely confession in the sense of testimony or witness.[15] It is normal for belief in the heart to give rise to confession with the lips (Rom. 10:9-10; see also 2 Cor. 4:13). A person who sincerely believes will normally be impelled to profess his or her faith, at least when the occasion requires. A culpable silence about—or denial of—one's beliefs can be a sin against the virtue of faith itself.

The concept of confession need not be limited to verbal statements. In a certain sense the whole life of the committed Christian is an external profession of faith. Good works are not only proofs and consequences of sincere faith; they may be called acts of faith in the secondary sense explained by Saint Thomas.

## FORMAL AND MATERIAL OBJECTS OF FAITH

Just as virtues are known by their acts, so acts are known by their objects, the realities in which they terminate. Superficially, it is correct to say that faith has a number of objects—all the truths revealed by God. But on a deeper level, the object of faith is one, for in every assent of faith the believer is intending to achieve, and actually achieving, union with the mind of God, who is the first truth and the witness to everything accepted in faith. In believing we assent primarily to God who reveals and only secondarily to this or

---

14. Thomas Aquinas *Summa Theologiae* 1a-2ae, q. 62, art. 3.
15. Ibid., 2a-2ae, q. 3, art. 1.

that particular truth that we believe on the authority of God. Saint Thomas and other Scholastic theologians distinguished between the formal and material objects of faith. The formal object is the ultimate reason for the assent to any particular truth that we accept on the authority of God. In more technical language, the authority of God the revealer is the "formal" object of faith, whereas that to which God attests is the "material" object. The formal object is the inner reason or ground for assent to the material object.

From this analysis it should be evident that there can be no faith without both a formal and a material object. To make an act of faith in the theological sense is to believe something on the authority of God. One submits to God's authority precisely in accepting what God vouches for.

The material object, revealed truths, requires further discussion. Faith is not an acceptance of a miscellaneous body of disconnected truths but an acceptance of the order of salvation as seen and disclosed by God. In God's mind the truth is one and undivided. God knows everything knowable by a single comprehensive idea. The human mind, however, knows piecemeal. It breaks up the totality of revealed truth into distinct truths, separately enunciated in judgments or statements. The articles of the creed and the dogmas of the church are enunciations of revealed truth.

When we make an act of faith we do not adhere to propositions or statements as the objects of faith, but rather to the reality designated by those propositions or statements. Primarily and directly we believe in the God who is triune, and in the Son who became incarnate, rather than in the statements that express these realities. Yet the believer does assent, in a secondary way, to the propositions, for without them the reality would not be humanly affirmable.[16]

As stated above, there can be no faith without revealed truth, the self-expression of the mind of God. But because of the human element in the articulation of revelation it is possible for a person of faith to accept an incorrect formulation as though it were God's word or to reject a correct formulation, not recognizing it as God's word. An authentic act of faith can coexist with opinions that are partly incorrect.

The formal object of faith as a theological virtue is the authority of the revealing God. Under this aspect faith is called "divine." God's authority, however, is normally grasped in some persons or institu-

---

16. In the words of Thomas Aquinas: "The act of the believer does not terminate in the propositions but in the reality, for we do not formulate propositions except in order to know things by means of them, whether in science or in faith" (*Summa Theologiae* 2a-2ae, q. 1, art. 2, ad 2).

tions who speak in God's name. The preeminent bearer of revelation is Jesus Christ, who, as the incarnate Logos, gives human utterance to the word of God. Faith may be called "Christian" as well as divine to the extent that it submits to the authority of Christ as the truth of God incarnate. For the Christian the truth of God is found not simply in the recorded words of Christ, but primarily in the very being of Christ, who could say of himself, "I am the truth" (John 14:6).

Christ, then, is not simply one among many material objects of faith. As Christians we believe God as God speaks to us in Christ. Christ in his humanity is not the formal object of faith but is the locus, so to speak, in which the formal object is preeminently encountered. In accepting the word of God the Christian accepts concurrently the word or self-expression of Christ.

Besides being divine and Christian, faith is, for many Christians, "Catholic." The Catholic Christian adheres to the church because God's word resounds in it. The church is not only a particular content (material object) of revelation; it is a trusted organ through which God's word comes to the faithful. The formal object of faith, according to Thomas Aquinas, is "the first truth [God] as this is made known in Scripture and in the doctrine of the Church, which proceeds from the first truth."[17] The Bible and approved doctrine are the means whereby the church proposes to the faithful the contents of divine revelation.

In brief, then, faith may be called "divine" insofar as it assents to the word of God, "Christian" insofar as it takes Christ to be "the Mediator and fullness of all revelation" (DV 2), and "Catholic" insofar as it submits to the church as the authoritative organ of revelation since the time of Christ. In the Catholic Christian's act of faith, these three dimensions are simultaneously present. When professing a particular article of the creed, the believer accepts it as part of God's revelation given in Christ and proclaimed by the church. Acceptance of particular doctrines would not be an act of faith unless they were accepted precisely on the word of a witness—either God directly encountered or God as represented by some person or organ through whom God chooses to speak.

## FAITH AND KNOWLEDGE

In the text on faith quoted above from Vatican Council I (DS 3008) a distinction is made between assent based on reason's grasp of the intrinsic truth of the contents and assent based on the authority of God

---

17. Ibid., 2a-2ae, q. 5, art. 3c.

the revealer. The distinction may be clarified by an analogy from the classroom. A teacher could either tell his or her students the correct answer to a problem in mathematics or else take the students through a series of steps by which they could see for themselves why this must be the answer. In the first case the students would have a highly imperfect knowledge of the answer, knowing what the solution is without knowing why. Yet they would not be without knowledge. A great deal of what we consider ourselves to know about secular matters depends on an acceptance of the word of others—often very fallible witnesses, such as schoolmasters, books, newspapers, broadcasters, friends, and neighbors. If we discounted all these sources, our knowledge would shrivel to a very small fraction of itself.

It is proper, therefore, to distinguish between two kinds of knowledge. There is evidential knowledge, in which one understands the grounds of one's assent, and faith-knowledge, in which one assents because of the trustworthiness of a witness. Faith-knowledge is imperfect as regards its mode, but it can be certain if the witness is evidently reliable and evidently vouches for what is believed. In divine faith we assent to something on the word of God, who can neither be deceived nor deceive.

Strictly speaking, we cannot "believe" what we know evidentially. If I could prove by conclusive argument that there are three divine persons, I could not "believe" it. Faith is by nature an obscure form of knowledge in which the inner grounds for the thing believed are hidden from the believer.

Does this mean that faith is irrational? Some Christians have portrayed faith as an arbitrary decision to believe in which proof or evidence plays no role at all. In the Catholic understanding, however, faith and reason work together. Even though reason cannot by its own powers establish the contents of faith, it can point to adequate motives for believing. Vatican Council I insisted very strongly on this point. The same God, it stated, is the author of faith and reason. Since God is not self-contradictory, truth cannot contradict truth (DS 3017). Faith, therefore, is not against reason. More than this, faith and reason mutually support one another, for right reason is capable of demonstrating the rational grounds of faith and of achieving some understanding of the revealed mysteries. Conversely, faith helps reason by enabling it to avoid certain errors and by giving it access to truth that would otherwise lie beyond its range (DS 3019).

Although faith cannot be an achievement of reason alone, the right use of reason can prepare for faith and confirm it. Reason can show how the contents of faith offer coherent answers to persistent questions to which merely human philosophies give no satisfactory solution. The answers of faith can be seen as having practical value in enabling people to cope with difficulties and reverses and in motivating them to live up to high standards and ideals. Faith gives steadiness, direction, and purpose to human life.

Christian revelation, moreover, is accredited by remarkable signs in history, including the prophecies and miracles of Scripture, the resurrection of Jesus from the dead, and the remarkable qualities of the church itself, which Vatican Council I described as a "great and abiding motive of credibility and an irrefragable witness to its own divine mission" (DS 3013). In this connection the council referred to the wonderful expansion of the church, its exceptional holiness and fruitfulness in good works, its catholic unity and unshakable stability (ibid.). The extent to which all these qualities are apparent is of course variable, depending on the fidelity of Christians to their own divine calling.

To conclude this section, then, we may say that although the contents of the Christian message cannot be proved by strict rational argument, they may reasonably be believed. Thanks to the qualities of the Christian message itself and the many signs given in history, the Christian religion may be described as "evidently credible" (Vatican I, DS 3013). That is to say, there are solid rational motives for deciding that one ought to become or remain a believer. To spell out the evidence of credibility by constructing arguments and refuting objections is the task of a special theological discipline known as apologetics. The extent to which any individual believer finds it necessary or useful to articulate the rational grounds of credibility varies enormously from case to case. As John Henry Newman never tired of asserting, the arguments set forth in manuals of apologetics rarely correspond to the spontaneous movement of the mind and heart that commonly brings conviction in matters of religion.[18]

## PROPERTIES OF FAITH:
## SUPERNATURALITY, CERTAINTY, FREEDOM, OBSCURITY

The signs of credibility have their importance in disposing a person to make an act of faith, in supplying some human confirmation for faith, and in enabling believers to give an account of their faith to others. At most, however, the study of the external evidence can yield only a theoretical assurance that it would be reasonable to believe. Faith itself, as a loving and reverent submission to the testimony of

_____

18. See especially Newman's *Fifteen Sermons Preached before the University of Oxford*, 3d ed. (London: Longmans, Green, 1871; London: SPCK, 1970). Later, as a Catholic, Newman expressed similar ideas in his *Essay in Aid of a Grammar of Assent* (1870).

God the revealer, requires a personal preparation that is more than intellectual.

The Catholic church, in its official teaching, has always insisted that any salutary act of faith depends on the prevenient gift of divine grace. In A.D. 529 the Second Council of Orange insisted on the necessity of "the illumination and inspiration of the Holy Spirit, who gives to all [believers] joy [or ease: *suavitatem*] in consenting to the truth and believing it" (DS 377). The Council of Trent in A.D. 1547 spoke of God touching the human heart through the enlightenment of the Holy Spirit, and added that the grace of God leaves the recipient free either to accept or to reject the gift of faith (DS 1525–26). The same doctrine is repeated in other words by Vatican Council I (DS 3010) and by Vatican Council II (DV 5).

Theologians explain that God's grace, working on the human heart, produces an existential affinity or connaturality with the good news of the gospel. A person thus prepared by grace feels an inner inclination to believe and is able to reach the practical conviction: It would be good for me to become a believer here and now; I have an obligation to believe. It is not necessary for this realization to be articulated in a distinct judgment, but some such realization is presupposed by the act of faith itself, for, as Saint Augustine said, "No one believes anything without first thinking that it ought to be believed."[19]

The illumination of the Holy Spirit does not make the contents of faith demonstrably true; nor does it negate the freedom of the person to reject, for whatever motives, the evidence of credibility. Its specific effect is to make clear to the recipient that he or she is called to become a believer. In so doing grace overcomes what would otherwise be a hesitation or disinclination to make the full commitment of faith. Grace thus confers a sense of peace and satisfaction upon the assent of faith.

The question whether faith is certain has been much discussed. If by certainty one means a firm commitment, certainty is an ingredient in the very concept of faith. On the other hand, faith is compatible with an acute realization that the evidence is far from compelling and that there are objections that the believer cannot answer. If the signs were so overwhelming that unbelief were impossible, faith, as a free assent, would also be impossible. Assent forced upon a person by stringent proofs would not be faith in the theological sense of reverent submission to the authority of the divine witness.

---

19. Augustine *De Praedestinatione Sanctorum* 2:5 (*Patrologia Latina*, ed. Migne, 44:963).

Since faith is by definition a firm assent, it excludes doubt in the usual sense of that word. But because faith lacks intrinsic evidence, it coexists with a kind of mental dissatisfaction or restlessness that Thomas Aquinas called *cogitatio* (pondering).[20] Without actually doubting the truth of the revealed content, the believer can continue to question how it is possible for things to be as faith asserts that they are; he or she can seek further signs confirming the truth of what is believed and can wrestle with objections that seem to defy solution. Because of these factors a believer will often feel tempted to doubt. This temptation, though painful, can have a purifying effect; it can banish the illusion that faith rests on strict rational proof.

Faith, therefore, is a *supernatural* assent. It adheres to the revealed message because of the majesty and authority of God the revealer. The *certitude* of faith is proportioned to the reliability of the divine witness, whose voice is heard not only in the externally proclaimed message but in the inner inclination to believe. Faith is reasonable because it is supported by external motives of credibility. It is *obscure* because its essential content, the mystery of God and salvation, surpasses the power of human reason either to discover without revelation or to fathom even after revelation. Finally, faith is *free* both because the grounds of credibility are not stringent and because the grace of God, inclining the mind and will to assent, can be resisted.

## IMPLICIT AND EXPLICIT FAITH

In the Christian theological tradition the term *implicit faith* is frequently used to convey some important but elusive ideas. The term *implicit* comes from logic, where it describes how a conclusion is contained in its premises. Applying this to theology, we can say that believers implicitly adhere to the logical consequences of the propositions they accept in faith. Thus in believing that Jesus Christ has a complete human nature, one implicitly believes that he had the powers of reasoning, speaking, and laughing. Once the logical consequences of our beliefs are brought to our attention, faith impels us to accept them.

To confine the concept of implicit faith to the logically implicit would, however, be too restrictive. As mentioned above, faith is not a mere assent to propositions. Above all else, it is a mysterious union of the mind with God, the first truth, who is both the formal object and the primary material object of faith.

---

20. Thomas Aquinas *Summa Theologiae* 2a-2ae, q. 2, art. 1.

Formally considered, faith is a submission to God's authority as manifested by certain divinely accredited witnesses or organs. The individual believer may be ignorant of many things actually taught by Christ or the church, but in professing to be a Christian or a Catholic one implicitly accepts everything that God teaches through these mouthpieces.

Faith, however, should not be understood as a blank check that we sign without any intimation of what will be written on it. The material object of faith, as previously stated, is one. Every act of faith terminates in the one mystery of salvation. Because God is one and the plan of salvation has an inner unity, every authentic act of faith puts us in a living relationship with aspects of the revealed mystery of which we are not explicitly conscious.

Even among Christians, not all know the contents of faith with the same degree of explicitness.[21] To the extent of their capacities, all Christians should explicitly profess the principal mysteries of faith, which are spelled out in the creed and celebrated in the liturgy. Those set over the community as teachers are required to know explicitly some points of faith that the uneducated believe only implicitly.

Taking the doctrine of implicit faith one stage further, Saint Thomas maintained that the ancient Israelites, though the gospel had not yet been proclaimed, had essentially the same faith as Christians, since the real object of their confession was the same.[22] Quoting Hebrews 11:13, he asserted that the Israelites of the early centuries beheld the promises from afar, and that the hopes of Israel became more distinct as the time of Christ drew nearer. Thus an increase in the articles of faith need not involve a change in the real object of faith.

The primary and irreducible content of explicit faith, for Saint Thomas, is that stated in Hebrews 11:6, "Whoever would draw near to God must believe that he exists and that he rewards those who seek him." Anyone who accepts this content through supernatural faith may be said to have an implicit grasp of the entire mystery of salvation, including the existence of the triune God, the incarnation, and the resurrection. The implication here is obviously not a matter of formal logic but one of real objective connection, arising out of the affinity between the virtue of faith and its real object.

---

21. Ibid., arts. 5 and 6.
22. Ibid., q. 1, art. 7.

## FAITH AND SALVATION

So often and so emphatically is the connection between faith and salvation stated in the New Testament that the necessity of faith has never been a matter of doubt in Catholic teaching. Relying on texts such as Mark 16:16, Romans 3:30, and Hebrews 11:6, popes and councils have repeatedly taught that no one can be saved without faith. The councils of Trent (DS 1529) and of Vatican I (DS 3010) stated in almost the same words that no one attains justification without faith.

The relationship of faith to justification and salvation is not a mere matter of God's positive decree, as though God had arbitrarily laid down faith as a condition. The purpose of the present life is that we may prepare ourselves for, and freely orient ourselves to, the goal for which we are destined. The goal is to behold God by the light of glory. Faith justifies because by means of it the future for which we are destined takes hold of us in an inchoative way. "Faith," says Saint Thomas, "is the habit of mind by which eternal life is begun in us, making the intellect assent to things that do not appear."[23]

The anticipation of the beatific vision in this life is necessarily partial and incomplete. We cannot by faith assent explicitly to everything that will be manifested by the light of glory. Thus it is legitimate to ask what the explicit content of saving faith must be. Saint Thomas, following Saint Augustine and the medieval Augustinian tradition, held that the necessary content varies according to different eras in salvation history and according to the capacities and status of individual persons.[24] In every age and for all persons, according to this theory, it has been necessary to believe that God exists and rewards those who seek God (see Heb. 11:6). Before the time of Christ unlearned persons were not required to have explicit belief in the mysteries of the Trinity and the incarnation, but in the present age of grace even uneducated people are bound to have explicit faith in the principal mysteries of Christ's life, especially those solemnly celebrated in the liturgy. While holding this in a general way, Saint Thomas also recognized the principle that people could not be required to have explicit faith in matters they were not in a position to learn.

With the discovery of new continents and civilizations unknown to the theologians of old, the problem of the salvation of the unevangelized has attracted increasing attention. Pius IX, in the course of a severe condemnation of religious indifferentism, conceded that per-

---

23. Ibid., q. 4, art. 1c.
24. Ibid., q. 2, arts. 7 and 8.

sons invincibly ignorant of the true religion could by the power of divine grace and enlightenment attain to eternal life, provided that they obeyed the natural law inscribed in their hearts.[25] The pope thus made it clear that God does not demand the impossible.

Several documents of Vatican Council II applied the same line of reasoning more specifically to the question of faith. The Decree on Ecumenism (*Unitatis Redintegratio* [hereafter UR]) teaches that Christians who are not members of the Catholic church can possess the gift of faith (UR 3). The Decree on Missionary Activity (*Ad Gentes* [hereafter AG]) declares that God "in ways known to himself can lead those inculpably ignorant of the gospel to that faith without which it is impossible to please him (Heb. 11:6)" (AG 7). The Pastoral Constitution on the Church in the Modern World affirms that the grace of God works in an unseen way in all human beings, and that the Holy Spirit offers to everyone the possibility of being associated with the paschal mystery (GS 22). The Constitution on the Church goes so far as to declare that people who without blame on their part have not yet arrived at an explicit knowledge of God are given the helps necessary for salvation (LG 16). Apparently the intended meaning is that an atheist in good conscience can have the faith required for justification and salvation.

Going back to certain very concise texts in Thomas Aquinas, several modern Catholic thinkers have tried to explain how even the professed atheist might be justified by faith.[26] Jacques Maritain maintained that at the dawn of reason each individual is offered the possibility, by grace, of orienting himself or herself to eternal beatitude by a movement of love. In tending toward that to which human nature is ordered, one orders oneself in fact toward God, even without knowing God in a conceptual way. Maritain contended that this real, nonconceptual knowledge of God, gained through the élan of the will under the leading of grace, satisfies the requirements of Hebrews 11:6 and can be salvific for persons who have not as yet been able to attain speculative certainty about God and God's redemptive action.

To affirm the necessity of faith is not to affirm its sufficiency. In the Catholic tradition it is taught that faith is sufficient for justification and salvation if, and only if, it is informed by charity (*fides caritate*

---

25. Pius IX, encyclical *Quanto Conficiamur Moerore*, Aug. 10, 1863 (DS 2865–67).

26. Jacques Maritain, *The Range of Reason* (New York: Scribner's, 1952), pt. 1, chap. 6, pp. 66–85. This is essentially a commentary on two texts from the *Summa Theologiae*, 1a-2ae, q. 89, art. 6, and q. 109, art. 3. A somewhat similar approach, based on the same texts, may be found in Max Seckler, *Instinkt und Glaubenswille nach Thomas von Aquin* (Mainz: Matthias-Grünewald, 1962).

*formata*). "Dead faith," which lacks the vivifying element of charity, is insufficient. I have referred earlier to the statement of the Council of Trent that "faith, unless it be joined by hope and charity, does not perfectly unite one to Christ or make one a living member of Christ" (DS 1531).

As biblical warranty for this position, Catholic authorities usually appeal to the teaching of James that faith without works is dead (James 2:17) and to Paul's statement that only "faith working through love" avails for salvation (Gal. 5:6). Sometimes also reference is made to Paul's hymn to charity in 1 Corinthians, chapter 13, in which the faith that moves mountains is declared unavailing in the absence of charity. Paul's teaching in Romans that justification is given by faith (Rom. 3:28), which might seem to constitute an objection to the Catholic position, is interpreted as referring to what Catholics call "living faith."

## SUMMARY: FAITH AND REVELATION

As may be seen from the preceding exposition, faith, in Catholic theology, is the correlative of revelation as provisionally given in the present life. Revelation as such becomes actual when it is accepted in faith, for until it is believed it has a merely potential or virtual existence.

The formal and material objects of faith are determined by the nature of revelation as God's self-disclosure and as manifestations of the divinely established order. The obscurity of faith corresponds to the mysterious content of revelation and to the symbolic modes whereby this content is communicated. The certainty of faith comes from its divine origin and attestation, both exterior and interior. The external signs of revelation constitute the outward call to faith; the interior illumination and attraction of grace give the inner vocation to faith. The freedom of faith follows from the noncoercive nature of the signs of revelation and of the interior solicitation to believe. The culmination of revelation in Jesus Christ and its mediation through the church give rise, respectively, to the Christian and Catholic character of faith. The universality of revelation accounts for the possibility of faith that is not explicitly Catholic or even Christian. The inner unity of revelation is the foundation for implicit faith.

Faith, in its theological meaning, issues into belief as its primary and internal act, but faith flows secondarily into external acts of confession by word and deed. Thus faith, without ceasing to be an assent of the mind, involves a trusting commitment of the whole person to

God who reveals, together with fidelity and obedience to the saving message.

The provisionality of revelation in the present life accounts for the orientation of faith toward the eternal vision of which it is a foretaste. The consummation of revelation in the light of glory will do away with the very possibility of faith.

## TRANSMISSION OF REVELATION

### TESTIMONY

Revelation, which reaches its term in the interior act whereby it is believed, spontaneously comes to expression in a bodily and social manner through external acts of confession. It achieves a public and historical existence when the testimony of the first witnesses becomes constitutive of an enduring community of faith. For the testimony to evoke the response of faith it must be both humanly credible and divinely fructified by the assistance of the Holy Spirit, who moves the witnesses to give testimony and at the same time enlightens the minds of the hearers. The mediation of revelation, therefore, is not a purely natural process but one that depends on God's continuing activity. To indicate this, some theologians speak in this connection of "dependent" or "repetitive" revelation.[27]

Among the original witnesses to revelation the prophets of the Old and New Testaments, and the apostles of the New Testament period, hold a preeminent place. According to the biblical understanding, accepted by the church, these witnesses were empowered, directed, and accredited by God. They were God's agents or instruments. Their words, without being less human than those of other men and women, were in some sort divine, since they gave verbal expression to revelation itself. According to the Gospels, Jesus was able to assure the twelve and the seventy, when he sent them on missions, that to receive and hear them was to receive and hear Jesus himself, who in turn spoke for the Father (Matt. 10:40; Luke 10:16; John 20:21). This apostolic mission did not cease with the ascension. Jesus promised to remain with the apostolic leaders (Matt. 28:20; Acts 1:8). Paul, conscious of God's self-communication through his

---

27. The theme of *dependent revelation* was proposed by Paul Tillich in his *Systematic Theology* (Chicago: University of Chicago Press, 1951), 1:126–28, and has been taken up in contemporary Catholic theology by Gerald O'Collins (*Fundamental Theology* [New York: Paulist, 1981], 100–102), among others. The term *repetitive revelation* was used by the Anglican John Macquarrie in his *Principles of Christian Theology* (New York: Scribner's, 1968), 80–81, 93.

own preaching, was able to congratulate the Thessalonians for having accepted the word they had heard from him "not as the word of men but as what it really is, the word of God, which is at work in you believers" (1 Thess. 2:13).

The expression *word of God* applies most obviously to the spoken and written words of those who are divinely inspired to put the divine message into human language. In a broader sense, however, it is a virtual synonym for revelation. The Hebrew term for "word," *dabar* (and sometimes its Greek equivalents, *logos* and *rhema*), when applied to God, includes not only speech and writing but all the external signs by which the mind of God is communicated to human beings. Thus the symbolic gestures of prophets and the expressive actions of inspired believers are forms of the word of God, insofar as these agents are taken up in the process of God's self-communication.

The word of God abides in the church in two closely connected forms, Scripture and tradition. The Council of Trent in one of its first decrees (A.D. 1546) asserted that the Catholic church accepts sacred Scripture and apostolic traditions with equal devotion and reverence as embodiments of the gospel truth (DS 1501). The first and second Vatican councils have reaffirmed the same doctrine (DS 3006; DV 9).

## THE BIBLE

The Bible, as understood in Catholic theology, is a fully human work, produced by human authors in the course of a long and complex history.[28] It is a kind of anthology of the sacred literature of Israel and of the primitive church. The selection was made under divine guidance by successive generations of the community of faith and ultimately confirmed by bishops in council and by popes. The Catholic church accepts as normative for its faith and practice the books that were received as Holy Scripture by the church of the first five centuries and were officially proclaimed as canonical by the councils of Florence (DS 1334–35) and Trent (DS 1502–3).

The Bible is frequently called, in official Catholic teaching, the "written word of God" (Vatican I, DF, chap. 3 [DS 3011]; Vatican II, DV 9, 21, and passim). God is said to be the "author" of the Bible not in the sense of having taken the place of the human authors, but in the sense that God's grace impelled the human authors to write

---

28. For recent overviews see in Frederick E. Greenspahn, ed., *Scripture in the Jewish and Christian Traditions* (Nashville: Abingdon, 1982): Avery Dulles, "The Authority of Scripture: A Catholic Perspective," 13–40, and Bruce Vawter, "The Bible in the Roman Catholic Church," 111–32.

and directed them to give a pure and reliable expression of the faith of the people of God at their particular stage of salvation history. In many cases the biblical books are attributable to the prophets, apostles, and other inspired leaders who helped to shape the faith of Israel and of the early church. In other cases the biblical authors owed their inspiration, at least in part, to such charismatic leaders. Although much of the inspired literature of the formative period has no doubt perished, a sufficient body of that literature has survived to enable the church to test its own teaching and piety against that of the period when the revelation was freshly given. The Bible thus serves as a critical reference point for the proclamation of the church. Christian faith is historical in the sense that the church, in transmitting it, continues to depend on reliable records of what was originally received.

Biblical inspiration, as Catholics understand it, is the entire complex of interior graces and external helps that enabled the writers and editors of the biblical books to produce normative texts for the church's guidance.[29] The concept of inspiration is often connected with that of inerrancy, meaning freedom from error. In accepting the Bible as the basis for its own belief and teaching, the church certifies that the Bible, taken as a whole, is a reliable witness to God's revelation as communicated in the formative period. The inspiration given to the sacred writers prevented them from falsifying what God had revealed. According to Vatican Council II: "Since, therefore, all that the inspired authors, or sacred writers, affirm should be regarded as affirmed by the Holy Spirit, we must acknowledge that the books of Scripture, firmly, faithfully, and without error, teach that truth which God, for the sake of our salvation, wished to see confided to the sacred Scriptures" (DV 11, Flannery ed.). This statement is carefully phrased. It affirms the value of the Bible as a whole for transmitting in its purity the truth that leads to salvation, but it leaves open the possibility that individual authors may have erred, especially with regard to scientific and historical matters not connected with salvation. This does not mean that the Bible is a patchwork of errant and inerrant passages. As understood by the council the whole Bible is authoritative and trustworthy in what it affirms about the revelation of God and the plan of salvation. Individual passages, however, must be interpreted according to the intentions of the authors and in their historical and literary context. Vatican Council II does not

---

29. On biblical inspiration see Karl Rahner, *Inspiration in the Bible*, rev. trans. (New York: Herder and Herder, 1964); also Bruce Vawter, *Biblical Inspiration* (Philadelphia: Westminster Press, 1972).

favor a fundamentalistic literalism in which each sentence, taken in itself, tends to be absolutized.

Some Christians have raised doubts about whether the Old Testament, written prior to the final revelation, still retains its authority. According to a Christian reading the Old Testament is the inspired literary expression or sedimentation of the faith of the people of God prior to the advent of Jesus Christ. Not everything contained in the Old Testament is directly normative for Christian faith. Certain ideas and practices that were appropriate or perhaps inevitable in an earlier period, before the revelation was complete, are now outdated. This is notably true of the ceremonial prescriptions of the Mosaic Law, which are not binding on Christians. The Old Testament, however, retains its value both because the history of Israel foreshadows and prepares for Christ and because many of the profound religious insights in the Old Testament are not repeated in, or supplanted by, the New Testament. The New Testament, indeed, would not be intelligible except in the light of the Old Testament, which it presupposes.

## TRADITION AS A SOURCE OF DOCTRINE

Since revelation is an organic unity, in which the whole is latently present in all the parts, the totality of revelation may be said to be given in the Bible. In bearing witness to Jesus Christ as the definitive disclosure of God, the New Testament presents him who is the "fullness of all revelation." But revelation is never contained in a book alone. The Bible would not be rightly understood if it were taken apart from the living community of faith in and for which it was written. The church, which collected and identified the books of Scripture with the help of the Holy Spirit, has the task of discerning their true meaning, with the help of the same Spirit, in the light of its own history and experience.

The Council of Trent, as we have seen, insisted that traditions that come down from the apostles have no less authority than the books of Scripture.[30] In the next few centuries many Catholic theologians spoke of revelation as being partly contained in Scripture, partly in tradition, as in two independent sources. Yet neither Trent nor any other council speaks of "two sources" or asserts that tradi-

---

30. The teaching of the Council of Trent on tradition has been much discussed. See, for example, Yves Congar, *Tradition and Traditions*, 156–69, and Joseph Ratzinger, "On the Interpretation of the Tridentine Decree on Tradition," in Karl Rahner and J. Ratzinger, *Revelation and Tradition* (New York: Herder and Herder, 1966), 50–68, 73–78.

tion teaches anything that is not in some way contained in Scripture. Vatican Council II insisted on the unity and coinherence of Scripture and tradition. The two, it asserted, are intimately connected, "for both of them, flowing from the same divine wellspring, in a certain way merge into a unity and tend toward the same end" (DV 9). As a consequence, "Sacred tradition and sacred Scripture form one sacred deposit of the word of God, which is committed to the Church" (DV 10).

Several other shifts in the Catholic theology of tradition should also be noted here.[31] It had become common, especially since the Counter Reformation, to think of tradition objectively, as a collection of truths communicated to the apostles and preserved in the church. Without rejecting this notion, contemporary Catholicism shows a deeper awareness that tradition cannot be adequately understood as a body of explicit teaching. Many doctrines are contained in a merely implicit way in tradition considered as an activity or process whereby faith is expressed and transmitted. In the words of Vatican Council II, tradition "includes everything that contributes to the holiness of life and the increase of faith of the people of God" (DV 8). The church "in its teaching, life, and worship, perpetuates and hands on to all generations all that the Church itself is, all that it believes" (DV 8). Authentic tradition is to be found not only in formal statements but also in "the practice and life of the believing and praying Church" (DV 8).

Tradition, finally, is not static or simply preservative. It develops dynamically. "This tradition which comes from the apostles progresses in the Church with the help of the Holy Spirit" so that, by means of it, the church "constantly moves forward toward the fullness of divine truth until the words of God reach their complete fulfillment in her" (DV 8). Because revelation has an eschatological dimension, tradition too can be future-oriented. It propels the church forward to the day of the Lord, when the church will fully come into its own.

## LOCI OF TRADITION

As may be seen from the quotations in the preceding paragraph, the process of "traditioning" the faith includes practically everything that the church does. Before we consider formal teaching it may be appropriate to mention some of the ways in which the church teaches

---

31. See Avery Dulles, "Vatican II and the Recovery of Tradition," in his *The Reshaping of Catholicism* (San Francisco: Harper and Row, 1988), 75–92.

informally or implicitly. Among the most important of these is the life of worship. The liturgy is the place where many of the faithful most vividly experience the saving mysteries and prayerfully reflect on the contents of their faith. For example, the rite of baptism with its accompanying prayers imparts a sense of the universal need for redemption and the removal of sin by grace. The repetition of the words of institution at each eucharist, together with the elevation of the consecrated elements and the genuflections, impresses on the faithful a realization of the "real presence." Throughout the centuries a vital interaction between worship and belief has continually occurred, as the maxim *lex orandi lex credendi* (the rule of prayer is the rule of faith) indicates. Sometimes the approved modes of worship give rise to doctrines, and sometimes worship is deliberately modified to reflect and inculcate the church's teaching.[32]

A second important vehicle of tradition is the writings of the fathers—writers of Christian antiquity distinguished for sanctity and orthodoxy and approved, at least implicitly, by the church as exceptional witnesses to the tradition.[33] The fathers played a providential role in establishing the canon of Scripture, the articles of the creed, the basic dogmas of the faith, the basic structures of the church, and the essential forms of the liturgy. Their theology was closely related to Scripture, prayer, worship, and preaching, and was less abstract than the academic theology of later centuries. They spoke with a freshness and unction that appeal to many contemporary readers. Although as individuals many of the fathers erred on particular questions, they more often achieved answers of lasting value. To the extent that they agreed among themselves the fathers enjoy strong authority.

A third locus of tradition, not totally separable from the two just mentioned, is the sense of the faithful.[34] Life within the church as the body of Christ has a profound influence on the ways in which people feel and think. The Holy Spirit, animating the church, produces in faithful members an instinctive sense of what agrees or disagrees with

---

32. See Aidan Kavanagh, *On Liturgical Theology* (New York: Pueblo, 1984), esp. 88–95; also Edward J. Kilmartin, *Systematic Theology of Liturgy*, vol. 1 of *Christian Liturgy: Theology and Practice* (Kansas City: Sheed and Ward, 1988), 96–99, with references to other literature. For an ecumenical treatment of the relation between *lex orandi* and *lex credendi*, see Geoffrey Wainwright, *Doxology* (New York: Oxford, 1980), 218–83.

33. On the concept and authority of church fathers, see Walter J. Burghardt, "Fathers of the Church," in *New Catholic Encyclopedia*, 5:853–55; Yves Congar, *Tradition and Traditions*, 435–50.

34. On the "sense of the faithful" see William M. Thompson, "*Sensus Fidelium* and Infallibility," *American Ecclesiastical Review* 167 (1973): 450–86; Jean M. R. Tillard, "*Sensus Fidelium*," *One in Christ* 11 (1975): 2–29.

revelation. Vatican Council II, in its Constitution on the Church, stated that the sense of the faithful, when it manifests universal agreement in matters of faith and morals, is unerring. Spelling out the effects of this supernatural sense, the same constitution declared that by means of it the faithful are able to recognize the word of God, to adhere to it unfailingly, to penetrate its true meaning, and to apply it in practice (LG 12). The sense of the faithful has often contributed to the clarification of Christian doctrine either when it arouses protest against certain errors or when it anticipates the official magisterium in discerning truths not yet officially taught.[35]

The sense of the faithful is not a totally autonomous source of doctrine, since it depends in part on the other bearers of tradition and overlaps with them, but it can often help to identify the true content and meaning of tradition, especially when it confirms what is also attested by the other sources. Thus Pius IX, in defining the immaculate conception of the Blessed Virgin, enumerated as witnesses "Holy Scripture, venerable tradition, the constant mind of the Church, and the remarkable convergence [*conspiratio*] of the Catholic bishops and faithful" (apostolic constitution *Ineffabilis Deus*, A.D. 1854). Because of the close connection between the two, the sense of the faithful leads naturally to the hierarchical magisterium as a teaching organ in the church.

## THE HIERARCHICAL MAGISTERIUM AND INFALLIBILITY

Since revelation is public, the church requires a way of publicly proclaiming the doctrine that expresses or safeguards that revelation. Catholics find evidence in the New Testament that Christ commissioned Peter and the apostles with the responsibility of overseeing the life and witness of the church. The pope and the other bishops are regarded as successors, respectively, of Peter and the other apostles.[36] One of their most important tasks is to keep the church in the truth of the gospel by proclaiming sound doctrine and condemning doctrinal deviations. In this function the hierarchy constitutes the church's official teaching body, or magisterium. To perform its doctrinal task successfully the hierarchy must take the necessary means. It must study the sources and the tradition, consult the sense of the faithful, and make use, on occasion, of the advice of qualified experts.

---

35. Still classic is the essay of John Henry Newman, *On Consulting the Faithful in Matters of Doctrine* (1859), rev. ed., 1871. It has been reprinted with an introduction by John Coulson (Kansas City: Sheed and Ward, 1985).

36. These points, which will be developed in the chapter on church, are taken up by Vatican II in LG 19–24; see also DV 10.

But it is not left to merely human resources. Christ has promised that the powers of death will not prevail against the church founded on the faith of Peter (Matt. 16:18) and that he will remain with the successors of the apostles to the end of time (Matt. 28:20). He has sent the Spirit of truth to guide the apostolic body in bearing witness to his revelation (John 15:26-27; 16:13). In view of these promises Catholics believe that the magisterium is generally reliable and that it will never lead the church into error by definitively teaching what is false or contrary to revelation.

When Catholics speak of the infallibility of the magisterium they mean that in certain specified acts the popes and bishops, teaching doctrine concerning faith and morals in a way that binds the whole church, are divinely protected from falling into error.[37] As explained in the dogmatic constitutions on the church issued by Vatican Councils I and II, the pope can teach infallibly when, in his capacity as successor of Peter (ex cathedra), he proclaims by a definitive act some doctrine to be held by all the faithful on the basis of divine revelation (DS 3074; LG 25). The same two councils teach that infallibility resides in the whole body of bishops when they exercise their supreme teaching power in union with the successor of Peter. The college of bishops can define matters of faith when it gathers in ecumenical councils. When the college is dispersed it can teach infallibly if all the bishops are unanimous in holding some doctrine as a matter of faith or morals to be held by all with irrevocable assent (DS 3011; LG 25).

When a pope or ecumenical council defines a dogma, the resulting definition is a human formulation of revealed truth. Catholics accept such teaching as irreversibly true and in that sense as irreformable. Every dogma of the church expresses an authentic aspect of Christian revelation, but the way in which the indivisible divine mystery is parceled out in dogmas depends on human modes of thinking and speaking that are to some extent culturally conditioned. It is always possible to plumb the truth of revelation more deeply and to express it more aptly in relation to the needs and possibilities of new times and situations. Thus the "irreformability" of dogma does not prevent its reformulation and further refinement. Since John Henry Newman wrote his great *Essay on the Development of Christian Doctrine* (1845), the idea that dogma "develops" has gained general acceptance in the Catholic church.

---

37. On the infallibility of the magisterium, see Francis A. Sullivan, *Magisterium: Teaching Authority in the Catholic Church* (New York: Paulist, 1983), esp. chaps. 5 and 6.

## NONINFALLIBLE TEACHING, RELIGIOUS SUBMISSION, AND DISSENT

Although a great deal of attention has been devoted to infallibility, it should be kept in mind that the vast majority of the church's official statements are not infallible. They are subject to correction in the light of further evidence. According to most theologians the popes of the past hundred years have uttered only one sentence of clearly infallible teaching—the definition of the dogma of the assumption of the Blessed Virgin by Pope Pius XII in 1950 (DS 3903). Vatican Council II issued some seven hundred pages of statements, but it chose not to invoke its infallibility for any of its teachings. Roman congregations, individual bishops, episcopal conferences, particular councils, and local or national synods issue many doctrinal utterances but have no power to speak infallibly.

Because popes and bishops are set over the church as official teachers, their pronouncements are always to be received with reverence and respect.[38] For Catholics, the teaching of the magisterium has a clear presumption of truth in its favor. It sometimes happens that popes or bishops, when teaching authoritatively though not infallibly, call upon their subjects to submit to their judgment and to cease defending contrary opinions. In such cases the faithful will strive to adhere sincerely to the teaching of the magisterium and will normally avoid publicly contesting it. The appropriate response to authoritative but noninfallible teaching is frequently called, in Latin, *obsequium animi religiosum* (religious submission of mind [LG 24; *Codex Iuris Canonici*, canon 753]). By this is meant a sincere acceptance based on the authority of the teacher, but one that falls short of the irrevocable assent of faith, which is given to dogmas as revealed truths taught with the charism of infallibility.

While assent to noninfallible doctrine is in principle required, cases arise in which this response is not forthcoming.[39] Doubt or disagreement on the part of the faithful is possible because, even after making an effort to submit, a person may be unable to attain sincere conviction, since the will cannot always force the mind to assent, especially where the special guarantee of infallibility is lacking. In exceptional cases dissent can be not only subjectively excusable but objectively justified, for, as the very term *noninfallible* implies, such teaching can in fact be erroneous. Historians of doctrine point out

---

38. On the response due to noninfallible teaching see ibid., chaps. 7–9. Sullivan discusses the meaning of *obsequium animi religiosum* on pages 158–61.

39. On dissent see ibid., 166–71 and 215–16; also Avery Dulles, *The Reshaping of Catholicism*, chap. 6, 93–109.

a number of cases in which noninfallible teaching has clearly been in error.[40]

What is the proper conduct for a Catholic who honestly disagrees with some point of official but noninfallible doctrine? First of all, one should critically review one's own contrary opinion. As stated by the German bishops in their pastoral letter of September 22, 1967:

> The Christian who believes that he has a right to his private opinion, that he already knows what the church will only come to grasp later, must ask himself in sober self-criticism before God and his conscience, whether he has the necessary depth and breadth of theological expertise to allow his private theory and practice to depart from the present doctrine of the ecclesiastical authorities. The case is in principle admissible. But conceit and presumption will have to answer for their willfulness before the judgment-seat of God.[41]

Assuming that a serious effort to come to agreement with the authoritative teaching has failed, several options remain. One of these is "submissive silence" (*silentium obsequiosum*), in which one keeps one's doubt or dissent to oneself. A second option is to express one's nonacceptance privately to one person or a small number who can prudently evaluate one's difficulties and possibly initiate some steps to clarify or correct, if necessary, the current teaching. A third possibility is to make one's dissent known in a public way by disseminating one's views through speeches and the press. In some cases public dissent may be "organized" in the sense that one seeks to mobilize public opinion against the official teaching. Public dissent, especially when organized, inevitably inflicts some harm. It weakens the church as a community of faith and witness; it spreads distrust in the hierarchical magisterium, and is often a source of scandal to Catholics and others. For all these reasons public and, especially, organized dissent requires special warrants—namely that the dissenter be firmly convinced that the official teaching, if unopposed, would cause grave harm and that other less destructive forms of dissent be unavailing.

---

40. The most celebrated error is no doubt the condemnation of Galileo by the papal inquisition in 1633. Many of the decrees of the Pontifical Biblical Commission issued between 1905 and 1915, dealing chiefly with historical and textual questions, are no longer defended. Other alleged errors and reversals in official Catholic teaching are discussed, for example, in Charles E. Curran and Robert E. Hunt, *Dissent in and for the Church* (New York: Sheed and Ward, 1969), 66–80.

41. The letter of the German hierarchy is here quoted from the article "Magisterium" by Karl Rahner in *Encyclopedia of Theology: The Concise "Sacramentum Mundi,"* 878.

# CONCLUSION:
# FAITH, REVELATION, AND THEOLOGY

The present chapter on faith and revelation is not a self-enclosed unit. It opens up toward all the other themes that are taken up in systematic theology.

Faith, as we have seen, has God as its formal object and as its primary material object. In the chapter on God, therefore, faith itself will be more fully elucidated. The chapter on creation, in turn, will provide an occasion for the reader to probe more deeply into what I have been calling God's revelation through nature. In treating the question of christology, this volume will fill out what has been suggested already concerning Jesus Christ as the Mediator and fullness of all revelation.

The chapter on church will amplify the observations already made about the church as the witness and home of faith. The church will be described as believer, as teacher, and as a symbolic realization of revelation in the world. In taking up the themes of sin and grace (theological anthropology) the reader will gain a fuller understanding of the obstacles to faith and of faith as a gift. What will subsequently be said about Mary and the saints will show how exemplary members of God's faithful people serve to mirror God's revelation in Christ. The chapter on the sacraments will illustrate how the church becomes most tangibly a symbolic presence of Christ in the world, actualizing its essential being, when its pastors and faithful gather in liturgical worship. And finally, in the chapter on eschatology it will be shown how faith passes into vision, overcoming the imperfections that necessarily accompany it under the conditions of this present life.

# FOR FURTHER READING

Congar, Yves. *The Meaning of Tradition.* Sec. 1, vol. 3 of *Twentieth Century Encyclopedia of Catholicism.* New York: Hawthorn, 1964.

A condensation, slightly updated, of material given in greater detail in Congar's masterful work, *Tradition and Traditions.* More concise and better organized than its longer and more informative predecessor.

Coventry, John. *The Theology of Faith.* Notre Dame, Ind.: Fides, 1968.

A simple but thoughtful systematic presentation that stands firmly in the Catholic tradition.

Dulles, Avery. *Models of Revelation*. Garden City, N.Y.: Doubleday, 1983.

A systematic work that proposes a symbolic approach and tests this by comparison with prevalent twentieth-century theories of revelation, both Protestant and Catholic.

Latourelle, René. *Theology of Revelation*. Staten Island, N.Y.: Alba House, 1966.

A standard historical and systematic treatment, especially valuable for its presentation and analysis of official Catholic teaching and of the Catholic theological tradition.

Newman, John Henry. *Fifteen Sermons Preached before the University of Oxford*. With introductory essays by D. M. MacKinnon and J. D. Holmes. London: SPCK, 1970.

A series of sermons preached between 1826 and 1843, showing the author's movement from an evangelical Protestant position on faith and reason to the position he was to maintain as a Catholic.

Rahner, Karl. *Foundations of Christian Faith: An Introduction to the Idea of Christianity*. New York: Crossroad, 1982.

An introduction to theology as a "first level reflection" on Christian faith. Gives a rather full presentation of Rahner's transcendental theology of revelation and a helpful summary of his views on faith, Scripture, and magisterium.

Sullivan, Francis A. *Magisterium: Teaching Authority in the Catholic Church*. New York: Paulist, 1983.

A balanced, carefully reasoned, and clearly written work that concentrates on the exposition and interpretation of official Catholic teaching concerning the magisterium.

Thomas Aquinas. *Faith: Summa Theologiae*. Vol. 31 (2a2ae, Questions 1–7). English translation, introduction, and notes by T. C. O'Brien. London: Blackfriars, 1974.

Still the most authoritative and incisive Catholic treatise on faith. The terminology is somewhat technical but richly repays those who take the pains to master it.

Vawter, Bruce. *Biblical Inspiration*. Philadelphia: Westminster Press, 1972.

A lucid survey of the history of the theology of inspiration by a prominent biblical scholar. Combines fidelity to the tradition with openness, in the final chapters, to recent developments.

*3*

# GOD

# 3.1

# Approaching the Christian Understanding of God

# 3.1

## Approaching the Christian Understanding of God

### David Tracy

## GOD AND THE REVELATION OF JESUS CHRIST

### GOD AND THEOLOGY

A Christian theological understanding of God merges with the question of the identity of God: Who is God? For the Christian, God is the one who revealed Godself in the ministry and message, the cross and resurrection, of Jesus Christ. A Christian theological understanding of God cannot be divorced from the revelation of God in Jesus Christ. The theological doctrine of God discloses the divine reality that must inform every symbol and doctrine just as the doctrine of God is informed by every symbol and doctrine (creation-redemption, Christ, eschatology, church, sacrament, revelation). A theological insistence on the interconnection of the central mysteries of the faith is true, of course, of the understanding of every great

**133**

symbol of Christian faith, but is especially crucial on the question of God. For Christian theology must be radically theocentric so that no single symbol or doctrine in the whole system of doctrines can be adequately understood without explicitly relating that symbol to the reality of God.

The theological understanding of God, therefore, may bear a distinct and explicit study only as long as one always recalls that the full Christian theological understanding of God occurs only in and through an entire systematic theology encompassing all the great symbols of the tradition.[1] One way to remind ourselves of this systematic theological insight is to initiate the discussion of God first with the question of the identity of God as disclosed in Jesus Christ rather than with the traditional questions of the existence and nature of God. The traditional separation of the tracts *De Deo Uno* and *De Deo Trino* now seems problematic.[2] The questions and concerns of the tract *De Deo Uno* remain, as we shall see below, vital questions for Christian theology. It also remains possible, as the division of essays in this volume shows, to have a distinct study of the trinitarian understanding of God. But even that practical need must prove a distinction, never a theoretical separation for systematic theology. For the Christian understanding of God is none other than a trinitarian understanding. Any theology of God that does not affirm that trinitarian self-understanding may, indeed, possess a concept of theism, even radical monotheism, but becomes a concrete Christian monotheism only as trinitarian.

The present essay is written in the context of that trinitarian conviction. This essay will affirm *that* such a trinitarian understanding of God is the properly Christian one but will not develop *what* analogies are most fruitful for contemporary trinitarian understanding.[3] Further theological understanding of the tri-une God will be addressed in the essay of Catherine LaCugna. However, the need for this practical division of labor among essays (following the earlier and even less happy division of whole tracts) for an adequate Christian systematic theology of God is not best resolved, as too often in the past, by analyzing the existence and nature (including attributes) of God first and only then analyzing the concrete identity of God as that identity is revealed in the event and person of Jesus Christ. In sum, the con-

---

1. The "placement" of the doctrine of God throughout systematic theology (and not as a single "locus") is one of the signal strengths of Schleiermacher's *Glaubenslehre*.

2. The problem is not merely the "manual" genre of traditional manual theologies but the temptations (not necessity) to separate rather than distinguish "theistic," "monotheistic," and "trinitarian" understandings of God.

3. For those developments, see the article of Catherine LaCugna in this volume.

cerns of the traditional tract *De Deo Uno* on the one God (insofar as there should continue to be a separate tract at all on the subject—which I admit I doubt) should begin even its own understanding of the "one God" through an analysis of God's self-revelation in Jesus Christ if it is to prove faithful to the *Christian* understanding of God.

To take this revelational approach to the question of God, however, need not deny the fruitfulness of traditional metaphysical and theological understandings of the nature of God or the fruitfulness of the insistence of Vatican I on the "knowability" of God in natural theology.[4] Rather both these important theological concerns (generically, the nature and attributes of God treated in the tract *De Deo Uno*, and the arguments on the existence of God studied in the discipline of "natural theology") should be developed since they clearly are legitimate. However, these questions should find a more appropriate locus or place in the fuller system of Christian systematic theology.[5] The proper "place" for these legitimate concerns on the nature and existence of God is after an analysis of the scriptural-revelational understanding of God. More exactly, on a Catholic understanding, we understand God foundationally in and through Scripture-in-tradition.

This revised ecclesial principle of Scripture-in-tradition is neither the older Reformation principle "Scripture Alone" nor the earlier Roman Catholic formulation "Scripture *and* Tradition."[6] For the common confession of the Christian church that clarifies the meaning of the creedal belief "We believe in one God" is the confession "We believe *in* Jesus Christ *with* the apostles" (i.e., with the apostolic tradition).[7] More exactly, the ecclesial confession on God can

---

4. In its Constitution on the Catholic Faith (*Dei Filius*), the First Vatican Council affirmed the church's faith in God's omnipotence, eternity, and incomprehensibility, and taught that God can be known from created things by the natural light of human reason (Denzinger-Schönmetzer, *Enchiridion Symbolorum* [hereafter DS], 3001–4, 3021, 3026). The chief study of *Dei Filius* is Hermann J. Pottmeyer, *Der Glaube vor dem Anspruch der Wissenschaft* (Freiburg: Herder, 1968); see also Heinrich Ott, *Die Lehre des I. Vatikanischen Konzils: Ein evangelischer Kommentar* (Basel: Reinhardt, 1963). The teaching of Vatican I is reflected in Karl Rahner's observation that "there is a knowledge of God which is not mediated completely by an encounter with Jesus Christ" (*Foundations of Christian Faith* [New York: Seabury, 1978], 13).

5. There are few more crucial issues for any systematic theology than the judgment of the proper "place" or "locus" of a particular theological issue.

6. The earlier Catholic-Protestant disputes are well-known. The phrase "Scripture-in-tradition" would demand separate theological defense; for the present essay, it may serve as a purely descriptive phrase in the actual practice of many contemporary Catholic and several Protestant theologians. For a representative discussion, see the essays in Richard John Neuhaus, ed., *Biblical Interpretation in Crisis: The Ratzinger Conference on Bible and Church* (Grand Rapids, Mich.: Eerdmans, 1989).

7. For a fuller explanation, see Robert M. Grant with David Tracy, *A Short History of the Interpretation of the Bible* (Philadelphia: Fortress Press, 1984), 174–87, and my

be rendered: "We believe in the God of Jesus Christ with the apostles." We so believe by believing with the apostles *in* Jesus Christ as the very self-revelation of God. This common ecclesial confession, which informs all the classic creeds, finds its scriptural foundation as well as its clearest rendering in the plain sense of the passion narrative of the New Testament.[8] That "plain" sense is the plain ecclesial sense, i.e., the obvious and direct sense these proclamatory narratives of God's actions in the cross and resurrection of Jesus of Nazareth have possessed for the Christian community that over the centuries has read these narratives *as Scripture*.[9] Christians as Christians understand who God is first and foundationally in and through their experience and understanding of Jesus Christ. Christians discover that experience and understanding mediated to them in Word and sacrament through the primary mediation of the ecclesial tradition.[10] Thus do they believe *in* Jesus Christ *with* the apostles. Christian tradition affirms the Jesus Christ proclaimed in the passion narratives of the original apostolic communities and mediated in Word and sacrament in the present ecclesial community in fidelity to the apostolic tradition as truly God and truly human (Chalcedon). Only by thus understanding Jesus Christ does the Christian hope to reach a properly Christian understanding of God.

## GOD AND CHRIST

Christian theology further understands the person and salvific event of Jesus Christ as the very self-revelation of who God is and who we are commanded and empowered to become. A systematic theological understanding of God, therefore, will be developed in direct relationship not only with the doctrine of Christ but also with the doctrines of revelation and salvation. A systematic theological understanding of both revelation and salvation, in turn, is

---

essay "On Reading the Scriptures Theologically," in Bruce D. Marshall, ed., *Theology and Dialogue: Essays in Conversation with George Lindbeck* (Notre Dame, Ind.: University of Notre Dame Press, 1990), 35–68.

8. See Hans Frei, *The Identity of Jesus Christ: The Hermeneutical Basis of Dogmatic Theology* (Philadelphia: Fortress Press, 1975); idem, *The Eclipse of Biblical Narrative: A Study in Eighteenth and Nineteenth Century Hermeneutics* (New Haven: Yale University Press, 1974).

9. See David Kelsey, *The Uses of Scripture in Recent Theology* (Philadelphia: Fortress Press, 1975). There is need for a parallel study of the use of Scripture in Catholic theology: see the forthcoming study (on both Catholic and Protestant biblical interpretation) of Werner Jeanrond.

10. The category "mediation" is central to the Catholic understanding of all reality: the primary mediations of Word and sacrament through the mediations of church and tradition.

also grounded in the common ecclesial confession and the plain sense of the passion narratives of the Gospels.[11] That "plain sense" remains the surest foundation and clearest explication of the Christian understanding of God. For, by understanding the proclamatory passion narrative[12] in its details and its unity, Christians begin to understand who God is. They do so by understanding first the identity of the one (Jesus of Nazareth) whose presence as Jesus Christ they experience in Word and sacrament as the very presence of God.

The passion narratives, justly described as "history-like" and "realistic,"[13] disclose the basic Christian understanding not only of the identity of Jesus Christ but, in and through that identity, the identity of the God who acts as agent in and through the actions and sufferings of Jesus of Nazareth.[14] As in any realistic narrative, so too in the passion narrative an identity is rendered through the plotted interactions of an unsubstitutable character (Jesus) and the unique events (betrayal, cross, resurrection) he undergoes. The fact that the Christian understanding of God is grounded not in a general theory of theism but in the concrete history of God's self-disclosure as loving agent in the cross and resurrection of Jesus of Nazareth is the theological foundation of all properly Christian understandings of God.

The passion narrative, moreover, should not remain isolated from the rest of the Scriptures or from the later creeds.[15] Rather, the passion narrative, as foundation and focus of all properly Christian understanding of God, should open up to the larger gospel narratives of the message and ministry of Jesus and the incarnation of the Logos, the theologies of Paul and John, the pastorals, the Book of Revelation, and all the rest of the New Testament. Again, as focused and grounded in the understanding of God's agency in the passion narrative, the Christian understanding of God should also open anew to the complex and profound disclosures of God's identity in the history of Israel rendered in the many genres (narrative, law,

---

11. For further reflections on the relationships of "confession" and "narrative," see my "On Reading the Scriptures Theologically."

12. The phrase "proclamatory passion narrative" refers to the genre "gospel."

13. Frei, *The Identity of Jesus Christ.*

14. Ibid., for a sensitive hermeneutical and theological account of "identity."

15. The temptation of the retrieval of the "passion narrative" as central can lead to a seeming failure of detailed attention to the rest of the individual Gospel—as, for example, in the study of Matthew in Ronald F. Thiemann, *Revelation and Theology: The Gospel as Narrated Promise* (Notre Dame, Ind.: University of Notre Dame Press, 1985), esp. 112–56.

praise, lamentation, wisdom) of the Old Testament.[16] This is clearly
not the place to review and interpret the extraordinary complexity
of a fuller scriptural understanding of God. This much, however,
does need to be affirmed: For the Christian, God is the one who
raised Jesus of Israel from the dead. God, for the Christian, is the
one who revealed decisively who God is in and through the message
and ministry, the incarnation, cross, and resurrection of none other
than Jesus the Christ. The most profound New Testament metaphor
for who God is remains the metaphor of 1 John: "God *is* love" (4:16).
To understand that metaphor (which occurs, let us note, in the first
theological commentary on the most theological and meditative of
the four Gospels)[17] is to understand, on inner-Christian terms, what
has been revealed by God of God's very identity as agent and as love
in the incarnation, cross, and resurrection of Jesus Christ.

Therefore, for the Christian faithful the answer to the question
"Who is God?," asked in relation to the self-disclosure of God in Jesus
Christ, is: God is love, and Christians are those agents commanded
and empowered by God to love. However, if this classic Johannine
metaphor (i.e., "God is love") is not grounded in and thereby interpreted by means of the stark reality of the message and ministry, the
cross and resurrection of this unsubstitutable Jesus who, as Christ,
is God's self-disclosure as love, then Christians may be tempted to
think that the metaphor is reversible into "Love is God." But this
great reversal, on inner-Christian terms, is hermeneutically impossible. "God is love": This identity of God the Christian experiences
and knows in and through the proclaimed and narrated history of
God's actions and self-disclosure as the God who is love in Jesus
Christ, the parable of God.

To affirm that "God is love" is also to affirm, now in the more abstract terms proper to postscriptural metaphysical theologies,[18] that
God, the origin, sustainer, and end of all reality, is characterized by
the radical relationality of that most relational of categories, love.
God, the one Christians trust, worship, and have loyalty to, can be
construed, in more abstract terms, as the radically relational (and,
therefore, personal) origin, sustainer, and end of all reality. To affirm
that the Christian understanding of God includes the affirmation

---

16. See Paul Ricoeur, "Toward a Hermeneutic of the Idea of Revelation," in
Lewis L. Mudge, ed., *Essays in Biblical Interpretation* (Philadelphia: Fortress Press,
1980), 73–119.

17. Although technically in the genre "letter," 1 John reads more like a commentary on the understanding of God present in the Gospel of John.

18. The appropriateness of such abstract categories is demonstrated best by the
classic developments of patristic and medieval theologies, as the magisterial work of
Bernard Lonergan on Nicaean and medieval developments shows.

that God is the origin, sustainer, and end of all reality is to "place" the Christian understanding of God on the language-map of all developed philosophical theisms. To affirm that the Christian understanding of God refers to the one whom Christians worship, trust, and are loyal to is to "place" this Christian understanding on the language-map of radical monotheism (shared by Judaism and Islam). To affirm, with 1 John, that "God is love"—an affirmation made in and through the gospel narrative and the ecclesial confession of the incarnation, cross, and resurrection of Jesus Christ—is to affirm the radical relationality of God's nature as personlike (i.e., characterized by intelligence and love).[19] The latter affirmation, moreover, both grounds a theological understanding of the economic Trinity in the primal Christian confession of Jesus Christ and also suggests how the immanent Trinity is to be understood in and through the economic Trinity.[20] For the trinitarian understanding of God is the fullest Christian theological understanding of the radical, relational, loving, kenotic God who revealed Godself in and through the incarnation, the ministry (healing, preaching, actions), the message (the "reign of God"), the fate of the cross, and the vindication of resurrection of Jesus of Nazareth.[21] Who God is—God's identity—is revealed decisively in this Jesus the Christ. In that precise theological sense, it is impossible to separate theo-logy and christology. In that same sense, the Christian understanding of the "existence" and "nature" of God is grounded in the "identity" of the God disclosed as kenotic love in Jesus Christ.

## GOD AND THE HUMAN QUEST FOR GOD

### CREDIBILITY AND INTELLIGIBILITY

The Catholic theological understanding of God is, therefore, grounded in the self-revelation of God in Jesus Christ. Jesus Christ is both the self-disclosure of God and God's quest for human beings. Jesus Christ is, therefore, the divine response to the question human

---

19. For a representative treatment of the understanding of God as person, see E. Schillebeeckx and B. van Iersel, eds., *A Personal God?* (entire issue of *Concilium* 103 [New York: Crossroad, 1977]).

20. Karl Rahner, "Remarks on the Dogmatic Treatise 'De Trinitate,' " in *Theological Investigations* (London: Darton, Longman, and Todd, 1966), 4:77–102; idem, *The Trinity* (New York: Crossroad, 1970).

21. It is to be noted that the full scriptural history of Jesus is needed for understanding the identity of God: the retrieval of the centrality of the passion narrative (H. Frei et al.) and the cross (E. Jüngel, J. Moltmann) should not become the occasion to eliminate additional attention to the message and ministry of Jesus.

beings are to themselves.[22] The further theological question occurs, in the Catholic tradition, of how this christic understanding of God's identity as love correlates with the human quest for God. The word *correlation* here does not imply that the Christian understanding of God must be made to "fit" some already existing understanding of theism or some already completed anthropology or ontology.[23] Rather the word *correlation* logically allows for the categories identity (of meaning), nonidentity, or similarity-in-difference. The Catholic theological tradition has ordinarily (but not always, e.g., Meister Eckhart) argued for a similarity-in-difference or analogy[24] between the properly Christian understanding of God and a coherent philosophical (i.e., inevitably metaphysical) understanding of God based on some aspect of the human quest for ultimate meaning and truth.[25] In the modern period, metaphysical accounts of the question of God have often (e.g., Karl Rahner, Edward Schillebeeckx, Bernard Lonergan) also involved an anthropology (the quest for God in the question the human being is to itself). More philosophically stated, classical ontology, in the modern period, often emphasizes an epistemological starting point.

Even Catholic theologians (e.g., Hans Urs von Balthasar) who remain doubtful of the fruitfulness of anthropological "starting points" for the question of God in Christian theology, nevertheless also tend to provide some theological anthropology that is argued to correlate with the Christian understanding of God (e.g., the "glory" of God disclosed in the visible form of Jesus Christ and disclosed in other beautiful and true visible forms).[26] An analogy may prove illuminating here.[27] Just as a great work of art may be said to "disclose"

22. In contemporary Catholic theology, the work of Karl Rahner is especially persuasive here; see *Foundations of Christian Faith* (New York: Seabury, 1978).

23. The debates on the "method of correlation" from Paul Tillich's model to the present are well documented in recent theological literature (G. Lindbeck, F. Schüssler Fiorenza, D. Tracy, H. Küng, et al.).

24. For some further analysis here, see David Tracy, "The Analogical Imagination in Catholic Theology," in David Tracy and John B. Cobb, Jr., *Talking about God: Doing Theology in the Context of Modern Pluralism* (New York: Seabury, 1983), 17–29.

25. The phrase "some aspect" refers to the use of the modern "reformed subjectivist principle" (A. N. Whitehead) on some "aspect" of the human person (e.g., "freedom" or "intelligence") to find one's initial analogy for developing a metaphysics (as "descriptive generalization" or "transcendental analysis") for understanding God.

26. The "disclosure" in other "visible forms" is, of course, understood for von Balthasar only in and through the definitive "visible form" of God, Jesus Christ. See the brilliant studies of classic and contemporary "visible forms" in this christological light in Hans Urs von Balthasar, *The Glory of the Lord: A Theological Aesthetics*, 6 vols. Volume 1, 2, and 3 are thus far published in English by Crossroad.

27. The analogy is dependent on the tradition of hermeneutics for understanding truth as manifestation (Paul Ricoeur) or disclosure-concealment (Martin Heidegger) in the work of art.

both beauty and truth so, too, the revelation (disclosure) of God in Jesus Christ is experienced as both beautiful and true. But just as we legitimately want to know how our experiences of an "event" of rev-elatory truth in and through a work of art may "correlate" with the rest of our experience, so too the question of how to correlate what we otherwise know or believe to be true with the strictly revelatory event of God's self-disclosure becomes the quest of the human for God.[28] Besides "criteria of appropriateness" for a properly *Christian* understanding of God's identity, therefore, there remain theological criteria of credibility or intelligibility for correlating the question of God and God's self-disclosure in Jesus Christ.[29] In Catholic theol-ogy, the decrees of Vatican I on the "knowability" of God as well as the decrees on the possibility of some "analogous" understanding of the mysteries of faith demonstrate the same conviction: Human beings, in their quest for God, do not quest in vain.[30] Christians should be willing to give "reasons for the hope that is in them" (see 1 Peter 3:15).[31] One theological way to give such reasons for hope is to attempt to correlate the human quest for God (in all the limit-experiences and limit-questions of human beings as human)[32] with God's own self-disclosure in Jesus Christ.

## GOD AND NATURAL THEOLOGY

The classical tradition of "natural theology" and the concerns of the traditional tract *De Deo Uno* may be interpreted, therefore, as Catho-lic theological responses to these questions of intelligibility and cred-ibility. In natural theologies, the "arguments" for the "existence" of God (ontological, cosmological, teleological, and moral) constitute part of the tradition of developing adequate criteria of credibility or intelligibility for the question of God.[33] In theological analyses

28. The "coherence" in question will ordinarily claim only a "rough coherence" (Reinhold Niebuhr) with one or another limit-question or limit-experience of human beings.

29. On criteria of appropriateness and criteria of intelligibility, see Schubert Ogden, *On Theology* (San Francisco: Harper and Row, 1986).

30. The decrees of Vatican I were formulated, of course, in the nineteenth-century context of the debates on "faith" and "reason." Nevertheless, they still serve both to articulate the mainline Catholic tradition (e.g., Thomas Aquinas) on these issues and to encourage contemporary Catholic theologies. See, for example, Hans Küng, *Does God Exist? An Answer for Today* (Garden City, N.Y.: Doubleday, 1980).

31. It is striking how often this scriptural saying is appealed to by Catholic theologians.

32. For further analysis, here, see David Tracy, *Blessed Rage for Order* (New York: Crossroad, 1975).

33. For a classical Thomist position here, see Jacques Maritain, *Approaches to God* (New York: Harper, 1954).

of God's nature as "one," moreover, the use of various metaphysics
or ontologies (e.g., Aquinas's transformation of both Aristotle and
Neo-Platonism into his brilliant metaphysics of "esse" whereby the
God of Exod. 3:14 is construed as "Ipsum Esse Subsistens")[34] is part
of that same tradition of intelligibility. In the modern period, the
"turn to the subject" of much modern thought (as of Augustine in
classical theology) has also occasioned several correlational anthropologies (both transcendental and dialogical) that attempt to develop
those same classic traditions of credibility and intelligibility in more
explicitly modern anthropological directions.[35] None of the classic
attempts of natural theology or apologetic theology (as distinct from
some exercises in a decadent Neo-Scholasticism) can be read as deductive proofs *sensu stricto*. Rather the arguments for the existence of
God should be read as reflective attempts to show to any reasonable
person the intelligibility or credibility of the ultimate mystery who
is the God of Jesus Christ. As such the traditional "proofs" remain
fruitful exercises: "reflective inventories" (Blondel) clarifying how
our most basic beliefs and convictions as thinking, existing human
beings are rendered intelligible only by grounding them in a basic
belief in God (e.g., as the necessarily coaffirmed horizon of ultimate
intelligibility and being of all our acts of knowing [Karl Rahner];
or the necessary ground of our most fundamental trust in existence
itself [Schubert Ogden]).[36]

United to the traditional and modern arguments on the "existence" of God there are the various philosophical and theological
attempts to find credible or intelligible analogies for understanding the nature and attributes of God. Here the theological criteria
remain twofold: first, the coherence of any conceptual-theological
understanding of God with the revelation of God's identity in Jesus
Christ (criteria of appropriateness); second, the internal coherence
of the metaphysical concepts employed for understanding God as
well as the coherence of those metaphysical concepts with our other
knowledge and basic beliefs.[37] In no responsible theological position
is there any claim to understand completely the divine mystery (ra-

---

34. For a helpful recent study of Aquinas, see W. J. Hankey, *God in Himself: Aquinas'
Doctrine of God as Expounded in the Summa Theologiae* (Oxford: Oxford University Press,
1987).

35. The "linguistic turn" and the "turn to the political" have, of course, rendered
earlier "transcendental" approaches more controversial.

36. On the development of Rahner's position from his early emphasis on "intelligibility" to his later emphasis on "holy mystery," see the essays in Leo O'Donovan,
ed., *A World of Grace: A Introduction to the Themes and Foundations of Karl Rahner's Theology* (New York: Crossroad, 1980); for Ogden, see Schubert M. Ogden, *The Reality of
God* (New York: Harper and Row, 1977).

37. A proper metaphysics will address both kinds of coherence.

tionalism). At the same time, the antifideist character of Catholic theology encourages any reasonable attempt to find proper analogical language for understanding the divine mystery more adequately and more intelligibly.

For example, it is correct to insist (as above) that, abstractly considered, the God of Jesus Christ, who *is* love, may also be conceptually construed as the radically relational origin, sustainer, and end of all reality, whose relationality, as love and intelligence, bears all the marks of agency and thereby makes "person" language (God is "who" not "which") appropriate.[38] In that conceptual context, the category of relationality will become the most necessary abstract category for understanding the divine reality. Indeed, how, most adequately, to understand the divine relationality is the central theological question of God's nature in our period. On the one hand, the recovery of the centrality of the trinitarian understanding of God is the prime instance of the importance of the concept of relationality. This is especially the case in those theologians who have rethought the intrinsic unity of the "economic" and "immanent" Trinity (Karl Rahner, Walter Kasper, et al.).[39] It is also the case in those trinitarian theologians who have rethought the nature of the divine relationship of suffering love in the light of the theology of the cross (Eberhard Jüngel, Jürgen Moltmann).[40] In every case of this contemporary trinitarian recovery, the category of relationality has become central for understanding the Christian God. In terms of criteria of appropriateness, therefore, an emphasis on trinitarian relationality is an entirely fruitful and now widespread theological advance.

In terms of criteria of intelligibility, moreover, the new trinitarian theologies have been joined by other theologies (some trinitarian, some not) where ontologies of relationality have come to the forefront of philosophical and theological attention.[41] Process theology (as well as some revisionary forms of Hegelian theology) has led the way in insisting upon relationality as the primary concept needed to render more intelligible the Christian understanding of God for

38. To claim "person" language as appropriate is not to deny that, like all analogous language for God, it is also finally inadequate for understanding divine intelligence and love.

39. See Rahner, "Remarks on the Dogmatic Treatise 'De Trinitate'"; idem, *The Trinity*; see also Walter Kasper, *The God of Jesus Christ* (New York: Crossroad, 1984), esp. 233–316.

40. Eberhard Jüngel, *God as the Mystery of the World* (Grand Rapids, Mich.: Eerdmans, 1983); Jürgen Moltmann, *The Trinity and the Kingdom: The Doctrine of God* (New York: Harper and Row, 1980).

41. For example, John Cobb's theology is not explicitly trinitarian; Norman Pittenger's process theology is.

modern persons for whom process, relationality, and freedom are prominent ideals.[42] The question of God, for the Christian, is not primarily (as some classical theists held) the question: How can the absolute one be intelligibly conceived as also relational? The question is: How can the unsurpassably related one best be conceived as absolute? It is to be noted that on the modern process theological view, God—and God alone—is related to all reality: both affecting all reality and affected by all reality.[43] In that sense, the metaphor "God is love" is rendered in explicitly relational terms. At the same time, this same emphasis on love as relationality helps to clarify how God's kenotic love disclosed in the cross of Jesus Christ can be expressed in theological terms that seem both appropriate (to Scripture) and intelligible (to any modern person who believes in the radically relational character of all reality and the centrality of love for human self-constitution).[44]

Part of this issue of intelligibility is, in fact, as much anthropological as it is ontological.[45] The concept of God, for the Christian as for any radical monotheist, must be conceived in terms of perfection-language. (Anselm: "id quo maius cogitare non potest.")[46] Otherwise one is not referring to God as understood by Jews, Christians, and Muslims. The question of God, if the discussion is really on God, must be the question of the perfect one. It must, therefore, always be formulated in terms of perfection-language. Here the language of relationality, even in terms of the human analogue, is a helpful analogous language for the divine nature.[47] Indeed, in a culture of possessive individualism, the theological defense of the relational concept of the human "person" and not the modern concept of the purely autonomous individual is crucial for those searching for models of human perfection. In the case of God's perfection, of course, any human analogue of perfection, as the Fourth Lateran Council insists on all analogies for God, must realize that "the greater the

---

42. For an important study here, see John Macquarrie, *In Search of Deity: An Essay in Dialectical Theism* (New York: Crossroad, 1985).

43. See John Cobb and David Griffin, *Process Theology: An Introductory Exposition* (Philadelphia: Westminster Press, 1976); Norman Pittenger, *Catholic Faith in a Process Perspective* (Maryknoll, N.Y.: Orbis Books, 1981).

44. It should be emphasized that process theologians characteristically appeal not only to a "modern" worldview but also to a biblical hermeneutic on God's relationality to the world.

45. Note Whitehead's use of the "reformed subjectivist principle" here.

46. See Charles Hartshorne, *The Logic of Perfection* (LaSalle, Ill.: Open Court, 1962); idem, *Anselm's Discovery* (LaSalle, Ill.: Open Court, 1965).

47. For further analysis here, see David Tracy, "Analogy and Dialectic: God-Language," in Tracy and Cobb, *Talking about God*, 29–34.

similarity, the greater still the difference."[48] At the same time, some human analogies for perfection are more fruitful than others: For example, the relational, affecting, and affected person of modern process, Hegelian, and dialogical philosophies does provide more helpful candidates for possible models of human "perfection" than the ancient Greek models of the unaffected (*a-patheia*) person (e.g., of the Stoics) or the modern liberal model of the purely autonomous individual. A relational model of human perfection is clearly a more adequate one for understanding divine perfection than either an ancient individualist or modern autonomous one.[49]

The full Christian theological appropriateness of modern relational thought (Whiteheadean, Hegelian, and dialogical) remains an open question. But the insistence in all these forms of thought on the centrality of relationality (as freedom and love) in finding appropriate human analogues for the radical relationality of the Christian God who is love seems a genuine advance beyond some earlier emphases on "absoluteness" alone in *De Deo Uno* followed (coherently?) by "relationality" in *De Deo Trino*.

## THE FUTURE OF THE THEOLOGY OF GOD

In my own judgment, only a fully trinitarian understanding of God is an adequate Christian theological understanding. In that understanding the concept of relationality as love and freedom will prove to be the central one for understanding—always analogously and always with the caution of the Fourth Lateran Council in mind—the holy mystery. All forms of theology that employ both criteria of appropriateness for the identity of God and criteria of intelligibility or credibility for understanding the nature and attributes of God (omniscience, omnipotence, omnibeneficence, etc.) cannot but aid in the contemporary Catholic theological struggle to understand more adequately the God who revealed Godself as love in Jesus the Christ. In this contemporary effort, moreover, the recovery of the prophetic-apocalyptic traditions in new theologies of the cross, as well as in political, liberation, and feminist theologies, promises new ways to understand the hidden-revealed God: revealed under God's opposite—the cross, suffering, and oppression—and revealed best to those "preferred" by God—the marginal, the suffering, the

---

48. "For no similarity can be asserted...unless an even greater dissimilarity is included" (DS 806).

49. Feminist theologies have been especially prominent in developing relational concepts of the "person" and criticizing the "maleness" of many "autonomy" and "individualist" models of the self.

oppressed.[50] At the same time, the recovery of the mystical traditions of reflection on God (the image mystics, the trinitarian mystics, the love mystics, and the radically apophatic mystics) promises further retrievals in contemporary theology of the classic mystical theological understandings of the comprehensible-incomprehensible God.[51] The prophetic and apocalyptic trajectories of the tradition will always develop the central Christian insight that "God is love" into more explicitly cross-centered understandings of that very God as revealed *in* hiddenness.[52] The mystical trajectories of the tradition will always develop that same central Christian insight into deeper and often radically apophatic understandings of God's very incomprehensibility in and through comprehensibility.[53]

As these two great strands of the tradition come into clearer dialectical relationship with one another as well as with the noble tradition of natural theology, one may hope that the theology of God of the future will be a full-fledged mystical-prophetic theology.[54] That systematic theology of God will be both grounded in the revelation of God in Jesus Christ and credible to the quest for God that *is* the ultimate meaning of all the classic limit-experiences and limit-questions of human beings, who become human by facing both the personal questions of finitude, anxiety, transience, guilt, and death and the historical questions of oppression and massive global suffering.[55] A future mystical-prophetic theology of God, moreover, will prove daring in its very fidelity to the central Christian meaning of the holy mystery: God *is* love. That classic Christian metaphor will inform every new naming of the hidden-revealed, the comprehensible-incomprehensible God of Jesus Christ. As the Christian theology of God recovers its own identity more fully through attention to the whole tradition, moreover, we may also hope that

---

50. See Victorio Araya, *God of the Poor: The Mystery of God in Latin American Liberation Theology* (Maryknoll, N.Y.: Orbis Books, 1988).

51. For the recovery of the mystical tradition in theology, see Louis Dupré, *The Deeper Life: An Introduction to Christian Mysticism* (New York: Crossroad, 1981); idem, *The Other Dimension: A Search for the Meaning of Religious Attitudes* (Garden City, N.Y.: Doubleday, 1972).

52. Contrast, here, the different notions of God's "hiddenness" in Jüngel's theology of the cross (see his *God as the Mystery*) and Araya's focus on God in the poor and oppressed (see his *God of the Poor*).

53. See Karl Rahner, "Thomas Aquinas on the Incomprehensibility of God," in David Tracy, ed., *Celebrating the Medieval Heritage: A Colloquy on the Thought of Aquinas and Bonaventure* (*Journal of Religion Supplement* [1978]: S107–S126).

54. Thus hope depends largely on the ability of "prophetic" orientations to learn new ways to appreciate the "mystical" traditions—and vice versa.

55. The choice of a particular focus for theology depends largely on a theological assessment of the present "situation" most needing attention.

the promise of genuine interreligious dialogue[56] with the other great traditions—theistic and nontheistic—will teach Christians yet further ways to understand God, the holy mystery who is the origin, sustainer, and end of all reality and who is disclosed to us in Jesus Christ as pure, unbounded love.

## FOR FURTHER READING

Araya, Victorio. *God of the Poor: The Mystery of God in Latin American Liberation Theology*. Maryknoll, N.Y.: Orbis Books, 1988.

A major study from a liberation theology perspective.

Bouillard, Henri. *The Knowledge of God*. New York: Herder and Herder, 1968.

By a leading Roman Catholic French representative of *la nouvelle théologie*; underscores the relation between language about God and the public nature of theology.

Burrell, David. *Knowing the Unknowable God*. Notre Dame, Ind.: University of Notre Dame Press, 1986.

An important exposition of Aquinas that highlights his relation to and difference from Moses Maimonides and Ibn-Sina.

Cobb, John B., Jr., and David Tracy. *Talking about God: Doing Theology in the Context of Modern Pluralism*. New York: Seabury, 1983.

A study of some central issues that emerge from Protestant and Catholic standpoints.

Cone, James. *God of the Oppressed*. New York: Seabury, 1975.

A major study of God from the perspective of African-American theology.

Daly, Mary. *Beyond God the Father*. Boston: Beacon Press, 1973.

A significant work of feminist theology in regard to metaphor and language about God.

Gilkey, Langdon. *Naming the Whirlwind: The Renewal of God-Language*. Indianapolis: Bobbs-Merrill, 1969.

Discusses the problem of God for modern secular culture.

---

56. For one example here, see Raimundo Panikkar, *The Trinity and the Religious Experience of Man: Icon, Person, Mystery* (Maryknoll, N.Y.: Orbis Books, 1976).

Hogdson, Peter C. *God in History: Shapes of Freedom*. Nashville: Abingdon Press, 1989.

Attempts to rethink the relationship between God and history through a reconstruction of Hegel's trinitarian understanding of God.

Jüngel, Eberhard. *God as the Mystery of the World*. Grand Rapids, Mich.: Eerdmans, 1983.

An elaboration of the centrality of the Trinity and of a theology of the cross for the Christian understanding of God.

Kaufman, Gordon. *God the Problem*. Cambridge: Harvard University Press, 1972.

A major study of the problem of God for modern thought.

Küng, Hans. *Does God Exist? An Answer for Today*. Garden City, N.Y.: Doubleday, 1980.

Articulates many of the central concerns of modern thinkers about God.

Lonergan, Bernard. *The Philosophy of God and Theology*. Philadelphia: Westminster Press, 1973.

Lonergan rethinks the relation between philosophy and religious experience for the question of God.

Lonergan, Bernard. *The Way to Nicea*. London: Longman and Todd, 1976.

A dialectical study of the emergence of the early conciliar understanding of God.

McFague, Sallie. *Models of God: Theology for an Ecological, Nuclear Age*. Philadelphia: Fortress Press, 1987.

A study of God in relation to the ecological crisis that suggests mother, friend, lover as new models of God.

Macquarrie, John. *In Search of Deity: An Essay in Dialectical Theism*. The Gifford Lectures, 1983. New York: Crossroad, 1985.

A major attempt to recover the Neo-Platonic tradition on the question of God.

Ogden, Schubert. *The Reality of God*. New York: Harper and Row, 1977.

A major articulation of the reasons for a process understanding of God.

Rahner, Karl. *Foundations of Christian Faith*. New York: Crossroad, 1978.

Rahner's most systematic treatment of divine incomprehensibility.

Ruether, Rosemary. *Sexism and God-talk: Toward a Feminist Theology*. Boston: Beacon Press, 1983.

A major feminist study of the doctrine of God/ess.

# 3.2

# The Trinitarian Mystery of God

# 3.2

## The Trinitarian Mystery of God

### *Catherine Mowry LaCugna*

# INTRODUCTION

Writing in the fourth century, Gregory of Nyssa reported that one could not go into the marketplace to exchange money, buy bread, or discuss the merits of bathing without getting involved in a discussion with merchants and others about whether "God the Son" is subordinate to "God the Father," begotten or unbegotten, created *ex nihilo* or an ordinary man. Gregory wondered whether this enthusiasm for "divine things" was the result of perversity, delirium, insanity, or some other kind of evil producing intellectual derangement.[1]

For nearly fifteen hundred years our situation has been quite the reverse of Gregory's world. The late Karl Rahner once remarked that one could dispense with the doctrine of the Trinity as false and the major part of Christian literature could well remain virtually unchanged.[2] The majority of Christians, including many theologians, have not been eager to inquire into the doctrine of the Trinity. Those who are ordained probably associate it with the difficulties of preaching on Trinity Sunday; most homilies on that day confirm the impression that the doctrine of the Trinity is not a very useful teaching.[3] Others tell stories about catastrophes in parish education programs where people tried to incorporate into the curriculum some mention of trinitarian doctrine.

Why has the doctrine of the Trinity, often claimed to be the center of Christian faith, been neglected, evaded, or even derided in what Rahner has called an "anti-trinitarian timidity"?[4] Critics throughout the centuries have suggested that Christianity would suffer no noticeable loss of coherence, and might even become more intelligible and more widely accepted, if it were to abandon the doctrine of the Trinity. Even within circles sympathetic to retaining a trinitarian schema for Christian faith, many writings in christology, ecclesiology, and other areas remain notably reserved about the doctrine of the triune God.

Is it that the doctrine of the Trinity is a hopelessly complicated

---

1. Gregory of Nyssa *De Deitate Filii et Spiritus Sancti* (*Patrologia Graeca*, ed. Migne [hereafter PG], 46, 557).

2. Karl Rahner, *The Trinity* (New York: Herder and Herder, 1970), 11. See other writings by Rahner, "Theos in the New Testament," in *Theological Investigations* (Baltimore: Helicon Press, 1961), 1:79–148; "Remarks on the Dogmatic Treatise 'de Trinitate,'" in *Theological Investigations* (New York: Crossroad, 1982), 4:77–102; "The Mystery of the Trinity," in *Theological Investigations* (New York: Crossroad, 1976), 16:255–59.

3. See Catherine M. LaCugna, "Making the Most of Trinity Sunday," *Worship* 60 (1986): 210–24.

4. Rahner, *The Trinity*, 13.

problem in speculative theology (or higher mathematics: God + God + God = God) that has no bearing on the practice of faith?

Like most caricatures, this one strikes a vulnerable point, particularly in the Western (Latin) theology of God. In the recent past, theological education in Catholic seminaries often went no further than requiring students to memorize the 5-4-3-2-1 formula, a mnemonic device for retaining the essential elements of the Thomistic doctrine of the Trinity: God is "five notions, four relations, three persons, two processions, and one nature."[5] When Bernard Lonergan taught this he is reported to have added, "and zero comprehension!"

Today trinitarian theology is being recovered as a fruitful and intelligible way to articulate what it means to be "saved by God through Christ in the power of the Holy Spirit." In the past few years virtually every theological journal, and many others oriented to pastoral, liturgical, and spiritual questions, have begun to include significant scholarly articles on issues related to the Trinity.[6] This trend is due in part to the rising interest in liturgy, spirituality, and world religions, as well as to the realization that political and feminist theologies require a solid theological basis for their praxis.

---

5. According to Scholastic theology, a notion is what distinguishes each person. The five notions are: innascibility or ingenerateness; paternity; filiation; spiration; procession. Four of the five describe relations; innascibility is the absence of relation. Three of these relations are "person-constituting": paternity, filiation, spiration. The ternary of relations is derived from the two processions, being begotten and being spirated. There is only one God, therefore only one divine essence.

6. Some recent works include: Joseph Bracken, "Process Philosophy and Trinitarian Theology," *Process Studies* 8 (1978): 217–30; (1981): 83–96; and idem, *The Triune Symbol* (Lanham, Md.: University Press of America, 1984); David Coffey, "The 'Incarnation' of the Holy Spirit in Christ," *Theological Studies* 45 (1984): 466–80; Yves Congar, *The Word and the Spirit* (New York: Harper and Row, 1987); idem, *I Believe in the Holy Spirit*, 3 vols. (New York: Seabury, 1983); Bertrand de Margerie, *The Christian Trinity in History* (Still River, Mass.: St. Bede's Publications, 1983); William Hill, *The Three-Personed God* (Washington, D.C.: University Press of America, 1983); Robert Jenson, *The Triune Identity* (Philadelphia: Fortress Press, 1982); Eberhard Jüngel, *God as the Mystery of the World* (Grand Rapids, Mich.: Eerdmans, 1983); Walter Kasper, *The God of Jesus Christ* (New York: Crossroad, 1984); Catherine M. LaCugna, "The Relational God: Aquinas and Beyond," *Theological Studies* 46 (1985): 647–63; idem, "Philosophers and Theologians on the Trinity," *Modern Theology* 2 (1986): 169–81; James Mackey, *The Christian Experience of God as Trinity* (London: SCM, 1983); Kilian McDonnell, "A Trinitarian Theology of the Holy Spirit?" *Theological Studies* 46 (1985): 191–227; Jürgen Moltmann, *The Trinity and the Kingdom* (New York: Harper and Row, 1981); Heribert Mühlen, *Una Mystica Persona* (Munich: Schoningh, 1964); idem, *Der Heilige Geist als Person* (Münster: Aschendorff, 1963); John O'Donnell, *Trinity and Temporality* (New York: Oxford University Press, 1983); Wolfhart Pannenberg, "Problems of a Trinitarian Doctrine of God," *Dialog* 26 (1987): 250–57; Piet Schoonenberg, "Spirit Christology and Logos Christology," *Bijdragen* 38 (1977): 350–75; idem, "Trinity, the Consummated Covenant: Theses on the Doctrine of the Trinitarian God," *Studies in Religion* 5 (1975–76): 111–16; George Tavard, *The Vision of the Trinity* (Washington, D.C.: University Press of America, 1981).

Excluding the present introductory material and a very brief conclusion, this essay is divided into six major sections. The first of these sections is meant to establish the claim that the doctrine of the Trinity *is* the Christian doctrine of God. Christian doctrine does not present two Gods—one a God "in general" and the other a triune God. The Christian doctrine of God concerns the God of Jesus Christ, and vice versa: The mystery of redemption points to the mystery of God as such.

The second section considers what it means to say that the God revealed in Christ is incomprehensible mystery.

The third section begins with the biblical and liturgical origins of trinitarian doctrine, retracing the steps by which the church, East and West, came to articulate its faith within a trinitarian framework. The purpose is to see how trinitarian doctrine made it possible to affirm the essential unity between "economy" and "theology," between the mystery of salvation and the mystery of God. Eventually Eastern and Western theology weakened the connection between "economy" and "theology" that fourth-century theologians had put in place. This led to the current situation in which the doctrine of the Trinity is not seen to be of existential importance.

The fourth section outlines some of the elements of a systematic trinitarian theology.

The fifth section reconsiders three topics—the meaning of "person" language, the *filioque* clause in the creed, and the fatherhood of God. Each of these has received fresh consideration with the aid of new categories of thought.

Finally, the sixth section spells out some of the practical dimensions of living trinitarian faith. The doctrine of the Trinity is a prime instance in which worship, spirituality, ethics, and doctrine are intimately bound up with each other, even if classical presentations of trinitarian doctrine do little to make this evident. The guiding principle in this essay is that the mystery of grace and redemption and the mystery of God must be thought of together. Only then is it plain that the doctrine of the Trinity is an eminently practical doctrine.

# CONFESSING FAITH
# IN THE GOD OF JESUS CHRIST

The doctrine of the Trinity is a summary statement of faith in the God of Jesus Christ. It identifies the God in whom Christians believe and the God whom Christians worship; it is the specifically Christian way of speaking about God. The focus of the doctrine of the Trinity is the God who acts and is present in the "economy" (*oikonomia* = plan or administration) of salvation, especially in Christ. Christ is the revelation of God, the culmination of the economy of salvation in which the reality and mystery of God are made manifest.

The mystery of God is revealed in Christ to be the mystery of love offered for the sake of life, even amid rejection and death. Those who believe in Christ are offered the possibility of sharing in divine life and love. Eastern theology expresses this in the language of deification (*theosis*): We are made partakers in divine life through the power of the Holy Spirit, as we grow in conformity to the image and likeness of God (1 Peter 2:4; 1 Cor. 3:18). The heart of Christian life is the encounter with a personal God who makes possible both our union with God and communion with each other. The Spirit of God gathers us together into the body of Christ, incorporating us into a new relationship with each other. Everything is created by God through Christ; all of creation is to be reunited with God (Father) through Christ in the Spirit.[7]

The economy of salvation is the basis, the context, and the criterion for Christian theology of God. Christian theology is the human attempt to speak truthfully and meaningfully about the God who is with us in Christ. Trinitarian theology focuses on the relationship between "economy" and "theology," or between what contemporary Western theologians refer to as the "economic" Trinity and the "immanent" Trinity, and Eastern theologians somewhat analogously refer to as "divine essence" and "divine energies" (see the section on tradition, below).

Trinitarian doctrine is not concerned exclusively with *theologia*, with the nature of God considered apart from who God is revealed to be in the actual economy of salvation; nor is it concerned with *oikonomia* to the exclusion of the question about God's nature. Since *theologia* (mystery of God) is what is revealed in the *oikonomia* (mystery of redemption), contemplating the mystery of the economy means contemplating the mystery of God. Therefore the basic principle of theological knowledge is that the starting point is the economy of salvation; there is no independent insight "into" God. Still, the mystery of God in the economy permanently remains ineffable mystery. Indeed, one could say that the purpose of the discipline of theology is not to produce a fully understood God, but to remind us of the inadequacy of our ideas of God.

---

7. "Father" is a synonym for God in Scripture, the older creeds, the eucharistic prayers, and Greek patristic thought.

# GOD WHO IS MYSTERY

The assertion that God is incomprehensible mystery arises out of the revelation of the *personal* character of God in the economy of salvation. Moses was almost unpardonably bold when he asked God to reveal God's name to him. In ancient Semitic cultures, name indicated essence, and to know the name of something meant to have control over it. God responded to Moses' request by giving a virtually unpronounceable tetragrammaton, YHWH, a name so sacred that only rarely could it be uttered. The name is often translated as "I Am Who Am," or "He Who Is," but it may also be translated as "I will be with you there as Who I Am will I be with you."[8] The name of God, which expresses the essence of God, amounts to a promise to be there (with Israel) always.

The incomprehensibility of God has to do with the inaccessibility of God, but not in the sense of God's remoteness or distance from us. Sometimes transcendence and immanence are played off against each other, as if transcendence and incomprehensibility go on one side, and immanence and comprehensibility on the other. But God's transcendence does not mean God out of relationship to us; God is transcendent because God's nearness to us does not exhaust the mystery that God permanently remains. The unfathomable mystery is that God is bound to humanity and its history through an unalterable covenant that was freely initiated out of love and is destined to be upheld despite the sin of the world. For Christians, the incomprehensibility of God takes on a new dimension in Christ: The invisible God is made visible in the humanity of Christ. And yet, God who is completely disclosed in Christ remains nonetheless veiled. The deep mystery, the wisdom that remains folly, is that God who dwells in light inaccessible (1 Tim. 6:16) should enter history, be limited by time and culture, experience longing and joy, even suffering and death, and yet remain God.

To speak of God as mystery is another way of saying that God is "personal." An analogy can be drawn with our knowledge of other (human) persons. We speak of a person revealing herself or himself to us. By that we do not chiefly mean learning facts about that person's past or present but seeing with the "eyes of the heart" who that person is, grasping through love her or his ineffable and inexhaustible mystery. The more intimate our knowledge of another, the more we are drawn to that person's unique mystery and the deeper that mys-

---

8. See John Courtney Murray, *The Problem of God* (New Haven: Yale University Press, 1964), 8–10.

tery becomes. The same is true of God; God is not less mystery on account of God's radical immanence in Christ. Indeed, the God who is absolutely other, absolutely transcendent but also absolutely near to us—this God is absolute mystery.

Both Eastern and Western traditions affirm that we cannot know the essence of the unknowable God. What God is must be respected by silence. While this strong and widespread conviction may appear to be motivated by the need for philosophical coherence (God by definition cannot be grasped by the finite intellect), its deepest root is to be found in an insight that comes from prayer, not philosophy: The more nearly one approaches God, the more one must bow down and cover one's face. The unknowable divine essence is God's holiness, God's glory, more than essence conceived strictly philosophically as nature or substance. The divine essence in this sense is what is meant by the term *theologia*, the mystery of God given and manifested in *oikonomia*. The economy of salvation is as ineffable, therefore, as is the eternal mystery of God (*theologia*).

The emphasis on apophatic theology in the Orthodox tradition springs out of the recognition of the poverty of human language face to face with divine mystery. Apophasis means the negation of all definitions of God. This darkness of "unknowing" is not agnosticism but a kind of knowing. Moses' vision of God in the cloud of darkness at the top of Mt. Sinai (Exod. 20, 24, 34) is a favorite image used in Greek patristic theology to explain that the utter brilliance of God, the effulgence of God's glory, can appear to us only as darkness.[9]

Even words like *God* and *creator* do not designate what God is *in se*, but describe God's face turned toward the world (what Orthodox theology calls the divine energies). Gregory of Nazianzus and others remind us that "God" is a relative (relational) term; God must be God-of-someone in order to be God.[10] By emptying ourselves of concepts and images of God, or of expectations about what God is or should be or should be doing, we become free to know and love the real living God instead of the God of our projections. Apophasis, therefore, leads us not into absence but into the presence of the God who far exceeds our thoughts and words and even our desires.

Negative theology, which proceeds by saying what God is not, is not just a remedy designed by theology to exercise control over

---

9. An analogy might be the experience of momentary blindness when we come out of a movie theater into bright daylight.

10. Gregory of Nazianzus *Orat.* 29.12 (Third Theological Oration) (PG 36, 90); Gregory of Nyssa *Against Eunomius* 1.38 (PG 45, 419–41); Thomas Aquinas *Summa Theologiae* Ia, q. 13, a. 8.

its concepts; nor is it a devaluation of images and concepts of God. Kallistos Ware compares negative theology to the sculptor who by chipping away at a piece of marble does not produce a heap of random fragments but "through the apparently destructive action of breaking the stone in pieces...ends up by unveiling an intelligible shape."[11]

A positive or cataphatic approach characterizes Latin theology, the tradition to which most North Americans and Europeans belong. This approach proceeds by analogy. Because of the ontological difference between what God is and what we are, words that apply to finite reality cannot univocally be applied to infinite reality. By acknowledging that the way of signifying (*modus significandi*) never adequately attains to the reality signified (*res significata*), theology is freed to predicate certain attributes of God (such as "wisdom") with the caveat that God is not wise as we are wise. Latin theology also admits the permanent inaccessibility of the divine essence. Thomas Aquinas spoke for all his predecessors when he said that we do not know what God is, only that God is; we know God only from God's effects.[12] In this one sees the apophatic dimension underlying the way of analogy. Words like *simple* or *omnipotent* do not provide positive content about God but convey how far beyond human concepts God is. As Augustine put it, something that can be called ineffable is not ineffable.[13]

Both Greek and Latin approaches preserve the ineffability of God. But negative theology must never be detached from the positive record of biblical revelation. Negation must be a way of affirmation. An excessive apophaticism tends to disengage theological reflection from the events of redemptive history and can devolve into agnosticism. Similarly, an excessive form of analogical theology also collapses the distinction between economy and theology and can devolve into an overconfident "description" of the mystery and reality of God. Since God whose face we seek is God whose face is already turned toward us, cataphatic theology is as necessary as apophatic. At the same time, all images and concepts of God must be chastened by apophasis, not just as a technical method but as the fruit of contemplative theology whose purpose is to bring us into the presence of the living God, into the region of love of God that surpasses images and concepts. As a method, Paul Evdokimov says, apophasis teaches

---

11. Kallistos Ware, *The Orthodox Way* (Crestwood, N.Y.: St. Vladimir's Seminary Press, 1981), 167.

12. Thomas Aquinas *Summa Theologiae* Ia, q. 12, a. 12.

13. Augustine *De Doct. Christ.* 1.6.

the correct attitude of all theologians: One does not speculate about God but is transformed by God.[14]

In sum, theology, and especially trinitarian theology, is not a concept about God but, as M. D. Chenu would say, a *scientia* ( = way of knowing) by means of and within the economy of salvation.[15] The incomprehensible mystery of *theologia*, the mystery of God, is approached through the economy of salvation, particularly if we take "economy" in Irenaeus's sense as a synonym for the incarnation of Christ and the deification of the human person. *Oikonomia* and *theologia* cannot be separated from each other because they are two ways in which the one God "is" God.

# RETRACING THE STEPS
# OF THE TRADITION

How did Christianity move from its belief that the mystery of God was fully revealed in Christ, to a doctrine of the Trinity? This section looks at the biblical and liturgical roots of later doctrine.

## BIBLICAL ORIGINS OF TRINITARIAN DOCTRINE

Recent developments in biblical studies have fostered an appreciation for the historical conditioning of texts, as well as a hermeneutical sensitivity to the intentions and thought-forms available to writers of a given era. These developments, along with the fact that the doctrine of the Trinity did not emerge until the fourth century, have made it necessary to clarify in what sense the doctrine of the Trinity may be said to be biblical.

Dogmatic manuals of the nineteenth and twentieth centuries routinely began the tract entitled *De Deo Trino* (on the triune God) by asserting that the God of the Hebrew Bible was a Trinity of persons, that it was the Trinity that was manifested in all pre-Christian theophanies. Genesis 1:26 ("Let *us* make man in *our* image and likeness") and similar texts (Gen. 11:7: "Come let *us* go down and there confound their tongue") were classical loci. The trisagion of Isaiah 6:3 ("Holy, Holy, Holy, the Lord God of Hosts, all the earth is full of his glory") was regarded as "the clearest allusion to the mystery

---

14. Paul Evdokimov, *L'Ésprit Saint dans la tradition orthodoxe* (Paris: Éditions du Cerf, 1969), 25.

15. M. D. Chenu, *L'Evangile dans le temps* (Paris: Éditions du Cerf, 1964), 666.

of the Blessed Trinity."[16] In an exegesis that many today would find fanciful, the Isaiah text was said to refer "to an ecstatic vision of the Godhead, by which Isaias was solemnly called and consecrated as the Prophet of the Incarnate Word."[17] When it came to establishing the divinity of the preexistent Son, the manuals appealed mainly to "messianic" and wisdom texts.[18] The divinity of the Spirit was more difficult because of the paucity of *dicta probantia* (proof-texts) for the divinity of the Holy Spirit in either Jewish or Christian Scriptures.

Exegetes and theologians today are in agreement that the Hebrew Bible does not contain a doctrine of the Trinity. Although the Hebrew Bible depicts God as Father of Israel and employs personifications of God such as Word (*dabar*), Spirit (*ruah*), Wisdom and Presence (*shekinah*), it would go beyond the intention and spirit of the Hebrew Bible to correlate these notions with later trinitarian doctrine. At the same time, the revelation of God's holy name to Moses, the election of Israel for covenant with God, and God's saving and prophetic action on behalf of Israel are formative elements in what will later become the specifically Christian theology of God.

Exegetes and theologians are likewise agreed that the New Testament does not contain an explicit doctrine of the Trinity, though most would maintain that the trinitarian doctrine of the fourth century and beyond has its origins in the testimony of Scripture.

Some of the exegetical difficulties associated with the proof-text approach of the manuals are bypassed by appreciating the genuinely liturgical nature of many texts. Most New Testament texts used to support later trinitarian doctrine were originally liturgical and creedal texts and fragments. God is called "Father of our Lord Jesus Christ," and the opening greetings in Paul and Deutero-Paul indicate that praise is to be rendered to God *through* Christ (e.g., Eph. 5:20: Give thanks "in the name of our Lord Jesus Christ to God the Father"). Other "binitarian" texts include Romans 4:24; 8:11; 2 Corinthians 4:14; Colossians 2:12; 1 Timothy 2:5; 6:13; 2 Timothy 4:1.

---

16. Joseph Pohle, *The Divine Trinity*, adapted by Arthur Preuss, 6th rev. ed. (St. Louis: Herder, 1911), 11.

17. Pohle, *Divine Trinity*, 12.

18. For example, Pohle, *Divine Trinity*, interprets Ps. 109:1–3 ("The Lord said to my Lord: 'Sit at my right hand.... From the womb before the day star I begot thee'") in an exegetically strained way: "If the future Messias is the 'Son of God,' and at the same time Jehovah, it is obvious that there must also be a 'Father' who is Jehovah. Consequently, there must be two Divine Persons in one Divine Nature. This notion was so familiar to the Jews that Jesus, in order to prove His Divinity, had merely to advert to the fact that He was the Son of God to provoke them to anger and blasphemy" (p. 16).

There are some triadic texts. The strongest are the baptismal formula in Matthew 28:19; Paul's closing benediction of 2 Corinthians 13:14 ("May the grace of our Lord Jesus Christ, the love of God, and the communion of the Holy Spirit be with you"); the description of Jesus' baptism in Matthew 3:16-17; the liturgical fragments in Galatians 4:6 and Romans 8:15 (the Spirit praying in us calls God *Abba*); the description of the economy of salvation in Ephesians 1:3-14. Others include 1 Corinthians 6:11; 12:4; 2 Corinthians 1:21f.; 1 Thessalonians 5:18f.; and Galatians 3:11-14. The high-priestly prayer of Jesus in John 17, while not triadic, contains important elements of the later theology of the relationship between the Father and the Son.

Many of the phrases that made their way into later creedal statements derive from liturgical settings (e.g., 1 Cor. 15:3ff.). For example, the phrase "the God and Father of our Lord Jesus Christ" (Rom. 15:6; 2 Cor. 1:3, 11, 31; Eph. 1:3; 1 Peter 1:3) probably originated in liturgical practice.[19]

It would be a mistake to think that only those texts that contain *three* names are authentically trinitarian. This is like looking for Jesus' teaching on the kingdom of God only in those texts where the word *kingdom* is found; one risks missing the real stories of the kingdom. Every testimony to any aspect of the mystery of redemption is important for a trinitarian theology of God. Again, the central concern of the doctrine of the Trinity is not to point to a numerical mystery but rather to name the God who redeems us in Christ and deifies us through the Holy Spirit. Trinitarian doctrine recapitulates Christian faith as found, for example, in Ephesians 1:3-14: We were chosen before the foundation of the world to be sons and daughters through Jesus Christ "to the praise of God's glorious grace freely bestowed on us in the Beloved [Christ]" (v. 6). In Christ we were redeemed by the blood of the cross and our trespasses were forgiven. In this "plan" or *economy* of salvation, all of creation is to be reunited with God (Father) in and through Christ. The path of salvation is the glorification of God: "We who first hoped in Christ have been destined and appointed to live for the praise of God's glory" (cf. Isa. 43:7; Phil. 1:11). Because of our faith in Christ we are sealed with the Holy Spirit "which is the guarantee of our inheritance until we acquire possession of it, to the praise of God's glory" (v. 14).

The New Testament writers were not concerned to develop a metaphysics of God; the New Testament does not contain the technical language of later trinitarian doctrine (*hypostasis*; *ousia*; *substantia*;

---

19. J. N. D. Kelly, *Early Christian Creeds*, 3d ed. (New York: Longman, 1972), 21.

*subsistentia*). Because the language of the Bible is "economic," focused on the concrete history of creation and redemption, some theologians have concluded that all postbiblical developments in the direction of a trinitarian metaphysics of God are therefore arbitrary.[20] While it is incontestable that the New Testament does not contain a comprehensive theology of God, much less a trinitarian doctrine of God, the origins and even the main lines of later doctrine may legitimately be sought in the Bible. This is not the same as proof-texting or claiming biblical warrant for one's metaphysics. However, the Bible is the authoritative record of God's redemptive relationship with humanity. That record, together with what is confessed in creeds and celebrated in worship, is the wellspring of later trinitarian doctrine. It is important to recall that there are many doctrines of the Trinity; no one doctrinal formulation, either that of Augustine and the church councils or that of Gregory of Nyssa and John Damascene, is mandated by the New Testament. At the same time, all doctrinal references to the nature of God must be measured by and checked against the biblical witness to God's self-revelation in the economy of salvation.[21]

## LITURGICAL ROOTS OF TRINITARIAN DOCTRINE

Histories of the doctrine of the Trinity sometimes leave the impression that a purely rational or logical difficulty arose in the minds of early Christians: If God is one, how can Christ also be God? Similarly, if the Holy Spirit is God, how can three be God without violating the unity of God?

It is doubtful that this is the level at which the problem arose. The most enduring and the most intellectually perplexing doctrinal disputes have always been those entangled with liturgical practices. Movements like Arianism, Hesychasm, the dispute over the *filioque*, and today's controversy over the fatherhood of God are interest-

---

20. For example, Maurice Wiles, *The Making of Christian Doctrine* (Philadelphia: Westminster Press, 1978), 21–39; idem, "Some Reflections on the Origins of the Doctrine of the Trinity," *Journal of Theological Studies* 8 (1957): 92–106 (reprinted in *Working Papers in Doctrine* [London: SCM, 1976], 1–17); Geoffrey Lampe, *God as Spirit* (Oxford: Clarendon, 1977); Cyril Richardson, *The Doctrine of the Trinity* (Nashville: Abingdon, 1958). They seem to equate "immanent Trinity" with "inner nature of God" and therefore take the view that all speculation about the "immanent Trinity" is illegitimate, that theology must confine itself to the "economic Trinity." They fail to see that both an "economic" and an "immanent" doctrine of God refer to the economy, not to "God as such" apart from the economy.

21. "The Filioque Clause in Ecumenical Perspective," in Lukas Vischer, ed., *Spirit of God, Spirit of Christ*, Faith and Order Report No. 103 (London: SPCK; Geneva: World Council of Churches, 1981), 10.

ing in their own right as theological questions. But their liturgical dimension makes them not only more intriguing but of greater consequence, and in some ways, more intractable. As Maurice Wiles says about the Arian crisis, people "do not normally feel so deeply over matters of formal doctrinal statement unless those matters are felt to bear upon the practice of their piety."[22]

The first Christians did not understand themselves to be part of a new religion; Christian prayer was derived from Jewish practice but was adapted to fit the belief that Christ is the mediator of God's work and will. The new doxologies directed praise to God *through* Christ the mediator. The mediatory order of prayer is especially prominent in letters of Paul and Deutero-Paul (see Eph. 5:20; 1 Cor. 15:57; Col. 3:17; Rom. 1:8; 16:27; 7:25; 2 Cor. 1:20; Heb. 13:15; 1 Peter 4:11). Although there is little explicit reference to the Holy Spirit, in its liturgical life as a whole the early church was very much aware of the Spirit. Early liturgical texts like Romans 8:15 and Galatians 4:6 show that Christians saw themselves as invited to become like Christ, sons and daughters in relation to the Father *in the Holy Spirit*: "And because you are sons God has sent the Spirit of God's Son into our hearts, crying, 'Abba! Father!' " (Gal. 4:6). The mediatory pattern of prayer is found in the anaphoral (anaphora = eucharistic prayer) and doxological portions of virtually all extant liturgical texts of the pre-Nicene church. In general, praise and thanksgiving were offered to God *through* Christ.

In contrast to the binitarian and mediatory form of public prayer, Christians baptized "in the name of the Father and of the Son and of the Holy Spirit" (Matt. 28:19b). The arrangement of prepositions in this phrase is unprecedented and unparalleled in the New Testament. Biblical scholars disagree about whether this text is authentically Matthean, or is an interpolation by a later (ca. second to fourth century) hand, or is a traditional baptismal formula that has been incorporated with other elements.[23] Most scholars think Matthew 28:19 reflects early baptismal practice in which the candidate was asked a triple set of questions: Do you believe in God the Father the Almighty...? Do you believe in Jesus Christ...? Do you believe in the Holy Spirit...? The "interrogation" was followed by a triple immersion in water.[24]

---

22. Wiles, *Making of Christian Doctrine*, 62.

23. Jane Schaberg, *The Father, the Son, and the Holy Spirit: The Triadic Phrase in Mt. 28:19b* (Chico, Calif.: Scholars Press, 1981), 9–58. Also Georg Kretschmar, *Studien zur frühchristlichen Trinitätstheologie* (Tübingen: Mohr, 1956).

24. See Kelly, *Early Christian Creeds*; Mark Searle, *Christening: The Making of Christians* (Collegeville, Minn.: Liturgical Press, 1980); Oscar Cullmann, *Baptism in the New Testament* (London: SCM, 1954).

Baptism was the original setting of early Christian creeds. From its apostolic origins, the Christian church was a confessing church, possessing a "creed" in the broadest sense of the term: a commonly held kerygma that was distinctive from the teaching of Judaism.[25] While in the New Testament there is no creed in the strict sense of the term, with the possible exception of "Jesus is Lord," there are what J. N. D. Kelly calls "creed-like slogans and tags" that are early evidence of the tendency to crystallize apostolic teaching into conventional summaries.[26] The creed was a "symbol" (*symbolum*), a sign, a token, a reminder of the God into whose name Christians were baptized. Only gradually did creeds evolve into uniform and fixed summaries of doctrine designed to exclude heretical interpretations.

Baptism notwithstanding, official and public Christian prayer in its earliest stages and without important exception was directed to God (Father) with Christ as its *mediator*.[27] It is easy to see why Arius and his followers would have considered the mediatory form of prayer to support their view that Jesus was inferior to God. Numerous New Testament texts seemed to support the idea of an "inequality" between Jesus and God: for example, "The Father is greater than I" (John 14:28), and texts indicating that God created *through* Christ (1 Cor. 8:6; John 1:2; Heb. 1:2; Col. 1:16). The Arians also liked to cite Proverbs 8:22, "The Lord created me at the beginning of his work, the first of his acts of old." Arianism seemed, *prima facie*, to have a stronger biblical basis than what later became "orthodoxy." As a result, the liturgy quickly became an arena in which various doctrinal stances struggled to establish themselves.

In reaction to Arianism, Eastern liturgies of the fourth century began to exhibit explicitly anti-Arian characteristics. (The Eastern churches were threatened by Arianism to a far greater extent than Western churches.) At some point after 340 in Antioch, some Christians for polemical reasons began to pray to the Father *and* the Son *and* the Holy Spirit.[28] Bishop Leontius, sympathetic to the Arians but trying not to offend others, is reported to have recited the doxology in public worship so quietly that no one could hear him utter the important concluding words.[29] The situation escalated when Basil, bishop of Caesarea, coined another anti-Arian doxology: "to God the Father *with* [*meta*] the Son, *together with* [*sün*] the Holy Spirit." The

---

25. For what follows, see Kelly, *Early Christian Creeds*, 1–29.

26. Kelly, *Early Christian Creeds*, 13.

27. There are exceptions, doxologies in which Christ is not named: Gal. 1:5; Phil. 4:20; 1 Tim. 1:17; 6:16.

28. For what follows see Josef Jungmann, *The Place of Christ in Liturgical Prayer* (New York: Alba House, 1962), 175ff. Also Wiles, *Making of Christian Doctrine*, 85.

29. Jungmann, *Place of Christ*, 176; Wiles, *Making of Christian Doctrine*, 85.

innovation caused an uproar and prompted Basil to write a treatise, *On the Holy Spirit*, in defense of the new doxology.

Western (Latin) liturgies as a whole did not change as drastically as a result of Arianism. In part this is because the West had no firsthand knowledge either of the texts expounding the Arian position or of their orthodox counterparts, and only a general knowledge of the Council of Nicaea.

## DEVELOPMENT OF TRINITARIAN DOCTRINE

Within the context of these liturgical and creedal developments, and against the background of the philosophies of the day, especially Stoicism and Neo-Platonism, trinitarian doctrine gradually developed. Prior to the fourth century, theology had been focused on christological and soteriological questions: Who is Christ in relation to us? How does Christ accomplish our salvation? Does Christ have a complete humanity, including a human soul? Who is Christ in relation to God? Is Christ equal to God? Is Christ less than God but greater than other creatures? How, within a monotheistic framework, is Christ the divine savior? At first, little attention was paid to the question of the divinity of the Holy Spirit; not until the Council of Constantinople in 381 would there be an official pronouncement that the Spirit is God.[30]

### *The Question Put by Arius*

Arius was a priest from Alexandria. Although his writings are not extant, his opponents tell us that his theology rested on the premises that God (the Father) is absolutely unique and transcendent, and that God's essence (*ousia*) cannot be shared by another or transferred to another (such as the Son).[31] For Arius the distinction between Father and Son was one of substance (*ousia*). If Father and Son are of the same substance, there would be two gods. The catch-phrase of Arianism, "there was when he was not," meant that Christ was begotten of God in time, not from all eternity. As part of creation, Christ is

---

30. The third article of the Creed of Nicaea reads simply: "And I believe in the Holy Spirit."

31. On Arianism, see Kelly, *Early Christian Creeds*, and idem, *Early Christian Doctrines*, 2d ed. (New York: Harper and Row, 1960); George Leonard Prestige, *God in Patristic Thought* (London: SPCK, 1952); Robert C. Gregg and Dennis E. Groh, *Early Arianism: A View of Salvation* (Philadelphia: Fortress Press, 1981); Frances Young, *From Nicaea to Chalcedon: A Guide to the Literature and Its Background* (Philadelphia: Fortress Press, 1983); R. P. C. Hanson, *The Search for the Christian Doctrine of God: The Arian Controversy 318–381* (Edinburgh: T and T Clark, 1988).

inferior to God but greater than other creatures. As we saw above, the church's public prayer at this time did not directly contradict a subordinationist interpretation of the relationship between God and Christ.[32]

Some elements of the fourth-century answer had already been worked out. The second-century Apologists had used Stoic philosophy to explain the preexistence of Christ. The distinction between the immanent Word (*logos endiathetos*) and the expressed Word (*logos prophorikos*) enabled Justin Martyr (d. 165) and others to formulate a "Logos christology." In the third century, in the writings of Tertullian and Origen especially, a technical vocabulary (*hypostasis, subsistentia, ousia, natura*) began to be developed. Origen, who has been called the father of both Arianism and orthodoxy,[33] contributed the idea that the Son is eternally generated within the being of God. Though open to an Arian interpretation, Origen's theology prepared the way for late fourth-century, orthodox trinitarian theology.

To refute Arius, the Council of Nicaea (325) taught that Christ was not created but "begotten of the substance of the Father."[34] Few words in the history of doctrine have provoked greater controversy than *homoousios*, a word inserted in the Nicene profession of faith at the insistence of Emperor Constantine.[35] Resistance to Nicaea's formulation was intense. Greek theologians objected that not only was the word *homoousios* not biblical, but it also could be interpreted as indicating numerical identity. This was the Sabellian position, that the one substance of divinity (the "Father") makes two different appearances in history, one as Son, another as Spirit. In order to highlight the distinctive "personhood" of Father and Son, some suggested that *homoiousios* (of similar substance) be substituted for Nicaea's word. But other theologians (especially in the West) took exception to the Eastern proposal, since *homoiousios* could be interpreted in a subordinationist way (the Son is different from the Father and therefore less than the Father).

The positions of Arius (and Sabellius) were developed in a philosophical milieu that understood the absolute transcendence of God

---

32. Subordination can be ontological, in which case one type of being is superior to another type of being. There is also a nonontological subordination of the emanationist kind; "God the Father" is logically prior to "God the Son," but this does not necessarily entail inferiority or superiority between Father and Son.

33. Prestige, *God in Patristic Thought*, xiv.

34. Notice, from the substance of the *Father*, not from the substance of Godhead. The "Father" is the substratum of divinity.

35. See Kelly, *Early Christian Creeds*, 205–95; Prestige, *God in Patristic Thought*, 197–218.

to preclude any traffic with temporal reality. Arianism might thus appear at first glance to have been a welcome defense of divine transcendence and strict monotheism. Already in the third century there was a suspicion that Logos christology compromised the absolute unity of God, and monarchianism arose to meet this fear.[36] But on second look, Arianism more closely resembled a philosophically based unitarianism; God is a monad who *cannot* enter time and history except through intermediaries. The "error" of Arius, the point at which his views conflicted most obviously with Christian experience, was his premise of the inability of God to submit to the vicissitudes of time and matter. As a philosophy of God this certainly is defensible. But it was far less compelling *religiously*, compared with the conviction of Athanasius and others of God's absolute presence in Christ. For them, Christ was not simply one instance of God's immanence in history; nor was Christ simply a bridge between the atemporal God and human history; rather, Christ was the coming of *very God* into the world, and our means of transformation and union with God.

## Greek Theology after Nicaea

Whether the *homoousios* is seen as the triumph of Hellenistic philosophy over the gospel[37] or as a desirable rejection of Arianism, there is a noticeable shift in the Christian theology of God after Nicaea. For better or for worse, Arius pushed theology toward ontology: Is Christ the same as God, or similar? Is Christ the same as us, or greater? Would "the same as" mean same in will, same in being, same in manner of being?

Athanasius (d. 373), the great defender of Nicene orthodoxy, put the issue directly: If Christ is not divine, he can neither save nor make us like God. And yet, "God became human that we might become

---

36. Monarchianism can be divided into two types, "dynamic" and "modalist." Dynamic monarchians, like Paul of Samosata, denied that Christ was any more than a man inspired by divine wisdom. Modalistic monarchianism was more widespread; its adherents (Noetus, Praxeas, Sabellius) believed both in the absolute oneness of God and in the divinity of Christ. The problem was to reconcile these two ideas. Since "Father" was synonymous with Godhead, to assert that the Divine Word (Son) was other than the Father would imply that there were two gods. The solution was to deny that the Father was other than the Son; indeed, "Father" and "Son" were interchangeable names for the Godhead. In a sophisticated version of modalism, Sabellius insisted on the oneness of God but allowed that the Godhead manifests itself in three distinct operations in history. "God the Father" was associated with creation and the giving of the law; "God the Son" with redemption; "God the Spirit" with inspiration and grace.

37. This was the view of Adolf von Harnack, *A History of Dogma*, 4 vols. (New York: Dover, 1961).

God."[38] Therefore the Logos incarnate in Jesus must be eternally with God the Father and of the same substance.

It fell to the Cappadocians, Basil (d. 379), Gregory of Nyssa (d. 394), and Gregory of Nazianzus (d. 390), to formulate trinitarian doctrine in its classic form: God is one nature, three persons (*mia ousia, treis hypostaseis*). The Arian crisis had necessitated a clear teaching about what Father, Son, and Spirit share in common (divinity, *ousia*). The late fourth-century concern was to specify what differentiates Father, Son, and Spirit from each other and from the divine nature (personhood, *hypostasis*). The speculatively gifted Cappadocians were able to fix the meaning of certain terms, especially *hypostasis* and *ousia* (roughly equivalent to particular and universal). A sharper distinction between nature and person was unavoidable.

Further, against the Arian position, the Cappadocians made a clear distinction between being begotten (*gennesia*) and being made or created (*genesia*). This settled the question of whether the Son was begotten from all eternity, and therefore is equal to God, or was made, and therefore is a creature. The Son is begotten from the *substance* of the Father, whereas the world is created by the *will* of God.

Greek trinitarian theology has a dynamic understanding of God and retains the biblical emphasis on the economy of salvation. God creates through Christ in the power of the Holy Spirit; the Spirit leads us back to God through Christ. God the Father is the "monarch," the unoriginate origin, source, and principle of Godhead (*fons et origo divinitatis*). The eternal being of God derives from the person of the Father; every act of God in creation originates with the Father, proceeds through the Son, and is perfected by the Holy Spirit (Gregory of Nyssa's formulation).

We are not able to say, however, what God is or what the divine persons are. The persons can be described only obliquely in terms of their origin, the "from whence" they come (*hypostasis* = relation of origin). Indeed, Gregory of Nazianzus says "Father" is not the name of the divine essence but the name of a relation.[39] Thus the personal property of the Father, that which makes the Father unique, is unbegottenness (coming from no one); the personal property of the Son is begottenness (coming from the Father); the personal property of the Spirit is procession (coming from the Father).

---

38. Athanasius *De Incarnatione* 54 (PG 25, 191); also Irenaeus: "Because of his immeasurable love God became what we are that he might fit us to be what he is" (*Adv. Haer.* 5, praef.).

39. Gregory of Nazianzus *Orat.* 29.16.

God the Father eternally produces, brings forth the Son. Jesus Christ, the personal Word of God, is eternally being begotten out of what God is. The Spirit is the bridge to the world, eternally proceeding from the Father (through the Son), opening the divine communion of love to what is not divine. The metaphors of "begetting" and "proceeding" suggest the ecstatic (out-going) and fecund nature of God the Father.

The Cappadocians never tired of repeating that we cannot know what God is, but we know God from God's "operations" (*energeia* or "energies"). When they wrote about the divine persons in relation to each other, they always had in mind the persons in the economy of salvation. In the course of discrediting Arianism and Eunomianism,[40] the Cappadocian theology of divine relationality emphasized the secondary meaning of "Father" as eternal begetter of the Son. The ubiquitous biblical, creedal, and anaphoral use of *Father* as a synonym for *God* was amplified in emerging trinitarian doctrine. "God the Father" now had two meanings: (1) the one who comes from nothing, from nowhere, from no one, principle without principle, and (2) the one who eternally begets the Son.

The expanded meaning of divine fatherhood forced an adjustment in the understanding of the "monarchy" of the Father. While the Father is the principle of unity, the unity of God was more and more understood to reside in the perichoresis (mutual interdependence) of three persons in each other. At the close of the patristic period John of Damascus (d. 749) summarized Greek theology up to that point with the idea of perichoresis, hoping to hold in tension divine unity and plurality, persons and nature.

## Latin Theology after Nicaea

With Augustine (d. 430) Latin theology pursued a different trajectory. Augustine, too, was greatly influenced by the Neo-Platonists, especially Plotinus. Augustine believed that because the soul was a reflection of its creator, contemplating the image of the Trinity in the soul was a means of return to God. By knowing itself, the soul knows God. In addition to the cycle of emanation of the soul from God and its return to God, there is the cycle within the soul by which the soul knows and loves itself. Augustine was unique in formulating a number of psychological analogies (such as lover-beloved-love; memory-understanding-will) to explain how one substance (the soul)

---

40. Eunomius claimed that since we know the name of the unoriginate God to be "Ungenerateness," we know what the essence of God is.

could exist in distinct representations or operations (knowing and loving) without partitioning the substance (thus the knower and lover are the same person). The psychological analogy was extended to the Trinity: the one God exists in the generation of the Word and procession of the Spirit.[41]

In the more strictly philosophical part of *De Trinitate* (books 5–7) Augustine's starting point, in sharp contrast with the Cappadocians, is the one divine substance, the "Godhead" that the three persons share in common. The Holy Spirit is understood not as the bridge between God and world but as the "bond of love" between the Father and the Son. The Augustinian model left no room for Arian subordinationism since each divine person fully shares the same divine essence. At the same time, distinctions among the divine persons tended to disappear since each is defined in relation to each other ("relations of opposition") instead of in terms of a specific role in our salvation. Augustinian theology is the basis for the axiom that "all works of the Trinity *ad extra* are indivisible."[42] Thus the Trinity creates, the Trinity redeems, and the Trinity sanctifies. The "doctrine of appropriations" became necessary to reinvest the divine persons with distinctive content. Thus creation is "appropriated" to the Father, redemption to the Son, and sanctification to the Spirit.

Augustine's focus on the interior illumination of the soul tended to move the doctrine of the Trinity away from the concrete details of salvation history, away from other areas of theology, and away from liturgy. Even though the psychological triads serve a modest role in Augustine's overall theology of God, they were adopted and made central to subsequent Latin tradition, even to the point of being elevated to the status of dogma.[43]

## General Characteristics of Greek and Latin Thought

Although there are always important exceptions to any typology,[44] in general, Greek theology emphasizes the divine hypostases (persons), whereas Latin theology emphasizes the divine nature. The emana-

---

41. Augustine *De Trinitate*, esp. bks. 8–15.

42. Denzinger, *Enchiridion Symbolorum*, 254, 281, 284, 421, 428; "the entire Trinity accomplished the Incarnation of the Son of God" (284, also 429). See *The Sources of Catholic Dogma*, from the 13th ed. of Denzinger's *Enchiridion Symbolorum*, trans. R. Deferrari (St. Louis: Herder, 1957).

43. Oliver du Roy, *L'Intelligence de la foi en la Trinité selon saint Augustin* (Paris: Études Augustiniennes, 1966), 459.

44. The classic elaboration of the differences between Greek and Latin theology is found in Théodore de Régnon, *Études de théologie positive sur la sainte Trinité*, 3 vols. (Paris: Retaux, 1892–1898). For a summary see Congar, *I Believe*, 3:xv–xxi.

tionist theology of the Greek tradition is often schematized as a line, and the self-enclosed Trinity of Latin theology as a circle:

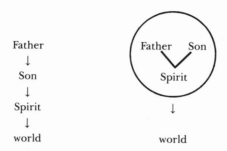

After Nicaea, theology in both traditions shifted from the question of function (what God does) to ontology (what God is). Christian theology thereafter pondered the economy of salvation only indirectly, from an "immanent" perspective. "Economic" Trinity refers to the life and work of God in salvation history, and "immanent" Trinity refers to this same life and work of God in the economy but from the point of view of their eternal ground in the being of God. There are not two ontologically distinct trinities; as the well-known axiom of Karl Rahner states, "The 'economic' Trinity is the 'immanent' Trinity, and *vice versa*."[45] Orthodox theology prefers the patristic language of "essence" and "energies." What God is (essence) can never be known, but the essence is revealed and manifested through the energies, which are God's actions in creation and redemption.

The subsequent history of trinitarian doctrine in the East and West is the history of a gradual de-emphasis on the economy of salvation in the Christian theology of God. In the West, Augustinian theology was given further elaboration in medieval theology, especially by Anselm (d. 1109) and in the Scholastic synthesis of Thomas Aquinas (d. 1274). Aquinas developed a sophisticated ontology of person and relation; person is defined as "subsistent relation" (to be God is to be relational).[46] He also used Augustine's psychological analogy to develop a theory of the intentionality of a subject; the divine processions of begetting and spirating are analogous to the two intentional activities of knowing and loving.[47]

---

45. Rahner, *The Trinity*, 22.
46. Thomas Aquinas *Summa Theologiae* Ia, q. 40, a. 2.
47. For a summary of Aquinas's theology see Hill, *Three-Personed God*, 62–78. Also LaCugna, "The Relational God," 647–63.

Others were deeply influenced by Augustine yet had a more Greek than Latin understanding of "person," and developed a "social" rather than psychological analogy for the Trinity. Richard of Saint Victor (d. 1173) taught that God is the supreme exemplification of charity.[48] To be perfect, the two coeternal and coequal divine persons must, without jealousy or competition, love a third coequal person. Bonaventure (d. 1274), like the Greeks, emphasized the monarchy of the Father whose self-diffusive fecundity is expressed in the intradivine processions of Son and Spirit, and the creation of the world in the triune image.[49]

Imitating Aquinas, medieval Christianity in the West adopted the practice of writing two distinct "tracts" on God: "On the One God" (*De Deo Uno*) followed by "On the Triune God" (*De Deo Trino*). This arrangement made the doctrine of the Trinity appear as an afterthought, as something added on to a prior, independent philosophical concept of God.[50] Soteriology, christology, and pneumatology evolved as discrete areas of theology. And insofar as divine personhood was conceived of as ancillary to the divine substance, Western Christianity failed to be wholly trinitarian in its doctrine of God. Trinitarian theology became abstract and impractical, immune to the concerns of ecclesial, spiritual, and liturgical life, thereby producing the situation with which this essay began. For many people today, the term *Trinity* evokes some image of the "internal" self-relatedness of God, rather than the life of God that permeates every moment and aspect of our existence. As Rahner says, "The treatise

---

48. Richard of Saint Victor, *The Trinity* (New York: Paulist, 1981); Ewert Cousins, "A Theology of Interpersonal Relations," *Thought* 45 (1970): 56–82.

49. Bonaventure, *Disputed Questions on the Mystery of the Trinity*, trans. Zachary Hayes (St. Bonaventure, N.Y.: Franciscan Institute, 1979); Ewert Cousins, *Bonaventure and the Coincidence of Opposites* (Chicago: Franciscan Herald Press, 1978); Etienne Gilson, *The Philosophy of St. Bonaventure* (New York: Sheed and Ward, 1938); Zachary Hayes, *The Hidden Centre: Spirituality and Speculative Christology in St. Bonaventure* (New York: Paulist, 1981).

50. Christian thought patterns continue to reflect this divided mind. For example: Who created the world? God? One of the divine persons? All of them together? One person through another person?

Who or what became incarnate in Jesus Christ? Did God (the nature) take on flesh? Was it the "second person of the Trinity"? Could *any* divine person have become incarnate?

Is the beatific vision a vision of "God" (Godhead), or of three persons, or of a tripersonal nature?

In the epiclesis of the eucharistic prayer, why is just the Holy Spirit invoked to "come down upon these gifts and make them holy"?

In grace does "God" indwell? Do one or two or three persons indwell? How might we differentiate among divine "persons" in the experience of grace?

Evidently, Christianity is an admixture of unitarian, binitarian, and trinitarian thought patterns.

of the Trinity locks itself in even more splendid isolation, with the ensuing danger that the religious mind finds it devoid of interest."[51]

The story in the East is not dissimilar. About one hundred years after the death of Thomas Aquinas and Bonaventure (1274), a controversy arose over Hesychasm (*hesychia* = silence). The Hesychasts practiced a method of contemplation that was believed to lead to an inner vision of uncreated divine light, like the light on Mount Tabor. Opponents of Hesychasm feared that this practice obliterated the unbridgeable difference between God and creature.

Gregory of Palamas (d. 1359), a monk from Mount Athos, defended Hesychastic prayer by distinguishing three aspects of God's being: the permanently unnameable and imparticipable divine essence; the three hypostases, Father, Son, Spirit; the uncreated "energies" that are the mode by which God enters into unmediated union with the creature. The energies are "God as such," God's self-communication and action; the energies are both what one sees and the power by which one sees. The creature participates in the divine energies, not the divine essence. This is not meant to deny true knowledge of God; through the energies we know God as God is, but not as God is in Godself.[52]

Palamism has been criticized as leading to the same "loss of the soteriological" that characterizes Latin theology after Augustine.[53] If the distinction between essence and energies is ontological and not merely epistemological (which seems to be the view of Orthodox theologians today), then the divine hypostases belong to the imparticipable essence of God. Therefore it is the energies, not the hypostases, that enter into communion with the creature. Even if the energies are "enhypostasized" (the energies express what the persons are), the three persons are one more step removed from our salvation.

Though not well-known in the West, Palamism is regarded by many Orthodox theologians as the summary of Greek patristic thought and an indispensable part of their faith. Some even consider it a dogma, not just normative in the way that Roman Catholicism

---

51. Rahner, *The Trinity*, 17.

52. For a summary of Palamism see Kallistos Ware, "God Hidden and Revealed: The Apophatic Way and the Essence-Energies Distinction," *Eastern Churches Review* 7 (1975): 125–36; Congar, *I Believe*, 3:61–71.

53. Dorothea Wendebourg, "From the Cappadocian Fathers to Gregory Palamas: The Defeat of Trinitarian Theology," in Elizabeth Livingstone, ed., *Studia Patristica* (Oxford: Pergamon, 1982), 17/1:194–97, which summarizes her argument in *Geist oder Energie? Zur Frage der innergöttlichen Verankerung des christlichen Lebens in der byzantinischen Theologie* (Munich: Chr. Kaiser, 1980); Rowan Williams, "The Philosophical Structures of Palamism," *Eastern Churches Review* 9 (1977): 27–44.

for a time considered Thomas Aquinas's theology as normative. Neo-Palamite theologians, like Vladimir Lossky, John Meyendorff, and others, have made Palamas's work better known in the West in the last half century.[54]

After the medieval period, the history of trinitarian thought is remarkable only for its peripheral role. Friedrich Schleiermacher, sometimes called the father of modern theology, relegated the doctrine to an appendix in his work *The Christian Faith*. Not until very recently has the doctrine of the Trinity again attracted notice and has effort been made to retrieve its central insight: that God's self-communication in Christ and the ongoing presence of God as Spirit are grounded in the essential and eternal being of God as God.

# TOWARD A REVITALIZED THEOLOGY OF GOD

The decline in vitality of the doctrine of the Trinity resulted from the preoccupation with the internal and eternal aspects of the "immanent" Trinity apart from the economy that was its original basis. Reconceiving the Christian theology of God as the mystery of salvation through Christ requires a return to the biblical and patristic affirmation that "theology" (the incomprehensible mystery of God) is to be found in the mysteries of incarnation and deification.

## THE ECONOMIC AND IMMANENT TRINITY

The distinction between economic and immanent Trinity (or energies and essence in Orthodox theology) is a framework for securing the essential relationship between economy and theology while preserving the freedom and incomprehensibility of God. Rahner's axiom that the economic Trinity is the immanent Trinity, and vice versa, is widely accepted. There are not two ontologically distinct trinities but only one trinitarian mystery of God that may be con-

---

54. John Meyendorff, *A Study of Gregory Palamas* (Crestwood, N.Y.: St. Vladimir's Seminary Press, 1964); idem, *Byzantine Hesychasm: Historical, Theological and Social Problems* (London: Variorum Reprints, 1974); Vladimir Lossky, *In the Image and Likeness of God* (Crestwood, N.Y.: St. Vladimir's Seminary Press, 1974); idem, *The Mystical Theology of the Eastern Church*, 2d ed. (Crestwood, N.Y.: St. Vladimir's Seminary Press, 1976); idem, *Orthodox Theology: An Introduction* (Crestwood, N.Y.: St. Vladimir's Seminary Press, 1978); Michael Fahey and John Meyendorff, *Trinitarian Theology East and West: St. Thomas Aquinas–St. Gregory Palamas* (Brookline, Mass.: Holy Cross Orthodox Press, 1979); Kallistos Ware, "The Debate about Palamism," *Eastern Churches Review* 9 (1977): 45–63; idem, "God Hidden and Revealed," 125–36.

sidered under two aspects. The economic-immanent distinction is epistemological, not ontological, since an "immanent" theology of God is nothing other than a theology of the economy, albeit considered from a non-economic point of view. By implication, the immanent Trinity is not the same as the divine essence.[55]

If the identity between economic and immanent Trinity were understood as a strict identity (A = A), the economic Trinity would be emptied of its own historical reality, as if it were simply the temporal reflection of an eternal immanent Trinity. Or, theology would be licensed to focus only on the immanent Trinity,[56] or only on the economic, remaining skeptical about whether the distinctions in the economy are "real" in God.[57] Rahner's axiom precludes thinking that the threefold distinction in God's self-communication exists only on the side of the creature. If the self-communication of God is truly a *self*-communication, if God is the *content* of that self-communication, then its mediation in Word and Spirit must derive from a real distinction in God.[58]

Yves Congar accepts Rahner's axiom but qualifies the "vice versa."[59] Congar agrees that God's self-communication is truly a *self*-communication, and that there is a divine self-communication both *ad intra* and *ad extra*, but he notes an asymmetry between theology and economy. "The Trinity is the same in each case and God is really communicated, but this [self-communication] takes place in a mode that is not connatural with the being of the divine Persons."[60] Moreover, God's self-communication "will not be a full self-communication until the end of time, in what we call the beatific vision."[61]

Congar's fundamental reservation about Rahner's axiom is that, taken at face value, it does not convey that there is "something new"

---

55. In the Palamite schema, a theology of the uncreated divine energies is a theology of the economy; the energies are not the same as the divine essence.

56. In the effort to make ancient doctrine more accessible some theologians have revised classical analogies of the "immanent" Trinity by using a more contemporary metaphysics, or semiotics, or interpersonal psychology (see the works listed above in note 6). These proposals leave behind some of the more arcane elements of Scholastic trinitarian doctrine. However, by pursuing an exclusively "immanent" theology of God, there is still no real connection between "theology" and "economy," apparently because of a misinterpretation of Rahner's axiom.

57. See, for example, Marjorie Suchocki, "The Unmale God: Reconsidering the Trinity," *Quarterly Review* 3 (1983): 34–49, and Norman Pittenger, *The Divine Trinity* (Philadelphia: United Church Press, 1977).

58. Rahner, *The Trinity*, 36–38.

59. Congar, *I Believe*, 3:13–18.

60. Ibid., 3:15. Congar gives the example that "the Father is 'omnipotent' but what are we to think of him in a world filled with the scandal of evil?"

61. Ibid.

about God because of God's self-communication in history. Walter Kasper makes the same point. In order to allow the economic Trinity its full historical distinctiveness we must "take seriously the truth that through the incarnation the second divine person *exists in history in a new way*."[62] He is careful to add that it would be an error to dissolve the immanent in the economic Trinity; the immanent Trinity did not come into existence for the first time in salvation history. Kasper thinks this is a tendency in Piet Schoonenberg's thought.[63] Kasper rephrases Rahner's axiom this way: "In the economic self-communication, *the intra-trinitarian self-communication is present in the world in a new way*, namely, under the veil of historical words, signs, and actions, and ultimately in the figure of the man Jesus of Nazareth."[64]

Congar, Kasper, and Schoonenberg use Rahner's axiom to emphasize God's real involvement with the world, over and against a previous theology that wanted to protect God from all "real relationship" with finite reality. They boldly assert that there is something "new" for God because of God's involvement with history and humanity. They do not mean that God becomes something other than God; nor do they make God "dependent" on the world for identity or being. They do, however, take fully into account the *historicity*, the *economy*, of God's being as triune mystery. This seems to be Rahner's understanding as well. He writes, "God's self-communication consists precisely in the fact that God really arrives at man, really enters into man's situation, assumes it himself, and *thus* is what he [God] is."[65]

## THE MYSTERY OF SALVATION AS THE MYSTERY OF GOD

As a first step toward restoring the soteriological dimension to trinitarian theology, we might revise the schema of patristic Greek theology in light of Rahner's axiom. The relationship between economy and theology may be conceptualized as in a parabola (see model 1, which is in contrast to the static Latin model [model 2]):

---

62. Kasper, *God of Jesus Christ*, 275.

63. Ibid., 276. Schoonenberg writes, "In the salvation history before Christ the distinction between God and the Logos was already present. In the incarnation, however, this distinction became fully interpersonal, a distinction between the Father and the Son. In the same way the Spirit was already working before Christ but became the Paraclete only through Christ, being with and in Christ's church and hence in some personal relation to the Father and the Son" (in "Trinity, the Consummated Covenant," 112).

64. Kasper, *God of Jesus Christ*, 276.

65. Rahner, *The Trinity*, 88–89.

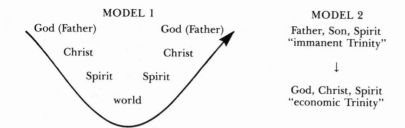

The parabolic model (*parabola*: to throw outward) expresses the one ecstatic movement of God whereby all things originate with God and are returned to God. The model admits neither a Neo-Palamite nor a Neo-Scholastic separation between "God" and "God-for-us." The subject matter of trinitarian theology is the one dynamic movement of God, *a Patre ad Patrem* (from the Father, to the Father), in the economy of incarnation and deification. There is no reason to single out one point as if it could be fixed or frozen in time. Christology is no more prominent than pneumatology; nor is the immanent Trinity conceived of as a reality separate from the economy of salvation. Rather, an immanent theology of God is a theology of the economy but from the point of view of its internal logic or its eternal ground.

The second model, in contrast, depicts the immanent Trinity as a distinct ontological reality, as a reified, timeless version of the economic Trinity, and as virtually identical with the essence of God. The subject matter of trinitarian doctrine in the second model is the "intradivine" relations, how God is related to God, apart from the economy of salvation. But the preceding pages have shown that by taking an epistemological distinction, whether in the Latin or Greek versions, and turning it into an ontological one, trinitarian theology loses its basis in salvation history. The only legitimate ontological distinction (and this must be carefully qualified) is between *theologia* and *oikonomia*, *not* between immanent and economic Trinity. This is the import of Rahner's axiom, as Kasper, Schoonenberg, and Congar suggest.

Theologies that speculate about God's self-relatedness without reference to the economy of salvation no longer are defensible.[66] Even if this approach has been taken by some of the most profound thinkers in the tradition, it is difficult to align with the Bible, early Christian creeds, and patterns of Christian prayer. Moreover, this trinitarian doctrine remains detached from the Christian life.

---

66. Rahner, *The Trinity*, 119, makes this criticism of Bernard Lonergan's *De Deo Trino* (Rome: Gregorian University Press, 1964).

Nor are theologies defensible that are agnostic about the eternal ground of God's self-communication in history. Rahner's axiom is useful if it conveys that God truly *is* what God has shown God's self to be. This should not be construed as impinging on the graciousness of divine freedom. God's freedom means fidelity to what God is, namely, self-communicating love.[67] God can be nothing other than what God is. If God comes to us through the economy of salvation, it is not out of constraint but because, as Dionysius the Areopagite or Bonaventure would have said, Goodness is self-diffusive, overflowing, fecund. If God's *ad intra* self-communication is expressed *ad extra* as well, this can only be the result of God's freedom.[68]

In sum, a trinitarian theology of God is ineluctably a theology of the economy. The existential reality that trinitarian doctrine articulates is that participation in the triune reality of God in history means participation in the eternal relationality of God. Everything that is literally exists in the permanent perichoresis between theology and economy. "I pray . . . that they may all be one, as you, Father, are in me and I in you, that they also may be in us" (John 17:21).

## ONGOING POINTS OF DISCUSSION

Doctrinal formulations help to clarify the "rules for correct speech about God," which is why the doctrine of the Trinity is sometimes called the "grammar" of theology.[69] At the same time, doctrinal formulations should serve the pastoral well-being of the church. To this end, a more contemporary and suitable interpretation may be given to the content of prior doctrinal assertions.

### MODERNIZING THE LANGUAGE OF "PERSON"

The affirmation that the one God exists (subsists) in three persons was a commonplace from the late fourth century on. Boethius (d. 524) formulated the classic Latin definition of person: "individual substance of a rational nature." Richard of St. Victor added that a person is what is "incommunicable" in a rational substance.

---

67. God's absolute fidelity is the religious way of expressing what philosophy calls divine immutability (unchangeability).

68. Contrary to libertarianism, which defines freedom as unlimited choices, the freedom of the person means conformity to self, to the deepest truth about oneself and to one's proper end (*telos*).

69. Kasper, *God of Jesus Christ*, 311, 304; George Lindbeck, *The Nature of Doctrine* (Philadelphia: Westminster Press, 1984).

Aquinas defined person as "subsistent relation." In antiquity, speaking of God as "three persons" was open to misunderstanding, and so it remains to this day. Since the Enlightenment "person" has been understood psychologically rather than ontologically, as "individual conscious subject." If God is three persons, God is three centers of consciousness, or three gods.[70]

Both Karl Barth and Karl Rahner suggested that if we are to use *person* in the plural, we must redefine what a person is. Barth proposed substituting "modes of existing," and Rahner, "distinct manners of subsisting."[71] Both phrases attempt to recapture some of the original meaning of *hypostasis*, especially the idea that each of the three persons is not just a different person but is a person in a different way. Both theologians presupposed that God is a single divine subject, possessing a single consciousness, who exists in three ways. Although these recommendations are theologically precise, they are unintelligible for nonspecialists and unsuitable for preaching.

Other contemporary theologians highlight the relational aspect of "person."[72] Contemporary object relations psychology[73] and relational philosophy[74] support this emphasis. According to these interpretations, "person" is more than "individual"; "person is relation." John Zizioulas, a contemporary Orthodox theologian, has restated Greek patristic theology in light of Heideggerian anthropology. Person is the "there" of being (*Dasein*). Because the ontological principle of God is the Father, "God 'exists' on account of a person . . . and not on account of a substance."[75] God's being is therefore inherently ecstatic and exists or is structured as a communion of persons. In Kasper's view, the trinitarian affirmation of God as personal implies that relation/love, not substance, is the highest ontological category.[76] Christian theology originally contributed the idea of per-

---

70. On the history of the term, see Kasper, *God of Jesus Christ*, 152–57, 285–91.

71. Karl Barth, *Church Dogmatics* (Edinburgh: T and T Clark, 1936), 1/1:412; Rahner, *The Trinity*, 106–15.

72. Kasper, *God of Jesus Christ*, 285–90, 153–57; Hill, *The Three-Personed God*, 255; Heribert Mühlen, *Der Heilige Geist als Person*.

73. John McDargh, *Psychoanalytic Object Relations Theory and the Study of Religion* (Lanham, Md.: University Press of America, 1983); D. W. Winnicott, *The Maturational Processes and the Facilitating Environment* (London: Hogarth Press, 1965); William R. D. Fairbairn, *Psychoanalytic Studies of the Personality* (London: Routledge and Kegan Paul, 1952).

74. See the classic works by John Macmurray, *Self as Agent* (New York: Harper and Brothers, 1957); idem, *Persons in Relation* (New York: Harper and Brothers, 1961); Martin Buber, *I and Thou* (Edinburgh: T and T Clark, 1937); Harold Oliver, *A Relational Metaphysic* (The Hague: Martinus Nijhoff, 1981).

75. John Zizioulas, *Being as Communion* (Crestwood, N.Y.: St. Vladimir's Seminary Press, 1985), 42.

76. Kasper, *God of Jesus Christ*, 310.

son to culture; trinitarian theology helps to emphasize the inherently relational aspects of person.

Even though the term *person* can be applied to God only analogically or apophatically, *person* indicates relationship, freedom, ineffability, mystery, the capacity to love and know, and the capacity to be loved and known. God is someone rather than something. Trinitarian doctrine is above all a theology of relationship and the affirmation that God's absolute mystery is carried out in absolute freedom; trinitarian doctrine is therefore inescapably a theology of personhood, regardless of how this is formulated. Without discarding the language of person, it is important not to make its content so abstract that we lose sight of the tripersonal God of the economy who comes to us as sovereign freedom, boundless love, and unfathomable mystery.

## BALANCING MASCULINE LANGUAGE FOR GOD

The metaphors of "Father" and "Son" trouble many feminist theologians. For some, trinitarian language promotes a social world based on hierarchy and inequality between men and women.[77] Mary Daly, for example, regards the personification of God as Father as the foremost symbol of patriarchy.[78]

The Father-Son analogy has been dominant in speculative theology. Well-attested in Scripture, especially in John's Gospel, and better than material analogies (sun-ray-light), the Father-Son analogy communicates that God is personal, and that God and Christ are equal: Just as human fathers and sons have the same human nature, the divine Father and Son have the same divine nature. Although maternal images for God and Christ are not unknown in antiquity, until recently the male was considered the active force in begetting new life; thus it was to be expected that the begetting of the Son be attributed to the Father. Any analogy, however, would have sufficed if it expressed relationship between persons of the same nature (e.g., Mother-Daughter, Father-Daughter, Mother-Son).

Few people seriously believe that God is male, yet most call God "he" and would resist calling God "she." Nor do most think that God the Father is male, even though this metaphor of paternity closely

---

77. See Rosemary Radford Ruether, *Sexism and God-Talk* (Boston: Beacon, 1983); Sallie McFague, *Metaphorical Theology: Models of God in Religious Language* (Philadelphia: Fortress Press, 1982); Naomi Goldenberg, *The Changing of the Gods* (Boston: Beacon, 1978). Exceptions would be Patricia Wilson-Kastner, *Faith, Feminism and the Christ* (Philadelphia: Fortress Press, 1983), chap. 6, and Gail Ramshaw-Schmidt, "Naming the Trinity: Orthodoxy and Inclusivity," *Worship* 60 (1986): 491–98.

78. Mary Daly, *Beyond God the Father* (Boston: Beacon, 1973), 13.

links God to what we know of nondivine fathers. Yet every statement we make about God must be negated; if we say that God is a father, we must acknowledge that God is unlike a father because God is neither male nor female.[79] Theological feminism is in part a critique of the propensity to literalize metaphors for God and to forget the dissimilarity in every analogy.

The meaning of God's fatherhood was at the heart of the Arian controversy. The tendency to understand fatherhood literally, and according to a biological analogy, threatened the proper use of this name of God. Sons always come after their fathers, and no son exists before his own generation; therefore, said the Arians, the Son must be less than God. Arius, it has been remarked, did not know a metaphor when he saw one.

It is impossible to say what God is or what God the Father is, except negatively. Gregory of Nazianzus ridiculed his opponents who thought that God was male because God is called Father, or that deity is feminine because of the gender of the word, or that the Spirit is neuter because it does not beget. Both philological and materialistic conceptions were ruled out: God's fatherhood, Gregory tells us in the same homily, has nothing to do with marriage, pregnancy, midwifery, or the danger of miscarriage.[80]

Some claim that because in the New Testament Jesus addressed God as Father, God *is* a Father and must be called "Father" or "he." These same persons claim that if God had wanted to reveal "himself" as a Mother, God could have done so. This interpretation has scant exegetical warrant. Without doubt, Jesus called God *Abba*,[81] although dogmatic positions based on this often are exaggerated.[82] By addressing God as *Abba*/Father we are using a term of intimacy that was a characteristic feature of Jesus' own prayer. The import of the two liturgical texts in which the word occurs (Rom. 8:15; Gal.

79. For a view from the Orthodox perspective, see Deborah Belonick, "Revelation and Metaphors: The Significance of the Trinitarian Names, Father, Son and Holy Spirit," *Union Seminary Quarterly Review* 40 (1985): 31–42.

80. Gregory of Nazianzus *Orat.* 31.8 (PG 36, 142).

81. See the classic studies by Joachim Jeremias, *New Testament Theology* (New York: Scribner's, 1971), and *The Prayers of Jesus* (London: SCM, 1967). See also Robert Hamerton-Kelly, *God the Father: Theology and Patriarchy in the Teaching of Jesus* (Philadelphia: Fortress Press, 1979); Edward Schillebeeckx, *Jesus* (New York: Crossroad, 1979), 256–71; Witold Marchel, *Dieu, Père, dans le Nouveau Testament* (Paris: Éditions du Cerf, 1965); idem, *Abba, Père, la prière du Christ et des chrétiens* (Rome: Institut Biblique Pontifical, 1963); H. W. Montefiore, "God as Father in the Synoptic Gospels," *New Testament Studies* 3 (1956–57): 31–46; James D. G. Dunn, *Christology in the Making* (Philadelphia: Westminster Press, 1980); Johannes B. Metz and Edward Schillebeeckx, eds., *God as Father* (entire issue of *Concilium* 143 [1981]).

82. James Barr, "Abba Isn't 'Daddy'," *Journal of Theological Studies* 39 (1988): 28–47.

4:6) pertains to the order of the economy of salvation: Through the Spirit we are given access to the one whom Jesus called *Abba*.[83]

Others refuse to address God as Father because they find this symbol corrupted by patriarchy. Some feminist scholars regard unitarianism as the only viable alternative to traditional trinitarian doctrine. Nonetheless, "to refuse ever to use Father as a personal name for God concedes that God the Father is male as patriarchy has defined it. It also duplicates the unitarianism of the Arians. Patriarchy is a unitarian monotheism, as opposed to a trinitarian monotheism where the centerpiece is God's kenotic self-revelation in Christ."[84] If nothing else, the doctrine of the Trinity declares that God is eminently God-for-us, whereas the unitarian God is for "himself" alone. One can affirm the doctrine of the Trinity, and also use the metaphors of Father and Son, without consenting that God is male.

In many worship services today, one hears "Creator, Redeemer, Sustainer" as a substitute for "Father, Son, Holy Spirit." While many forms of public prayer are possible and desirable, and while every effort must be made to avoid language that excludes or hurts, the Creator-Redeemer-Sustainer triad may not be as advantageous as it first appears. According to Scripture, God creates *through* the Son (Col. 1:16; Heb. 11:3; John 1:1-3) and *by* the Spirit (Gen. 1:1-2); God redeems *through* Christ (2 Cor. 5:19; Eph. 1:7; Col. 1:14).[85] Functional language (creator) is not necessarily economic (God creates through Christ). And functional language, following the Augustinian model, "appropriates" certain activities to the persons, which reinforces thinking of the divine persons as discrete individuals.

Moreover, distinguishing persons only by their function with respect to us shies away from the central claim of trinitarian doctrine— that God *as God* is triune mystery. The problem with functional language is not that it is not metaphysical; the problem is that it can destroy the essential connection between *theologia* and *oikonomia*. As Rahner puts it, the distinctions among God, Christ, and

---

83. "Holy Father, keep them in your name that you have given me, so that they may be one just as we are one" (John 17:11).

84. Catherine M. LaCugna, "The Baptismal Formula, Feminist Objections and Trinitarian Theology," *Journal of Ecumenical Studies* 26 (1989): 243. See also Moltmann, *The Trinity and the Kingdom*; idem, "The Motherly Father: Is Trinitarian Patripassianism Replacing Theological Patriarchalism?" in Metz and Schillebeeckx, eds., *God as Father*, 51–56, esp. 53.

85. While it is true that the Bible sometimes "appropriates" certain functions to one of the divine persons (e.g., Christ is called Savior [Acts 5:31] and the Spirit is called Counselor and Teacher [John 14:26]), more often than not a variety of actions is mentioned in connection with each name (sometimes Christ is called Savior, at other times God is called Savior [Luke 1:47; John 4:42; Acts 5:31; 1 John 4:14]).

Spirit must belong to God as God, otherwise the reality of God's *self*-communication is jeopardized.[86]

Recently some writers have stressed the "feminine" characteristics of the Holy Spirit as a way to counterbalance masculine pronouns for Father and Son.[87] But feminine imagery for God in the Bible or in some mystical writers does not establish that God has "feminine aspects" any more than masculine imagery establishes that God has "masculine aspects." In addition, this type of interpretation tends to incorporate sex-stereotypes (women are compassionate, men are strong) and to suggest that God is primarily masculine but with a feminine side.

Further, feminine imagery for God or for the Holy Spirit can be taken as literally as masculine imagery. Calling only the Holy Spirit "she" may hide the deeper truth that each divine person is as much "he" as "she," which is to say, not at all. A sufficiently apophatic use of feminine as well as masculine imagery can free the imagination of the Christian community. There is ample precedent to explore many different relational trinitarian analogies.[88] An interesting precedent has already been provided by the Eleventh Council of Toledo in 675, which stated that the Son was begotten *"de utero Patris* [from the womb of the Father], that is, from the substance of the Father."

In sum, trinitarian theology need not be looked upon as inherently sexist and patriarchal. Indeed, trinitarian doctrine articulates a vision of God in which there is neither hierarchy nor inequality, only relationships based on love, mutuality, self-giving and self-receiving,

---

86. This does not vitiate the earlier defense of God's incomprehensible essence nor the reluctance to make the economic-immanent distinction an ontological one. Rahner's point, with which I fully agree, is that God's way of being God is to be "self-communicating," a synonym for "trinitarian." The trinitarian self-communication of God must be what God really is as God. But what God is "apart from" that self-communication ("apart from" means, what God is as God, which explains why God's nature is to be self-communicating) must remain unsaid.

87. Robert Murray discusses the evidence in Syriac literature in *Symbols of Church and Kingdom* (London: Cambridge University Press, 1975), 312–20; see also Peter A. H. DeBoer, *Fatherhood and Motherhood in Israelite and Judean Piety* (Leiden: Brill, 1974); more recently, Congar, *I Believe,* 3:155–64; Donald Gelpi, *The Divine Mother: A Trinitarian Theology of the Holy Spirit* (Lanham, Md.: University Press of America, 1984).

88. In addition to works already cited, see Rebecca Oxford-Carpenter, "Gender and the Trinity," *Theology Today* 41 (1984): 7–25; Mary Collins, "Naming God in Public Prayer," *Worship* 59 (1985): 291–304; Letty Russell, "Inclusive Language and Power," *Religious Education* 80 (1985): 582–602; Barbara Brown Zikmund, "The Trinity and Women's Experience," *The Christian Century* (April 1987): 354–56; Gracia Grindal, "Reflections on God 'the Father,'" *Word and World* 4 (1984): 78–86; Geoffrey Lilburne, "Christology: In Dialogue with Feminism," *Horizons* 11 (1984): 7–27; Gail Ramshaw-Schmidt, *"De divinis nominibus*: The Gender of God," *Worship* 56 (1982): 117–31.

freedom, and communion. These values are the leitmotif of theological feminism. The Christian community is the image or icon of the triune God when the pattern of its relationships imitates what God is. In sharp contrast to the unitarian God who is the first choice of some Christian feminists, the God who exists as an eternal communion (*koinonia*) of love is a surer foundation for authentic *koinonia* of the body of Christ in which "there is neither Jew nor Gentile, slave nor free, male nor female" (Gal. 3:28; Col. 3:11).

## TOWARD ECUMENICAL AGREEMENT
## ON THE *FILIOQUE* CLAUSE IN THE CREED

One of the most sensitive issues still separating East and West from ecumenical unity is the *filioque*: "The Holy Spirit proceeds from the Father *and from the Son*."[89] According to the East, the Holy Spirit proceeds from the Father (through the Son).[90]

At first this may seem to be nothing more than a quibble over language. But because it touches directly on how we understand the person and work of the Holy Spirit in the economy of salvation, the *filioque* has a bearing on every aspect of Christian life.[91] The Spirit is the one who makes us a new creation (John 3:5), giving us through

---

89. Most people in the West do not realize that this one word in the Western interpolated version of the Niceno-Constantinopolitan Creed arouses deep feelings of animosity on the part of the Orthodox. One reason is the different importance East and West attach to reciting creeds. In the West, the Niceno-Constantinopolitan Creed is regarded primarily as a doctrinal statement, even in the setting of liturgy, whereas the Orthodox venerate creeds as having almost the same status as the Scriptures.

The *filioque* clause was introduced into the Western creed in Spain to counter various heresies that denied the full divinity of Christ (Arianism, Adoptionism, Priscillianism). Its advocates considered it to be a local adaptation to a specific need, not a change in doctrine. From Spain the *filioque* spread to Gaul, where it was included in the Preface of the Mass before being introduced into the creed itself. The Roman church resisted its inclusion longer than other Western churches. Pope Leo III, in response to a delegation from the court of Charlemagne in 810, refused to sanction the interpolation even though he approved the singing of the creed during the Mass. The inclusion of the *filioque* was allowed in Rome around 1014 and was officially declared licit by the Council of Florence in 1439 (see Kelly, *Early Christian Creeds*, 338–67).

90. The body of literature on the *filioque* seems endless. An excellent starting point is Vischer, ed., *Spirit of God, Spirit of Christ*. The text includes the memorandum drawn up by Eastern and Western theologians in 1979, as well as several readable essays by theologians from Orthodox, Catholic, and Protestant traditions.

91. Yves Congar quotes Vladimir Lossky as claiming that because of the *filioque*, in the Western church "the people of God are subjected to the body of Christ, the charism is made subordinate to the institution, inner freedom to imposed authority, prophetism to juridicism, mysticism to Scholasticism, the laity to the clergy, the universal priesthood to the ministerial hierarchy, and finally the college of bishops to the primacy of the Pope" (in Congar, *I Believe*, 3:208). Lossky's statement may be exaggerated but it helps to show that the *filioque* or other formulations have a direct bearing on ecclesiology.

Christ access to the Father (Eph. 2:15; Gal. 4:6; Rom. 8:15). Life in the Spirit is life in Christ; thus there must be full reciprocity between christology and pneumatology within a trinitarian perspective.[92]

Studying the *filioque* is one point of entry into pneumatology. The doctrine of the Spirit is particularly pertinent today, given the vitality of the charismatic movement, epidemic fundamentalism, and the flourishing interest in spirituality, mysticism, and world religions. These questions are beyond the scope of the present essay; only the main elements of the *filioque* controversy can be presented here.

Eastern and Western theology view the procession of the Holy Spirit differently because of the fundamental incompatibility of their trinitarian frameworks.[93] According to Eastern theology, because of the monarchy of the Father, the hypostasis of the Father is the cause (*aitia*) of the Spirit. According to Western theology, the cause (*principium*) of the Spirit is the essence of God. The West appears to the East to be positing *two* sources of divinity.

At the Council of Lyons (1274) and the Council of Florence (1439), the West tried, unsuccessfully, to impose the *filioque* on the East. The offense of this remains to this day. Some Orthodox insist that the West renounce the *filioque* as an error before there can be any restoration of *koinonia*. Yves Congar has suggested that as a gesture of humility the West omit from the creed the clause that it unilaterally inserted.[94] The Faith and Order Commission that studied this question recommended that the creed be restored to its ancient form, without the *filioque* clause, so that East and West may confess a common faith. The following formulations, many of them rooted in early patristic sources, have been suggested as meeting ecumenical concerns while maintaining the integrity of both traditions:

- The Spirit proceeds from the Father of the Son.
- The Spirit proceeds from the Father through the Son.
- The Spirit proceeds from the Father and receives from the Son.
- The Spirit proceeds from the Father and rests on the Son.
- The Spirit proceeds from the Father and shines out through the Son.[95]

---

92. See Catherine M. LaCugna and Kilian McDonnell, "Returning from 'The Far Country': Theses for a Contemporary Trinitarian Theology," *Scottish Journal of Theology* 41 (1988): 191–215.

93. In his classic work from the 1890s, Théodore de Régnon wrote that "we ought to regard the Greek and the Latin churches as two sisters who love and visit each other, but who have a different way of keeping house and who therefore live apart" (*Études*, 3:412).

94. Congar, *I Believe*, 3:214.

95. "The Filioque Clause in Ecumenical Perspective," p. 16 of the final memorandum of the Faith and Order Commission.

Any new formulation must attend to the proper relationship between theology and economy, taking care not to exaggerate or collapse the essence-energies or immanent-economic distinctions. Every theology of the procession of the Spirit must be anchored in the economy of salvation.[96] While it is by no means illegitimate to speculate on the eternal ground of some aspect of the Spirit's mission in the economy, we must be scrupulous not to confuse the reality of God with our meager efforts at understanding. As Gregory of Nazianzus wrote,

> What then is Procession? Do you tell me what is the Unbegottenness of the Father, and I will explain to you the physiology of the Generation of the Son and the Procession of the Spirit, and we shall both be frenzy-stricken for prying into the mystery of God.[97]

## LIVING TRINITARIAN FAITH

The development of trinitarian doctrine has been explained as the effort to bring together the mystery of God and the mystery of salvation. It remains to indicate briefly some of the ways in which trinitarian theology is related to the praise and worship of God, ethical transformation in Christ, and Christian spirituality.

### WORSHIPING THE GOD OF JESUS CHRIST

The glorification of God is the goal of creation and the fulfillment of humankind (Eph. 1:12; 2 Cor. 3:18). Economy and theology, economic and immanent Trinity, essence and energies, belong together in doxology. Doxology is the praise of God, the appreciation of God as God apart from the benefits of God. In praising God we make no distinction between who God is as God, and who God is for us; we

> turn and open ourselves to the God who is none other than He has revealed himself in his Word. This calling upon [God's] name is the essential expression of doxology, that is, of trust, praise and thanks that the living God from eternity to eternity was, is and will be none other ("immanent Trinity") than He has shown himself to be in history ("economic Trinity").[98]

---

96. Congar points out that if every detail of the incarnation "were transposed into the eternity of the Logos, it would be necessary to say that the Son proceeds from the Father and the Holy Spirit—*a Patre spirituque*" (*I Believe*, 3:16).

97. Gregory of Nazianzus *Orat.* 31.8 (PG 36, 142).

98. "The Filioque Clause in Ecumenical Perspective," 10. Only within the doxological context does the phrase "inner life of God" make sense.

Walter Kasper points out that the intention of the trinitarian confession of faith is "not really a teaching about God but the doxology or eschatological glorification of God."[99] The opening prayer of the Roman eucharistic rite ("May the grace of our Lord Jesus Christ, the love of God, and the communion of the Holy Spirit be with you all" [2 Cor. 13:13]) is a confession of faith in the God of Jesus Christ and signals our entry into the very life of God. Through prayer we are united to God's triune mystery and to all believers throughout time, as we place ourselves into the whole history of redemption, particularly its eschatological movement of return to God.

Baptism into the name of God, Father, Son, and Spirit, is the first of two central symbols of living trinitarian faith.[100] Baptism is the outward sign of our common vocation to holiness and friendship with God, as well as a sign that we belong to a community and a tradition. Previous patterns of relationship are reordered when we "put on Christ" (Gal. 3:27). Alienating patterns of relationship (Jew-Greek, slave-free, male-female [see Gal. 3:28]) are overcome; unity in Christ transcends the dictates of culture, ignorance, and prejudice. To undertake baptism means submitting to the transforming and deifying work of the Spirit who perfects us in the image of God.

The eucharist is the second central symbol of new life through Christ. In the eucharistic prayer we give thanks to God for what God has done in the history of salvation, especially in Christ. Christ offers our prayer to God (the Father); we invoke the Spirit upon the gifts and upon the community (epiclesis) so that a new basis for community is forged. The eucharistic prayer ends with the great trinitarian doxology, the *Per Ipsum*: "Through him and with him and in him, in the unity of the Holy Spirit, all glory and honor is yours, almighty Father, forever and ever. Amen." The eucharistic celebration concludes with the missionary charge to "go in peace to love and serve...." Trinitarian faith is incomplete until what is confessed in faith is enacted in life.

In addition to sacraments of initiation, the rhythm of the entire liturgical year is occupied with remembering and commemorating the activity of God in redemptive history. Beginning with Advent and culminating with Easter and the giving of the Spirit at Pentecost, Christians "relive" these events of salvation and commit themselves to living what they mean.

Through public worship we walk along the "path of glory." However, the praise of God extends beyond the assembly, beyond

---

99. Kasper, *God of Jesus Christ*, 304.
100. See LaCugna, "The Baptismal Formula."

prepared formulas of prayer. Whole lives, including "all forms of thought, feeling, action and hope directed and offered by believers to the living God," can praise God.[101] Through Word and sacrament we celebrate the mystery of God among us; through lives of loving service we show what it means to "live for the praise of God's glory" (Eph. 1:11).

## BEING TRANSFORMED IN CHRIST

Humanity is created in the image of God, and God exists as the communion of love, as a reciprocal exchange of love and persons in which humanity has graciously been included as a partner. Christ is the image of the invisible God, reflecting the glory of God (Col. 1:15; cf. 2 Cor. 4:4; Heb. 1:3). Followers of Christ are exhorted to be icons of Christ, even sharing in his suffering, and thereby glorified (1 Cor. 15:49; Col. 3:10; Rom. 8:29; 2 Cor. 3:18). When we are Christ to each other, the kingdom of God is made present for the sake of the transformation of the world.

The Council of Chalcedon (451) affirmed that Christ is complete in divinity and complete in humanity. The *person* of Christ is divine; his way of "subsisting" (hypostasis) is the same as God's mode of subsistence. This means that the "being-there" of Christ is the "being-there" of God. For Christians, Christ is the fulfillment of the covenant promise of God "to be there with you as Who I Am." The divinity of Christ lies in his perfect humanity, which is why he can be seen as the perfect fulfillment of our own humanity.

The person of Jesus Christ—how he is in relationship with others—is the criterion of what we are to become. In Christ, divine love is shown to be inclusive, healing and uniting, and on the side of the poor. The power and presence of God in Christ are neither coercive nor divisive nor under the control of the privileged. Christ's life is characterized by perfect self-giving, even amid rejection, jealousy, and all other forces that conspire against infinite love. The cross is the central symbol of Christianity because it expresses, by way of a seeming contradiction, that the "heart" or essence of God, that which makes God to be God, is love that triumphs over nonbeing.

## LIFE IN THE SPIRIT

Life in the Spirit is life in Christ. The life of God is bestowed on us as love, grace, and communion, as Paul's closing benediction

---

101. "The Filioque Clause in Ecumenical Perspective," 10.

(2 Cor. 13:13) declares. Eastern theology, from the patristic period to the present, has described salvation as "deification" (*theosis*). Deification means participating in the very life of God,[102] being made like Christ ("ingodded" or "christified"), for through Christ we are made sharers in the divine nature (2 Peter 1:4).

Cyril of Alexandria coined the oft-cited phrase, "We become by grace what God is by nature."[103] Our "personhood" is to become what God's personal reality already is: boundless self-giving, love poured out for the sake of life, and that which creates inclusive communion among persons. The "deified" human being is the totally free human being, one who can embrace the enemy and help bring about the kingdom of God.

In Western spirituality the "contemplative" and "active" are often played off against each other, with the higher regard going to the contemplative. In a trinitarian spirituality this dualism passes away. To participate in the economy of history *is* to participate in the eternal mystery of God. Likewise, contemplating the eternal mystery of God means contemplating the God whose life is carried forth into the history of the world. A trinitarian spirituality leaves no place for a self-preoccupied concern to "develop one's spiritual life." Life in the Spirit of God is communitarian, ecstatic, and eccentric (de-centering).

Union with God (deification) is therefore union with the life of God in the economy. It is at once mystical and active. In a trinitarian spirituality neither a pneumatological nor a christological focus may overtake the other. Christ and the Spirit are the two foci of Christian life. The economy of the Spirit (deification) and the economy of the Son (incarnation) comprise the one divine economy,

> for God has made known to us in all wisdom and insight the mystery of the divine will, according to the purpose which God set forth in Christ as a plan for the fullness of time, to unite all things in Christ, things in heaven and things on earth.... In Christ you also, who have heard the word of truth, the gospel of your salvation, and have believed in Christ, were sealed with the promised Holy Spirit, which is the guarantee of our inheritance until we acquire possession of it, to the praise of God's glory [Eph. 1:9, 13-14].

---

102. Participation is in the divine energies, not the essence. As was explained above in the discussion of Palamism, the purpose of the distinction is to avoid pantheism (God = world) while affirming that we truly share in what God is.

103. Cyril of Alexandria *De Trin. Dial.* (PG 4, 520c).

# CONCLUSION

This essay has reaffirmed what Christianity has regarded as the center of its faith. The doctrine of the Trinity expresses, often with the aid of the specialized language of ontology, that God who redeems us through Christ in the Spirit is from all eternity self-communicating and creative love. Baptism initiates us into the life of God so that we may be transformed by grace and perfected in the image of God. The Spirit gathers the baptized into the body of Christ, bringing about union with God and new relationship with each other. The doctrine of the Trinity is the specifically Christian way to explicate the meaning of participation in the life of the triune God. As such, this doctrine is intrinsically linked to liturgical and confessional expressions of faith.

# FOR FURTHER READING

Congar, Yves. *I Believe in the Holy Spirit.* 3 vols. New York: Seabury, 1983.

A masterful synthesis of Greek and Latin theology and history, ecumenically oriented, with an emphasis on pneumatology.

Hill, William. *The Three-Personed God.* Washington, D.C.: University Press of America, 1983.

A modern restatement of Thomas Aquinas's trinitarian theology.

Jüngel, Eberhard. *God as the Mystery of the World.* Grand Rapids, Mich.: Eerdmans, 1983.

A philosophical and theological trinitarian theology based on the centrality of the cross and the hermeneutics of word-as-event.

Kasper, Walter. *The God of Jesus Christ.* New York: Crossroad, 1984.

A magisterial summary of classical and contemporary trinitarian theology (with emphasis on the Latin tradition) developed against the backdrop of contemporary atheism.

Kelly, J. N. D. *Early Christian Creeds.* 3d ed. New York: Longman, 1972.

A fascinating study of the historical development of Christian creeds.

Kelly, J. N. D. *Early Christian Doctrines.* 2d ed. New York: Harper and Row, 1960.

An overview of the development of doctrine during the first five centuries of Christianity.

Lossky, Vladimir. *The Mystical Theology of the Eastern Church.* 2d ed. Crestwood, N.Y.: St. Vladimir's Seminary Press, 1976. Idem. *Orthodox Theology: An Introduction.* Crestwood, N.Y.: St. Vladimir's Seminary Press, 1978.

Two works that introduce and survey Eastern Orthodox theology.

Moltmann, Jürgen. *The Trinity and the Kingdom.* New York: Harper and Row, 1981.

A theology of the Trinity centered on the cross as a divine event.

Murray, John Courtney. *The Problem of God.* New Haven: Yale University Press, 1964.

An excellent introduction and a classic in Catholic theology.

Prestige, George Leonard. *God in Patristic Thought.* 2d ed. London: SPCK, 1952.

A study of the early development of patristic terminology.

Rahner, Karl. *The Trinity.* New York: Herder and Herder, 1970.

A pivotal work that set the agenda for most contemporary trinitarian theologies.

Richardson, Cyril. *The Doctrine of the Trinity.* Nashville: Abingdon, 1958.

A critical study by a respected Protestant patristic scholar who points out the division between the doctrine of the Trinity and the life of most Christians.

Rusch, William, ed. *The Trinitarian Controversy.* Philadelphia: Fortress Press, 1980.

A collection of key texts representing the debate over the doctrine of the Trinity.

Schoonenberg, Piet. "Spirit Christology and Logos Christology." *Bijdragen* 38 (1977): 350–75. Idem. "Trinity, the Consummated Covenant: Theses on the Doctrine of the Trinitarian God." *Studies in Religion* 5 (1975–76): 111–16.

Two articles proposing a creative reinterpretation of the traditional Christian understanding of the relationship of God, Christ, and Spirit.

Wainwright, Arthur. *The Trinity in the New Testament*. London: SPCK, 1962.

A study of monotheistic, binitarian, and trinitarian formulas found in the New Testament; treats the sources, context, and meaning of those formulas.

Ware, Kallistos. *The Orthodox Way*. Crestwood, N.Y.: St. Vladimir's Seminary Press, 1981.

An introduction to basic themes in Eastern theology.

Welch, Claude. *In This Name: The Doctrine of the Trinity in Contemporary Theology*. New York: Scribner's, 1952.

A summary of Protestant trinitarian theology.

# 4

---

# CREATION

---

# 4

## CREATION

### Anne M. Clifford

The doctrine of creation expresses the belief that God is the origin, ground, and goal of the world and of everything in it. Creation is a fundamental belief from which flows much of what Christians profess about God, about the cosmos we inhabit, and about our destiny and hope. The doctrine of creation is shaped by presuppositions about God—fundamental beliefs that are difficult to conceptualize, and yet make a profound difference in how Christians view the world. In turn, creation is presupposed in revelation, the primary source for what Christians profess to believe about God. This is succinctly expressed in the Book of the Wisdom of Solomon: "For from the greatness and beauty of created things comes a corresponding per-

ception of their Creator" (Wisd. of Sol. 13:5). For the Christian,
creation itself is the self-revelation of God.

In biblical revelation the very first line introduces the theme of
creation: "In the beginning God created the heavens and earth"
(Gen. 1:1). The creation theme recurs again and again in the prophetic and wisdom literature, in the Pauline epistles, and in the
Gospels. Finally, in the Bible's last book we find a hymn in praise
of the creator:

> You are worthy, our Lord and God,
> to receive glory and honor and power,
> for you created all things,
> and by your will they existed and were created [Rev. 4:11].

The belief in the God who created all things, celebrated in this
hymn, is expressed in the first article of the Nicene Creed, as revelation continued to unfold as the tradition of the church developed.
The first lines of the creed are at once a prayer of praise and a confession of one of the church's core beliefs: that God is "maker of
heaven and earth, of all that is seen and unseen." Although there
was no early doctrine of creation as such, this articulation of the
Christian belief that the God of Jesus is creator is part of a long
process of the church's struggle to make its faith intelligible.

To understand Christian creation faith requires that we address
it with an eye on a diversity of questions that have emerged in a long
and complex history. The one most immediate to us is the question of
the relation of science and religion in an advanced scientific and technological culture. This question finds itself expressed in two major
forms: the challenge of evolutionary science to religious faith and the
concern for ecology. Evolution and ecology are obviously intercon-
nected. Ecology both learns from the study of biological evolution
and in turn contributes much to it. Evolution and, to a lesser extent, ecology will provide us with lenses for surveying major recent
developments in theologies that address creation.

A presentation of the theology of creation requires a survey of
historical developments with some attention to their social context
and to their underlying philosophical assumptions. This task can be
executed only in a limited fashion in this essay. I will begin by presenting some of the major currents of interpretation of the biblical
sources on creation; then I will survey major Roman Catholic theological and church traditions; and finally I will give some highlights
from contemporary theological discussion.

# THE BIBLE ON CREATION

The Bible contains passages that focus on creation and numerous verses that touch on it in the context of other topics. Given the diversity of these texts, it is not possible to speak about a theology of creation in the Bible. It is more appropriate to speak of a biblical creation faith than a systematic biblical theology as such. In a sense, biblical creation faith is a broad canvas against which can be seen God's dealings with humanity. Biblical creation faith, which is presented in stories and statements about faith in creation, has significantly influenced the creation doctrine of the Christian tradition and continues to be addressed by theologians today. Therefore it is deserving of a careful treatment. Due to the limitations of this essay, I will focus my presentation of the Old Testament only on the Genesis texts, on Deutero-Isaiah, and on carefully selected passages from wisdom literature. The New Testament creation material will include examples drawn from Pauline literature, the Synoptic Gospels, and John.

## THE OLD TESTAMENT

Although the Bible opens with the story of the world's creation, it has been treated as a topic of secondary importance until recent years. This was due largely to Gerhard von Rad's highly influential essay (1936) in which he forcefully argued that the Old Testament has no "independent" theology of creation, that creation is subordinate to human redemption in biblical thought.[1] In von Rad's interpretation the history of human salvation (*Heilsgeschichte*) is the most important hermeneutical category for interpreting biblical faith.[2]

Many scholars today criticize this position because their reading of the data leads them to conclude that creation of the world was very much a part of ancient Israel's concerns. Claus Westermann has argued that creation should not be entirely subsumed under soteriology.[3] In his judgment the Old Testament has something of its very own to say about the creator and creation. This must be left

---

1. Gerhard von Rad, "The Theological Problem of the Old Testament Doctrine of Creation," in *The Problem of the Hexateuch and Other Essays* (New York: McGraw-Hill, 1966), 131–43. Later von Rad qualified his views, but not before his statement influenced many scholars.

2. Richard J. Clifford ("The Hebrew Scriptures and the Theology of Creation," *Theological Studies* 46 [1985]: 507n) notes that von Rad likely took this position to counter the National Socialist manipulation of the doctrine of creation.

3. Claus Westermann, *Creation*, trans. John J. Scullion (Philadelphia: Fortress Press, 1974), 175.

intact and must not be presented merely in its relationship to salvation history. Otherwise we will not perceive accurately what is being said about the activity of God.

The wide acceptance of von Rad's position by a generation of scholars may be due in large part to the hermeneutical presuppositions of his day. The glaring disparity of the cosmogony of the Genesis accounts and the positivistic scientific world view of the early decades of this century militated against a theology that places creation faith in the foreground. In contrast, the scholars of Westermann's generation no longer subscribe to these presuppositions. Westermann finds no disparity between the scientific and biblical explanations of the origins of the world.[4] He advocates another hermeneutical approach. He views the creation texts, especially those found in Genesis, as a relatively self-contained expression of faith that can be best understood through an analysis of their relationship to the myths of the ancient Near East.

The Genesis creation texts were not composed to answer the scientific question of how the world came to be. On the contrary, they proclaim the relationship of God to reality, a relation of creator to creation. The people for whom these texts were written did not base their views of the universe on the critical use of empirical data. Rather their thinking was imaginative and their expressions of thought concrete, pictorial, and poetic. Furthermore, Genesis was not intended to give a final, single answer to the question of how God created the earth. In fact, in Genesis a number of different presentations of the matter can be found. There is good reason to conclude that each age of ancient Israel's faith reflection expressed its understanding of creation in a way intelligible to itself. This point is illustrated in the initial chapters of Genesis, which present two distinct narratives on creation written in different centuries, and in the other creation texts found in the Old Testament.

Since the Bible begins with the two accounts of creation, they will be our starting point. Literary-critical study of the Bible in the late nineteenth century resulted in a distinction being made between the two creation accounts in the initial chapters of Genesis. Among biblical scholars there is universal agreement that the creation narratives beginning in Genesis 1:1 and in Genesis 2:4b are examples of the Priestly (P, sixth–fifth centuries B.C.) and Yahwist (J, tenth–ninth centuries B.C.) traditions, respectively. Each account has a long prehistory; the writers of these accounts received a tradition and shaped what they received into a new form. Each narrative is a

---

4. Ibid., 78.

product of a different period in Israelite history, a period that expressed its belief in God in a manner that reflects its own concerns and needs. Therefore, each addresses issues that are peculiar to its own situation.

A cursory look at Genesis 1 in its historical context will make it clear that it is written as a vigorous protest against the then accepted notions of creation. The historical context of the Priestly account of creation is the Babylonian exile in the sixth century B.C. The exile was a devastating experience for Israel politically and theologically. Those who survived the trauma reasserted their belief in God's power over chaos. They did this by developing their own creation narrative. This narrative was influenced by the Babylonian epic poem *Enuma Elish* and possibly by earlier motifs from Egyptian accounts of creation.

Parallels in the progression of events in *Enuma Elish* and in Genesis 1 led scholars to conclude that the former is an important part of the prehistory of Genesis 1. The general succession of events in both accounts is this: chaos at the beginning, then creation of the firmament, of dry land, of the heavenly bodies, and of people. The Babylonian creation myth was reshaped by the authors of the Priestly account in such a way as to portray the God of Israel establishing an orderly cosmos out of chaos for the elect people of Israel. The rekindling of confidence in this God, rather than the reporting of the history of primordial times, seems to be the major intent of the narrative.

Aside from the overarching structural parallels, there are differences worthy of note. In *Enuma Elish* creation unfolds through conflict between the deities.[5] The conflict between Marduk and Tiamat gives rise to the world out of the slain Tiamat, whose body is severed. It is only because of Marduk's struggle with Tiamat that heaven and earth are created.[6] In contrast to the Babylonian myth, Genesis 1 shows no conflict. In Genesis 1 creation takes place simply through God's word. It is through God's word that a good and orderly world is created.[7]

---

5. For the text of this epic poem see Alexander Heidel, *The Babylonian Genesis: The Story of Creation* (Chicago: University of Chicago Press, 1951), 18–60.

6. Ibid., 42–43.

7. Ibid., 45. Westermann notes that the depiction of the creation of man and woman through God's word in Gen. 1:26-31 is the exception. The passage is set off from what has gone on before with a new introduction: "Let us make humankind..." In most passages that deal with the subject, the creation of human beings does not appear as creation through the word. This peculiarity is likely due to the history of this tradition; the narration of the creation of the human was once independent and

The motif of creation through God's word has theological importance in this text. Westermann points out that the power of God's word is characteristic of the Priestly tradition as a whole. The purpose of the Priestly tradition is misunderstood if one has a general and abstract notion of God's word. Creation through the word as such is not the point. The purpose of the text is to arrange God's work of creation into a network of sentences whose succession follows the pattern of the fulfillment of a command given by God. The word of command has a special significance that colors the whole of Priestly theology. Everything that happens has its source in God's word of command. The only difference between God's action in history and God's action in creation is that in the one case God's command is directed to a person (Abraham) or mediator (Moses) while in the other it is without an addressee, and hence is a creation command.[8]

Another difference between the Priestly view of creation and that of Israel's neighbors has to do with the creation of the heavens. Given the cosmologies of Israel's neighbors, which envisioned the astral realm as inhabited by a multiplicity of deities, it is significant that Israel envisions the heavens as created through God's command. The emphasis on the creatureliness of the heavenly bodies serves to exalt Israel's God as creator.

The fulfillment of God's command is celebrated in Israel's own cultic form. The narrative with its six days of activity culminating in a day of rest moves in successive stages of creation to Sabbath celebration. This movement points to the continuation of a process as it moves toward a goal that transcends the works of creation. The purpose of the creation story is to praise God. The text is a narrative about world creation expressed as doxology.

In *Enuma Elish* the liturgical elements are also clear, particularly when it comes to the creation of humans. In the Babylonian myth the purpose of human creation is the service of the gods. In contrast, Genesis 1:26-31 views humans, male and female, as made in God's image.[9] Humans are the crowning species with a dual relationship, a

---

only later became part of the story of the creation of the world. See Westermann, *Creation*, 45.

8. Claus Westermann, *Genesis 1–11: A Commentary*, trans. John J. Scullion, 2d ed. (Minneapolis: Augsburg Publishing House, 1984), 85. Besides Genesis 1, passages that speak of creation through the word are found in Pss. 33:6, 9; 147:15; 148:5; as well as Isa. 48:13.

9. Dianne Bergant points out that it appears that Israel, like its neighbors, understood image/likeness in relational terms. The primary significance of this notion was divine relationship, not the possession of a divine element. See Dianne Bergant and Carroll Stuhlmueller, "Creation according to the Old Testament," in Ernan McMullin,

relationship to God and to their earthly coinhabitants. As creatures who image God, humans have a special purpose within the plan of creation. They are to act as God's representatives and are charged by God with dominion over the other orders of animals with whom humans share the same habitat.[10]

This survey of some major elements in the Priestly creation narrative clearly demonstrates that the author of Genesis 1 was unaware of any opposition between a scientific and a theological explanation of the origin of the world and of humanity. One might argue that the Priestly account demythologizes the traditions it received by stripping the heavens and the earth of their divine character and, in a sense, by thus making them accessible to human research. While not being a work of science itself, it certainly does not preclude scientific theories of origins.

The second creation account, found in Genesis 2:4b—3:24, is the literary and theological product of a much earlier generation. It reflects the concerns of the united kingdom of David and his successor, Solomon (ca. 1010–930 B.C.). Unlike the Priestly teaching, which grew out of the exile experience of dissolution, the Yahwist tradition reveals biblical Israel's appropriation of a royal ideology and its development as a national entity. Dianne Bergant points out that Israel's tenth-century theology contains a refashioning of royal ideology that both legitimized the monarchy and at the same time held it accountable to the Mosaic Law. The creation narrative found within this tradition is a statement that is theological and anthropological; it is not an account of the historical origins of the then-known world.[11]

A careful reading of the Yahwist creation narrative clearly indicates that it is not concerned with providing answers to questions about cosmogony. Rather, the Yahwist account is an etiology,[12] a story rich in symbolism that attempts to locate and give expression to the causes for the present condition of the people. This etiology encompasses both the experience of goodness and intimate relatedness with God, the benevolent Gardener, and the contrasting experience of sin and estrangement from that God. Borrowing stories and themes from other Near Eastern religions, the Yahwist author refashioned

---

ed., *Evolution and Creation* (Notre Dame, Ind.: University of Notre Dame Press, 1985), 161.

10. Phyllis A. Bird, "'Male and Female He Created Them': Gen 1:27b in the Context of the Priestly Account of Creation," *Harvard Theological Review* 74 (1981): 137–45.

11. Bergant, "Creation according to the Old Testament," 156.

12. For more on the etiological character of this Genesis text, see Karl Rahner, *Hominization: The Evolutionary Origin of Man as a Theological Problem* (New York: Herder and Herder, 1965), 32–44.

them in response to the people's concerns and in the light of Israel's own religious faith. The Yahwist account uses symbols in order to disclose dimensions of experience that otherwise would remain closed and hidden.

The second creation narrative is likely a combination of two stories that the Yahwist author brought together into a unified whole. The combination results in a story that is at once a creation narrative and a primeval narrative of crime and punishment. Westermann hypothesizes that one story tells how God put the human into the garden, provided this first human with nourishment, and forbade this creature to eat the fruit of one of the trees in the garden. This tradition tells of the creation of humankind and the crisis of alienation.[13]

The other narrative tells how at the beginning God formed the first human creature (ha'adam) from the earth and breathed into this creature the breath of life (Gen. 2:4b-17). The creation of humans from the earth was a widely spread notion, found in Egypt and in the Babylonian version of the Gilgamesh epic of the creation of Enkidu.[14] Having made the first earth-creature, God then noticed that this creature was not yet complete. God tried to make up for what was lacking by the creation of the animals; but they were not adequate. God then created woman out of the human creature's rib (Gen. 2:18-25). Westermann contends that the creation of humankind is complete only when woman is created and the man and the woman are together.[15] Elsewhere, Westermann points out that the depiction of the creation of humans, male and female, in Genesis 2 reflects a stage of civilization that was aware of the great importance of the role of woman in the existence of humankind. Genesis 2 is unique among the creation myths of the whole of the ancient Near East in its appreciation of the meaning of woman, i.e., that human existence is a partnership of man and woman.[16]

About these same verses, Phyllis Trible argues that the creation of woman is a second full creation story that is necessary to the completion of creation. Through God's activity of fashioning a creature from the first human creature, ha'adam becomes male ('is) and female ('issa). Trible asserts:

In the very act of distinguishing female from male, the earth creature describes her as "bone of my bones and flesh of my flesh" (2:23). These

---

13. Westermann, *Creation*, 72.
14. Ibid., 76.
15. Ibid., 72.
16. Westermann, *Genesis 1–11*, 232.

words speak unity, solidarity, mutuality and equality. Accordingly, in this poem the man does not depict himself as either prior to or superior to the woman. His sexual identity depends on her even as hers depends upon him. For both of them sexuality originates in the one flesh of humanity.[17]

Although the Genesis creation narratives are usually given the most attention, a discussion of Old Testament creation faith would be unnecessarily limited if it focused only on those texts. Creation is a theme that is found in the prophets and in the wisdom literature, as well. In the texts of the classical prophets such as Amos (see 4:13; 5:8) and Jeremiah (see 27:5; 31:35-37) the theme of creation occurs, but no prophet stresses the theme as much as the unknown prophet referred to as Deutero-Isaiah. To the scroll of Isaiah a message was added when the Babylonian exile was nearing an end (540 B.C.). In contrast to the sharper words spoken in chapters 1-39, likely dating to the eighth century, chapters 40-55 offer no judgment and condemnation of Israel, but rather a message of confident hope that the exile will soon end. For this reason these chapters are often called the Book of Consolation.

In the introductory chapter of this book, the prophet is advised by God to speak tenderly to Jerusalem because its service as an exile is coming to an end. Deutero-Isaiah proclaims that the very earth will be re-created: "Every valley shall be lifted up and every mountain and hill be made low; the uneven ground shall become level and the rough places a plain" (Isa. 40:4). The glory of God will be revealed; all will see it together.

Richard J. Clifford suggests that the theme of new creation in Deutero-Isaiah is a renewal of the theme of the exodus-conquest— the first act that brought Israel into existence.[18] Creation in Deutero-Isaiah does not refer to the act that brought the world of the nations into being. Deutero-Isaiah's preaching focuses intensely on Israel and God's plan of salvation. The people do not properly exist scattered in exile apart from God, without land and temple, ritual and officials. Their God will create a people a second time.

This perspective differs from that in Genesis, where the creation of the world took place once and for all. Deutero-Isaiah's concern is predominantly Israel, the beloved nation that has fallen into non-existence as a people. This prophet speaks of a renewed existence for the people, a new exodus-conquest, a new creation. Creation is not

---

17. Phyllis Trible, *God and the Rhetoric of Sexuality* (Philadelphia: Fortress Press, 1978), 98-99.

18. Clifford, "The Hebrew Scriptures and the Theology of Creation," 517.

simply an act of God in the beginning, but rather God's continual involvement throughout history. This is brought out in the prophet's linking of creation with redemption. The link between creation and redemption is explicitly made in the opening verse of Isaiah 43: "But now thus says the Lord, he who created you, O Jacob, he who formed you, O Israel: Do not fear, for I have redeemed you; I have called you by name, you are mine." The redemptive word by which Israel was created as the people of God is none other than the creative word by which God made earth and heaven.

In Deutero-Isaiah the great themes of Israel's faith—God as creator, as liberator from slavery under Egypt at the exodus, as redeemer from all enemies, and as giver of covenant promise—are intertwined. They are presented in hymns of praise. Through them Israel is invited to remember the great deeds of the past and believe that God will do a "new thing" on their behalf.

We have seen that during the exilic period creation as an activity was connected to redemption (Deutero-Isaiah) and was viewed as having been effected simply through God's word (Gen. 1). Later in Israel's history creation is spoken of as an activity of God's wisdom, whereby God created a world of wondrous design.

In the wisdom literature God is viewed primarily as creator.[19] Walther Zimmerli's insight that wisdom theology is creation theology has gained wide acceptance.[20] It is true, if it is properly understood. Within the wisdom literature there is not a great deal of interest in the question of origins. Rather, the interest is in creation's order. The ability to perceive this order and the discernment of how to live in harmony with it are what constitute wisdom. The close connection between creation and wisdom in wisdom literature makes it necessary to inquire first about wisdom.

In the wisdom literature, wisdom itself is presented with multi-faceted nuances. Sometimes wisdom is a divine quality or entity, not

---

19. The term _wisdom literature_ refers to Proverbs, Job, Ecclesiastes (Qoheleth), Sirach (Ecclesiasticus), the Wisdom of Solomon, and some of the Psalms. Although dating these books has posed some difficulties, there is general agreement that they are postexilic or at least took their final form after the exile. See Roland E. Murphy, _Wisdom Literature and Psalms_ (Nashville: Abingdon Press, 1983), 13–17.

20. Walther Zimmerli, "Ort und Grenze der Weisheit im Rahmen der altestamentlichen Theologie," in _Gottes Offenbarung, Gesammelte Aufsätze zum Alten Testament_, Theologische Bücherei, vol. 19 (Munich: Kaiser, 1963), 302. For commentary on the significance of Zimmerli's position, see Leslie J. Hoppe, "Biblical Wisdom: A Theology of Creation," _Listening_ 14 (1979): 198; Hans-Jürgen Hermisson, "Observations on the Creation Theology of Wisdom," in Bernhard W. Anderson, ed., _Creation in the Old Testament_ (Philadelphia: Fortress Press, 1983), 118–19; and Roland E. Murphy, _The Tree of Life: An Exploration of Biblical Wisdom Literature_ (New York: The Anchor Bible Reference Library, 1990), 118.

distinct from God, but not totally identified with God either. In other instances, particularly in texts focused on creation, such as Proverbs 8, Sirach 24, and Wisdom of Solomon 7, the figure of Wisdom appears to have taken on the status of a second divine person.[21]

Much debate has surrounded the figure called Wisdom. Is Wisdom merely a personification of an attribute in God in the sense of a literary device? Although this has been the most common interpretation, Roland Murphy questions whether personification does justice to the figure of Wisdom. Is Wisdom here a hypostatization? That is, has a personal trait been transformed into a person with her own existence? Murphy is cautious about accepting this interpretation due to the complexity of this concept. He argues that the figure of Wisdom cannot be conceived as a hypostatization or as a person because of the strict monotheism of the postexilic period. He concludes: "Whatever associations Wisdom may have had in an earlier era, she is best understood in her biblical expression as a communication of God."[22]

The main and longest speech of Wisdom that focuses on creation is Proverbs 8. What is unusual about this passage is that Wisdom is personified as a woman who is distinct from God. This passage harkens back to the first chapter of Proverbs where Wisdom is introduced as a female figure who carries a message into the streets (Prov. 1:20-33). The passage opens with this figure speaking and offering truth and righteousness (Prov. 8:1-8). Here Wisdom speaks at length in her own name. The climax of the passage comes in verses 22-31 when Wisdom describes her origins and her functions. She existed prior to creation, was present when God began the preliminary actions of creation (vv. 27-29), served as the fashioner of creation beside God (v. 30), and rejoiced in the inhabited world and took delight in the human race (v. 31).

In Proverbs 8, Wisdom is within creation, yet transcends the human creature. At the same time, Wisdom is also turned toward human creatures soliciting their adherence to her divine ways. She declares: "Happy are those who keep my ways. Hear my instruction and be wise, and do not neglect it" (vv. 32-33).

In the Book of Sirach, Wisdom once again appears as a female figure mysteriously produced by God "in the beginning" before the

21. For a treatment of other wisdom texts, such as creation texts in Job and Psalm 104, see Richard J. Clifford, "Creation in the Hebrew Bible," in Robert J. Russell, William R. Stoeger, and George V. Coyne, eds., *Physics, Philosophy and Theology: A Common Quest for Understanding* (Vatican City State: Vatican Observatory, 1988), 160–64.

22. Murphy, *The Tree of Life*, 133.

creation of external reality (Sir. 24:9). In a speech she reveals her origin, status, and special role in creation. She declares:

> I came forth from the mouth of the Most High,
> and covered the earth like a mist.
> I dwelt in the highest heavens,
> and my throne was in a pillar of cloud.
> Alone I encompassed the vault of heaven
> and traversed the depths of the abyss [24:3-5].

The figure of personified Wisdom reached its peak of development in the Book of the Wisdom of Solomon. Its description of Lady Wisdom, Sophia, is composed of elements from the Israelite tradition (e.g., Prov. 8), from the cult of the Egyptian goddess Isis, and from Hellenistic thought. At the outset Sophia is depicted as a people-loving spirit who will not enter deceitful souls (Wisd. of Sol. 1:4-6). In her creative role she is described as the mother of all things (7:12), responsible for their existence and thus knowing their secrets. Later, unlimited power is ascribed to Sophia: Though she is but one, she can do all things and is the fashioner of all things (7:22). Her image is given further contours as she is described as a spirit that loves the good and that is intelligent, holy, unique, subtle, and steadfast (7:22-23). Through her extraordinary power, she reaches from one end of the earth to the other and orders all things well (8:1). Wisdom knows that God has ordered all by measure and number and weight (11:20). Therefore, it is foolish, in looking at the works of creation and perceiving their regularity, not to recognize their creator.

By way of summary, this survey of texts in the Old Testament makes it clear that its understandings of creation are rich and varied. The creation texts represent distinct literary forms and present different religious insights into the relationship between God and the world. This is the case because these texts were profoundly affected by the questions, concerns, and world view current when they were formulated. Old Testament perspectives on creation do not necessarily conflict with contemporary scientific theories about the origins of the world and its development. The tensions between the two can be greatly diminished if we attend to their fundamental differences. Richard Clifford astutely analyzes four significant differences between the concepts of creation in the Old Testament and in modern science: the process, the product or emergent, the description, and the criteria for truth.[23]

---

23. Clifford, "The Hebrew Scriptures and the Theology of Creation," 509, and idem, "Creation in the Hebrew Bible," 155.

Attention to the process that underlies the formation of biblical creation texts discloses the first important difference in how creation is treated by the biblical authors and by the scientific-minded. In the case of Genesis 1, for example, we have noted that the creation faith of Israel contrasts with that of its neighbors, who envision creation as the result of conflict among the gods. Creation flows purposefully from God's word. Modern science, on the other hand, sees creation as the impersonal interaction of physical forces extending over eons.

In regard to the product or emergent, to the ancients of the biblical world, an organized human society was the primary emergent of the process. In the case of Deutero-Isaiah, that society is re-created by the intervention of God. By way of contrast, moderns usually view creation as issuing in the physical world. The focus is primarily on planet Earth amid the solar system.

The description of the process and product that emerge is also distinctly different for the biblical authors and modern science. The biblical writers reported creation as drama. They devised new stories, or presented variations of existing ones, in order to respond to the questions and concerns that arose in their situations. In contrast, modern scientific conceptualizing of creation is impersonal; it proceeds according to laws. It seeks to describe by making models of or hypotheses about nature.

Finally, it logically follows that the criteria of truth for each are different. The criteria for truth in biblical texts are the plausibility of the story and what it illumines about the God-human relationship. The text need not offer a complete account. The story can focus on one element of concern and omit others. The scientific-minded expect a creation theory that has empirical reference and that can explain all the data. A complete explanation that is compatible with other verifiable theories is of utmost importance. Failure to do so makes the hypothesis suspect.

Richard Clifford's analysis highlights the fact that creation in the Old Testament and modern science represent different world views expressed in two distinctive modes of discourse. If they are said to conflict in an age in which science is the dominant mode of discourse that has shaped the world view, in large measure that is due to the simple fact that neither religious beliefs nor scientific theories exist in isolation from other perceptions about the world and ourselves.

## THE NEW TESTAMENT

Unlike the Old Testament, the New Testament does not focus extensively on creation as an isolated topic. Creation is related to other themes, principally to the saving significance of Jesus. It is believed that one of the earliest theological interpretations of Jesus associated him with Wisdom, which, as we have noted, was closely associated with the activity of creation. James Dunn argues that wisdom christology provided the early Christians with a way of speaking about Christ's relationship with the cosmos. Christ is interpreted to be the embodiment of the creative activity of God. He represents and manifests all that God is in God's outreach to humanity.[24]

Elisabeth Schüssler Fiorenza argues that early Palestinian Christians, as they struggled to illumine their understanding of Jesus, reinterpreted Sophia-Wisdom and viewed Jesus as the prophet of Sophia-God.[25] It is likely that the early church saw Jesus in this way because Jesus saw himself as the prophet and child of Sophia. As the agent of Sophia's creative power, Jesus is able to manifest her reign in the deeds he performs. He extends the reign to the poor, the outcasts, and those who suffer injustice. In turn, the followers of Jesus-Sophia continued what Jesus did; namely, they took up the mission of making the reign (*basileia*) of God a reality. The theme of the reign of God, common in the Synoptic Gospels, reflects the Old Testament tradition of creation. The reign of God is the goal that God "intends from the creation of the world" (Matt. 25:34).

The earliest written application of Sophia-God to Jesus is found in the Pauline epistles. A connection between Sophia and Christ is found in Colossians. In an early hymn Christ is presented as the preexistent agent of the invisible God (Col. 1:15; see Wisd. of Sol. 7:26; Prov. 8:27). Paul proclaims the creative activity of Christ with these words: "For in him all things in heaven and on earth were created, things visible and invisible, whether thrones or dominions or rulers or powers—all things have been created through him and for him" (Col. 1:16).

Paul explicitly refers to Christ as the wisdom of God (1 Cor. 1:24, 30). Elsewhere, in 1 Corinthians 8:6, Jesus is said to be the one "through whom are all things and through whom we exist." This early creedal statement, which proclaims the creative activity of Jesus

---

24. James D. G. Dunn, *Christology in the Making: A New Testament Inquiry into the Origins of the Doctrine of Creation* (Philadelphia: Westminster Press, 1980), 163. It is important to note here that Dunn claims that while it is possible to say that divine wisdom became incarnate in Christ, this does not necessarily mean that Wisdom was a divine being.

25. Elisabeth Schüssler Fiorenza, "The Sophia-God of Jesus and the Discipleship of Women," in Joann Wolski Conn, ed., *Women's Spirituality, Resources for Christian Development* (New York: Paulist Press, 1986), 265. She interprets Sophia as "Israel's God in the language and *Gestalt* of the goddess" (p. 264).

Christ, appears to parallel the activity of Wisdom in Proverbs 8:4-6, 22-31.

No doubt, it is largely through interpreting Jesus as Sophia-God that he came to be linked with the activity of creation. Perhaps the most obvious example of reinterpretation of Sophia-God in the Gospels is found in John. Here we find Jesus described in ways that Sophia had been depicted earlier: as the Word who was with God in the beginning before the world existed (John 1:1; 17:5; see Wisd. of Sol. 2:22). The claim of Sophia to exist with God from eternity is applied to Jesus. In addition, the creative function of Sophia is now the function of Jesus. Jesus is the agent of creation: "Through him all things came into being, and apart from him nothing came to be" (John 1:1-3).

The Johannine "Logos made flesh" christology is therefore the identification of Jesus as Sophia-God incarnate. Elizabeth A. Johnson points out that this identification had profound theological consequences. It enabled the early Christian communities to attribute cosmic significance to the crucified, risen Jesus, relating him to the creation and governance of the world.[26] The revelation in Jesus is so fundamental to the sense and purpose of the cosmos that he must be conceived as the shaping force in the very beginning of existence.

In conclusion, just as the primary purpose of the Old Testament accounts of creation is not to report the physical beginnings of the world but is to express faith in God, so the New Testament creation theology is a reflection of the meaning of Christ. Its purpose is to provide an interpretation of salvation in Jesus that is closely linked with creation, so closely linked that salvation is looked upon as a renewal of the original creation through the saving presence of God in Jesus (see 1 Cor. 15:45-49; 2 Cor. 5:17; and Rom. 8:18-23).

# CREATION IN THE HISTORY
# OF ROMAN CATHOLIC THEOLOGY

Roman Catholic theology of creation is characterized by the development of official statements of belief, creeds, and doctrines about creation in response to questions that have been raised in the course of time. These doctrines are the vehicle by which the Roman Catholic church develops and transmits its belief as a living tradition. While official church doctrines are important for understanding Roman

---

26. Elizabeth A. Johnson, "Jesus, the Wisdom of God: A Biblical Basis for Non-androcentric Christology," *Ephemerides Theologicae Lovanienses* 61 (1985): 261.

Catholic creation theology, beliefs about creation cannot be limited to the formulations of official pronouncements. The consensus these pronouncements represent has its roots in the life and practices of the believing community and in the teachings of theologians who reflect on them. Therefore, this section of this essay will present theologians' ground-breaking insights on creation as well as a survey of official church teaching.

## CREATION IN THE PATRISTIC AGE

One of the most central creation doctrines for Christianity is the belief that creation by God is *ex nihilo*, a statement that articulates faith in the transcendence of God and in the agency of God in creation. This doctrine is an interpretation of God's creative activity that is not explicit in the biblical creation texts themselves. At best it is hinted at in 2 Maccabees,[27] in Romans,[28] and in Hebrews.[29] The notion of creation in the biblical texts was taken up by early theologians who, with the help of ancient philosophy, sought to grasp this faith more deeply. However, they were soon faced with a major challenge, for the notion of creation was foreign to the thinkers of antiquity.

The formulation of the Christian response to this challenge will be surveyed here because it has become normative for Roman Catholic theology. The period of the formulation of these early teachings is known as the patristic age. This period encompasses the end of the New Testament era until roughly the middle of the eighth century. The theologians of this period contributed extensively to Christian belief. Roman Catholics have long given considerable weight to their insights. This is particularly evident in the documents of the Second Vatican Council, which cite them frequently.

The notion of *creatio ex nihilo* was developed in the second century as the Christian response to Greek cosmology and its religious and philosophical visions of the nature of the world. The ancient Greeks commonly taught that God was not a creator, but rather a world architect who ordered preexistent material. What is called creation in the Bible, for them was an ordering and setting in motion of already present, eternal matter. *Creatio ex nihilo* is found in the writings of theologians such as Theophilus of Antioch, Tertullian, and Irenaeus,

—————————————

27. "I beg you, my child, to look at the heaven and the earth and see everything that is in them, and recognize that God did not make them out of things that existed" (2 Macc. 7:28).

28. "God . . . gives life to the dead and calls into existence the things that do not exist" (Rom. 4:17).

29. "By faith we understand that the worlds were prepared by the word of God, so that what is seen was made from things that are not visible" (Heb. 11:3).

and in the Shepherd of Hermas.[30] Because of the far-reaching significance of the writings of Tertullian and Irenaeus, their contribution
will be treated here. The arguments of these early theologians center on opposition to the Platonic idea of the coeternity of God and
matter and to the dualism of the Gnostics.

Tertullian, a North African apologist who shaped much of the
theological vocabulary in the Latin West, proposes *creatio ex nihilo* as
an argument against the eternity of matter. Tertullian holds that matter could not have existed before creation. God had to have created
matter out of nothing and not out of preexisting matter. Tertullian
argues that although *creatio ex nihilo* is not explicitly stated in the
Bible, it is clearly implied. To make his case Tertullian presents an
argument from the logic of silence. He reasons:

> For I say that, though Scripture did not clearly proclaim that all things
> were made out of nothing—just as it does not say either that they were
> made out of matter—there was not so great a need to declare that all
> things had been made out of nothing as there would have been, if they
> had been made out of matter.[31]

He goes on to argue that the first possibility would have been completely understandable, but the second would be doubtful unless it
was explicitly stated.[32]

Tertullian's dismissal of the Platonic doctrine of the coeternity of
matter and the divine had a profound influence on Christianity's rejection of two ideas closely related to the concept of creation. One is
the pantheistic notion that God and matter are the same.[33] Tertullian
recognized that if Christianity accepted this, God's transcendence
would be compromised. *Creatio ex nihilo* expresses the belief that
God transcends the world.

The other idea is a naturalism that posits the divine as necessary
for explaining the natural processes. This sense of the divine conflicts
with the Christian appropriation of biblical revelation in which God's
agency in creation is depicted as freely chosen. Tertullian writes:
"Thus you see how the universe exists by the operation of God who
made the earth by His power, prepared the world by His wisdom,

---

30. Jaroslav Pelikan, *The Emergence of the Catholic Tradition (100–600)*, vol. 1 of
*The Christian Tradition: A History of the Development of Doctrine* (Chicago: University of
Chicago Press, 1971), 36–37.

31. Tertullian *The Treatise against Hermogenes* 22.2 (trans. J. H. Wasznik [Westmin-
ster, Md.: The Newman Press, 1956], p. 55). In an introduction Wasznik notes that
Hermogenes, influenced by Platonism, believed that God created all things out of
preexistent, "unborn" matter (pp. 4–9).

32. Tertullian *The Treatise against Hermogenes* 21.4 (p. 56).

33. Pelikan, *The Emergence of the Catholic Tradition (100–600)*, 36.

and stretched out the heaven by His understanding."[34] He argues further that creation was not a necessity but rather was freely chosen by the operative functions of God's mind.[35] The force of Tertullian's argument illustrates that the early Christian theology of creation, with its claim that everything is due to God's freedom and goodness, was for Greek antiquity a foreign and new notion.

The other major concern of the church in the second century was Gnostic dualism. Gnostics believed in a supreme God, who was the source of the fully spiritual, invisible world, and in a lesser God, who created material reality. The creator was the God of the Old Testament, the demiurge, and enemy of the supreme God of Jesus Christ.

Irenaeus, bishop of Lyons, argued against the Gnostic teachers Valentinus and Marcion; he was convinced their polytheism and dualism were contrary to biblical faith. Irenaeus affirmed the unicity of God the creator and the God of Jesus, the unity of creation and redemption, and the continuity of the old dispensation and God's plan for salvation. Irenaeus's strong commitment to arguments that emphasized unity led him to view creation in the context of the economy of salvation. For Irenaeus, the central affirmation that God redeemed the world by taking on the materiality of human existence, thereby recapitulating its history,[36] meant that matter could not have an independent existence apart from the God of Jesus.

Inherent in the Gnostic belief in the God of creation as a demiurge is an ontological dualism that posits material reality as evil and spiritual reality as good. Against the Gnostics' extreme pessimism about matter, Irenaeus argues for the inherent goodness of creation. These words of Irenaeus illustrate themes of his creation theology:

> If...He (the Creator) made all things freely, and by His own power, and arranged and finished them, and His will is the substance of all things, then He is discovered to be the one only God who created all things, who alone is omnipotent, and who is the only Father founding and forming all things, visible and invisible, such as may be perceived by our senses and such as cannot, heavenly and earthly, "by the word of His power" (Heb. 1:3); and He has fitted and arranged all things by His wisdom.... He [is] the Creator, He the Lord of all; and there is no one besides Him.[37]

---

34. Tertullian *The Treatise against Hermogenes* 45.2 (p. 84).

35. Ibid.

36. Irenaeus *Against Heresies* 3.8.6–7 (in *The Writings of Irenaeus*, trans. Alexander Roberts and W. H. Rambaut [Edinburgh: T and T Clark, 1880], pp. 342–43).

37. Ibid., 2.30.9 (p. 238); see also 3.4.2 (p. 264) and 4.20.2 (p. 429).

The theological positions of Tertullian and Irenaeus are aimed at resolving the questions of their day. They articulate the doctrine of creation as part of a cosmic vision. This cosmic vision sees the existence of the world as dependent on a transcendent God who created and fashioned it as a free exercise of divine will. *Creatio ex nihilo* succinctly expresses this vision of the God-world relationship. In this unified cosmological picture, the creator transcends the world and is not to be identified with it. But the creator is not remote from the world either. Creation has been designed through God's wisdom and its course is directed by that wisdom.

In the fourth century major threads of this developing creation tradition found expression in the first article of the Niceno-Constantinopolitan Creed. Here we find the confession of faith that begins with an affirmation of the oneness of God, maker of heaven and earth. Although the Council at Nicaea was called to resolve the question of the relationship of Jesus Christ to God the Father, its initial statement, adopted from an earlier baptismal confession, explicitly confesses against the dualism of the Gnostics that one God made all of reality, spiritual as well as material. In addition, it implicitly argues against a pantheism that envisioned the world as coeternal with God. God transcends the world and is "maker" of it.[38]

The Niceno-Constantinopolitan Creed represents a heritage shared broadly by Christians of both East and West. Although all Christian churches do not explicitly endorse the creed, belief in God as creator is the starting point of belief in God for many Christians. God, the creator, is the ultimate source of the existence of the world and of ourselves.

During the subsequent centuries of the patristic age theologians continued to respond to pantheism and dualism in their various forms as the tradition unfolded. One major response came at the turn of the fifth century from Augustine, who found himself confronted with the pantheism of the Neo-Platonists and the dualism of the Manicheans. According to his *Confessions*, he was intimately acquainted with each.

---

38. The choice of the word *maker* is significant for the tradition and was the product of much debate between Arius and Athanasius about the identity of Jesus Christ. Athanasius chose the verb *beget*, reserving *make* for creation in reference to Jesus, because he believed that *beget* was the word that best expressed the unity and equality of the Son with the Father. The choice of terms must be interpreted in the light of Athanasius's argument for *homoousios*. The significance of the choice of *make* vis-à-vis *create* and *generate* has been a topic of discussion over the centuries. The struggle over language underscores the fact that the Christian sense of creation is that the divine act of origination has no proper analogies in any act of the creature.

Augustine's conception of God was deeply affected by Neo-Platonism. This is particularly evident when he speaks of God's immutability, eternity, and incomprehensibility.[39] For Augustine, the immutability of God encompasses the other traits. In his interpretation of God's revelation to Moses as "I am who I am" (Exod. 3:14), Augustine stresses that only the essence of God is unchangeable.[40] Therefore, being is in the highest and truest sense only proper to God. As unchanging, God is eternal, and for humans, who change, God is incomprehensible.

In his speculative theology Augustine appropriates the hierarchically ordered universe of Neo-Platonism. He pictures the universe as a scale of being that reaches down from the supreme being of God to creatures. However, he rejects the emanationist pantheism of the Neo-Platonists. He finds that the idea of emanation conflicts with the doctrine *creatio ex nihilo*. He argues: If God made creation out of God's self, then creation would be equal to God.[41] For Augustine, divine creation is a far more radical activity than making creatures from preexisting matter.

Augustine's theology of creation was not shaped only by his dialogue with Neo-Platonism; he also rigorously argued against the dualism of the Manicheans.[42] The Manicheans were a sect to which Augustine belonged in his youth, and their dualism resembled that of the Gnostics. For example, they rejected the Old Testament and attributed good and evil to two distinct, ultimate principles: light and darkness. They disdained material reality and were particularly hostile to marriage. In opposition to Manichean dualism Augustine defended the teaching of Genesis that God created from nothing all that is outside of God and saw that it was good. The goodness of material creation is underscored in Augustine's works. This is especially clear in his speculative reflections on the Trinity; in those reflections he argues that traces or vestiges of the Trinity are found in the human body ("outer man").[43] It seems that Augustine believed that all of creation bears the mark of the Trinity.

---

39. Augustine *The Trinity* 5.1.2. (trans. Stephen McKenna [Washington, D.C.: Catholic University of America Press, 1963], pp. 175–76).

40. Ibid., 5.2.3 (p. 117).

41. Augustine *The Confessions* 12.7 (trans. John K. Ryan [Garden City, N.Y.: Image Books, 1960], p. 308). Augustine's writings on creation in the *Confessions* are found in books 11–13. For a succinct treatment of Augustine on creation see Leo Scheffczyk, *Creation and Providence*, trans. Richard Strahan (New York: Herder and Herder, 1970), 94–105.

42. Augustine pointedly argued against the Manicheans in *A Commentary on Genesis: Two Books against the Manicheans*; *The Literal Meaning of Genesis: An Unfinished Book*; and *The Literal Meaning of Genesis: A Commentary in Twelve Books*.

43. Augustine *The Trinity* 11 (pp. 315–41).

However, Augustine's optimism about creation in his speculative writings is not the total picture. Although Augustine does not share the low opinion of material reality of the Manicheans, in his ethical writings his appraisals of the human body and of sexuality have a characteristically somber tone.[44]

Closely related to Augustine's interpretation of *creatio ex nihilo* are his reflections on the nature of time. Time is God's creature and is the condition under which all of creation exists. Since time is created, the creator is outside the temporal process.[45] The creator, who is immutable, brings past, present, and future to be in a single act. Thus God made everything together. However, Augustine also argues that God continues to sustain all things. He brings these two distinct ideas together by describing the divine agency in terms of two "moments of creation,"

> one in the original creation when God made all creatures before resting from His works on the seventh day, and the other in the administration of creatures by which He works even now. In the first instance God made everything together without any moments of time intervening, but now He works within the course of time.[46]

Calling these "moments" can contribute to the confusion because Augustine also holds that God is not governed by time as are creatures. Ernan McMullin argues that "aspects" might have been a better way to highlight the distinction Augustine wishes to make.[47] What the two "moments" indicate is that for Augustine *creatio ex nihilo* by God is not a singular event in the past, over and done with, but also *creatio continua* by God whose agency continues to sustain creation. Augustine writes: "Let us, therefore, believe and, if possible, also understand that God is working even now, so that if His action should be withdrawn from His creatures, they would perish."[48]

In this same work, in the context of additional reflections on time and the creator, Augustine employs an important hermeneutical principle in interpreting Genesis 1–3. He argues that the Genesis

---

44. For more on this point I recommend Peter Brown, "Augustine: Sexuality and Society," in *The Body and Society: Men, Women and Sexual Renunciation in Early Christianity* (New York: Columbia University Press, 1988), 387–427.

45. Ernan McMullin, "Natural Science and Belief in a Creator: Historical Notes," in Russell, Stoeger, and Coyne, eds., *Physics, Philosophy, and Theology*, 57.

46. Augustine *The Literal Meaning of Genesis: A Commentary in Twelve Books* 5.11 (trans. John Raymond Taylor [New York: Newman Press, 1982], vol. 1, p. 162).

47. Ernan McMullin, "Introduction: Evolution and Creation," in McMullin, ed., *Evolution and Creation*, 10. My analysis is dependent on that of McMullin; see also his valuable explanatory footnotes on pp. 49–50.

48. Augustine *The Literal Meaning of Genesis: A Commentary in Twelve Books* 5.20 (vol. 1, p. 171).

account of creation in six days could not be taken as literal history. He asserts: "We should not think of those days as solar days."[49] God brings all things into existence with a single act, disposing them in an order based not on intervals of time but on causal connections, which can be discovered by us.[50] What is implied in this passage is that if there is a conflict between a literal reading of Scripture and a well-established truth about nature, then there is sufficient reason to interpret the scriptural passage metaphorically.[51]

## CREATION IN THE MIDDLE AGES

Augustine's hermeneutical principle seems to have gone unnoticed in the Middle Ages when theology found itself challenged by the newly available works of Aristotle. At the universities, such as those at Oxford and Paris, Aristotle's thought was taught to all students. Areas of Aristotle's philosophy were soon judged to be incompatible with the theology of the day. Ernan McMullin expresses the problem succinctly: "Aristotle's world was . . . not a created world. It depended on nothing other than itself for its existence. Aristotle's science took the world as a *given*, and what was more, assumed its structure to be a necessary one."[52] Aristotle's necessary structures for the world seemed to exclude the long-held Christian belief in the freedom of God in the act of creation.

Thirteenth-century university teachers made great efforts to reconcile Christian doctrine and Aristotelian philosophy. For the Roman Catholic tradition, the most significant of those teachers was, of course, Thomas Aquinas. Although Aquinas's theology was condemned in 1277, three years after his death, his condemnation did not last long. Even before he was canonized in 1323, his Christianizing of Aristotle gained wide acceptance. Aquinas later became the theologian of choice for Roman Catholics when in 1879 Pope Leo XIII wrote the encyclical *Aeterni Patris*, which inaugurated a Neo-Thomist revival.

Thomas Aquinas was not a strict Aristotelian; Plato, Augustine, and the Neo-Platonist Dionysius the Areopagite play significant roles in his arguments. For example, in the overarching structure of the *Summa Theologiae* Aquinas adapts the Platonic schema of emanation

---

49. Ibid., 5.5 (p. 154).
50. Ibid.
51. For an analysis of the different levels of meaning in this work (e.g., literal, metaphorical, and allegorical meanings), see Taylor's introduction, pp. 9–12. *Literal* for Augustine has a different meaning than is common today; he uses the term more broadly as a contrast to an allegorical interpretation.
52. McMullin, "Natural Science and Belief in a Creator," 59–60.

and return, *exitus et reditus*. All things are presented in their relation to God, whether in their production or in their final end. Aquinas did, however, find one major aspect of Aristotle's thought to be foundational for his own work. In contrast to Plato's idealism, Aristotle refused to withdraw from the realities present to the senses, refused to be distracted from what is evident to the eyes. Aristotelian realism is a principle Aquinas wholeheartedly accepted because he found it compatible with the Christian affirmation of creation.[53]

For Thomas Aquinas, the acceptance of Aristotle is not merely a choice between rival philosophies. It is a theological decision for a mode of reasoning that would enable him to make faith in God and Christian revelation more intelligible. This is evident in the beginning of the *Summa Theologiae*. In the second question Thomas Aquinas uses Aristotle's understanding of the first or unmoved mover as a way to explain and affirm the existence of a being whom all Christians would understand as God.[54] On the surface, this creative appropriation of Aristotle may seem to present Aquinas with a problem. How is one to proceed from the first mover of Aristotle to the creator God of the Christian tradition?

Aquinas is able to bring the two together because his reflection on Aristotle's first mover is only one element in a more complete picture that focuses on God as the first cause, a cause that is efficient, necessary, and universal. The analysis that leads Aquinas to these conclusions underscores the transcendence of God and leaves no opening for pantheistic conceptions of the universe. God cannot be confused with the creation God sets in motion.

Even more importantly, at the core of Aquinas's understanding of God is the insight that God is the pure act of being. This insight is derived from his interpretation of Exodus 3:14: "I am who I am." In this regard Aquinas chooses a point of emphasis that distinguishes him from Augustine, who made God's immutability a central notion. Viewing God as the pure act of being is a position unique to Aquinas. While it bears the influence of Aristotle's metaphysics, it has priority over Aquinas's use of Aristotelian concepts.[55] Aquinas views God not as any sort of essence having existence, but as the sheer act of

---

53. See Thomas Aquinas *Summa Contra Gentiles* 2.1–4 (trans. James F. Anderson [Garden City, N.Y.: Hanover House, 1956], pp. 29–36).

54. Thomas Aquinas *Summa Theologiae* Ia, q. 2, a. 3 (in vol. 2, *Existence and Nature of God*, trans. Timothy McDermott [London: Blackfriars, 1964], pp. 13–15). Note: I have avoided the term *proof* here because the modern understanding of that term contributes to a misunderstanding of what Thomas is doing. The *Summa Theologiae* presupposes the existence of the God of revelation; it does not seek to prove that existence.

55. Ibid., Ia, q. 2, a. 3 (p. 13).

existence itself.[56] This is what distinguishes God's being from all the beings that God causes to exist.

In causing creation to exist God's agency is unique: God exists in everything. Paradoxically, God is never really distant from creation, although creatures, since they are unlike God in nature, are necessarily distant from God.[57] The distinction lies in this: God is being, but all created things only have being. And they have being as a participation in what God is fully and perfectly.[58] With this line of reasoning, Aquinas artfully combines likeness and distance.

Aquinas's understanding of God as pure being and giver of all existence is interrelated with his understanding of *creatio ex nihilo*. God's creation presupposes nothing in the being that is created. God did not create out of matter; on the contrary God posited all of finite being, matter as well as form, from nothing. Therefore, creation by God is different from any becoming and is the proper activity of God alone. Reality is called forth by God where previously there was a void. Creation is the emanation of all being from a universal cause. God causes all being without exception and accordingly creates out of nothing.[59]

Thomas Aquinas's application of Aristotelian causality allows him to explain the difficult idea of creation from nothing as an act of God. One of his key insights is that God as first cause is an efficient cause. As efficient cause, God causes effects—creatures—in a way that involves no change from nothingness to being and yet is complete effect. As efficient cause, God has transcendence over creatures, and creatures from their side have their own autonomy.[60] One might argue that creation freely created by God is also gifted with freedom. As Walter Kasper has succinctly expressed it in reflecting on Aquinas's creation theology: "So in Aquinas theonomy presupposes the autonomy of human beings."[61]

Although this treatment of Thomas Aquinas does not begin to do justice to his thought, it is clear that he was addressing a different set of issues than Augustine. The shift in emphasis in Aquinas does not mean, however, that Augustine had succeeded in dispelling Manicheism and its dualistic influences. Dualism continued to re-

---

56. Ibid., Ia, q. 3, a. 3 and a. 4 (pp. 29–34).

57. Ibid., Ia, q. 8, a. 1 (pp. 111–13).

58. Ibid., Ia, q. 44, a. 1 (in vol. 8, *Creation, Variety and Evil*, trans. Thomas Gilby [Cambridge: Blackfriars, 1968], pp. 6–9). Aquinas's incorporation of participation is, of course, an example of the influence of Platonic doctrine on his thought.

59. Ibid., Ia, q. 45, a. 1 (pp. 24–29).

60. Ibid., I, q. 44, a. 1 (pp. 4–9).

61. Walter Kasper, *Theology and Church*, trans. Margaret Kohl (New York: Crossroad Publishing Co., 1989), 37.

main a concern during the Middle Ages. A decade prior to Thomas Aquinas's birth the church again found it necessary to respond to concerns about dualism.

At the Fourth Lateran Council (1215) the church condemned the creation theology of the Cathari and the Albigenses; successors of the Manicheans, these sects believed that matter is evil and was created out of nothing by the devil. The council drafted a statement of faith that confessed belief in one triune God, creator of all things, visible and invisible, who, by divine and omnipotent power, created each creature from nothing.[62] Here in highly condensed form we have the Catholic doctrine against dualism. Over two hundred years later, at the Council of Florence (1442), Manichean dualism was addressed again in a reaffirmation of the belief that God created a good creation out of nothing (DS 1333 and 1336).[63] Only after that pronouncement did dualistic ideas about creation cease to trouble the Roman Catholic church.

## CREATION IN THE ENLIGHTENMENT AND EARLY MODERN PERIODS

The creation theology of the patristic and medieval periods was engaged primarily in explaining the relation between God and the world, and it did so by employing its central symbol, *creatio ex nihilo*. These explanations provided Christianity with responses to the questions of who God is and with affirmations of the goodness of the world this God created. With the Enlightenment a set of challenges emerged that caused Christian theologians to ask anew: What does it mean to say that God created all things out of nothing? The challenge now focused on the questions from science, particularly hypotheses concerning the origins of the solar system, geological explanations of the earth's development, and theories regarding the emergence of the forms of life. Of the three, the final proved to pose the greatest challenge.

Some philosophers of the eighteenth century responded to the challenge posed by new scientific theories by viewing the doctrine *creatio ex nihilo* as primitive mythology. They ceased to talk

---

62. H. Denzinger and A. Schönmetzer, *Enchiridion Symbolorum, Definitionum et Declarationum de Rebus Fidei et Morum* (hereafter DS), 36th ed. (Rome: Herder, 1976), no. 800.

63. The Council of Florence was primarily concerned with the reunion of the separated East with Rome. In its decrees it also condemned old heresies, with a specific focus on Manicheism.

of God as a personal being and began to talk of the creator as the rational architect of the universe. This deist interpretation rejected the authority of the Bible and presented God as the first cause of all things. Deism contributed a chronological component to the doctrine of *creatio ex nihilo:* Deists argued that God caused the world in a singular event in the more or less distant past.[64] In the nineteenth century some philosophers began to rationalize the idea of creation by stripping from it almost all of its anthropomorphic, mythical terms. God was presented as an impersonal principle identical with the developing universe. Thus we find pantheism emerging anew. Still others viewed the Christian God as mere projection and argued that the world is not governed by intelligence, purpose, or final causes, but rather by material processes.

By the late nineteenth century we find the Roman Catholic magisterium responding to some of these philosophical challenges. The responses manifest the influence of the Enlightenment on Roman Catholic thought. In apologetical writings of this era there was a considerable emphasis on the reasonableness of the Roman Catholic tradition.

At the First Vatican Council (1869–70) the church once again addressed creation. The language of the council's statements on God and creation corresponds closely to the Fourth Lateran Council's decree and contains themes expressed at the Council of Florence. Although there is continuity with the earlier statements, the canons make the particular concerns of this council clear: Those positions that equate God and the world, or dispute that God made the world from nothing, free from all necessity, are condemned (DS 3023–25). The whole of reality comes from God's action; all reality originates in the free initiative of God's love. Pantheism is incompatible with Christian belief.

In addition to the condemnation of pantheism, atheism and materialism are also condemned (DS 3021 and 3022). Although we cannot know what was in the minds of the theologians at the council, it is likely that the materialism condemned in the conciliar decree was closely linked with evolution, a theory that was widely believed to be incompatible with the doctrine *creatio ex nihilo*. In the assessment of Leo Scheffczyk, the repudiation of materialist evolution had the unfortunate result "that the Catholic mind did not for a moment con-

---

64. Jaroslav Pelikan, "Creation and Causality in the History of Christian Thought," in *Evolution after Darwin,* vol. 3 of Sol Tax and Charles Callender, eds., *Issues in Evolution* (Chicago: University of Chicago Press, 1960), 38.

sider whether there might be something to be said for the theory of evolution."[65]

The condemnations of pantheism, atheism, and materialism by Vatican I did not make the Catholic doctrine of creation responsive to the major movements in nineteenth-century thought. Very importantly, there was no attempt to address the problem that faced Christian thought on creation: How to respond to the tenets of evolutionary science.

Since evolution, more than any other scientific theory, has posed a major challenge to creation theology for the Christian churches, it seems appropriate to examine why this has been the case. To answer this question requires examining Darwin's theory in the context of how science and religion were commonly viewed during the Enlightenment period by scientists themselves. The most common approach was "concordism," an effort to interpret the Bible as if it corresponded to scientific data.[66] For example, the eighteenth-century scientist Buffon engaged in research that led him to conclude that the development of the earth and of the life forms that inhabit it took place over a long period of time and not in six days, as Genesis 1 indicated. Buffon, rather than reject the Bible, set about reconciling his findings with it. He argued that the "days" of creation were actually epochs and charted the successive phases in the history of the earth against the six days of creation.[67] Such attempts at concordism were common at the end of the eighteenth century.

The threads of concordism that bound science and religion together began to unravel, however, in the nineteenth century, particularly with the work of scientists such as Charles Lyell. On the basis of the geological data Lyell gathered, he claimed that the physical composition of the earth was the result of gradual geological processes. Lyell argued against cataclysmic geology, the most widely held theory at the time, which proposed that geological change was due to the direct intervention by God, such as in the case of the flood.

---

65. Scheffczyk, *Creation and Providence*, 240. During this period Roman Catholic theology was allied with a philosophy that allowed room for some science, but rarely for new science.

66. The concordism of the early Enlightenment period commonly took the form of explanations that presented religion and science in harmony or in continuity. Belief in the biblical account of divine creation of the world provided scientists with presuppositions about divine intervention that colored their scientific inquiry. See Charles Coulston Gillispie's *Genesis and Geology: A Study in the Relations of Scientific Thought, Natural Theology and Social Opinion in Great Britain, 1790–1850* (New York: Harper and Row, 1959).

67. McMullin, "Introduction: Evolution and Creation," 32; see Buffon, *Epochs of Nature* (1778).

In its place he proposed "the principle of uniformitarianism."[68] He argued that all geological change could be explained by reference to natural forces or laws operating over a long span of time.[69] Divine intervention played no role in these changes. He did not, however, conclude that God was not at the direct origin of each living species. Lyell, typical of the scientists of his day, believed that science could not explain the origins of forms of life, especially of human life, in terms of laws. It was up to theology to explain the origin of species; the task of the scientist was to study and classify them.

Darwin's theory of biological evolution followed on the heels of the geological theory of Charles Lyell and challenged the division of labor that Lyell held sacrosanct. With the publication of *On the Origin of Species* in 1859, Darwin shook the last vestige of concordism, as scientists and theologians alike struggled to come to terms with the theory of the evolution of species through natural selection. In 1871 Darwin published his other highly controversial book, *The Descent of Man*, in which he argued that not only did the human body evolve naturally from its animal ancestors, but the human soul evolved as well. Darwin's naturalistic explanations for the origin of species, including human beings, made the theological explanations of his era untenable. Previously, humanity was set apart from the rest of nature, which was generally conceived in rather static or mechanistic terms. Since Darwin, humanity has been understood as a part of nature, the product of an evolutionary process in common with all life forms.

With Darwin the concordism between science and religion, which supported continuity between revelation and the Enlightenment sciences, was widely abandoned, and a conflict between science and religion about the historical and scientific origins of the universe, and of humanity, erupted. Darwinian evolution placed into doubt the trustworthiness of the Bible, particularly the literal accuracy of the creation narratives in Genesis and the doctrine *creatio ex nihilo* according to God's design.[70]

Seldom in the history of Christianity have churches reacted as violently to nontheological theories as they did to those of Darwin. If the universe and humans within it gradually evolved, then

68. Sir Charles Lyell, *Principles of Geology*, 3 vols. (London: J. M. Dent, 1830–33), vol. 1 (1830), passim.

69. Lyell, *Principles of Geology*, 1:144.

70. Due to the limitations of space, I made the decision not to focus on the doctrine of the human person as *imago Dei*. However, it is obvious that Darwin's proposal for the descent of humans from earlier and lower forms of life imperiled this traditional Christian belief.

Christian cosmogony, the affirmation of the origin of the world by God's intervention, based on a literal reading of the Genesis creation texts and long associated with the doctrine *creatio ex nihilo*,[71] was challenged. Prior to Darwin, this cosmogony, which emerged with the Enlightenment, was not widely questioned. Many Christian churches, including the Roman Catholic church, responded to the Darwinian challenge by attempting to uphold a literal interpretation of the Genesis creation texts. This response by the Roman Catholic church of the late nineteenth and early twentieth centuries marks a break from an older and long-held tradition that accepted a literal interpretation but also looked for the true religious meaning at the level of spiritual interpretation by means of allegory.

During the pontificate of Pius X, the Pontifical Biblical Commission issued official *responsa* to questions concerning the historicity of Genesis 1–3. These *responsa* bear evidence of the Roman Catholic church's movement to a more literalist interpretation.[72] The commission issued a negative response to a query asking whether the historical and literal sense of Genesis 1–3 can be put into question, specifically whether the creation of all things directly by God in the beginning of time can be disputed (DS 3514).[73] The replies published on the same date also include a response to a question asking whether the intent of the author of Genesis 1 was "to furnish his people with a popular account, such as the common parlance of that age allowed, one, namely, adapted to the senses and to human intelligence," or "to teach us in a scientific manner" the nature of visible things. The answer to the first is "in the negative" (DS 3518).[74] The Genesis 1 account of origin is not to be viewed as a fictional narrative; rather, when interpreting this text one should seek "scientific exactitude of expressions" (DS 3518). This "scientific exactitude" can be equated with a literal interpre-

71. Prior to and even after the mid–nineteenth-century theories of evolutionary science, the majority of Christians, including Roman Catholics, interpreted *creatio ex nihilo* as an affirmation that the world began through God's direct intervention in a singular event in the more or less distant past. See David Kelsey, "The Doctrine of Creation from Nothing," in McMullin, ed., *Evolution and Creation*, 181; see Pelikan, "Creation and Causality in the History of Christian Thought," 29–41.

72. The Pontifical Biblical Commission, "On the Historical Character of the Earlier Chapters of Genesis," June 30, 1909 (DS 3512–19).

73. In its assessment of the first chapters of Genesis, the Pontifical Biblical Commission is likely following principles of interpretation from *Providentissimus Deus*, the encyclical of Leo XIII (1893), to counter the "evil" of rationalism and the influence of science in biblical interpretation.

74. In reading these responses it is good to bear in mind that Pius X was vigorously antimodernist. Modernism was a movement perceived to be bent on making the Bible a set of beautiful sentiments or pious fables with no particular connection to reality.

tation that ruled out the derivation of this account from other mythologies.

These turn-of-the-century *responsa* of the biblical commission were designed to check the new methods of historical research into the Bible that scholars had begun to develop even prior to Darwin. Through the Darwinian period such research continued with heightened interest, as biblical scholars attempted to understand the Bible in its historical contexts and on its own terms.

In 1943 the magisterium gave official approbation to such biblical scholarship in an encyclical of Pius XII, *Divino Afflante Spiritu* (see DS 3825–30). An important example of the application of modern biblical scholarship called for in this encyclical is a 1948 letter of the secretary of the biblical commission to Cardinal Suhard, archbishop of Paris (DS 3862–64).[75] This letter addresses questions about the authorship of the Pentateuch and the historical character and literary form of the first eleven chapters of Genesis. It indicates that the positions concerning the authorship and historicity of these parts of the Bible previously taken in the earlier *responsa* of the commission are in no way opposed to further, truly scientific examination of these questions in accordance with the results obtained through scholarship during the past forty years (DS 3862). It specifically notes that Genesis 1–11 does not contain history in the modern sense of the term and calls for the biblical exegete to investigate how the "ancient peoples of the East" thought and expressed their ideas and how they conceived of historical thought itself (DS 3864).

A few years later, the positions articulated in this letter were repeated in Pius XII's encyclical *Humani Generis* (1950) (DS 3898). In this same encyclical the doctrine of evolution is addressed and held to be "an open question" as long as certain qualifications are met. The encyclical permits speculations about the development of the human *body* from other living beings already in existence, but it forbids such speculation regarding the human *soul* (3896).[76]

---

75. This document marks a movement from official *responsa* in the form of a cryptic positive or negative answer to "letters" with more nuanced and time-conditioned answers.

76. The concern here is with safeguarding Catholic doctrine on the spiritual nature of humans. This encyclical was also interested in preserving the doctrine of original sin. Due to the limitations of this essay, it is not possible to explore these areas.

# CREATION IN CONTEMPORARY THEOLOGY

## CREATION AND THE RELATIONSHIP
## OF THEOLOGY AND SCIENCE

Since the nineteenth century, the doctrine of creation has been en-
meshed in questions about the relationship of theology and science.
As noted above, these questions initially emerged when the theological community attempted to respond to the challenge of evolutionary
science to religious faith in creation. However, what resulted was
that creation, a topic usually addressed in systematic theology, has
often found itself on the periphery of discussions that are properly the concern of fundamental theology. These discussions, which
focused on methodology, epistemology, and the nature of biblical
revelation, sought to establish the foundations of the reasonableness
of theological discourse.

Arguments about the reasonableness of theological discourse led
theologians to examine carefully the very foundations on which theology is articulated. The discussions that ensued have led to the
emergence of four broad conceptions of the relationship of theology and science.[77] The first type envisions theology in continuity
with scientific theory. The second conception envisions science in
continuity with religious belief, particularly beliefs based on a literal
interpretation of the Bible. The third major type argues that theology and science are totally distinct and separate realms of discourse.
The fourth holds that theology and science are distinct but interact-
ing approaches to reality. Since these conceptions of the relationship
of theology and science continue to manifest themselves in theological discussions in varying degrees today, I will illustrate each with a
focus on how creation is addressed.

### Theology in Continuity with Science

The view that sees theology in continuity with science can be traced
to the liberal Protestantism of the nineteenth and early twentieth centuries. While the official Roman Catholic position at this
time was to withdraw from modernism, including Enlightenment
science, some Protestants began to sketch continuities between theology and science. Perhaps the most important early voice to shape

---

77. For related but different analyses of the relationship of theology and science,
see Ian Barbour, *Religion in the Age of Science* (New York: Harper and Row, 1990), 3–
30; and Arthur R. Peacocke, *The Sciences and Theology in the Twentieth Century* (Notre
Dame, Ind.: University of Notre Dame Press, 1981), xi'i–xv.

the contours of liberal Protestant thought was that of Friedrich Schleiermacher. Although Schleiermacher died over two decades before Darwin published *On the Origin of Species*, he had pointedly addressed Enlightenment skepticism about the doctrine of creation. This German theologian's perspective on the divine causality of God the creator was influential long after his death because it was progressive and in many ways evolutionary. This characteristic made his theology a good candidate for wide acceptance after Darwin.

In an effort both to counter deistic understandings of divine causality that put God's activity at the beginning of the world process and to respond to Enlightenment thought, Schleiermacher developed a reinterpretation of creation theology that stressed the world's continuing dependence on God. He began his description of God's relation to the world with a conception of creation that argued that what God did "at the beginning" in bringing the world into being out of nothing continues over time in a developmental process.[78] He argued that there is one creative divine decree and action spanning all of history. This decree brought the human race into being at a lower level of existence and gradually lifted it to higher levels of self-consciousness. Because humans are by nature religious, those higher levels of self-consciousness meant higher levels of God-consciousness.[79]

Liberal Protestantism's response to Darwin's theory of biological evolution drew on the earlier insights of Schleiermacher and articulated a faith in an evolutionary order of reality that made belief in a higher purpose of a creator intelligible to many late nineteenth-century Christians. The scientific concept of evolution provided liberal Protestants with an interpretative key that enabled them to illumine further the insights of Schleiermacher and to reformulate the Christian doctrine of creation and the related doctrine of divine providence. They held that God's creative and providential activities are not challenged by scientific theories such as those of Darwin; rather they are implied by them. Thus liberal Protestantism accommodated its theology to the science of its time by arguing that it was possible to discern an order of ultimate coherence and evolving process in the activity of God. The findings of science, such as those of Darwin regarding biological evolution, were viewed as evidence for an all-pervasive presence of a providential creator.

---

78. Friedrich Schleiermacher, *The Christian Faith*, ed. H. R. Mackintosh and J. S. Stewart (1928; reprint, New York: Harper and Row, 1963), vol. 1, secs. 36–39 (pp. 142–49).

79. Ibid., vol. 1, sec. 46 (pp. 170–78).

In the twentieth century the major instance of this type of thought is process theology, which in its interpretation of the Christian tradition utilizes the speculative philosophical system of Alfred North Whitehead and Charles Hartshorne, Whitehead's principal commentator. Process theology shares many of the presuppositions of the liberal Protestantism of the nineteenth century. Like its predecessor, it seeks to harmonize Christian belief with scientific ways of conceiving reality. Process theologians incorporate the metaphysical vision of reality opened up by modern science, particularly by biology and physics, and adapt the categories of process philosophy to rethink the relation of God to the natural world and to reinterpret certain core doctrines of the Christian tradition, such as creation. Process theology understands God to be the source of novelty and order, and creation to be a long and incomplete process.

One of the areas of process thought judged by many to be problematic for a Christian interpretation of creation is Whitehead's concept of creativity.[80] This central notion in his thought refers to a moment-by-moment emergence of an infinite variety of actual occasions of experience. He envisions creativity as a way of understanding the whole process of reality and not just the beginnings of reality. In this process, God is not the ultimate source of actual entities in the sense that they are produced or created by God. Rather, because God is a real and actual entity, God corresponds to the categories of all reality.

Since Whitehead believes that the process of creativity is the very nature of reality, he does not incorporate into his understanding of God the traditional Christian doctrine *creatio ex nihilo* because it depicts God as an eternal being who suddenly created all things out of nothingness. For Whitehead this doctrine does not explain whether or not God was a part of the nothingness out of which creation appeared. By affirming categorically that God is a real entity coextensive in time with the reality of the universe, Whitehead avoids the question about whether a creator God existed before the beginning of things. He argues: "He [God] is not *before* all creation, but *with* all creation."[81]

Whitehead does not believe it is possible to explain the existence of a first entity and how it originated because the beginning of real-

---

80. For an excellent critique of Whitehead on this point see Langdon Gilkey, *Reaping the Whirlwind* (New York: Seabury Press, 1981), 110–14.

81. Alfred North Whitehead, *Process and Reality: An Essay in Cosmology* (1929; reprint, New York: Macmillan Co., A Free Press Paperback, 1969), 405. "God and the World" (pt. 5, chap. 2), in which this quote appears, is the major source for my presentation of Whitehead on God and creation.

ity is ultimately unexplainable. Although Whitehead would not posit divine creation as an explanation of the temporal origin of reality, he does ascribe to God a creative function in the emergence of actual occasions. This function is God providing an initial aim to each actual occasion. In this way God is an integral element in the creative advance of the world and becomes as the world becomes. Ultimately, God includes the world in God's self. This is expressed in Whitehead's paradoxical axiom: "It is as true to say that God creates the world as the world creates God."[82]

In their reflections on Whitehead on *creatio ex nihilo*, John B. Cobb, Jr., and David R. Griffin indicate that process theology affirms instead the doctrine of creation of order out of chaos, which they argue is more true to the Old Testament. In their opinion *creatio ex nihilo* too easily depicts God as a controlling power. They prefer to conceive of God as a source of novelty who through persuasive love produces order. The first stage of the order of creation was the development of things or enduring individuals. As creation evolved beyond that initial stage, each new stage of the evolutionary process represented an increase in the actualization of divinely given possibilities for value. Cobb and Griffin argue that this conception of creation of order out of chaos can be a key to interpreting the evolutionary development of the world propounded by modern science in harmony with the character and purpose of God.[83]

Since the inception of process theology, the writings of Pierre Teilhard de Chardin have been frequently used by process theologians as a dialogue partner for refinement of their interpretations of Christian doctrine.[84] Teilhard is an appropriate choice because his thought represents another example of theological reflection in continuity with evolutionary science.[85] For Teilhard, a Jesuit paleontologist, evolution in many ways is a theological category and a hermeneutical principle that can be used to transform Christian belief from a static world view into one that recognizes the world as being in the process of becoming.

The theory of evolution, however, does not just provide Teilhard with a speculative framework. In the preface of *The Phenomenon of Man*, Teilhard says he wants to have his ideas judged by their con-

---

82. Ibid., 410.

83. John B. Cobb, Jr., and David Ray Griffin, *Process Theology: An Introductory Exposition* (Philadelphia: Westminster Press, 1976), 63–68.

84. For example, Cobb and Griffin draw upon Teilhard's thought in their presentation of a creation theology; ibid., 68.

85. For his position on the relationship of science and religion, see Pierre Teilhard de Chardin, *The Phenomenon of Man*, trans. Bernard Wall (New York: Harper and Row, 1959), 283–85.

formity to the observable patterns of the universe.[86] In this work Teilhard presents his understanding of these patterns and argues that the universe has an intrinsic tendency to evolve and in so doing to develop more complex structures. He calls this process "complexification," with its final observable stage being the appearance of human beings.

Like process thought, Teilhard speaks of a continuing creation with God immanent in an incomplete world. However, unlike process theology, his evolutionary vision includes a final convergence, an "Omega Point," which he identifies with God. This concept is, at one and the same time, an extrapolation of scientific evolutionary theory and an unique interpretation of the Christian doctrines of creation and eschatology.[87] For Teilhard, the creator is the God of evolution.

Although Teilhard's ideas were rejected by the Roman Catholic magisterium during his lifetime, they have continued to live on. Ervin Nemesszeghy and John Russell argue that Teilhard's ideas influenced the text of Vatican II's Pastoral Constitution on the Church in the Modern World. As a basis for their claim, they cite the following sentence from article 5: "Thus the human race has passed from a rather static concept to a more dynamic, evolutionary one."[88]

These distinctive representatives of a view that sees theology in continuity with science have both strengths and weaknesses. To their credit they are responsive to the challenges posed by science, such as evolution. Divine activity is viewed not in conflict with science, but as behind and within the processes traced by science. Their articulations of an order of ultimate coherence makes sense to many persons in a scientific culture. The difficulty with this view, however, is that it tends to harmonize religious truth with the prevailing spirit of the culture. The result of theology's accommodation to scientific evolution is that progressive development becomes the ontological basis for this type of theology. Put simply, theology in continuity with evolutionary theory too easily promotes an optimistic view about historical progress and about the rational and moral perfectability of humanity. This optimism cannot stand up to the test of human experience.

---

86. Ibid., 29–30.
87. Ibid., 267–72. For more on the interconnectedness of these doctrines see also a collection of Teilhard's essays entitled *Christianity and Evolution*, trans. René Hague (New York: Harcourt Brace Jovanovich, 1971).
88. Ervin Nemesszeghy and John Russell, *The Theology of Evolution* (Butler, Wis.: Clergy Book Service, 1971), 48.

## Science in Continuity with Religion

The second type of conception of the relation of theology and science stands in sharp contrast to the first type, for it argues for a science that is in continuity with religious beliefs about creation. This view harkens back to the pre-Darwinian concordism noted above. It was developed by evangelical, fundamentalist Protestants in the United States to counter the accommodation of theology to evolutionary science and is known as scientific creationism or creation science. It is militantly antimodernist. It opposes explanations of life and its origins in terms of natural evolution, even if that evolution is theistically conceived. Instead, creation scientists stress supernatural intervention in the origin of all things and propose scientific explanations for the universe that are compatible with their commitment to the inerrancy of biblical revelation.

Against the acceptance of evolutionary science by the scientific community and by more liberal Christians, creation scientists argue that the Bible is a book of scientific merit. Creation scientists believe that their role as scientists is to defend the biblical account of creation against intellectual attack and ridicule, and to demonstrate that the Bible is undergirded by solid knowledge.[89]

Creation science traces its origins to the late 1960s and early 1970s; it was developed by scientists who were also evangelical, fundamentalist Protestants.[90] The immediate event that precipitated creation science was the 1968 U.S. Supreme Court decision that declared that a 1928 Arkansas law, which was passed on the heels of the famous Scopes-Monkey trial (1925) to prevent the teaching of Darwinian evolution in public schools, was unconstitutional.[91] Instead of trying to outlaw the teaching of evolution on the grounds that it was antibiblical and antireligious, these fundamentalists developed creation science to circumvent court rulings based on the First Amendment and argued for equal time with evolution in the public

---

89. This form of argument has been most thoroughly developed by Henry M. Morris in *The Beginning of the World* (Denver: Accent Books, 1977), 7ff., and in idem, *Scientific Creationism* (San Diego: Creation-Life Publishers, 1974), 203–4. The latter book contains a full account of the creation science position.

90. In 1970 Henry Morris founded the Christian Heritage College in San Diego as an educational center for creation science. In 1972 the Institute for Creation Research was founded in affiliation with the college. The institute has twenty Ph.D.'s on its staff, some of whom earned their doctorates at institutions such as Yale, the University of California, and Ohio State. See Warren D. Dolphin, "A Brief Critical Analysis of Scientific Creationism," in David B. Wilson, ed., *Did the Devil Make Darwin Do It?* (Ames: Iowa State University Press, 1983), 23.

91. For a full explanation of the events that led to the U.S. Supreme Court decision see Edward Larson, *Trial and Error: The American Controversy over Creation and Evolution* (New York: Oxford University Press, 1985), 98–119.

school curriculum. The Arkansas Balanced Treatment Act, passed in 1981, provides a list of the tenets of creation science; some of these tenets state that there is scientific evidence of the sudden creation of the universe from nothing; others state that changes in life forms have occurred only within the fixed limits of originally created kinds of plants and animals.[92]

Creation science, although obviously founded on religious convictions from a literal interpretation of Genesis 1–3, was set forth as a scientific theory because it contains no explicit reference to a creator God. Without explicitly mentioning God, creation scientists believed that they set forth a truly scientific model as an alternative to evolution through natural selection.[93] Their science, however, interprets empirical data in a way that serves their goal of verifying biblical statements about the natural world. In a very real sense, creation science is more concerned with the inerrancy of biblical truth than with articulating a theology of creation, per se. Those persons who are proponents of creation science today stand in continuity with their evangelical predecessors who, in the 1920s, attempted to safeguard the fundamentals of Protestantism by engaging in warfare against evolutionary science. Spokespersons for fundamentalism, such as William Jennings Bryan, did this primarily because they believed that evolutionary biology was inherently atheistic. They were concerned that its acceptance would surely weaken the moral fabric of the nation.[94] Creation scientists share the same concerns, but they also recognize that they cannot eliminate evolutionary theory. Therefore, they propose that their science be given equal treatment with biological evolution.

In 1987 the U.S. Supreme Court struck down the Louisiana Balanced Treatment Act, which sought to require that creation science be given equal time with the teaching of evolution science. In the court's judgment creation science was founded on a particular religious view and therefore violated the separation of church and state.[95] Despite this setback, the creation science movement among fundamentalist Protestants shows no signs of abating.

92. This act is quoted in Langdon Gilkey, *Creationism on Trial: Evolution and God at Little Rock* (Minneapolis: Winston Press, 1985), 260–65.

93. For a critical appraisal of this position see Langdon Gilkey, "The Creationist Issue: A Theologian's View," in David Tracy and Nicholas Lash, eds., *Cosmology and Theology* (entire issue of *Concilium* 166 [New York: Seabury Press, 1983], 56–69).

94. See C. Allyn Russell, *Voices of American Fundamentalism* (Philadelphia: Westminster Press, 1976), 162–89.

95. Colin Norman, "Supreme Court Strikes Down 'Creation Science' Law as Promotion of Religion," *Science* 236 (June 1987): 1620. The Louisiana act, "The Balanced Treatment for Creation-Science and Evolution-Science," was based on the Arkansas act.

Creation science is representative of the broad and largely unquestioned acceptance of the dominance of science in North American culture. To their credit creation scientists draw attention to the dominance of science in our culture. They recognize that to a great extent science provides the theoretical basis for what the culture accepts as knowledge and as its most valuable forms of praxis. Science, therefore, has been given a certain sacral character. Scientific evolution is not a theory that is confined to biology. It has had and continues to have an influence on other academic disciplines, on religion, and on the culture as a whole. Creation science in many ways is a reaction to this expansion of evolutionary science into these other areas.

A major problem with the science that the creation scientists present is that it does not conform to the canons of the wider scientific community. One of those canons rules out the appeal to supernatural forces or agents in scientific explanations. Creation science defies that canon when it states that a transcendent creator established the entire realm of nature in a unique act at the beginning of time. Even if "God" is not explicitly mentioned, to speak of a creator is to imply God and therefore is to speak religiously.[96]

In addition, the creationists' literal interpretation of the Bible misconstrues the meaning and purpose of revelation. Their treatment of Genesis creation texts as sources for scientific facts ignores the historical context of their formation, their nonscientific intent, and their symbolic and doxological richness.

### Theology and Science as Separate Realms

The third view of the relation of theology and science emerged from Protestant neo-orthodox theology's criticism of liberal Protestantism's incorporation of a modern scientific world view and its optimism about the progress of history. The proponents of this view argued that the crisis precipitated by two world wars in the first half of the twentieth century made the principles of liberal Protestantism untenable. Neo-orthodox Protestantism sought to recover the Reformation emphasis on the primacy of divine revelation and of redemption in Jesus Christ. What resulted was the development of a dialectical approach to theology that reconceived the relation of God to the world as discontinuous. There is discontinuity between human beings as radically sinful and the judgment of the transcendent God,

---

96. For more on the canons accepted by the scientific community and creation science see Langdon Gilkey, "The Creationist Issue," 60–61.

between human reason and faith based on the Word of God, and between science and biblical revelation. Emphasis on the primacy of revelation, conceived as the otherworldly Word of God received in faith, is foundational for neo-orthodox theology's conception of theology and science as radically distinct and separate.

Since neo-orthodox theology has been so extensively shaped both in Europe and the United States by Karl Barth, his treatment of creation is the most logical one to examine. Barth includes a lengthy treatment of creation in his *Church Dogmatics*. In the preface of part 1 of his four-part theology of creation, Barth clearly articulates his approach, as a theologian, to science. About his decision to engage in an exegetical exposition of the first two chapters of Genesis, Barth writes:

> It will perhaps be asked in criticism why I have not tackled the obvious scientific question posed in this context [i.e., the question of evolution]. It was my original belief that this would be necessary, but I later saw that there can be no scientific problems, objections or aids in relation to what Holy Scripture and the Christian Church understand by the divine work of creation.[97]

He continues to spell out the relationship of science and theology by saying that "there is free scope for natural science beyond what theology describes as the work of the Creator."[98] In turn, "theology can and must move freely where science...has its appointed limit."[99] The independent status of science and theology allows for no exchange between them. It logically follows that Barth's theology of creation rules out a natural theology.

Barth's theology of creation stresses that creation cannot be known or interpreted apart from divine election and salvation in Jesus Christ. He presents creation and redemption as joined in one work of grace. This position is illustrated in his extensive interpretation of Genesis 1 and 2 in relation to God's sacred covenant.[100] In presenting creation as "the external ground of the covenant," Barth subordinates creation to human redemption.[101] In commenting on Barth's creation theology, Ian Barbour argues that his main concern

---

97. Karl Barth, *The Doctrine of Creation*, trans. J. W. Edwards, O. Bussey, and Harold Knight, vol. 3, pt. 1 of *Church Dogmatics* (Edinburgh: T and T Clark, 1958), ix.

98. Ibid., x.

99. Ibid.

100. Ibid., 94–329.

101. In this regard Barth clearly has much in common with the position of von Rad already cited in this essay.

is with the doctrine of redemption. As a result, "nature is treated as the unredeemed setting for human redemption."[102]

In *Maker of Heaven and Earth*, Langdon Gilkey offers one of the clearest and most straightforward articulations of the neo-orthodox position on the separation of theology and science. In speaking with specific reference to the Christian doctrine of creation, Gilkey claims that "faith draws a sharp line of distinction between the created world and the Creator."[103] The warrants for this claim lie in his conception of theology's relationship to science. He states earlier in this work: "Science and religion are not in real conflict on the question of origin, for the hypotheses of the one are dealing with vastly different questions than the affirmations of the other."[104] He describes the differences in terms of the fundamental questions each asks. He argues that science merely asks about the character of the preceding affairs, and is therefore concerned only with secondary causes. In contrast, theology is concerned about ultimate origins or primary causes.[105] He also analyzes the distinction along the lines of the contrasting categories of "how" questions versus "why" questions. He holds that the "how" explanations of science are antithetical to theology, which responds to the deeper "why" questions of existential concern.[106]

To the credit of the proponents of this third type of view of the relation of science and theology, they are critically aware of many of the basic assumptions of the modern scientific world view. In addition they do recognize that a theology that accommodates itself to the science and prevailing thought forms of the culture will not maintain its identity. However, what these neo-orthodox Protestant theologians tend to ignore is the manner in which science affects their theology, because they too participate in their culture.

Neo-orthodox Protestant theology fails to attend to the manner in which prevailing attitudes in a scientific culture affect its interpretation of the Bible. Although neo-orthodox theologians view their theology as constructed on the biblical Word, it is in fact built on some basic assumptions of a modern scientific world view that holds that science is both independent from religion and the source for

---

102. Barbour, *Religion in the Age of Science*, 15.

103. Langdon Gilkey, *Maker of Heaven and Earth: The Doctrine of Creation in the Light of Modern Knowledge* (1959; reprint, Lanham, Md.: University of America Press, 1985), 149. In later works such as *Religion and the Scientific Future* (Macon, Ga.: Mercer University Press, 1970), Gilkey takes a position of dialogue with science. In *Catholicism Confronts Modernity* (New York: Seabury Press, 1975), he is explicitly critical of this earlier argument (see p. 126).

104. Gilkey, *Maker of Heaven and Earth*, 26.

105. Ibid., 16–21.

106. Ibid., 66–80.

determining what is true. The neo-orthodox position that revelation "happens" when it is received in faith and its perspective on the symbolic and paradoxical nature of religious language make its claims to truth problematic. Any statement about creation is knowable only through faith and is of a unique kind having no analogue in science or in other forms of knowing.

In addition, its tendency to emphasize existential experience and personal ethics contributes to the privatizing of religion. The outcome is that in areas of public discourse theological assertions are often held to be meaningless, or of little or no relevance. This emphasis on existential, revelatory experiences also results in neo-orthodox theology's rejection of natural theology on the grounds that it reduces the relation of God with the world to the status of familiar relations within the world. Consequently, neo-orthodox theology is not only removed from science and other areas of public discourse; it is also removed from the natural world. It rules out both natural theology and a theology of nature.

The conception of the relationship of theology and science as separate realms is also evident in the Roman Catholic magisterium's response to modern science. Although Roman Catholic theology has traditionally conceived of the relationship of faith and reason in a way that is markedly different from that of neo-orthodox Protestantism, its caution about modernism led it to treat theology as separate from the natural sciences and from Enlightenment philosophy. On the whole, the Roman Catholic magisterium relied on tradition and authority, rather than on modern criteria, for reasonableness. This is evident in Pius XII's words in *Humani Generis:*

> Let them strive with every force and effort to further the progress of the sciences which they teach; but let them also be careful not to transgress the limits which we have established for the protection of the truth of Catholic Faith and doctrine.[107]

Earlier in this same encyclical in the context of the question of evolution, Pius XII indicates that research in evolution is encouraged, provided that all engaged in it are prepared to submit to the judgment of the authority of the church.[108]

A major point of contrast between Roman Catholic theology and neo-orthodox Protestantism is their positions on natural theology. Roman Catholic theology has continued to retain natural theology.

---

107. Pius XII, *Humani Generis*, in *Four Great Encyclicals of Pope Pius XII* (New York: Paulist Press, 1961), no. 73 (p. 186).

108. Ibid., no. 64 (p. 184); see DS 3896.

Vatican I affirmed the possibility that human reason could gain a sure knowledge of God from created realities (DS 3004, 3206). Consequently humans would have some understanding of God's Word when it was announced to them. However, the predominant form of rationality well into the twentieth century was speculative philosophy. During the pre–Vatican II era the predominant response of the official church authority to science was to cling to a dualistic, Neo-Scholastic, philosophical construction of reality founded on distinctions between the supernatural and natural. However, most people, due to the influence of science on how reality is conceived, envisioned themselves as living in one world, a natural world. If science is said to have the final say about the natural world, then there is little room for theology. It is detached from an experiential grounding. Accordingly what was once viewed as supernatural easily becomes unnatural and, therefore, without meaning.

*Mutual Interaction of Theology and Science*

In Roman Catholic magisterial teaching, the Second Vatican Council replaced the third view of the relation of theology and science, described above, with a fourth view. This is evident in the Pastoral Constitution on the Church in the Modern World, which critiques views that hold theology and science to be mutually opposed. Such views are false because science and faith never truly conflict. "For earthly matters and the concerns of faith derive from the same God."[109] In recent years, Pope John Paul II has quoted this passage on several occasions in his repeated calls for constructive dialogue between theology and science.[110]

Among major contemporary Roman Catholic theologians, Karl Rahner has especially contributed to a constructive dialogue of theology with science. He has done this from the unique perspective of his "transcendental theological anthropology," a perspective that argues that in every act of knowing a person has an innate pregrasp of God, not as an object, but rather as a horizon of mystery. Since "the knowing subject" plays such a key role in Rahner's theological method it follows that his engagement with science would include epistemolog-

---

109. Vatican II, Pastoral Constitution on the Church in the Modern World, in Walter Abbott, ed., *The Documents of Vatican II* (New York: America Press, 1966), no. 36.

110. See in particular "Faith, Science and the Search for Truth" *Origins* 9 (1979–80): 389–92; and "Science and the Church: A Dialogue," *Origins* 10 (1980): 395–98. For more on the pope's views on this topic see "A Dynamic Relationship of Theology and Science," *Origins* 18 (1988): 375–79, and "The Links between Science and Faith," *Origins* 19 (1989): 338–40.

ical questions. In "Natural Science and Reasonable Faith" he argues that fundamental theology cannot do without ongoing dialogue with natural science about epistemological questions.[111]

For Rahner, theology and natural science cannot contradict since both are distinct from one another in their areas of investigation and in their methodologies. He accounts for the distinction of science and theology in this manner. Natural science investigates "a posteriori experiences" of individual phenomena and explores how a particular phenomenon is related to others. It should be methodologically atheistic because God is not an individual factor in a series of related phenomena. Theology for its part raises "a priori questions" about the ultimate ground of reality and affirms God as that absolute ground. Methodologically it is concerned with the transcendental relationship of the "original one and the whole."[112] Conflict occurs only when either science or theology fails to respect the proper domain of the other. For instance, when scientists who ascribe to a "mentality of positivism" confine knowledge to what can be demonstrated by direct experiment or hold that they can interpret and determine by their science the totality of their existence, then they have crossed over the boundaries of natural science.[113] But Rahner argues that theology has also overstepped its boundaries. Some of the examples Rahner cites have a direct bearing on theology of creation. He notes:

> For a long time it [the church] tried to hold onto a fixity of the kinds of living beings by appealing to the account of creation in the Book of Genesis. For a long time it rejected the biological emergence of humankind from the animal kingdom and fought against it. In *Humani Generis* and in a schema prepared for Vatican II it taught the origin of all human beings from a numerically single pair. In reprimanding Teilhard de Chardin and repressing his endeavors it manifested too little understanding for an ontology in which created being is conceived in principle and in the very beginning as being which is in the process of becoming within an entire evolution of the cosmos, which is still in the process of evolution.[114]

In each of these past cases the church's teaching office has placed itself in conflict with an individual affirmation of natural science.

---

111. Karl Rahner, "Natural Science and Reasonable Faith," trans. Hugh M. Riley, in *Theological Investigations* (New York: Crossroad, 1988), 21:16–55.

112. Ibid., 21:17–22.

113. Ibid., 21:23–24.

114. Ibid., 21:25. For more on how Rahner has addressed the topics listed here see *Hominization*; and idem, "Christology within an Evolutionary View of the World," in *Theological Investigations* (Baltimore: Helicon Press, 1966), vol. 5.

In the post–Vatican II era the church has adopted a much more dialogical stance in its dealings with natural science.

Rahner argues that dialogue between theology and science is possible if each respects the other's uniqueness and is also desirable, particularly about themes of ongoing interest, such as creation and evolution. Rahner writes from the perspective of theology: "That the world has been created is a theological affirmation, not one of natural science."[115] He argues that creation theology does not affirm that there has been a creation event of a specific kind. Rather, it affirms the continuing relationship of the world to its "transcendent ground." It follows that scientific theories of evolution that explain the continuous development of the cosmos from its simplest components to the most complex are acceptable to Christian faith as long as the presupposition of the transcendental relationship between absolute being (the creator God) and finite being (creatures) is not ruled out on scientific grounds.[116]

Among contemporary Protestant theologians, Wolfhart Pannenberg has long been engaged in dialogue with science. In opposition to neo-orthodoxy, he has attempted to find connections between the central claims of theology and the insights of science.[117] Although a great deal of his work in this area has focused on methodological issues and on rational criteria for examining religious beliefs, he has also focused on creation theology. In company with Rahner he views the proper subject of theology as "reality as a whole," with natural science concerned with particular questions. His theology explicitly lends itself to an evolutionary world view because he views reality to be an unfinished process whose future we can only anticipate. Unlike Rahner, Pannenberg is in dialogue with science not only about broad epistemological issues, but also about specific scientific theories.

This aspect of Pannenberg's theology is illustrated well in his probings of the meaning of the doctrine of creation. Pannenberg believes that it is possible to appropriate the scientific description of the world of nature in a theology of creation. He proposes the concept of contingency as a bridge between the doctrine of creation and the scientific understanding of the universe. He argues: "Any contemporary discussion regarding theology and science should first focus on the question of what modern science ... can say about the

---

115. Rahner, "Natural Science and Reasonable Faith," 31.
116. Ibid., 34–41.
117. See Wolfhart Pannenberg, *Theology and the Philosophy of Science*, trans. Francis McDonagh (Philadelphia: Westminster Press, 1976).

contingency of the world as a whole and of every part of it."[118] Pannenberg reflects on contingency on different levels: he sees it as the characteristic of any scientific law, as an aspect of historical reality, and as the first instant of a new sequence. In his reflections he incorporates different perspectives: empirical claims about the physical world, ontology, and laws of nature. For example, he argues that the laws of nature, especially those of physics, appear to the theologian as "contingent products of the creative freedom of God."[119]

In dialogue with evolutionary biology Pannenberg examines the order of creation in Genesis 1 and points out that the Priestly narrative presents a sequence that is evolutionary. Certainly Pannenberg is not noting a new insight by pointing this out. He does, however, have a definite reason for making this observation. He notes that while the details of that sequence are obsolete where science is concerned, the sequence itself appears from a modern perspective as an evolutionary process. Thus, although modern biology and biblical revelation are different forms of discourse, this does not rule out commonalities in their perceptions of reality. Elsewhere, Pannenberg asks: "Is there any equivalent in modern biology to the Biblical notion of the Divine Spirit as origin of life that transcends the limit of the organism?"[120] In engaging in these types of reflection Pannenberg seeks to demonstrate that if the Christian faith in God as creator is to be accepted as truth, this truth must somehow be present, even if only in oblique form, in modern biological descriptions of life.[121]

These reflections provide Pannenberg with a basis for reinterpreting the theological doctrine of creation. While the topics highlighted require much more systematic attention, particularly a more in-depth examination of what physicists are saying about contingency and biologists about the process of evolution, Pannenberg does envision theology and science as modifying each other while respecting each other's distinctive activities and contributions.

Theologians who engage in dialogue with scientists and the theories of science are performing an important service for the community of believers. It is desirable for theologians to explicitly attend to science in doing theology because the influence of science is a major factor in determining the meaning and validity of religious discourse. Attempts to draw dividing lines between science

---

118. Wolfhart Pannenberg, "The Doctrine of Creation and Modern Science," *Zygon* 23 (1988): 9.

119. Ibid., 11.

120. Wolfhart Pannenberg, "Theological Questions to Scientists," in Arthur R. Peacocke, ed., *The Sciences and Theology in the Twentieth Century* (Notre Dame, Ind.: University of Notre Dame Press, 1981), 11.

121. Ibid.

and theology are no longer necessary because science's earlier unquestioning faith in itself has disappeared. Science in the era of the theories of quantum physics and indeterminacy is far less mechanistic and positivistic than it was in the early phases of the Enlightenment. Therefore, science today is better able to engage in dialogue with plausible theological hypotheses than ever before. Scientists are slowly beginning to discover that Christian theology is not conserving an antiquated world view; rather it is a partner that deserves to be taken seriously. The dialogue between theology and science needs to continue about epistemological questions as well as specific scientific hypotheses.

This survey of major conceptions of the relationship of theology and science leaves a great deal unsaid. Many more variations of the four basic types treated here could be noted, as well as many more theological examples. The four types are representative of modern theoretical discussions about creation theology and science. In recent years creation theology has begun to focus also on ecology, in an effort to develop a faith-rooted praxis that will respect and preserve nature.

## CREATION AND ECOLOGY

The current ecological crisis, which threatens the future of the matrix of life forms on earth, has brought with it questions about the relationship of the doctrine of creation to Western attitudes about nature. Some have raised the criticism that the doctrine of creation has had a highly negative influence on attitudes about nature. In the eyes of these critics the doctrine of creation is one of the causes of the exploitation of the environment to further scientific and technological advance.

In the late 1960s Lynn White, Jr., a historian, wrote an essay on the ecological crisis. He argued that the exploitative outlook that has engendered the ecological crisis in Western industrialized nations is the direct result of the Judeo-Christian tradition's conception of humanity as having dominion over nature, a conception rooted in Genesis 1:16. As a result the Western world has determined that nature exists in order to serve humans. White asserted that Christianity's anthropocentric view of creation contributes to a dualism involving humankind and nature. By emphasizing the dominion of humanity over nature, Christianity has sanctioned an exploitative ethic. White further argued that Christianity has thereby fostered science and technology as instruments of that exploitation. Since both pose manifold threats to the environment and possibly even to the existence of the planet, it follows that Christianity bears a huge burden of guilt for our ecological crisis.[122]

In response to White's thesis, Arthur R. Peacocke, a biologist and theologian, argues that an exploitation of nature that is inimical to the ecosystem and to the welfare of subsequent generations antedates the Genesis text. It has occurred from the time of primitive societies onward and is not specifically associated with Judeo-Christian cultures.[123] He further claims that the Judeo-Christian tradition does not in fact depict humanity's dominion over nature as simply brutally exploitative, as if nature were there only for humanity's benefit. In the Genesis 1 text humanity exercises the dominion that is accorded it under a delegated authority from God. The dominion assigned to humanity is as God's vice-regent, steward, or manager.[124] This interpretation is made in the context of the human depicted as being made in the "image of God." As has been noted by many authors, the scholarly consensus is that the term *image of God* refers to the fact that the human is God's representative. There is one legitimate image whereby God shows God's self, and this is the human.[125]

Peacocke points out that in this era of ecological crisis the biblical concept of dominion that depicts humans acting on behalf of a transcendent creator needs to be reinterpreted in a way that would also highlight God's immanence. In developing this emphasis on God as immanent in creation Peacocke makes several proposals for the roles of human beings. He explores the role of "priest," proposing a sacramental understanding of creation with nature depicted as worthy of humanity's reverence.[126] The role of "prophet" is depicted as a charge to call others to recognize the meaning of God's action in the world.[127] Although these special roles for humans are important, the most critical one is that of "cocreator" with God. Peacocke believes that science itself will provide the means whereby humans can cooperate and act as cocreators in God's creative processes in nature. He dismisses the notion that science is the cause of the ecological crisis. However, to be committed to use science as cocreator with God implies intelligent use of scientific knowledge and requires the willingness to forgo selfish ends in order to make the sacrifice of love

122. Lynn White, Jr., "The Historical Roots of Our Ecological Crisis," in David Spring and Eileen Spring, eds., *Ecology and Religion in History* (New York: Harper and Row, 1974), 24–28. The essay was first published in *Science* 155 (1967): 1203–7.

123. Arthur R. Peacocke, *Creation and the World of Science* (Oxford: Clarendon Press, 1979), 277.

124. Ibid., 281.

125. Ibid., 282.

126. Ibid., 295–97.

127. Ibid., 301.

that is needed to achieve ecological wholeness.[128] This means that both as individuals and as a community, people must be willing to be sufferers with God in creation. It is this role that was uniquely illumined in the Christian doctrine of the incarnation of Jesus Christ, in God's "transcendence in immanence" in the world.[129]

Peacocke hopes that his interpretation of the doctrine of creation will encourage people to become committed to the creative activity of God, who in creation always actualizes new possibilities. He does not claim to know exactly how humans are to become cocreators with God. He has not developed a specific program of action. However, he does hope that Christian faith will inspire people to make wise ecological decisions and to act for the future good of humanity and the earth's ecosystems.[130]

A theologian who shares some of the perspectives, concerns, and hopes of Peacocke is Jürgen Moltmann. In *God in Creation* he also notes that the ecological crisis has been closely associated with the directive found in Genesis 1. Those who make this association see the charge of dominion over creation and the directive to subdue the earth as a command to dominate nature, to conquer the world, and to rule over it. Moltmann believes that this criticism must be taken seriously. He writes:

> Today a theological doctrine of creation which can responsibly be maintained must first of all come to terms critically with its own tradition and the history of its own influence, before it can face up to the dialogue with the modern sciences and the contemporary philosophy of nature.[131]

Moltmann presents research that leads him to conclude that the troublesome biblical concepts of "dominion" and "subduing the earth" have nothing to do with the charge to rule over the world that people for centuries interpreted as a call to domination of the earth. The Judeo-Christian tradition of dominion is not responsible for humanity's usurpation of power over nature. The allegedly anthropocentric view of the world found in Genesis 1 is more than three thousand years old; whereas modern science and technology began to develop in Western civilization barely four hundred years

128. Ibid., 304–5, 311–12.

129. Ibid., 315.

130. Ibid., 316–17.

131. Jürgen Moltmann, *God in Creation: A New Theology of Creation and the Spirit of God*, trans. Margaret Kohl (San Francisco: Harper and Row, 1985), 21. The social and ecological content of the doctrine of creation has also been developed by Franz Schupp, an Austrian Catholic theologian and philosopher. See his *Schöpfung und Sünde: Von der Verheissung einer wahren und gerechten Welt, vom Versagen des Menschen und vom Widerstand gegen die Zerstörung* (Düsseldorf: Patmos, 1990).

ago.[132] The biblical charge to subdue the earth is a dietary command: Human beings and animals alike are to live from the fruits that the earth brings forth in the form of plants and trees. A seizure of power over nature is not intended.[133]

More so than Peacocke and most theologians who have addressed the problem of ecology, Moltmann attends to the socio-political dimension of the ecological crisis. He astutely points out that the ecological crisis brings with it social crises, that is, crises of the value and significance of science and technology in human society. Moltmann calls for the examination of structures of societal power. His own examination indicates that science is not value free; scientific research is not a detached pursuit of pure knowledge. Science is linked with politics, and science and scientists belong within the political context whether they like it or not.[134]

Moltmann points out that the high status given to science as pure knowledge and as the source of progress has affected theologians and their conception of theology. Theologians have withdrawn to the field of history, leaving nature to the scientists. The development of theologies of history seemed an appropriate way of assimilating and interpreting the historical tradition of biblical promise and future hope. Moltmann asserts:

> The theology of history was also able to evaluate the practical behavior of men and women in history. Whereas nature took on the overtones of what is timeless, static and continually recurring, "history" was filled with remembrance and hope and the real meaning of human life. History became the symbol for the world when the notion "cosmos" ceased to fulfill this function, because it had been superseded by the concept of nature as the object of the sciences. The study of history became the universal science, both theologically and atheistically.[135]

In Moltmann's judgment, this emphasis on history in contemporary theology indicates that theology has let itself participate in a dualism that defines nature and history over against one another. Moltmann calls for a new stage in the relationship of theology and science. If human beings are to survive at all, these two areas of study must recognize that they are companions in the ecological crisis and together must search for new directions and work toward new goals. In a situation in which the stakes are the preservation or destruction of the world, science and theology cannot afford to divide

---

132. Moltmann, *God in Creation*, 26.
133. Ibid., 29.
134. Ibid., 24–25.
135. Ibid., 31.

reality. Theology and the sciences must work together to resolve the ecological crisis in our world.[136]

Moltmann argues that the task of the theologian in the midst of this ecological crisis includes answering the question: How is nature to be understood as God's creation? His response is that nature is neither divine nor demonic, but is "the world," a contingent and not a necessarily existent world. Knowledge of that world through science is itself contingent and never absolute. The visible part of creation accessible to science is only part of nature. An understanding of nature as God's creation includes not only what is visible or known scientifically, but also the sector of the invisible or not-yet-known.

Moltmann's ecological theology of nature has a forceful eschatological dimension. He argues that it is not enough for theology to focus on the protological declaration that in the beginning God's creation was "good" (Gen. 1:31). This must be joined by Paul's recognition of the anxious waiting and longing of creation that is subjected to futility, but which also has the strength of hope (Rom. 8:19-21). Moltmann incorporates eschatological hope—a recurring theme in his theology—into his theology of nature. He states: "To understand nature as creation means therefore discerning nature as the enslaved creation that hopes for liberty."[137] Creation is both in bondage and open to the future in anticipation of the fullness of God's glory.

Like Peacocke, Moltmann believes that it is important in an ecological theology of nature to recover the immanence of God in creation. In his reflections on the trinitarian God of creation, he seeks to bind together God's transcendence and immanence in his interpretation of the Christian insight that God created heaven and earth through the Son and in the Spirit. The Father is the creating origin of creation and the Son its shaping origin. The Son is "the Cosmic Christ," the ground for the existence of the whole of creation, human beings and nature alike. The Spirit is the life-giving origin. Moltmann stresses the immanence of the Holy Spirit in creation. Through the Spirit, God participates in the destiny of creation. Through the Spirit, God suffers with the sufferings of creatures. In the Spirit, God experiences their annihilation and sighs with the enslaved creation for redemption and liberty. The Spirit is capable of suffering with creation, for in the Spirit is the power of the love from which creation has issued and through which it is sustained.[138]

---

136. Ibid., 34.
137. Ibid., 39. The theme of eschatological hope receives an extensive treatment in Moltmann's earlier work *Theology of Hope* (New York: Harper and Row, 1967).
138. Moltmann, *God in Creation*, 94–103.

One of the major strengths of Moltmann's emphasis of the immanence of the Spirit is that it undercuts the dualism of God and nature
that has characterized the Western Christian tradition. In focusing
on creation and ecological theologies of nature, other theologians
also seek to overcome this dualism. For example, Sallie McFague underscores affinity between God and the world in her model of God
as mother, which includes the provocative metaphor of the earth as
"God's body." In her understanding of this metaphor she does not
claim that God creates by giving birth to the world as her body, but
rather that the earth is "bodied forth from God" in the sense that
the earth is expressive of God's very being.[139] She argues that if we
looked at the earth this way we would be less likely to abuse our
coinhabitants. For to do so would be to sin against God, "against
the body," by refusing to be part of an ecological whole whose existence and success depend on a recognition of the interdependence
and interrelatedness of all species.[140]

These distinctive interpretations present creation as an ecological doctrine, a doctrine that seeks to articulate what it means to
inhabit a world that is both gift and promise. It is not possible to
delve any further into an ecological theology of creation. In this
regard it does seem that cosmology is an area ripe for fruitful theological dialogue with science. Contemporary theology with its strong
focus on history could benefit greatly from a parallel focus on the
cosmos. Creation theology needs to attend to nature and to the cosmos not as a replacement for the concerns for human emancipation
and liberation, but as a complement to them. An ecological theology of creation would be of great benefit to the poor and oppressed
who suffer due to the technological advance and consumerism of the
wealthy and whose concerns theologies of emancipation and liberation explicitly address. For human history, as it runs its course, both
profoundly affects and is affected by the cosmos, the comprehensive
ecosystem.[141]

As we approach the dawn of the twenty-first century, creation theology will likely require both reflection on scientific cosmology and

---

139. Sallie McFague, *Models of God: Theology for an Ecological, Nuclear Age* (Philadelphia: Fortress Press, 1987), 110.

140. Ibid., 114.

141. In an address entitled "Peace with All Creation" (World Day of Peace, Jan. 1,
1990), Pope John Paul II reflected on the ecological crisis in the context of a search
for world peace. He called the international political and scientific communities to
exercise ecological responsibility and to work together in solidarity for the sake of the
poor and for the well-being of future generations. See *Origins* 19 (1989–90): 465–68.
See also John Paul II's encyclical *Sollicitudo Rei Socialis*, in *Origins* 17 (1988): no. 34,
p. 653.

concrete praxis that incorporates socio-political and ecological goals to use science and technology to replenish renewable resources for the benefit of humans and of all life forms. These two areas, cosmology and praxis, which are closely connected in the age of ecological crisis, will likely provide the guiding questions for the expression of belief in the God who is both source and ground for the world we inhabit and our destiny and hope. As cosmological concerns and ecological praxis assume the center stage of creation theology, may the following directive serve as a comfort and challenge: "I set before you life and death, blessing and curse; therefore choose life, that you and your descendants may live" (Deut. 30:19). May the choices for life—the "yeses" to creation through the study, dialogue, and difficult decisions that are required for the life and health of nature—be a living hymn of thanksgiving and praise for the creator, the God who is worthy of our glory and honor.

## FOR FURTHER READING

Barbour, Ian. *Religion in the Age of Science.* New York: Harper and Row, 1990.

Explores views of God, the creator, in relationship to understandings of the world from biology, physics, astronomy, and scientific cosmology.

Barth, Karl. *The Doctrine of Creation.* Vol. 3 of *Church Dogmatics.* Edinburgh: T and T Clark, 1958–61.

Presents the doctrine of creation from an anthropological perspective. Creation is viewed as the external ground of God's covenantal history with humanity. The four parts of this volume address God, the creator; the human creature; divine providence; and ethics and freedom.

Frye, Roland Mushat, ed. *Is God a Creationist? The Religious Case against Creation-Science.* New York: Charles Scribner's Sons, 1983.

A collection of essays that presents a detailed overview of the history and development of the creationist movement and critical analysis of creation science by Roman Catholic, Protestant, and Jewish theologians.

Gilkey, Langdon. *Maker of Heaven and Earth: The Doctrine of Creation in the Light of Modern Knowledge.* 1959. Reprint. Lanham, Md.: University of America Press, 1985.

A treatment of the doctrine of creation that takes into consideration challenges from the physical sciences and modern philosophy. For the most part Gilkey understands creation to be a symbol that illumines the meaning of human existence.

Hayes, Zachary. *What Are They Saying about Creation?* New York: Paulist Press, 1980.

A general introduction to the doctrine of creation that addresses the problems raised from the positive sciences; includes a survey of the development of the doctrine with a reinterpretation of it from a largely anthropological perspective.

Hefner, Philip J. "The Creation." In *Christian Dogmatics.* Ed. Carl E. Braaten and Robert W. Jenson. Philadelphia: Fortress Press, 1984, 1:269–357.

Addresses several topics including biblical witness to creation, creation and the world, and the continuing work of creation; written from a Lutheran perspective.

McMullin, Ernan, ed. *Evolution and Creation.* Notre Dame, Ind.: University of Notre Dame Press, 1985.

A collection of essays written from a variety of perspectives in science, philosophy, and theology. The essays present arguments in favor of the compatibility of the theory of evolution and creation theology.

Moltmann, Jürgen. *God in Creation: A New Theology of Creation and the Spirit of God.* San Francisco: Harper and Row, 1985.

The second volume of a proposed five-volume work entitled *Messianic Theology.* Moltmann develops an "ecological doctrine of creation" that stresses the immanence of God in the world.

Murphy, Roland E. *The Tree of Life: An Exploration of Biblical Wisdom Literature.* New York: The Anchor Bible Reference Library, 1990.

An excellent introduction to biblical wisdom literature. It includes sections devoted to creation (pp. 118–21, 134–35) and a whole chapter on "Lady Wisdom."

Peacocke, Arthur R. *Creation and the World of Science.* Oxford: Clarendon Press, 1979.

A collection of lectures that address specific scientific theories and explore the meaning of the doctrine of creation in an age that interprets reality in scientific terms.

Peacocke, Arthur R. *God and the New Biology.* San Francisco: Harper and Row, 1986.

Treats new developments in biology as a horizon for a reconsideration of the human, of God, and of evolution.

Schmaus, Michael. *God and Creation.* Vol. 2 of *Dogma.* London: Sheed and Ward, 1969.

A presentation of creation that places it as an introduction to the "event of Christ" and the offer of salvation. Subjects treated include biblical understandings of God as the creator, the Roman Catholic teachings on creation, and divine providence.

Westermann, Claus. *Creation*. Trans. John J. Scullion. Philadelphia: Fortress Press, 1974.

Argues that an understanding of Genesis 1–3 can best be gained by examining these texts in relationship to other primeval religious myths and their depictions of the divine.

# 5

## JESUS CHRIST

5

# JESUS CHRIST

# 5

# JESUS CHRIST

## *John P. Galvin*

---

1. For a survey see John Macquarrie, *Jesus Christ in Modern Thought* (London: SCM, 1990), 175–303, 320.

# INTRODUCTION

At the center of Christian creeds and Christian faith stands the figure of Jesus Christ. For this reason, the study of christology needs
no prolonged justification. While no theology can confine itself exclusively to christology, no Christian theology would be complete
without serious reflection on Jesus Christ.

Yet, though christology is a perennial topic for theology, both the extent to which christological issues are debated and the form in which such issues are pursued have varied widely from one period of the church's history to another. Among Protestant theologians, christology has been the focus of impassioned debate for nearly two centuries.[1] Similarly, after a half-century in which first the doctrine of grace and then questions concerning the church had largely occupied the creative energies of Catholic theologians, the past two decades have witnessed an extraordinary proliferation of writing on christology in Catholic circles.[2] The results have included a reexamination of central and foundational christological issues once thought to have been definitively resolved.

Such changes do not occur accidentally. A brief comparison of past and present approaches to christology will help clarify the present situation; for practical reasons, I shall limit the discussion at this stage to the modern history of Catholic theology.

In the period between the First (1869–70) and Second (1962–65) Vatican Councils, Catholic theology was dominated by the movement known as Neo-Scholasticism. As its name suggests, this school of thought sought to revive, in modified form, the great speculative syntheses of the Middle Ages, especially the work of Thomas Aquinas (1224/25–74). During the hegemony of Neo-Scholasticism, Catholic christology was characterized by widespread consensus on central issues, such as the divinity of Christ and the interpretation of the crucifixion and the resurrection. With these questions considered settled, debate flourished only with regard to such comparatively peripheral matters as the nature and scope of Christ's human knowledge and the precise relationship of his divine and human natures. Yet the secure exterior masked a deep-seated malaise.

Neo-Scholastic theology, unlike its medieval forebears, divided doctrinal questions into two spheres of inquiry: fundamental theology and dogmatic theology. Each area had its own topics for investigation and a distinct method of argumentation. Fundamental theology, presupposing the results of Scholastic philosophy and

---

1. For a survey see John Macquarrie, *Jesus Christ in Modern Thought* (London: SCM, 1990), 175–303, 320–35.

2. As an indication of this development, see the following works, devoted entirely or in large part to christology, by major Catholic theologians: Walter Kasper, *Jesus the Christ* (New York: Paulist, 1976); Hans Küng, *On Being a Christian* (Garden City, N.Y.: Doubleday, 1976); Karl Rahner, *Foundations of Christian Faith* (New York: Seabury, 1978); Edward Schillebeeckx, *Jesus: An Experiment in Christology* (New York: Seabury, 1979); idem, *Christ: The Experience of Jesus as Lord* (New York: Seabury, 1980). For an informative study of the recent literature see William M. Thompson, *The Jesus Debate: A Survey and Synthesis* (New York: Paulist, 1985).

arguing by appeal to reason and history, examined the evidence for divine revelation, the status of Christ as divine legate, the inspiration of the Scriptures, and the foundation of the church. Its inquiry drew on the Gospels as reliable historical sources of information about Jesus' public life and his resurrection, and found historically credible both Jesus' claim to represent God and a confirmation of that claim through the fulfillment of prophecy and the performance of miracles. Building on bases established in fundamental theology, dogmatic theology studied other doctrinal issues by appeal to the authority of the Bible and of subsequent church teaching. Its treatment of Christ was in turn subdivided into two parts: christology (in the narrow sense) examined the person of Christ and consisted largely of a theology of the incarnation; soteriology (from the Greek *soteria*, salvation) explored Christ's salvific work, in particular his atoning death on the cross.

As a result of this organization, Neo-Scholastic study of Christ was fragmented, and many topics were divorced from their appropriate contexts. Jesus' public life and resurrection were considered solely from an apologetic perspective, as evidence for the validity of his divine mission, while the incarnation and crucifixion were studied in isolation. This procedure impeded development of a unified and comprehensive christology, and inhibited efforts to address contemporary christological problems in a constructive and creative manner.[3]

In sharp contrast to the Neo-Scholastic approach, current Catholic authors typically seek to overcome the artificial divisions of the recent past and to present a unified treatment of christological issues.[4] As a general rule, they devote much attention to questions emerging from biblical exegesis and strive to address specific challenges posed to Christianity by modernity. Both concerns promote increased interest in christology and require intensified consideration of its foundational questions.

---

3. Karl Rahner's seminal essay "Current Problems in Christology" (*Theological Investigations* [Baltimore: Helicon, 1961], 1:149–200), originally published in 1954, exposed the shortcomings of the prevailing approach and outlined a program for further investigation. The impact of this essay on Catholic theology can scarcely be overestimated. The treatment of Jesus in fundamental theology is thoroughly analyzed in Franz-Josef Niemann, *Jesus als Glaubensgrund in der Fundamentaltheologie der Neuzeit: Zur Genealogie eines Traktats* (Innsbruck: Tyrolia, 1983).

4. This comment is true of the works mentioned in n. 2. Exceptions to the rule are: Jean Galot, *Who Is Christ? A Theology of the Incarnation* (Chicago: Franciscan Herald, 1981); Johann Auer, *Jesus Christus—Gottes und Mariä "Sohn"* (Regensburg: Pustet, 1986); and idem, *Jesus Christus—Heiland der Welt; Maria—Christi Mutter im Heilsplan Gottes* (Regensburg: Pustet, 1988).

In order to address these concerns adequately, christology must maintain a broad scope in its inquiries. One issue that must be faced is the question of truth. Theologians cannot rest content with unfolding the implications of standard christological assertions, for these assertions are themselves subjected to challenge. Rather than taking such statements as an unquestioned point of departure, christology must explore the very basis of the traditional confessions. Indeed, as the Lutheran theologian Wolfhart Pannenberg has cogently argued, examining the grounds of Christian faith must take pride of place on the modern theological agenda.[5]

But questions of truth can be addressed only after questions of meaning have been clarified, at least to a degree. To offer an example, the truth of the assertions that "Jesus is the Christ" and that "Jesus is risen" can be considered only after their content has been specified. It may initially appear that the meaning of the words *Christ* and *risen* in these statements is clear, but this assumption will not withstand careful scrutiny. As the obscurity of the creedal references to Christ's descent into hell and his sitting at the right hand of God shows, even the presence of christological statements in such basic Christian sources as the creeds is no guarantee that their content is self-evident or easy to determine. Clarifying the meaning of Christian beliefs, while often the most arduous part of the theologian's task, can help remove many apparent obstacles to faith.

Among other effects of these developments, foundational questions such as "What does it mean to confess that Jesus is the Christ?" and "What are the grounds for belief that Jesus is the Christ?" have penetrated into the heart of systematic christology. Their presence inevitably modifies the nature of christological argumentation, for appeal to church teaching is not by itself an adequate response to them. One result is a widespread tendency among contemporary theologians to approach christology "from below," starting with the historical figure of Jesus, rather than beginning "from above," with the incarnation of the second person of the Trinity.[6] In addition,

---

5. Wolfhart Pannenberg, *Jesus—God and Man* (Philadelphia: Westminster Press, 1968), 21–37.

6. See ibid., 33–37, and Nicholas Lash, "Up and Down in Christology," in S. Sykes and D. Holmes, eds., *New Studies in Theology* (London: Duckworth, 1980), 1:31–46. The distinction between christology from below and christology from above refers to differing starting points and methods of argumentation; it should not be confused with the distinction between high christology, which affirms the divinity of Christ, and low christology, which stops short of that affirmation. A more complex typology is offered by Karl Rahner ("Die deutsche protestantische Christologie der Gegenwart," *Theologie der Zeit* 1 [1936]: 189–202), who distinguishes among "christology below," "christology from below," "christology from above," "christology from below and from above," and "christology above."

since similar concerns motivate recent Protestant authors,[7] addressing foundational issues leads to a certain ecumenical convergence in
christological questioning. Nonetheless, as we shall see in more detail, much variety remains, for different authors analyze the problems
in varying ways and propose differing strategies for addressing them.

The pages that follow present an introductory theological examination of Jesus Christ as foundation and content of Christian faith.
Following the present section, a relatively brief section will consider
diverse christologies reflected in the writings of the New Testament.
Against this background, the third section will examine the development and content of the classical Christian understandings of Christ's
person and work; here the focus will be upon patristic and medieval
thought. The exigencies of the contemporary state of christological
questioning will then lead to the fourth section, an investigation of
the historical foundations of Christian faith, with particular attention given to Jesus' public life, crucifixion, and resurrection. The
fifth section will look at two major modern christological conceptions, and the chapter will conclude with a summary of some basic
principles and guidelines for contemporary christology.

# NEW TESTAMENT CHRISTOLOGY

While efforts to pinpoint the origin of christology depend in part
on the precise meaning assigned to the term, a rudimentary form of
christology has existed since the public activity of Jesus of Nazareth
caused people to wonder what he was about and who he was. His
words and deeds provoked reaction—on the part of his wider audience, among the followers he attracted, and on the part of his foes.
What he said and did raised questions, which people answered in
different ways. An echo of some diverse responses may be found in
Mark 8:27-29, where Jesus' disciples report popular identification of
him as John the Baptist, Elijah, or one of the prophets, and Peter
confesses him as the Messiah.[8] Not all interpretations of Jesus can be

---

7. For representative examples of major different approaches to christology in
recent Protestant thought, see, in addition to Pannenberg, Jürgen Moltmann, *The
Crucified God* (New York: Harper and Row, 1974), and Schubert M. Ogden, *The Point
of Christology* (London: SCM, 1982).

8. The historical reliability of this passage is much disputed, but it can in any
case serve as an illustration of diverse assessments of Jesus. For an account of the
various exegetical positions and a treatment of the issues see Rudolf Pesch, "Das Mes-
siasbekenntnis des Petrus (Mk 8, 27-30): Neuverhandlung einer alten Frage," *Biblische
Zeitschrift* 17 (1973): 178-95; 18 (1974): 20-31.

called christology—some are based on rejection—but all do involve at least a tentative assessment of who Jesus is.

As far as Jesus' followers were concerned, this reflection continued during his lifetime, but developed more rapidly after his death, for only then was it possible to weigh the whole of his life.[9] It included, but was not limited to, attribution to Jesus of various titles (e.g., Messiah, Lord, Son of God), each of which was itself modified in the course of such application. As was inevitable, christological thought first developed in unwritten form. Only at a later stage, beginning with the epistles of Paul, did it acquire fixed literary expression.

Our access to the development of christology in these first twenty years (before and after the crucifixion) is inevitably limited and fragmentary; scholars must seek to retrace their way from material embedded in later documents, often in edited form, to its antecedents. Yet the thought of this foundational age is too decisive to be ignored; indeed, as Martin Hengel has noted, "one is tempted to say that more happened in this period of less then two decades than in the whole of the next seven centuries."[10] Various exegetes have therefore sought to provide plausible reconstructions of the course of christological development. From all indications, early thought about Jesus, on the part of his followers, was quite varied and complex.

Past efforts to analyze early christological development often chose the major christological titles of the New Testament as their point of reference and principle of organization. In an influential study, Oscar Cullmann distinguished titles that refer to Jesus' earthly work (prophet; servant; high priest), future work (Messiah; Son of man), present work (Lord; Savior), and preexistence (Word; Son of God; God). Cullmann summarized the background of each title in Judaism and Hellenism and traced the history of its application to

---

9. Some authors wish to reserve the term *christology* for later Christian thought. Thus Gerald O'Collins holds that "Christology properly began with what we can call the 'post-existent' Jesus" (*Interpreting Jesus* [New York: Paulist, 1983], 14). With somewhat different emphasis, Edward Schillebeeckx identifies christology as "a declaration, made in faith, about the totality of Jesus' life" and notes that such judgment is possible only after death (*Jesus*, 640; see also *Christ*, 831); elsewhere (e.g., *Jesus*, 741), Schillebeeckx's descriptions of christology lack this insistence on totality. In contrast, Hermann Dembowski maintains: "The task of christology can be formulated simply: christology has to speak properly of Jesus" (*Einführung in die Christologie* [Darmstadt: Wissenschaftliche Buchgesellschaft, 1976], 21). Illuminating comments on the origin and meaning of the term *christology* are provided by Gerhard Ebeling, "The Question of the Historical Jesus and the Problem of Christology," in *Word and Faith* (London: SCM, 1963), 288–89 n. 2, and idem, *Dogmatik des christlichen Glaubens* (Tübingen: Mohr, 1979), 2:10–12.

10. Martin Hengel, *The Son of God* (Philadelphia: Fortress Press, 1976), 2.

Jesus.[11] Similarly, Ferdinand Hahn investigated the major titles Son of man, Lord, Christ, Son of David, and Son of God, and treated in an appendix the theme of eschatological prophet.[12] Though varying significantly on specific points of interpretation, Cullmann and Hahn shared a common focus in their concentration on titles as the reference point for examining the origin and course of christological development.

While continuing to devote considerable attention to titles, Reginald H. Fuller adopted a significantly different principle of organization for his work.[13] Adapting Wilhelm Bousset's sharp dichotomy between Jewish and Hellenistic Christianity,[14] Fuller proposed a three-stage division among Palestinian Judaism, Hellenistic Judaism, and Hellenistic Gentile worlds. To each environment corresponded, in Fuller's judgment, particular christological patterns. The preaching of the earliest stage, the Palestinian church, had two foci: the past word and work of Jesus and his future coming in glory. The second stratum, in a Hellenistic Jewish context, transformed the primitive kerygma into a proclamation of Jesus' present work as exalted Lord and Christ; still more concerned with Jesus' functions than his being, its christology distinguished two stages in Jesus' activity, his historical ministry and his current reign. Finally, the Hellenistic Gentile mission replaced this twofold pattern with a three-stage framework of preexistence, incarnation, and exaltation. At this time affirmations about the being of Jesus, not simply his saving functions, began to develop.

Works such as these have significantly enhanced appreciation of the complexities of early christological thought. Yet the presuppositions on which such studies are based have in part been called into question. The sharp division between Palestinian and Hellenistic spheres, even in the modified form advanced by Fuller, overlooks the penetration of Greek influence into Israel during the centuries before Jesus' birth.[15] Discontent with past analyses of christologi-

---

11. Oscar Cullmann, *The Christology of the New Testament* (London: SCM, 1963). The first German edition was published in 1957.

12. Ferdinand Hahn, *The Titles of Jesus in Christology: Their History in Early Christianity* (Cleveland: World, 1969). This work, Hahn's dissertation at Heidelberg, was completed in 1961.

13. Reginald H. Fuller, *The Foundations of New Testament Christology* (London: Collins, 1965).

14. Wilhelm Bousset, *Kyrios Christos: A History of the Belief in Christ from the Beginnings of Christianity to Irenaeus* (Nashville: Abingdon, 1970). The original edition was published in 1913.

15. See Larry W. Hurtado, "New Testament Christology: A Critique of Bousset's Influence," *Theological Studies* 40 (1979): 306–17. Hurtado is strongly influenced by Martin Hengel, *Judaism and Hellenism*, 2 vols. (Philadelphia: Fortress Press, 1974).

cal development, contemporary exegetes have continued to propose new reconstructions.

Among the many efforts to outline early christological thought, a proposal advanced by Helmut Koester is worthy of note as an initially helpful way of classifying the data. Koester identifies four basic christological trajectories that arose, independently of each other, in different Christian circles in the years between Jesus' death and the writing of the New Testament.[16]

1. An initial type, possibly the most primitive of all, conceived of Jesus as Son of man and coming Lord. Eschatological in focus, this parousia christology continued Jesus' own future-oriented preaching, but also identified him as the divine agent who would soon return in glory to judge the world. This christological trajectory is reflected in such biblical passages as the apocalyptic discourse of Mark 13, the judgment scene of Matthew 25:31-46, and the Pauline exhortation of 1 Thessalonians 4:13—5:3. Ecclesiologically, it tends to foster separation of Jesus' followers from the rest of society.

2. In sharp contrast to the parousia christology's orientation toward the future, the second christological trajectory looks back on events in Jesus' public life, especially his miracles and exorcisms. Drawing on popular conceptions of the presence of divine powers in gifted religious figures, it understands Jesus as a "divine man" (*theios aner*). Divine-man christology, evident in references to "Jesus of Nazareth, a man attested to you by God with mighty works and wonders and signs which God did through him in your midst" (Acts 2:22), promoted the handing on and embellishment of miracle stories (see, e.g., Mark 1:23-45); it may also be detected in the opponents Paul criticizes in 2 Corinthians. While not conducive to the development of stable communal consciousness, this model has exerted strong influence on the piety of individual Christians.

3. A third trajectory, wisdom christology, parallels the second in its concentration on Jesus' public life, but sees him as teacher rather than miracle-worker. In this model, Jesus is identified as envoy of divine wisdom (e.g., Matt. 11:25-30; Luke 11:49-51) or even, in more developed forms, as wisdom incarnate (John 1:1-18; Phil. 2:5-11). The ecclesiological effect is a concentration on teaching, manifest in the development of the parable tradition, with corresponding focus on the theological school.

4. Lastly, a fourth christological model directed its attention to Jesus as crucified and raised from the dead. Reflected in early creedal

---

16. For the following see Helmut Koester, "The Structure and Criteria of Early Christian Beliefs," in James M. Robinson and Helmut Koester, *Trajectories through Early Christianity* (Philadelphia: Fortress Press, 1971), 205–31.

formulations (e.g., 1 Cor. 15:3-8) and liturgical tradition (1 Cor. 11:23-26), this paschal christology was strongly promoted by Paul. It took seriously the reality of human life and suffering, eventually created the literary genre of the canonical Gospels, and facilitated the Christian church's self-understanding as a new society created by God.

While approximately equal in age, these four christological models are not, in Koester's judgment, equal in quality. In the canonical New Testament, paschal christology predominates and functions as the unifying factor. Far from being fortuitous, its preeminence reflects inherent superiority: greater fidelity to the historical Jesus, greater church-building power, and the ability to provide a framework within which the other types could be incorporated and used to enable formation of the gospel tradition.

Reaction to Koester's reconstruction of early christological development has varied. Edward Schillebeeckx has adopted, with some modifications, much of Koester's analysis, but differs from Koester on two salient points. First, Schillebeeckx argues that prior to the emergence of any of the four trajectories, Jesus was identified as the long-awaited eschatological prophet, promised to Israel in words God addressed to Moses: "I will raise up for them a prophet like you from among their brethren; and I will put my words in his mouth, and he shall speak to them all that I command him" (Deut. 18:18). This initial identification of Jesus as the prophet like Moses undergirds the more differentiated models and accounts for the ability of the New Testament to unify them. Second, Schillebeeckx offers a different theological assessment of the various approaches. In his judgment, the identification of Jesus as eschatological prophet holds theological, as well as historical, pride of place. Paschal christology is placed on the same level as the other models, and Koester's conviction of its inherent superiority is abandoned.[17]

Exegetes have also questioned certain aspects of Koester's work. In an assessment of Schillebeeckx's adaptation of Koester's reconstruction, George MacRae observed that "it is not entirely clear that these and only these are the earliest conceptions," and wondered if "adoptionist" christology might be equally primitive.[18] Pointing in another direction, Petr Pokorny has stressed the centrality of the resurrection for all strands of christology and warned against exaggerating the extent of diversity within the New Testament.[19]

---

17. For Schillebeeckx's arguments see *Jesus*, 401–515.

18. George MacRae, *Religious Studies Review* 5 (1979): 270–73. The citation is from p. 271.

19. Petr Pokorny, *The Genesis of Christology* (Edinburgh: T and T Clark, 1987).

Appealing to 1 Corinthians 15:11, Martin Hengel has also emphasized the unity of the early apostolic preaching.[20] Thus Koester's reconstruction should not be taken as a definitive solution to the problem of christology's early development.

Yet, despite such criticisms, Koester's analysis of early christological trajectories can serve as a useful reference point in considering biblical interpretations of Jesus. At the very least, it draws attention to the depth and complexity of Christian thought in the formative years antedating the writing of the New Testament and serves as a warning against facile attempts to reduce christological reflection to a single title or a single perspective.

In the New Testament itself, interpretations of Jesus achieve canonical expression in more developed forms. While past studies of New Testament theology concentrated almost exclusively on Paul and John,[21] methods developed over the past four decades have led to the recognition of distinctive christologies in other biblical authors as well. Since its inception in the 1950s with the pioneering work of Willi Marxsen on Mark, Günther Bornkamm on Matthew, and Hans Conzelmann on Luke, redaction criticism has succeeded in detecting the theological positions of the individual Synoptic evangelists by studying the ways in which these writers modified the sources on which they drew.[22] More recently, application of the principles of literary criticism to gospel research has shed light on the evangelists' theologies by examining the techniques employed in structuring their narratives.[23] These approaches make clear that the authors of the Synoptic Gospels, far from being mere collectors of available material about Jesus, were accomplished theologians whose works contain rich presentations of christology not inferior to the more obviously theological reflections of the Pauline letters and Johannine writings. Each New Testament au-

---

20. Martin Hengel, *The Atonement* (Philadelphia: Fortress Press, 1981), 34–39.

21. See, for example, Rudolf Bultmann, *Theology of the New Testament*, 2 vols. (New York: Scribner's, 1951, 1955).

22. The classic texts are Willi Marxsen, *Mark the Evangelist: Studies on the Redaction History of the Gospel* (Nashville: Abingdon, 1969); Günther Bornkamm, Gerhard Barth, and Heinz Joachim Held, *Tradition and Interpretation in Matthew* (London: SCM, 1963); and Hans Conzelmann, *The Theology of Saint Luke* (London: Faber and Faber, 1961). For an informative account of the development, refinement, and use of redaction criticism see Raymond F. Collins, *Introduction to the New Testament* (Garden City, N.Y.: Doubleday, 1983), 196–230.

23. See Jack Dean Kingsbury, *Jesus Christ in Matthew, Mark, and Luke* (Philadelphia: Fortress Press, 1981); idem, *Matthew* (Philadelphia: Fortress Press, 1978); Paul J. Achtemeier, *Mark*, 2d ed. (Philadelphia: Fortress Press, 1986); and Frederick W. Danker, *Luke*, 2d ed. (Philadelphia: Fortress Press, 1987).

thor offers a distinctive and valuable interpretation of Jesus' life and work.[24]

New Testament christology thus spans a considerable range, as it includes the Pauline focus on Jesus' cross and resurrection, the Synoptic interpretations of his public life and passion, the Johannine account of the revelation of God in the Word become flesh, and the diverse reflections on Jesus embodied in the other canonical texts. This variety in perspective and content prevents distillation of a common christology that could be termed *the* biblical conception of Jesus and used as a unified basis for further thought. Nonetheless, the diversity is not without limit;[25] all New Testament authors share a common conviction that in and through Jesus something decisive for human salvation has occurred. The combination of diversity and unity suggests several elements of the New Testament's permanent legacy to the church's christological reflection.

First, nowhere in the New Testament is christology developed in isolation from other theological questions. It is inseparable from a theology of history (including an eschatology), a conception of salvation, and a perspective on the church. These interconnections are not a historical accident; they reflect relationships inherent in the nature of christology.

Second, the diversity of biblical christology and its close connection with specific issues confronting the church at the time it was developed imply that systematic theology cannot rest content with merely organizing New Testament thought into a more orderly form. The New Testament itself demands that we move beyond it—a fact that in no way detracts from its permanent importance. It is in this sense that Schillebeeckx has observed that "New Testament Christianity can only be a model indirectly, and not directly,"[26] for later Christians.

Third, the importance of the New Testament's references to history, to certain factual events of the past and certain expectations regarding the future, must not be overlooked. Christology is not an expression of timeless truths; it is an assertion of the universal sig-

---

24. For recent treatments of the christologies of the major New Testament authors, see Jerome H. Neyrey, *Christ Is Community: The Christologies of the New Testament* (Wilmington, Del.: Glazier, 1985), and Arland J. Hultgren, *Christ and His Benefits: Christology and Redemption in the New Testament* (Philadelphia: Fortress Press, 1987).

25. Gerhard Ebeling (*The Word of God and Tradition* [Philadelphia: Fortress Press, 1968], 151) has rightly insisted that "in the last resort there has not been an indiscriminate acceptance of anything into the canon." These issues are pursued further in Alex Stock, *Einheit des Neuen Testaments: Erörterung hermeneutischer Grundpositionen der heutigen Theologie* (Einsiedeln: Benziger, 1969).

26. Schillebeeckx, *Christ*, 561.

nificance of someone who lived and died in a particular time and place.

Fourth, tendencies to divide the New Testament into works that propose a "high christology" (affirming Jesus' divinity) and those content with "low christology" (stopping short of that affirmation) should be viewed with suspicion. Such divisions are likely to confuse biblical expressions with similar terminology from the church's dogmatic tradition (e.g., by taking "Son of man" as a designation for Christ's humanity) and to underestimate the christological content articulated in forms unfamiliar to later usage.

Finally, both the content and the diversity of New Testament christology inevitably pose the question of the legitimacy of the interpretations of Jesus given by the various biblical authors and by the early church in general. Karl Rahner has noted that if the New Testament evaluations of Jesus are valid, then the further step to the doctrine of the early councils is not especially problematic.[27] While the church recognizes the Scriptures as divinely inspired,[28] the validity of the New Testament's christological affirmations cannot simply be presumed in theological argumentation; it must be examined critically. One portion of that examination is, inevitably, a look at these affirmations' historical basis in Jesus' life and death.[29] Before considering these matters, however, we must first examine the postbiblical development of Christian thought on Jesus and his salvific work.


## CLASSICAL CHRISTOLOGY AND SOTERIOLOGY

The classical expression of the church's teaching about Jesus Christ was forged in the centuries immediately following completion of the New Testament. Christological reflection continued in the second and third centuries, especially in efforts to express Jesus' relationship to the Father and in conjunction with denials of Jesus' true humanity. Yet it was only in the fourth and fifth centuries that the development of classical christological doctrine reached its climax. The fourth-century controversy centered on Arianism and was addressed by the Council of Nicaea, the first ecumenical council, in 325. One hundred years later, the issues of Nestorianism and monophysitism were weighed by the councils of Ephesus (431) and Chalcedon (451). In

---

27. Rahner, *Foundations of Christian Faith*, 285–86.

28. On biblical inspiration see the Second Vatican Council's Dogmatic Constitution on Divine Revelation (*Dei Verbum*), nos. 11–13.

29. As will become clear later in the chapter, this last point is not undisputed; such theologians as Rudolf Bultmann and Schubert Ogden deny it.

the aftermath of these councils, some related christological matters were considered by the Third Council of Constantinople in 681. The first part of this section will consider the formation of christological doctrine during this decisive period.

Motivated by concern for human salvation but formulated in opposition to doctrines judged to be heretical, the teaching of the early ecumenical councils focused on the person of Christ rather than his salvific work. Interpretations of his salvific activity developed at a different pace and never achieved comparable dogmatic status. For this reason, despite the intrinsic connection between the person and work of Christ, I shall postpone consideration of classical soteriological thought until later in this section.

## CHRISTOLOGY

In the fourth century, the major christological issues were the divinity of Christ and the integrity, or completeness, of his humanity. The chief biblical point of reference was John 1:14: "The Word [*Logos*] became flesh [*sarx*]." In the terms of Koester's models, the christology of this period was largely a pursuit of one strand of primitive Christian thought: the incarnational type of wisdom christology reflected in the prologue to the Fourth Gospel.

About the year 318, Arius, a priest in Alexandria (the center of Egyptian Christianity), advanced the teaching that the Logos is not truly God, not equal to the Father. Instead, the Logos was created out of nothing by the Father as the first and highest creature, the only created reality made directly by God. The Word can be called Son and even God ("and the Word was God" [John 1:1]), but is not of the same substance as the Father. While the Word existed before all other creatures, his existence had a beginning; there was a time when he was not. In due course, the Logos functioned as the instrument of the rest of creation ("all things were made through him" [John 1:3]), while God remained in exalted distance from the world. In the incarnation, the Word became flesh through union with a human body. No human soul was present, for its place was taken by the Logos. Thus Jesus Christ, in Arian understanding, is an intermediary being, neither divine nor human.

An appealing figure, Arius quickly won popular support. In 320 he was condemned and excommunicated by a regional synod at Alexandria, but these measures proved ineffective, as his following was too large. Finally, in May 325, the emperor Constantine convened a general synod of bishops at Nicaea (in modern Turkey, not far from Istanbul). This first ecumenical council was well attended, with 220–300 participants. (Estimates vary; the traditional figure of 318 is symbolic, based on the number of Abraham's warriors in Genesis 14:14.)

After long and bitter debate, during which Arius was supported by several bishops, the anti-Arian party prevailed. An ancient creed of uncertain origin was reworked into the Nicene Creed, still used liturgically, though in expanded form. Subordination of the Logos to the Father was unambiguously rejected. The council professed that the Son is "true God from true God, begotten not made, of one substance (*homoousios*) with the Father." Of particular importance was the introduction of the nonbiblical term *homoousios*, which precluded diminution of the divinity of Christ and became the touchstone of fidelity to the conciliar teaching. To the creed itself the council appended an anathema directed against those who maintained characteristic Arian tenets.[30]

Despite condemnation at Nicaea, Arianism persisted for some time in many variants, as several compromise formulations were proposed. The controversy focused on Arianism's denial of Christ's divinity; those involved in the controversy took less account of the fact that Arianism also undercut Christ's humanity. In the ensuing disputes, the chief proponent of Nicaea's teaching was Athanasius, who had been present at the council as an Alexandrian deacon and in 328 became bishop of Alexandria. His chief argument against the Arians was soteriological. "He became man that we might be divinized."[31] Salvation is participation in divine life (see 2 Peter 1:4). Unless the Logos is divine, Athanasius argued, salvation through Christ is impossible; an adequate theology of salvation requires rejection of all forms of Arianism.

With much difficulty, Nicaea's rejection of Arianism won general acceptance in East and West over the course of the next half-century. Eventually, the climate became emphatically anti-Arian, with heavy stress on the divinity of Christ in theology and general piety.[32]

---

30. For the Greek text and an English translation see J. N. D. Kelly, *Early Christian Creeds*, 3d ed. (New York: McKay, 1972), 215–16. On Arianism and the Council of Nicaea see ibid., 205–62; Kelly, *Early Christian Doctrines* (New York: Harper and Row, 1960), 223–51; Leo D. Davis, *The First Seven Ecumenical Councils (325–787): Their History and Theology* (Wilmington, Del.: Glazier, 1987), 33–80; Alois Grillmeier, *Christ in Christian Tradition*, 2d ed. (Atlanta: Knox, 1975), 1:219–73; John Courtney Murray, *The Problem of God* (New Haven: Yale University Press, 1964), 31–60; and I. Ortiz de Urbina, *Nicee et Constantinople* (Paris: Éditions de l'Orante, 1963), 13–136.

31. Athanasius *De Incarn.* 54 (*Patrologia Graeca*, ed. Migne [hereafter PG], 25, 192b).

32. On the effects see Josef A. Jungmann, *The Place of Christ in Liturgical Prayer* (Staten Island, N.Y.: Alba House, 1965).

Before we proceed to the christological councils of the fifth century, a few remarks must be made about earlier thought on the humanity of Christ. At an early date, some denied the reality of Christ's body, often on the basis of a general conviction that matter is evil. Gnostics and Manicheans held that his body was only a costume worn to conceal his true identity (a position called docetism, from the Greek *dokeo*, seem). Among other things, these views entail denial of the reality of the crucifixion.

A more specifically christological rejection of the integrity of Christ's humanity is the denial of the presence in him of all or part of a human soul. Arianism held this position, along with its denial of his divinity. While affirming the divinity of the Logos, Apollinarianism (named after Apollinarius, bishop of Laodicea from ca. 360) held that the active principle of the soul, the *nous*, was replaced in Christ by the Logos. In its subordination to the Logos, Christ's humanity lacked its own active principle. This teaching was rightly repudiated by most Christians. The First Council of Constantinople (381), though more concerned to defend the divinity of the Holy Spirit against the Pneumatomachians, also rejected Apollinarianism in passing.[33] Operative in theological criticism of Apollinarianism was the soteriological principle already mentioned: If Christ does not have a human soul, then he is not truly human; if he is not truly human, then we are not truly saved.

Both Arianism and Apollinarianism, and also much orthodox christology, have a common basis in the use of what has been called a Logos-*sarx* (Word-flesh) christological model. Typical of Alexandria, this approach is represented by Athanasius, among others. The terminology is derived from John 1:14. There *sarx* does not mean body as distinguished from soul, but rather full human reality.[34] Later Logos-*sarx* christology, however, typically compared the unity of divinity and humanity in Jesus with the union of soul and body in all human beings, and either denied the presence of a human soul in Christ (Arius, Apollinarius) or affirmed the integrity of his humanity without seeing his human soul (intellect and will) as a major salvific factor (Athanasius). This Alexandrian christology continued into the fifth century, with Cyril (patriarch of Alexandria, 412–44) its major proponent. In this approach the unity of Christ, based on the rule of the Logos, is so emphasized that the role of Christ's humanity is obscured, though its reality is not denied.

---

33. On this council see Davis, *The First Seven Ecumenical Councils*, 81–133, and Ortiz de Urbina, *Nicee*, 137–242.

34. On this verse see Raymond E. Brown, *The Gospel according to John* (Garden City, N.Y.: Doubleday, 1966), 1:13, 30–35.

In the late fourth and early fifth centuries, a new type of christology arose further to the East. Centered in Antioch, this approach has been called a Logos-*anthropos* (Word-man) christology. Its chief early figures, Diodor of Tarsus (d. before 394) and Theodore of Mopsuestia (d. 428), were connected with Antioch's school of catechists. In contrast to Alexandria, the Antiochene school emphasized the distinction of two natures in Christ and sought to give full scope to his human nature. It encountered difficulty, however, in articulating clearly the unity of Christ.

Behind the thought of each school lie legitimate christological concerns. Yet, in the fifth century, when each school absolutized its position and ignored or rejected the intention of the other, serious problems arose. Christological debate raged from 428, when controversy erupted in Constantinople, to 451, when a widely accepted resolution was produced at the Council of Chalcedon. To understand Chalcedon's achievement, it is necessary to grasp the history of the dispute. The first stage is marked by the rise and rejection of Nestorianism.

In 428, Nestorius, an Antiochene monk, was appointed patriarch of Constantinople by Emperor Theodosius II. Later that year he was drawn into a dispute concerning the use of *theotokos* (bearer of God) as a title for Mary. Though the title was ancient and enjoyed considerable popularity, Nestorius supported its critics and recommended instead honoring Mary as *christotokos*, bearer of Christ. That term was certainly unobjectionable, but the legitimacy of *theotokos* remained a matter of contention.

While the language directly concerns Mary, the underlying issue is christological and was immediately recognized as such: Is the unity of Christ such that his mother can be called Mother of God? Aside from considerations of context, the word *theotokos* can have varying meanings. Its use as a Marian title cannot mean that Mary is divine or that she is the source of Christ's divinity. Nonetheless, since motherhood relates to a person and since the person of Jesus is divine, Mary is rightly called Mother of God. As far as Jesus' natures are concerned, she is the source of his human reality, not his divinity. Thus the term *theotokos*, ambiguous in itself, has a legitimate Christian sense.[35]

In 428, the christological terminology used in the preceding paragraph, especially *person* and *nature*, was not yet available for common use. The dispute quickly became bitter. Monks in Constantinople, Alexandrian in their theological orientation, opposed Nestorius,

---

35. These issues are discussed helpfully by Karl Rahner in remarks cited by Klaus Riesenhuber, *Maria im theologischen Verständnis von Karl Barth and Karl Rahner* (Freiburg: Herder, 1973), 72–73 n. 49.

and immediately sent excerpts from his writings to Alexandria and Rome. The patriarch of Alexandria, Cyril, and Nestorius then exchanged letters. Cyril offered a detailed commentary on the teaching of Nicaea, and urged Nestorius to alter his views. Nestorius in turn accused Cyril of misunderstanding Nicaea. Each wrote to Rome seeking support, but only Cyril strengthened his case by providing translations of the disputed texts. In 430, a local Roman synod under Celestine I condemned Nestorius's teaching and authorized Cyril to obtain from Nestorius a repudiation of his previous position. When Nestorius refused to comply, Cyril conducted a synod in Alexandria. The synod produced a christological confession and a list of twelve anathemas (see Denzinger-Schönmetzer, *Enchiridion Symbolorum* [hereafter DS], 252–63), which were sent to Constantinople for Nestorius to sign. In addition to speaking of Mary as *theotokos*, the text refers to a "natural union" in Christ and compares the union of his divinity and humanity to the union of soul and body in all human beings. The Alexandrians were apparently unaware that such language would inevitably awaken suspicions of Apollinarianism.

Hoping to reestablish peace, Emperor Theodosius convened a council to assemble in Ephesus on June 7, 431. On the appointed day over two hundred bishops, including both Cyril and Nestorius, were present, but the Eastern bishops, led by John of Antioch, had not yet arrived. On June 22, despite their continued absence, Cyril forced the opening of the council, over the protests of at least sixty bishops and the imperial representative. Under the circumstances, Nestorius refused to appear. On its first day, the council read the Nicene Creed, Cyril's second letter to Nestorius, and Nestorius's reply. The letter of Cyril was approved, and Nestorius's response was condemned as contrary to Nicaea. The twelve anathemas of the Alexandrian synod were received favorably, but not voted on. Finally, Nestorius was deposed.

Four days later, the Eastern bishops arrived in Ephesus. Upon hearing what had happened, they immediately assembled and condemned Cyril, both for his procedure and for favoring Arianism and Apollinarianism. In early July, the papal legates reached Ephesus and, in accordance with their instructions, confirmed the condemnation of Nestorius. Cyril's party then excommunicated the bishop of Antioch. At this point, the emperor's representative ended the council. Theodosius eventually took Cyril's part, and exiled Nestorius from Constantinople, first to Antioch and then to Egypt. Cyril returned to Alexandria a theological and political success.

The Council of Ephesus produced no new creed and no new christological formula. Its accomplishments were limited to condemning

Nestorianism, affirming the legitimacy of *theotokos* as a title for Mary, and accepting Cyril's second letter to Nestorius as an authentic interpretation of Nicaea. A complete victory for the Alexandrian school, the council was too one-sided to bring about reconciliation.[36]

From the conclusion of the council until Cyril's death in 444, efforts were made to reunite the two factions. Both John of Antioch and Cyril were anxious to bring about reconciliation. In 433 Theodoret of Cyrrhus, the last great Antiochene theologian, composed a creed of union and an explanation of proper christological vocabulary (DS 271–73), which were acceptable to Cyril. The creed speaks of two natures in Christ, yet also confesses that there is but "one Christ, one Son, one Lord." The title *theotokos* is applied to Mary. Drawing on the terminology of Nicaea but expanding its use, the creed teaches that Christ is *homoousios* with the Father according to his divinity and *homoousios* with us according to his humanity. While the creed of union was not universally accepted— some Alexandrians felt that Cyril conceded too much in accepting reference to two natures—the new formula resulted in a relatively peaceful period that lasted until Cyril's death in 444.[37]

Cyril was succeeded at Alexandria by his archdeacon Dioscorus, a foe of the two-natures terminology and of Cyril's policy of reconciliation. Four years later, Eutyches, the leader of the monks in Constantinople, rejected the formula of union and accused its defenders of Nestorianism; he taught instead the presence of one nature in Christ (monophysitism). Under the leadership of the patriarch Flavian, a synod in Constantinople condemned Eutyches, but he found support from Dioscorus and from Emperor Theodosius. Over the opposition of the bishop of Rome, Leo the Great (440–61), the emperor summoned a new general council, to meet again in Ephesus. Dioscorus was designated to preside, and the council was intended to repeat the condemnation of Nestorianism, condemn Flavian, and rehabilitate Eutyches.

The assembly convened on August 8, 449. Roman legates arrived with a dogmatic letter from Leo (DS 290–95), which stressed the unity of Christ and confessed the presence of two natures. The legates were not allowed to have the letter read. Instead, Eutyches defended his teaching and was declared orthodox by about 80 percent of the 130–40 bishops in attendance. When the minority protested efforts to have Flavian deposed, Dioscorus had

---

36. On Nestorianism and the Council of Ephesus see Grillmeier, *Christ in Christian Tradition*, 1:443–87.

37. For an English translation of the formula of union see Davis, *The First Seven Ecumenical Councils*, 161–62.

the assembly disrupted by imperial soldiers and a crowd of monks. A later meeting, which the papal legates refused to attend, condemned the major Antiochene theologians. Alexandria had once again triumphed, and the reunion of 433 was annulled.

Yet the meeting at Ephesus won no general acceptance. Both Flavian and the papal legates protested to Rome. Leo denounced the assembly as a gathering of robbers and demanded that a new council be convened. In July 450, the death of Theodosius brought with it a shift in imperial policy. Theodosius's influential and antimonophysite sister Pulcheria quickly married Marcian, a former military commander, and aided her husband to the throne. The new emperor exiled Eutyches from Constantinople and called a council, initially intended for Nicaea in deliberate imitation of Constantine, but finally convened at Chalcedon, very near Constantinople, on October 8, 451.

Chalcedon was the best attended of the early councils, with approximately 350 bishops in attendance, all but seven from the East. Influenced by Roman legates and imperial commissioners, its early sessions reaffirmed the Nicene Creed and Leo's letter to Flavian. Dioscorus was then tried and deposed. In the fifth session, a crisis developed, as the imperial representatives insisted on formulating a new creed, in order to achieve complete clarity. After a first draft was found ambiguous, especially by the Roman legates, a commission of bishops succeeded in drawing up an acceptable text, which was then adopted. This creed became the classical formulation of christological doctrine. Its purpose is to profess both the unity of Christ and the completeness of his divinity and humanity:

> Following then the holy Fathers, we all with one voice teach that it should be confessed that our Lord Jesus Christ is one and the same Son, the Same perfect in Godhead, the Same perfect in manhood, truly God and truly man, the Same (consisting) of a rational soul and a body; *homoousios* with the Father as to his Godhead, and the Same *homoousios* with us as to his manhood; in all things like unto us, sin only excepted; begotten of the Father before ages as to his Godhead, and in the last days, the Same, for us and for our salvation, of Mary the Virgin *Theotokos* as to his manhood;
>
> One and the same Christ, Son, Lord, Only begotten, made known in two natures (which exist) without confusion, without change, without division, without separation; the difference of the natures having been in no wise taken away by reason of the union, but rather the properties of each being preserved, and (both) concurring into one Person (*prosopon*) and one *hypostasis*—not parted or divided into two persons (*prosopa*), but one and the same Son and Only-begotten, the divine Logos, the Lord

Jesus Christ; even as the prophets from of old (have spoken) concerning him, and as the Lord Jesus Christ himself has taught us, and as the Symbol of the Fathers has delivered to us.[38]

The council expresses its doctrine in a variety of ways. The definition first professes belief in the unity of Christ with the simple confession that "our Lord Jesus Christ is one and the same Son." The phrase "one and the same" is used twice, the word *same* four other times, thus emphasizing the unity. Here the text draws on the creed of union of 433, but uses nontechnical expressions that both schools, Alexandrian and Antiochene, could understand, thus establishing a context for reconciling the conflicting terminologies.

In an equally understandable way, stress is laid on both the divinity and the humanity of Christ. To accomplish this, the most disputed word of the previous century, *homoousios*, is used twice: Christ is *homoousios* with the Father and *homoousios* with us. (The meaning is of course not the same in each case: There is only one divine nature, while there are many human beings.)

Yet the fifth-century debate had to be addressed more precisely. Chalcedon therefore spoke of Christ as one "in two natures" (not "from two natures"), a clear rejection of monophysitism. The creed then confesses that the difference of the natures (divine and human) is not removed by their union but rather preserved, as the two natures are united in one person (*prosopon*) and one hypostasis. The term *hypostasis* is used in addition to *prosopon* to stress that in this context *prosopon* signifies something real, and not what its original meaning in profane Greek would suggest: a mask, or appearance. In English it is customary to speak of the "hypostatic union" of the two natures in the one person of Christ.

Of special importance is the council's use of four adverbs, which express in summary form key characteristics of the union: *asygchytos*, without confusion; *atreptos*, without change; *adiairetos*, without division; *achoristos*, without separation. The first two adverbs contain a rejection of monophysitism, by insisting that neither nature is destroyed in the union; the final set rejects Nestorianism, by insisting on Christ's unity. The juxtaposition of the four words reflects Chalcedon's concern to oppose the extreme positions of both Alexandria and Antioch. The balance that results accounts in large part for the council's success.[39]

---

38. The translation is taken from Robert V. Sellers, *The Council of Chalcedon: A Historical and Doctrinal Survey* (London: SPCK, 1953), 210–11. For the original Greek text (with Latin translation) see DS 301–2.

39. For further indication of the issues Chalcedon's definition helps to clarify see Bernard Lonergan, "Christ as Subject: A Reply," in *Collection* (New York: Herder,

Chalcedon's use of *person* and *nature* is not identical with the way these terms were used in any particular ancient philosophy. Nor does the council seek to provide a precise definition of its technical vocabulary. Rather, the meaning of the terms is specified operatively, i.e., by the way they are used. Like other dogmatic definitions, Chalcedon's teaching entails an ecclesial regulation of language: In this case, the church determines authoritatively that certain words (*nature, person*) are to be used in a specific way in christological application. This decision contributes to preserving and promoting Christian unity in faith by providing a common language for use in speaking about Christ. Yet it does not preclude use of other terminology in speaking of Jesus. Nor does it imply that the words in question have always had the meaning attributed to them by the council.[40]

The standard argument in support of Chalcedon's teaching appeals to the "communication of idioms," or the exchange of attributes. Presupposing biblical christology, this argumentation notes that in the New Testament both divine and human attributes are predicated of the one subject, Christ. Reference is made to such passages as Acts 3:15 ("You have killed the author of life") and John 17:5 ("Father, glorify me with the glory which I had with you before the world was made"). Such statements are possible only if both natures, divine and human, are present and united in a single person; a merely moral union would not be sufficient to justify speaking in this way of death and suffering.

Despite its balance, Chalcedon was not universally accepted. Most Egyptian bishops rejected the two-natures terminology as a betrayal of Ephesus and Cyril, while Nestorians remained unwilling to accept *theotokos*. Both monophysite and Nestorian churches still exist; Coptic Christians (chiefly in Egypt and Ethiopia) remain monophysite, and there are Nestorians in Syria and India. In recent decades, ecumenical dialogue has reached considerable agreement on christological issues, but intractable ecclesiological matters remain a stumbling block to reunion.[41]

---

1967), 192–93. "Two natures" answers the question of "what" Jesus Christ is; "one person" answers the question of "who" he is.

40. On the regulation of language inherent in all dogmatic definitions see Karl Rahner, "What Is a Dogmatic Statement?" in *Theological Investigations* (Baltimore: Helicon, 1966), 5:42–66. On the council's use of words as technical terms see Frans Jozef van Beeck, *Christ Proclaimed: Christology as Rhetoric* (New York: Paulist, 1979), 131–33.

41. See Grillmeier, *Christ in Christian Tradition*, vol. 2, pt. 1 (Atlanta: Knox, 1987); W. de Vries, "The Reasons for the Rejection of the Council of Chalcedon by the Oriental Orthodox Churches," *Wort und Wahrheit*, supplement 1 (Vienna: Herder, 1972), 54–60; Ronald G. Roberson, "The Modern Roman Catholic–Oriental Orthodox Dialogue," *One in Christ* 21 (1985): 238–54.

In the years after Chalcedon, various efforts were made to reconcile the monophysites, chiefly by retaining Chalcedon's formula but placing greater stress on the unity of Christ. One such effort had significant doctrinal repercussions. To allay fears about division within Christ, the patriarch Sergius of Constantinople (610–38) taught that although there are two natures in Christ, there is only one operation of the will, which is both divine and human. Many monophysites found this formulation acceptable. The resulting reconciliation of several provinces with Constantinople won the approval of the emperor Heraclius (610–41), who in 638 signed a decree confessing "one will of our Lord Jesus Christ." This teaching is open to the interpretation that the exercise of Jesus' human freedom was always an act of the one person (in that case it is faithful to Chalcedon); but it could also be taken as a denial of the existence of a human will in Jesus (in which case the integrity of his human nature is abbreviated).

While Pope Honorius (625–38; see DS 487–88) did not object to the teaching, others—for example, Maximus Confessor and Sophronius of Jerusalem—saw the problem more clearly. In 649, a Lateran synod (DS 510) condemned monothelitism (one will in Christ) and taught instead the presence of two harmoniously united wills, one divine, one human. After fierce controversy, during which the aged Maximus was barbarically tortured at the hands of monothelites, the matter was finally addressed at the Third Council of Constantinople (680–81; DS 553–59). The christological definition of Constantinople III cites Chalcedon, teaches the presence of two wills and two operations of the wills in Jesus, and notes the submission of his human will to the divine will. This teaching does not add to the content of Chalcedon, for two natures implies two wills, but it was an important explicitation and defense of Chalcedonian doctrine. More than an abstract principle is at stake, for without a human will Christ could exercise no human freedom.[42]

With the Third Council of Constantinople, the development of church doctrine on the person of Jesus is substantially complete. Christological issues, in this sense, were not at stake in the division of the Eastern and Western churches or at the time of the Reformation, and thus did not evoke additional official reaction. More recently, such mid–twentieth-century Neo-Scholastic theologians as Paul Galtier and Pietro Parente have debated the implications of the

---

42. On the history of Constantinople III see Davis, *The Seven Ecumenical Councils*, 258–89. The theological significance of the issue is discussed by Raymund Schwager, *Der wunderbare Tausch: Zur Geschichte und Deutung der Erlösungslehre* (Munich: Kösel, 1986), 135–60.

hypostatic union for Christ's psychological constitution,[43] and many authors have analyzed the differences between the use of the terms *person* and *nature* in the ancient councils and the meaning of these words in contemporary usage.[44] But modern official statements on the person of Christ, such as Pope Pius XII's encyclical *Sempiternus Rex* (1951) and the Congregation for the Doctrine of the Faith's declaration *Mysterium Filii Dei* (1972), largely confine themselves to paraphrasing the teachings of the early councils and insisting on their continued validity.[45]

In recent centuries, the development of classical christological dogma has been assessed in widely varying ways, which can be grouped into three basic categories. A theologian's assessment of this issue is a reliable indication of that author's overall christological position.

1. Some authors consider the dogmatic development an aberration that replaced New Testament christology with philosophical reflection on the person and natures of Christ. From this perspective, the christology of the patristic period has been rejected as a Hellenization of Christianity, in which Greek metaphysical speculation supplanted the Bible's historical mode of thought and fostered an often intolerant preoccupation with doctrine. Criticisms of this sort were registered in the past by liberal Protestant theology; Adolf von Harnack (1851–1930), who opposed gospel to dogma, is an important historical example. More recently, Leslie Dewart has advocated a similar position, and Hans Küng's *On Being a Christian* reflects some similar tendencies.[46]

2. Diametrically opposed to this position is a conception that Avery Dulles has termed the dogmatic approach to christology.[47] Authors of this persuasion typically conceive the conciliar devel-

---

43. See Paul Galtier, *L'unité du Christ: Être, personne, conscience* (Paris: Beauchesne, 1939), and Pietro Parente, *L'Io di Christo* (Brescia: Morcelliana, 1951). On this debate see Alois Grillmeier, "The Figure of Christ in Catholic Theology Today," in *Renewal in Dogma*, vol. 1 of *Theology Today* (Milwaukee: Bruce, 1965), 92–97.

44. See, e.g., Karl Rahner, "Current Problems in Christology," 158–63, and Piet Schoonenberg, *The Christ* (New York: Herder and Herder, 1971), 50–105. Freedom and self-consciousness are now often associated with "person" rather than "nature."

45. For the original Latin texts see *Acta Apostolicae Sedis* 43 (1951): 625–44, and 64 (1972): 237–41; for English translations see *Eastern Churches Quarterly* 9 (1952): 229–44, and *Catholic Mind* 70 (1972): 61–64.

46. See Harnack's widely read lectures on the essence of Christianity, delivered at the University of Berlin in 1899–1900 and translated as *What Is Christianity?* (Philadelphia: Fortress Press, 1986), and L. Dewart, *The Future of Belief* (New York: Herder, 1966). For a telling critique of Dewart see Bernard Lonergan, "The Dehellenization of Dogma," in *A Second Collection* (Philadelphia: Westminster Press, 1974), 11–32.

47. Avery Dulles, "Contemporary Approaches to Christology: Analysis and Reflection," *Living Light* 13 (1976): 119–44.

opment as a movement from the New Testament's concern with more functional christology (Christ in his significance for us) to a more ontological christology (Christ in himself), and evaluate this step as progress from the order in which realities become known to us to the order in which they exist in themselves. The conciliar development can then be taken, not only as true, but also as providing the proper framework for further christological questioning. Bernard Lonergan's Latin writings on christology provide an example of this position, which is also reflected in more recent work influenced by Lonergan's conception of theological method.[48]

3. A third position judges the early councils' doctrine to be a true expression of the reality of Christ, and usually considers itself still bound by their authoritative regulation of christological language. Nonetheless, it finds the development of dogma marked by a gradual narrowing of the question. While issues concerning Christ's divinity and humanity are important, they are not the only significant questions for christology to address. Adherents of this third approach often note that, although the patristic period was moved by soteriological concerns, its final formulations do not incorporate an explicit soteriology. Thus the conciliar teaching, while true, neither exhausts the matter nor determines the agenda for all future christological investigation. This assessment is widespread among major contemporary theologians.[49]

In my judgment, only the third position does justice to all dimensions of the actual development. Christology is free to develop new terminology and to address issues that the early councils did not face. This is all the more necessary in view of the ease with which ancient terminology can be misunderstood in the modern world.[50] Yet contemporary christology should be measured against the conciliar teaching, especially that of Chalcedon, to ensure that its content does not fall short of expressing what the church has recognized in Jesus. Chalcedon's regulation of the christological use of the terms *person* and *nature* also continues to deserve respect.

---

48. See B. Lonergan, *De Verbo Incarnato*, 3d ed., 4 vols. (Rome: Pontificia Universitas Gregoriana, 1964), and Daniel A. Helminiak, *The Same Jesus: A Contemporary Christology* (Chicago: Loyola University, 1986).

49. See especially Karl Rahner, "Current Problems in Christology."

50. A particular danger is that reference to "one person" may be misunderstood as denial of Jesus' humanity. Conversely, of course, to speak of Jesus as a "human person" departs from the conciliar regulation of language and may be construed as a denial of his divinity.

## SOTERIOLOGY

To complete this survey of classical christology and soteriology, we must now turn explicitly to the question of Christ's work. While not completely separable from the person of Christ, soteriology has its own distinctive history and must be considered by itself. In this area we have no official teaching comparable to the dogmas of Nicaea and Chalcedon regarding Christ's person. Soteriology has been more varied (perhaps necessarily so) than christology, where a fixed terminology has been more firmly established.

In classifying soteriologies, it is useful to ask what aspect or aspects of Christ's existence are seen as salvific. The four major points of reference are Christ's incarnation, public life, crucifixion, and resurrection, either alone or in some combination.[51] Is salvation attributed to God's presence in Jesus? To Jesus' teaching and example? To his death on the cross? To his exaltation after death? Or must these items be drawn together more closely than this series of questions suggests? Various positions have been held in the history of Christian thought. Each choice reflects basic theological intentions; each choice has consequences and can be assessed in part with reference to those consequences. A sketch of the historical development will help clarify the issues.

In the patristic period there was no unified systematic soteriology. The fathers developed instead a wide variety of themes and images, each of which contributed something to the overall picture. Only a few significant features can be mentioned here, without any attempt to discuss individual authors in detail.

A basic theme is an antidualist principle, stressed especially in anti-Gnostic writing. The question of salvation is often cast in terms of a struggle between good and evil, between God and the devil. Yet this conception, much praised by such modern authors as Gustaf Aulen for its dramatic thrust and for its emphasis on salvation as the work of God,[52] is always accompanied by an insistence that creation is good. While patristic soteriology speaks of conflict and opposition in the history of salvation, and even of God's triumph over hostile powers (see also Col. 2:15), it rejects any metaphysical dualism in which the world is seen as evil by nature. Salvation is salvation of the world, not escape from the world.

---

51. See Cornelius Mayer, "Von der satisfactio zur liberatio?: Zur Problematik eines neuen Ansatzes in der Soteriologie," *Zeitschrift für Katholische Theologie* 96 (1974): 405–14.

52. See Gustaf Aulen, *Christus Victor: An Historical Study of the Three Main Types of the Idea of the Atonement* (New York: Macmillan, 1969). The book is based on lectures delivered at the University of Uppsala in 1930.

A more specific theory, perhaps the most important theme of the period, is the idea of recapitulation. This conception derives from Irenaeus of Lyons, though it has biblical foundation in Paul's epistles. Christ is seen as the new Adam (see Rom. 5; 1 Cor. 15), the new head of creation who summarizes or recapitulates in himself the whole of creation. His coming is the fullness of time (Gal. 4:4), the climax of human history. The central biblical text for this approach is Ephesians 1:10, which speaks of God's plan to sum up (*anakephalaiosasthai*) all things in Christ. In patristic thought, the incarnation is the beginning and foundation of such recapitulation, but there is also a resurrectional component; it is as "firstborn of the dead" (Col. 1:18) that Christ restores to the human race the existence in the image and likeness of God that had been lost in Adam.

This theory, which combines several biblical themes, especially from Pauline sources, remained influential throughout the patristic period. Closely connected with the principle that what is not assumed in Christ is not saved, it focuses attention on the incarnation. More ontological than juridical in its terminology, it conceives of salvation primarily as communication of and participation in divine life (2 Peter 1:3-4), not primarily as forgiveness of sin. Salvation is the perfection of creation.

Yet patristic thought is not exhausted in the notion of recapitulation. Many authors, including those who favored the theme of recapitulation, also accented the idea of divine education of the human race in and through Christ. Here emphasis is placed on the teaching and example of Jesus' public life. Irenaeus, for example, writes that Christ wanted to be our teacher so "that through imitation of his works and performance of his words we might have communion with him" and that "had the truth already been known, the coming of the Redeemer into the world would have been superfluous."[53] This theme, also to be found in later authors, prevents the idea of salvation through recapitulation from becoming an automatic physical process.[54]

Finally, the idea of divine triumph over the devil was often elaborated in detail. On the basis of Jesus' reference to giving his life as a ransom for many (Matt. 20:28; Mark 10:45), Origen and numerous other theologians developed the idea that Christ was a ransom

---

53. Irenaeus *Adv. Haer.* 5.1.1; 2.18.6.

54. This theme is particularly accented by Gisbert Greshake, "Der Wandel der Erlösungsvorstellungen in der Theologiegeschichte," in *Gottes Heil—Glück des Menschen* (Freiburg: Herder, 1983), 50–79; this essay is based on a widely noted lecture delivered in Munich in 1972. For a differing emphasis and critique of Greshake's position see Hans Urs von Balthasar, *Theodramatik 3: Die Handlung* (Einsiedeln: Johannes, 1980), 224–34.

offered to the devil for the fallen human race, which had become the devil's property through sin. Deceived through inability to perceive Christ's divinity, Satan swallowed the bait, exchanging control over the rest of the human race for Christ. When Christ rose from the dead, the devil was completely overcome. While popular at the time, the theory of ransom paid to the devil always met resistance; Gregory of Nazianzus, among others, rejected its notion of God as blasphemous.[55]

While patristic thought drew upon a multiplicity of images to suggest a variety of soteriological insights, medieval theologians, especially in the West, developed a more rigorously reasoned theoretical account of Christ's salvific activity. Salvation was envisioned as forgiveness of sin, attention fixed firmly on the cross, and theology developed in juridical categories. The chief figure in this process was Anselm of Canterbury (1033/34–1109).

A strong critic of any notion of ransom paid or offered to the devil, Anselm sought to show that the Christian idea of the incarnation is compatible with God's dignity. Entitling his work *Cur Deus Homo?* he divides his argument into two parts. First, he seeks to demonstrate that without the incarnation salvation of the human race would be impossible (bk. 1). Then, against this background, he argues that salvation is God's intention for the human race (bk. 2). The incarnation, far from being inappropriate for God, is in fact a necessary element in fulfilling God's purpose in creation. In the course of these analyses, Anselm develops his theory of satisfaction, which has influenced Western thought to the present day.

Anselm's starting point is an assessment of sin and its effects. Instead of concentrating on the content of specific sinful deeds, Anselm views sin formally, as an offense against God. Drawing on the legal theory of his day, he measures guilt and the resulting debt in qualitative terms, with reference to the dignity of the offended party. In the case of sin, the offended party is God, and the resulting debt is therefore infinite. Either punishment or satisfaction is necessary. As long as the matter remains unresolved, the proper order of the universe is disrupted, for God is not a private figure but creator of heaven and earth.

Like sin, payment of the appropriate satisfaction is also measured qualitatively; but here the point of reference is the one who offers satisfaction in repayment of the debt. Concretely, this means that the human race, left on its own, is unable to pay the debt it

---

55. The conception is analyzed in more detail by Raymund Schwager, *Der wunderbare Tausch*, 32–53.

has contracted. Any attempted satisfaction would remain finite and therefore insufficient, and in any case the human race has nothing that it does not already owe to God. On purely human terms, the disrupted cosmic order cannot be restored.

Yet punishment is no adequate solution. Punishment of humanity would leave God's plans for creation frustrated—an intolerable notion. To forget or ignore the debt is equally impossible, for divine mercy is inseparable from divine justice, and in any case ignoring the debt would leave the proper order disturbed. At the same time, since human dignity and freedom must be respected, satisfaction must be offered by a member of the human race.

From a combination of these ideas Anselm concludes to the necessity of the incarnation. The debt must be repaid, and a human being must repay it; yet apart from the incarnation no human being can do so. Therefore, given both God's initial free choice in creating the human race for a specific end and the fact of human sin, the incarnation of God's Son is needed to achieve the divine purpose. Since death is a consequence of sin and Christ is sinless, he did not have to die. Nonetheless, as a true human being composed of body and soul, he was able to die if he freely chose to do so. Because of the dignity of his person as true God, his death is of infinite value and constitutes the necessary satisfaction for sin. Incarnation is the necessary presupposition of a necessary redemption.[56]

In the centuries that followed, Anselm's theory achieved widespread acceptance in the West, though it has never been defined as a dogma by the church. In the course of its reception, however, various modifications were introduced into Anselm's conception. The most influential change derives from Thomas Aquinas. Aquinas in general supported Anselm, though he also used other models in his soteriology. Yet Thomas opposed Anselm's idea that the incarnation was necessary for redemption. In his judgment, the incarnation was very appropriate ("convenient"), a fitting and reasonable thing for God to do, but not strictly necessary. Thomas held that the incarnation was necessary only on the condition that God demands full satisfaction. Why God requires this and why satisfaction is accomplished precisely in Christ's death remain mysteries of divine freedom. Had God so willed, redemption could have been accomplished differently.

Later developments can be mentioned more briefly. While Martin Luther revived certain aspects of patristic thought on Christ's salvific work in criticism of Scholastic theology, this issue was not a central

---

56. An English translation of *Cur Deus Homo?* is available in *Saint Anselm: Basic Writings* (Lasalle, Ill.: Open Court, 1968), 171–288.

point of controversy at the time of the Reformation.[57] In classical
Protestant theology, atonement was often conceived as a punishment
of Christ (instead of others) by God. In Catholic thought, especially in
Neo-Scholasticism, different schools developed, as varying emphases
were placed on Christ's obedience and his physical suffering. In some
circles, a highly abstract evaluation of Christ's acts developed: It was
argued that, since Christ is divine, any free act on his part could
have infinite value as satisfaction. This approach, of course, sharply
reduces the significance of the crucifixion.[58]

Many modern theologians, especially liberal Protestants, have
criticized Anselm sharply, both for his reliance on legal categories
and for his concentration on the crucifixion. Much of this criticism
can itself be criticized: as to the first matter, liberal theology's dichotomy between legal and personal categories must be questioned,
for legal categories are personal; as to liberal theology's charge that
Anselm concentrated too much on the crucifixion, it is fair to reply that liberal theology has suffered from an opposing tendency
to reduce Christ's significance to the content of his ethical teaching
and the example of his life. Anselm does tend, however, to separate Christ's death from his public life. In addition, the choice of
the need to overcome sin and its consequences as his point of departure narrows the soteriological question, in comparison with the
patristic theme of divinization. Nonetheless, as Gisbert Greshake has
observed, there is much value in Anselm's stress on the exercise of
Christ's human freedom and in his insistence that salvation is a public
act, the removal of the public consequences of sin.[59]

There is more to be criticized in the reception of Anselm than
in Anselm himself. The various modifications of his thought separate incarnation and redemption, and make the actual salvific events
seem arbitrary. One effect of these modifications is a lack of intrinsic
connection between christology and the doctrine of grace. Excessive
efforts to safeguard divine freedom can lead to positions in which

---

57. On Luther's thought see Aulen, *Christus Victor*, 101–22, and Schwager, *Der wunderbare Tausch*, 192–231.

58. On developments after Anselm see Franz Lakner, "Salvation B: Satisfaction," in Karl Rahner et al., eds., *Sacramentum Mundi* (New York: Herder and Herder, 1970), 5:433–35.

59. Evaluations of Anselm's work range from Aulen's sharp criticism (*Christus Victor*, 84–92, 143–59) to Greshake's praise (*Gottes Heil*, 80–104; summarized under the title "Redemption and Freedom," *Theology Digest* 25 [1977]: 61–65). For further analyses see Schwager, *Der wunderbare Tausch*, 161–91, and Hans-Ulrich Wiese, "Die Lehre Anselms von Canterbury über den Tod Jesu in der Schrift 'Cur Deus homo,'" *Wissenschaft und Weisheit* 41 (1978): 149–79; 42 (1979): 34–55. For a thought-provoking assessment of common soteriological conceptions see Thomas Marsh, "Soteriology Today," *Irish Theological Quarterly* 46 (1979): 145–57.

God's actions are arbitrary and therefore border on intrinsic meaninglessness; if salvation of the human race can be accomplished in an infinite number of ways, then the actual history of salvation loses importance.

As the substance of Anselm's theory of satisfaction became widely accepted in the West, Scholastic theologians began to inquire thematically into the motive for the incarnation. The standard way of posing the question was to ask if the Word would have become flesh if Adam had not sinned. While broaching the subject in unreal terms and envisioning a hypothetical answer, this speculation was based on legitimate concerns about the role of Christ in world history. The traditional answers (no unanimity was reached) remain of interest, for the underlying issues are still important.

The answer of the Thomist school is negative: The Word would not have become flesh had Adam not sinned. The motive of the incarnation is the overcoming of sin; without sin to overcome, the incarnation would not have taken place. The biblical basis for this position is found chiefly in Paul's insistence that Christ died for our sins, though it is recognized that the New Testament does not precisely address the later question. An ancient liturgical expression of the idea is enshrined in the Exsultet of the Easter Vigil: "O happy fault!...O truly necessary sin of Adam." The Thomist position entails the consequence that both creation and the initial offer of grace are not intrinsically related to the incarnation. The incarnation is the divine response to a factor eternally foreseen but not willed by God.

The Scotists hold the opposite position: The Word would have become flesh even if Adam had not sinned. The motive of the incarnation is the perfection of creation. While not denying that Christ in fact overcame sin, the Scotists see this as a subordinate effect, accomplished in the process of fulfilling God's original design. The biblical basis is sought especially in the hymn of Colossians, which praises Christ as the "first-born of all creation" and confesses that "all things were created through him and for him" (1:15-16). The Scotist position sees creation and all grace in christological terms.[60]

Contemporary theologians rarely discuss this issue in the terms familiar to medieval thought. Yet the interrelationship of Christ, grace, and sin remains an object of questioning. Many recent authors, such as Karl Barth and Karl Rahner, favor the more christocentric Scotist view. Rahner even takes matters a step further by arguing that, while the offer of grace is a free act on God's part, grace itself is inherently

---

60. For a penetrating study of the issues see Felix Malmberg, *Über den Gottmenschen* (Freiburg: Herder, 1960), 9–26.

directed toward the incarnation of the second person of the Trinity as an indispensable component of the elevation of the human race to participation in the divine life. Edward Schillebeeckx, in contrast, develops a more Thomistic perspective; his soteriology focuses more on overcoming evil than on perfecting what is by nature good. But before examining such modern conceptions in more detail, we must first consider the background of all christological assertions: the life, death, and resurrection of Jesus of Nazareth.

## HISTORICAL FOUNDATIONS

To this point we have examined various Christian interpretations of Jesus' person and work. Such theological assertions are statements of faith, but they are not arbitrary; even if not susceptible of proof in a strict sense, they can be assessed by reference to the figure whom they claim to interpret. Against the background of the doctrinal history surveyed in the preceding sections, the following portion of this chapter will study the historical reference points of christology in the public life, death, and resurrection of Jesus.

Reference to these items as historical foundations requires some qualification. First, our historical knowledge of Jesus is mediated chiefly by documents written to promote theological understanding, not by works of history in the modern sense. The extent and the theological significance of our historical access to Jesus are subject to dispute and will have to be weighed in our treatment of Jesus' public life. Consideration of the crucifixion requires attention to issues ranging from Jesus' approach to death to the origin of theological interpretations of the crucifixion. Finally, since the resurrection can hardly be classified as a historical event in the same sense as Jesus' life and death, a series of different questions will demand attention on that score. Despite these complications, the three topics to be investigated here share common ground as foundational factors influential (or possibly influential) in the development of faith in Jesus.

### PUBLIC LIFE

The chief sources of information about Jesus' public life (almost nothing is known about his earlier years) are the four Gospels. For much of the church's history, the Gospels were taken in a straightforward manner as reliable sources of information about Jesus' actual words and deeds, though their theological content was recognized as well. Since its inception in the late eighteenth century, critical biblical scholarship has gradually led to recognition that the Gospels are primarily expressions of Christian preaching. To retrieve from them historical data about Jesus remains possible, but this task requires careful, methodical investigation and entails a willingness to settle for fragmentary results. Yet some historical knowledge of Jesus seems essential for christology, especially for examination of its foundational dimensions.

The following account of Jesus' public life will begin with a look at the chief stages of modern inquiry into this question, since familiarity with this background is indispensable for grasping current research. It must be borne in mind throughout that the range of possible historical investigation is not restricted to the issues selected for notice here, and that historical study of Jesus' life does not exhaust the task of interpreting the Gospels.

The work of Hermann Samuel Reimarus (1694–1768), a rationalist thinker and teacher of Near Eastern languages in Hamburg, is usually identified as the origin of critical research into Jesus. Between 1774 and 1778, Gotthold E. Lessing published seven lengthy excerpts from Reimarus's defense of rationalist religion, without revealing the author's name. Two of these *Fragments* considered the aims of Jesus and his disciples and the story of the resurrection. Their publication aroused a storm of controversy and shattered untroubled acceptance of the Gospels as historical documents.[61]

Distinguishing sharply between Jesus' aims and the later aims of his disciples, Reimarus identified Jesus as a messianic pretender who preached the nearness of the kingdom of heaven in a political, nationalistic sense. His activity was limited to Israel, and involved no break with the law (see Matt. 5:17-18). While the Messiah could be called Son of God, this royal title did not imply divinity. Jesus twice came close to achieving his goals, once during his ministry in Galilee and later at his triumphant entrance into Jerusalem, but the desired popular response ultimately failed to materialize and he was executed. His last words ("My God, my God, why have you forsaken me?" [Matt. 27:46]) are an admission of failure.

Jesus' disciples, who shared their master's hopes during his lifetime, were totally unprepared for his death. (Reimarus rejects the predictions of the passion as unhistorical, with the argument that the disciples' reaction to Jesus' arrest and crucifixion betrays no sign of advance preparation.) After Jesus' death, they had recourse to a different strand of Jewish messianic expectation. While Jesus had seen

---

61. For an English translation see C. H. Talbert, ed., *Reimarus: Fragments* (Philadelphia: Fortress Press, 1970). The full text of Reimarus's *Apologie* was not published until 1972.

himself as Messiah in the royal, Davidic sense, the disciples turned after his failure to an apocalyptic strand of hope for a messiah who would come twice, first in human weakness, then in divine glory: a supernatural Son of man coming on the clouds of heaven (see Dan. 7:13). To carry out this reinterpretation, the disciples stole Jesus' body (see Matt. 28:11-15, where the evangelist tries to refute this allegation) and after waiting fifty days so that their claims could not be disproved, proclaimed his resurrection from the dead and imminent return in power. Soon his death was proclaimed a redemptive event, and Christianity became sufficiently well established to survive Jesus' failure to return. As a final stage of the subterfuge, the Gospels seek to depict Jesus' life in conformity with the disciples' later ideas. Fortunately, elements of the true story continue to show through (especially in Matthew, which at the time of Reimarus was considered the oldest Gospel) and make exposure of the fraud possible.

Reimarus erred in many respects, especially in attributing nationalistic ideas to Jesus and deliberate deception to the disciples. His work remains important, however, for having questioned forcefully the relationship of what would later be called the historical Jesus to the Christ of faith. The issues that he addressed have remained matters of serious theological concern.

The period immediately after publication of Reimarus's *Fragments* did not produce important new insights. Instead, two types of literature on Jesus abounded: traditional harmonizings of the Gospels; and rationalist lives that sought to provide natural explanation for unusual events, especially the miracles. The next major contribution was the publication of David Friedrich Strauss's *The Life of Jesus Critically Examined* in 1835-36.[62]

Highly influenced by Hegel's philosophy, Strauss sought to contribute to systematic theology by developing a variant of the Hegelian notion of myth. As an initial step in this ambitious project, he subjected the Gospels to close examination. Proceeding scene by scene and accompanying each account with detailed criticism, he presented the traditional harmonizing of the different texts and the recent naturalist explanation. Against this twofold background Strauss advanced his "mythical" interpretation as the third stage of the dialectic. In his judgment, the Gospels result from application of Old Testament themes, especially messianic ideas, to the life of Jesus: Apart from a few basic facts about Jesus' life, they contain primitive Christian ideas expressed in historical form. Unlike Reimarus,

---

62. Strauss's work, published when the author was twenty-seven, eventually appeared in four editions. The English translation, *The Life of Jesus Critically Examined* (Philadelphia: Fortress Press, 1972), is by the novelist George Eliot.

Strauss did not consider the Gospels a product of deceit. That the gospel tradition is historically unreliable is due, not to fraud, but to the inevitable growth of poetic legend around a venerated figure.

In any case, for Strauss the important point is early Christian thought, not the history of Jesus. Critical historical examination of Jesus' life is but a means to an end, for Jesus is simply the vehicle used to express messianic ideas and is no more important than any other human being. The ideas that the Gospels present in mythical form by applying them to Jesus must now be reexpressed as truths about the human race as a whole, for no idea can be confined to one individual. "Humanity is the union of the two natures—God become man."[63] Within this framework, neither the historical Jesus nor any other individual can be the object of faith; christology, shorn of its reference to Jesus, is transformed into a theological-philosophical anthropology.

Despite Strauss's speculative goal, his major impact was as an exegete and historian. His *Life* sparked intense debate, especially among Protestant theologians,[64] and caused books on the historical Jesus to proliferate. The most fundamental objection to his recasting of christology is that Strauss failed to see the importance of Jesus for the development of the "christological idea": The Gospels are not the mere expression of existing ideas with reference to Jesus, but a critical adaptation of such ideas on the basis of who Jesus was. Nonetheless, Strauss remains important for urging two basic (perhaps the two basic) christological questions: What is the relationship of the historical Jesus to the Christ of faith? Is the Christian message of salvation separable from its historical origin in Jesus?

As the nineteenth century progressed, liberal Protestant thought came to dominate critical research on the life of Jesus. Liberal Protestantism was opposed to the dogmatic Christ of the early councils, and suspicious of the christologies of Paul and John. Judging these developments a falsification of the true picture of Jesus, it devoted its efforts to reconstructing from the Synoptic Gospels a biography of Jesus as an ethical teacher. Here inquiry into the historical Jesus is associated with a "low christology" that denies the divinity of Christ.

The resulting effort to uncover the historical Jesus soon concluded that the only suitable sources were the Synoptic Gospels. Methodical study of the texts gradually led to recognition of the priority of Mark and to identification of a common source, termed Q, behind the texts of Matthew and Luke. As the oldest material, Mark

---

63. Ibid., 780.
64. On the Catholic reaction see William Madges, "D. F. Strauss in Retrospect: His Reception among Roman Catholics," *Heythrop Journal* 30 (1989): 273–92.

and Q were presumed to be a reliable basis for reconstructing Jesus' public life. These liberal Protestant interpretations of the life of Jesus depict him as an ethical teacher who preached the kingdom of God as an interior, moral reality. Much attention is devoted to psychological description of his personality and inner development, which are seen as a model for our imitation. Biographical presentation is thus essential to the theological enterprise.

The most influential example of this unitarian theology is a series of lectures on the essence of Christianity delivered in 1899–1900 at the University of Berlin by the eminent church historian Adolf von Harnack. Harnack identified three basic principles in Jesus' teaching: the coming of the (ethical) kingdom of God; the Fatherhood of God and the infinite value of the human soul; and the better justice (see Matt. 5:20) and the command of love. Jesus' preaching is concerned exclusively with the individual, who is called to repent and believe. Dogmas, especially christological and trinitarian doctrine, are later Hellenizations of the gospel. In a famous, oft-criticized passage, Harnack states that "the Gospel, as Jesus proclaimed it, has to do with the Father only and not with the Son," though he does hasten to add that Jesus "was its personal realization and its strength, and this he is felt to be still."[65] Central to this position are a rejection of classical christology, an optimistic assurance that exegetes can reach the historical Jesus, and the image of Jesus as preacher and model of an ethical message of the kingdom of God. The apocalyptic, eschatological element in the Gospels is dismissed as an incidental residue of Jewish cultural influences.

Positions of this sort, while now discredited in theological circles, still exert a certain popular influence. It is important to note that they have been rejected not simply out of fidelity to postbiblical tradition, but due to internal deficiencies. Their inadequacy is best seen in conjunction with the development of research around the turn of the century, when the liberal quest was jolted by the publication of four books. Each in its own way challenged an essential element of the synthesis prevailing in liberal circles.

In 1892, the exegete Johannes Weiss published a brief but important study of Jesus' preaching. Weiss argued that Jesus' understanding of the kingdom of God was eschatological; the ethical interpretation of his message was a false modernization of his actual teaching. This critique called into question the liberal image of Jesus as an ethical teacher.[66]

65. Harnack, *What Is Christianity?* 144, 145.

66. The first edition was sixty-seven pages in length; an expanded second edition appeared in 1900. For an English translation of the original text see Johannes

In the same year, Martin Kähler, a systematic theologian opposed to liberal christology, rejected the quest for the historical Jesus as historically fruitless and theologically bankrupt. Kähler held that, given the limitations of our sources, finding the Jesus of history is impossible. Furthermore, even if better sources were available, no historian can reach what alone interests believers: the suprahistorical Savior. Fearing that liberal theology makes Christian faith dependent on the shifting sands of historical research, Kähler insists that "the real Christ is the Christ who is preached," not the product of a scholarly reconstruction.[67]

Shortly thereafter, in 1901, Wilhelm Wrede published his study of the messianic secret in the Gospels. Wrede argued that the structure of Mark and the Gospel's messianic material were the product of the evangelist, and could not serve as a guide to the actual events of Jesus' life. Details of Jesus' life, including the sequence of events, which is indispensable for psychological reconstruction, are unavailable to us. As Wrede realized, his insight into the character of the Gospels sounded the death knell for psychological biographies of Jesus.[68]

Finally, Albert Schweitzer summarized a vast amount of research on the Jesus of history and brought it into intelligible order. While sympathetic to liberal Protestantism's goals, he showed that its portrait of Jesus was a modernization unduly influenced by nineteenth-century theological views. Schweitzer did not deny the possibility of reaching the historical Jesus; he rejected Wrede's doubts on this point, and held that an accurate picture of Jesus could be obtained. But the Jesus of history was an apocalyptic preacher who mistakenly expected God's kingdom to arrive with cosmic force in the near future. As a high-water mark of Jewish apocalypticism, he is even more foreign to modernity than is the conciliar christology that liberal theology sought to supplant. Since the historical Jesus provides no support for liberal thought, the search for "the Jesus of history as an ally in the struggle against the tyranny of dogma" must be declared a failure.[69]

---

Weiss, *Jesus' Proclamation of the Kingdom of God* (Philadelphia: Fortress Press, 1971). Significant presence of eschatology in Jesus' teaching does not exclude ethics from his message, but it does rule out conceiving Jesus solely as a moral teacher.

67. For an English translation see Martin Kähler, *The So-Called Historical Jesus and the Historic, Biblical Christ* (Philadelphia: Fortress Press, 1964). The citation is taken from p. 66.

68. See Wilhelm Wrede, *The Messianic Secret* (Cambridge, Eng.: Clarke, 1971). Wrede's specific interpretation of Mark's theological activity is itself open to objection.

69. Schweitzer's work was originally published in 1906 under the title *Von Reimarus zu Wrede*. For an English translation see *The Quest of the Historical Jesus: A Critical Study of Its Progress from Reimarus to Wrede* (London: Black, 1911). The citation

The nineteenth-century quest of the historical Jesus never recovered from these assaults. Liberal theology, so accommodated to a particular culture, lost its prominence in the aftermath of World War I. In the period that followed, Paul and John again became the decisive voices of the New Testament, and pursuit of the historical Jesus receded in favor of focus on the preached Christ. Karl Barth, whose impassioned commentary on Romans inaugurated a new theological epoch in 1919, repeated Kähler's charge that the quest was both impossible and illegitimate. Wholeheartedly repudiating all that liberal theology stood for, Barth insisted that we know Christ only by faith. In a famous exchange of letters with Adolf von Harnack, he went so far as to maintain that the meager results of historical inquiry into Jesus could paradoxically serve a good purpose by demolishing a place where faith might be tempted to seek false support.[70] In a similar vein, Rudolf Bultmann opined that "we can now know almost nothing concerning the life and personality of Jesus,"[71] and insisted that theology needs knowledge only of the fact of Jesus' existence, not further information about his life.[72] While Bultmann offered an account of Jesus' message and spoke of a christology implicit in his words and deeds,[73] he was convinced that theology should focus on the preaching of the cross rather than on Jesus' public life.

Lack of theological interest in the historical Jesus prevailed in large part—never universally—for a generation.[74] In 1953, an important lecture by Ernst Käsemann, one of Bultmann's students, inaugurated the "new quest" of the historical Jesus.[75] Intense theological interest in the historical Jesus, now on the part of Catholic as well as Protestant scholars, has persisted since that time. Initially, Jesus' preaching was the focus of attention, but other major aspects

---

is from p. 4. This work is the classic history of the "quest." For a briefer informative account and critique see Ben F. Meyer, *The Aims of Jesus* (London: SCM, 1979), 25–59.

70. See H. Martin Rumscheidt, *Revelation and Theology: An Analysis of the Barth-Harnack Correspondence of 1923* (Cambridge: Cambridge University Press, 1972), 35, where Barth's text is translated.

71. Rudolf Bultmann, *Jesus and the Word* (New York: Scribner's, 1934), 8.

72. Rudolf Bultmann, "The Primitive Christian Kerygma and the Historical Jesus," in C. Braaten and R. Harrisville, eds., *The Historical Jesus and the Kerygmatic Christ* (Nashville: Abingdon, 1964), 20–21, 25.

73. See Bultmann, *Jesus and the Word*, and *Theology of the New Testament*, 1:43.

74. This generalization does not apply to Catholic theology, which in this period rightly rejected bifurcation of the historical Jesus from the Christ of faith but lacked adequate appreciation of the difficulty inherent in recovering historical data about Jesus from the New Testament. For official Catholic recognition of the theological interests that affect the work of the evangelists see the Second Vatican Council's Dogmatic Constitution on Divine Revelation (*Dei Verbum*), no. 19.

75. Ernst Käsemann, "The Problem of the Historical Jesus," in *Essays on New Testament Themes* (London: SCM, 1964), 15–47.

of his public life now attract equal interest. In view of the purpose of this chapter, the following recapitulation of the major conclusions of modern research emphasizes matters that bear directly on christology.[76]

The central content of Jesus' public life can be determined with great certitude. Addressing Israel as a whole, Jesus preached and exemplified in his conduct the coming of God's kingdom. The kingdom is expected to arrive in the (near) future, yet has already begun to be present among Jesus' hearers. Since preaching the coming of God's rule entails a summons to repent, Jesus' message has both eschatological and ethical dimensions.

Jesus did not make himself the focus of his own teaching. Nonetheless, the coming of the kingdom of God, and the message of the coming of that kingdom, are in Jesus' view inseparably tied to his person. The kingdom begins to arrive in and through his presence and conduct. His actions and words presuppose and reflect a conviction that he is God's definitive representative, not to be surpassed in the future. A prophetic figure, he is (in his own self-understanding) incapable of being replaced by a later prophet. Thus Jesus' preaching of the kingdom has christological presuppositions and implications.[77] Among other things, the link between his person and message implies that the truth of the message is inseparable from his personal destiny.

The indirect self-reference of Jesus' public preaching and conduct is often termed implicit christology: christology because of its personal claims about Jesus; implicit because the claims are not expressed through explicit use of titles. There is no consensus among contemporary exegetes about the existence of explicit christology during Jesus' lifetime.[78] In any case, however, the decisive theological issue is the presence of implicit christology in Jesus' words and deeds, for without this reference point any verbal claim to messianic status

---

76. For a succinct and balanced account see John P. Meier, "Jesus," in R. Brown et al., eds., *The New Jerome Biblical Commentary* (Englewood Cliffs, N.J.: Prentice Hall, 1990), 1316–28. For more detailed discussions see Meyer, *The Aims of Jesus*; Schillebeeckx, *Jesus*, 41–319; and E. P. Sanders, *Jesus and Judaism* (Philadelphia: Fortress Press, 1985).

77. In this context Edward Schillebeeckx (*Jesus*, 256–71) refers to Jesus' "abba-experience" as the foundation of his preaching and conduct, and Karl Rahner (*Foundations of Christian Faith*, 251–54) notes Jesus' consciousness of unsurpassable proximity to God. The intrinsic connection of Jesus' message and person is also expressed in Wolfhart Pannenberg's thesis: "The office of Jesus was to call men into the Kingdom of God, which had appeared with him" (*Jesus—God and Man*, 212).

78. On these issues see Raymond E. Brown, *Biblical Reflections on Crises Facing the Church* (New York: Paulist, 1975), 20–37. On the individual titles see Meier, "Jesus," 1323–25.

or to other christological titles would be hollow. Explicit christology cannot stand on its own; implicit christology can.

Like the rejection of the original quest, renewal of research on the historical Jesus is defended on both historical and theological grounds. On the historical side of the question, it is argued that our inability to write a biography of Jesus, as we might write a biography of a modern figure, does not preclude uncovering accurate historical information of more limited scope. While care must be taken neither to retroject later material into Jesus' life nor to divorce Jesus from his historical context, application of such criteria as multiple attestation (the presence of similar material in varying forms and in mutually independent sources) and dissimilarity (identification of material that cannot be ascribed either to early Christians or to Jewish sources other than Jesus) makes it possible to distinguish what stems from Jesus from other material attributed to him in the Gospels.[79] Moreover, the basic picture of Jesus obtained in this way is more certain and more stable than are judgments with regard to the origin of individual texts.

Perhaps even more important than this historical argumentation is the changed theological situation. The new quest's chief difference from Bultmann lies not in its description of the historical Jesus but in the theological importance it attributes to this information. "Kerygmatic theology" feared the original quest as an attempt to replace faith with historical research, and in some respects its suspicion was well founded. In contrast to both nineteenth-century research and its critics, modern scholars frequently assert that investigation into the historical Jesus, far from being excluded by faith, is a basic imperative arising from faith itself. This argument, common to exegetes and theologians, has two distinct aspects.

The first aspect of the argument, advanced especially in the early years of the new quest, is the need to ask if the Christian kerygma's reference to and interpretation of Jesus is legitimate. Since the biblical message is not self-justifying, the question of continuity between Jesus and the preaching of the church must be addressed. This point has been expressed emphatically by Gerhard Ebeling: "If it were to be shown that Christology had no basis in the historical Jesus, but was a misinterpretation of Jesus, then Christology would be ruined."[80] In a similar vein, Nicholas Lash has observed: "If I were to be-

---

79. For discussion of criteria see Meier, "Jesus," 1317–18; Meyer, *The Aims of Jesus*, 76–94; and Schillebeeckx, *Jesus*, 81–102.

80. Gerhard Ebeling, "The Question of the Historical Jesus," 289; translation slightly modified. See also idem, *Theology and Proclamation* (Philadelphia: Fortress Press, 1966), 54–81.

come convinced that Jesus did not exist, or that the story told in the New Testament of his life, teaching and death was a fictional construction ungrounded in the facts, or a radical *mis*interpretation of his character, history and significance, then I should cease to be a Christian."[81]

The second aspect of the argument, more emphasized now than in the initial phase of the revival of research on Jesus, is the need for historical knowledge of Jesus in order to understand christological assertions. To understand what is meant by confessing that "Jesus is the Christ" it is necessary to know something about his life. Historical knowledge of Jesus is important not only for studying the foundation of christological statements, but also for grasping their content. On both grounds, these scholars argue, Christian faith requires historical knowledge of its object.

As is clear from the history of research, the theological function attributed to the historical Jesus (whether to Jesus himself in past history, or to historical knowledge of Jesus in contemporary theology)[82] is an issue distinct from the question of the extent of our historical knowledge about him. While the terminology used in discussing these matters varies from one author to another, three basic positions may be distinguished.

1. Some authors, such as David Friedrich Strauss, have denied any theological significance to the historical Jesus. A position this extreme is not common.

2. Other theologians, such as Bultmann, restrict or seek to restrict theologically relevant historical material about Jesus to the mere fact of his existence. It is easier to articulate this position than to carry it out consistently; even Bultmann would hardly have been able to find significance in the preaching of the cross if Jesus had not been crucified.

The major contemporary representative of a position akin to Bultmann's is Schubert Ogden, who argues that the historical point of reference for Christian faith and theology is the earliest apostolic preaching, not the life of Jesus. Distinguishing between the empirical-historical Jesus and the existential-historical Jesus (Jesus as known through the earliest apostolic witness), Ogden holds that contemporary christology typically suffers from the flaw of "asking about the being of Jesus in himself, as distinct from asking about the meaning of Jesus for us." In fact, Ogden argues, the necessary and sufficient condition for the appropriateness of a christological

---

81. Nicholas Lash, *Theology on Dover Beach* (New York: Paulist, 1979), 84.

82. On the issues involved here see John P. Meier, "The Historical Jesus: Rethinking Some Concepts," *Theological Studies* 51 (1990): 3–24.

assertion is its compatibility with the earliest apostolic witness, not its basis in Jesus' self-understanding.[83]

3. Most contemporary authors attribute greater theological significance to Jesus himself and to our historical knowledge of him. For the reasons noted above, though with variations in detail, these authors consider certain elements of Jesus' life and of our information about him to be indispensable presuppositions of christological assertions.[84]

Divergences among theologians on the theological significance of the historical Jesus are closely related to differences on other theological issues. Authors who conceive of Christian faith as closely related to history tend to attribute more theological significance to the historical Jesus than do those who divorce faith from history and perhaps even see factual historical knowledge as inimical to faith conceived as risk. Similarly, theologians who profess the divinity of Christ may require more historical material to support their affirmations than do those content with a low christology depicting Jesus solely as teacher and example. Still, the divisions noted above do not follow strictly on these lines, for numerous factors influence such theological judgments.

In my opinion, only the third of these positions takes into adequate account the historical nature of Christian faith and the centrality of the basic Christian confession that *Jesus* is the Christ.[85] As described above, however, the third category is quite broad; it leaves within itself considerable room for pluralism. One disputed issue is of major importance: the sufficiency of the historical Jesus as the historical reference point of christology.

Most theologians concerned with foundational christological issues (Pannenberg, Kasper, Küng, O'Collins, Rahner in several writings) identify the public life of Jesus and the resurrection as the two major poles upon which christology is built; in their judgment, knowledge of Jesus' public life is a necessary but not a sufficient ba-

---

83. See Ogden, *The Point of Christology*; the citation is from pp. 15–16. For further assessment see my review in *Heythrop Journal* 26 (1985): 67–69. A position similar to Ogden's is represented by David Tracy, who holds with regard to christology that "the primary content criterion should be the Jesus-kerygma of the original apostolic witness" (*The Analogical Imagination: Christian Theology and the Culture of Pluralism* [New York: Crossroad, 1981], 272); see ibid., 248–338, esp. 300–301 n. 97, and idem, *Blessed Rage for Order: The New Pluralism in Theology* (New York: Seabury, 1975), 204–36.

84. Karl Rahner's reflections on the systematic issues and summary of major aspects of our historical knowledge of Jesus (*Foundations of Christian Faith*, 243–49) can serve as an example of this position.

85. See Elizabeth A. Johnson, "The Theological Relevance of the Historical Jesus: A Debate and a Thesis," *Thomist* 48 (1984): 1–43.

sis for christology.[86] Other authors equally interested in developing a high christology (Ebeling, Rudolf Pesch, Franz Schupp, some lines of thought in Rahner) consider the historical Jesus the exclusive historical reference point for christology; the resurrection, while not denied, is classified as a confession of faith rather than part of the historically establishable foundation of faith.

Differences on this score often reflect varying evaluations of the crucifixion as well as alternative conceptions of the role of the resurrection in christological argumentation. Authors who consider the resurrection the second pole on which christology is based frequently assess Jesus' death in negative terms, as an end that calls into question the validity of his entire life. Consequently, their references to the historical Jesus typically encompass his life up to but not including his crucifixion. Conversely, those who envision the historical Jesus as sufficient basis for christology typically include his death in their point of historical reference, for they find his crucifixion revelatory of God. Thus the question of the theological significance of Jesus' public life leads inescapably to consideration of his death.

## CRUCIFIXION

As is evident from even a cursory reading of the New Testament, Jesus' death on the cross has long been the focal point of vigorous controversy. That Jesus was crucified is beyond doubt, though the precise date of his death can no longer be determined.[87] At issue in theological discussion is not the fact of the crucifixion but its meaning, for "Christ crucified, a stumbling block to Jews and folly to Gentiles," is "to those who are called, both Jews and Greeks, Christ the power of God and the wisdom of God" (1 Cor. 1:23-24).

### Jesus' Approach to Death

As a prelude to considering theological interpretations of the crucifixion, we must first examine a historical issue with far-reaching theological implications: Jesus' personal stance toward death. The importance of this matter, accented in the reference to "a death he freely accepted" in the Second Eucharistic Prayer of the Roman liturgy, has been articulated clearly in a statement on christology issued in 1979 by the International Theological Commission: "If,

---

86. For a clear defense of this position see Pannenberg, *Jesus—God and Man*, 53–114.

87. On crucifixion as a means of punishment in antiquity see Martin Hengel, *Crucifixion* (Philadelphia: Fortress Press, 1977).

for Jesus, the Passion was a failure and a shipwreck, if he felt abandoned by God and lost hope in his own mission, his death could not be construed then, and cannot be construed now, as the definitive act in the economy of salvation. A death undergone in a purely passive manner could not be a 'Christological' saving event. It must be the consequence, the willed consequence, of the obedience and love of Jesus making a gift of himself."[88] As this passage suggests, the meaning of Jesus' crucifixion rests in part on its relationship to his earlier life.

The issues entailed in inquiry into this relationship are multidimensional. In a more objective respect, we can ask why Jesus was put to death and we can inquire into the compatibility of his message of God's kingdom with his own execution. More subjectively, we can ask if Jesus foresaw his death, and seek to determine if and how he interpreted it and incorporated it into his understanding of his mission.[89]

Answers to such questions may seem self-evident, for the Gospels show Jesus predicting his passion (e.g., Mark 8:31; 9:31; 10:33-34, 45; John 10:18) and interpreting his death as salvific (e.g., Mark 10:45; 14:22-24). But while these texts have traditionally been read as historical reports, they are suspect from a critical perspective of being creations of the early church. In addition, there is tension between Jesus' public preaching of the kingdom of God and an attribution, on his part, of salvific efficacy to his death.[90]

The strongest adversary of the traditional understanding is Rudolf Bultmann, who denies that we can establish a positive connection between Jesus' life and his death. Objectively, Bultmann considers

---

88. See "Select Questions on Christology," in Michael Sharkey, ed., *International Theological Commission: Texts and Documents 1969–85* (San Francisco: Ignatius Press, 1989), 197.

89. Scholastic and Neo-Scholastic theology deduced from the hypostatic union that Jesus' human intellect enjoyed the beatific vision and knowledge of all past, present, and future reality from the moment of his conception; to these authors, it is a priori clear that Jesus foresaw his death and recognized its salvific significance. In contrast, contemporary theologians typically ascribe to Jesus a consciousness of unsurpassable proximity to God that does not imply unlimited knowledge of factual data (see, e.g., Rahner, *Foundations of Christian Faith*, 249, 253–54); from this perspective, questions such as those noted above cannot be answered a priori. The issue was much discussed in the 1950s and early 1960s. Influential modern analyses include Engelbert Gutwenger, *Bewusstsein und Wissen Christi* (Innsbruck: Felizian Rauch, 1960), and Karl Rahner, "Dogmatic Reflections on the Knowledge and Self-Consciousness of Christ," in *Theological Investigations* (Baltimore: Helicon, 1966), 5:193–215. On the history of thought see Helmut Riedlinger, *Geschichtlichkeit und Vollendung des Wissens Christi* (Freiburg: Herder, 1966).

90. This point is urged especially by Anton Vögtle, "Todesankündigungen und Todesverständnis Jesu," in *Der Tod Jesu: Deutungen im Neuen Testament* (Freiburg: Herder, 1976), 51–113.

Jesus' crucifixion as a political criminal a sign that his religious message (in Bultmann's judgment, nonpolitical) was misinterpreted as a threat to Roman rule. On this view, Jesus' death is linked to his public activity only insofar as his purposes were misunderstood. On the subjective level, Bultmann insists that our sources permit no firm conclusions about Jesus' personal approach to death and even leave open the possibility that he suffered a complete collapse. The gospel passages that interpret the crucifixion as salvific are expressions of early Christian theology, developed after the crucifixion and retrojected into Jesus' life.[91]

Both aspects of Bultmann's position have rightly been challenged. As Jürgen Moltmann and others have argued, Jesus' death flowed from his public activity. It is not that Jesus wished to be executed or directed his actions toward that end. But his death resulted from rejection, not misunderstanding. To the Jewish religious leaders, Jesus' stance toward the Law was blasphemous and endangered their own status. To Roman civil authority, his efforts to gather Israel represented a political threat in a highly volatile situation, though Jesus himself was neither a political activist nor a revolutionary. Death was the inevitable result of fidelity to his own preaching, given the failure of his message to win general acceptance.[92]

Bultmann's views on Jesus' personal stance toward death have also been criticized, most notably in several closely reasoned studies of Heinz Schürmann. Schürmann argues that, given the historical context, Jesus must have realized from the start of his public life the possibility of provoking opposition and meeting death at the hands of his adversaries. As opposition mounted, he must have recognized the increasing danger, so that toward the end of his life the final outcome became clear. In addition to these general considerations, a text from the Last Supper plays an important role in Schürmann's argumentation. In a passage widely judged authentic, Jesus tells his disciples, "Amen, I say to you, I will not drink again of the fruit of the vine until that day when I drink it new in the reign of God" (Mark 14:25). This saying of Jesus both predicts death and expresses certitude that his death will prevent neither the coming of God's kingdom nor Jesus' own participation

---

91. See Bultmann, *Jesus and the Word*, 213–14, and "The Primitive Christian Kerygma and the Historical Jesus," 23–24.

92. On these issues see Jürgen Moltmann, *The Crucified God*, 126–45; the trinitarian aspect of Moltmann's interpretation of the crucifixion is not at issue here. Wolfhart Pannenberg observes more soberly that "Jesus' cross is . . . the not fortuitous consequence of his preaching" ("Den Glauben an ihm selbs fassen und verstehen," *Zeitschrift für Theologie und Kirche* 86 [1989]: 366).

in it.[93] Thus Jesus' faithfulness to his message remained constant to the end.

Positions akin to Schürmann's have been adopted by many theologians. Walter Kasper, Hans Küng, and Gerald O'Collins offer similar reflections, and Edward Schillebeeckx, though hesitant on some points, follows the same basic line of argumentation. Karl Rahner, enumerating the main points of our historical knowledge about Jesus, asserts that "he faced his death resolutely and accepted it as the inevitable consequence of fidelity to his mission and as imposed on him by God."[94] Thus it is possible to speak of a widespread consensus about Jesus' free acceptance of death on the part of recent Catholic theologians. While Jesus' death was not an explicit topic of his public preaching, we can be certain that he accepted personally the most radical consequences of the message he had proclaimed and embodied in his deeds.

## Interpretations of the Crucifixion

Against this background, it is possible to weigh various theological interpretations of the crucifixion. As a first step, drawing in large part on Edward Schillebeeckx's summary of exegetical studies, I shall identify three major early Christian assessments of Jesus' death and consider the relationship of these interpretations to Jesus himself. The present look at the crucifixion will then conclude by noting the thought of some modern authors on the immediate theological implications of the crucifixion.

**The Death of a Prophet-Martyr.** Consistent with Jesus' status as a prophetic figure, one pattern of thought took recourse to the Old Testament experience that prophets often encounter rejection and even violent death. The sufferings of Jeremiah are a case in point, though Jeremiah's trials stop short of execution. In the New Testament, Jesus' lament over Jerusalem (Luke 13:33-34) and Stephen's speech to the high priest (Acts 7:51-52) express the general theme of persecution of the prophets, and the parable of the vineyard (Mark 12:1-12) places Jesus' death in this traditional context. While devel-

---

93. See especially Heinz Schürmann, *Gottes Reich—Jesu Geschick* (Leipzig: St. Benno, 1983), 183–251. For a more detailed summary and for discussion of other authors see John P. Galvin, "Jesus' Approach to Death: An Examination of Some Recent Studies," *Theological Studies* 41 (1980): 713–44.

94. Rahner, *Foundations of Christian Faith*, 248; the sense is that God imposes death on Jesus inasmuch as it is entailed in fidelity to his mission. For the other authors see Kasper, *Jesus the Christ*, 114–21; Küng, *On Being a Christian*, 320–25; O'Collins, *Interpreting Jesus*, 79–92; and Schillebeeckx, *Jesus*, 294–312.

opment of this line of thought can suggest that a prophet-martyr's woes have salvific value for others, the basic point is that persecution and death do not undermine prophetic standing; on the contrary, genuine prophets must expect opposition. Jesus' crucifixion does not disprove his claim to represent God.

**The Death of the Righteous Sufferer.** Prominent in the psalms of lament (e.g., Ps. 22) and in the wisdom literature (e.g., Wis. 2:12-20; 5:1-23) is the theme of the current travail and eventual triumph of the righteous sufferer. To outward appearances utterly abandoned, the victim is eventually vindicated by God. The theme can involve simply the suffering of the innocent, as in the Book of Job, or persecution of the righteous precisely because of their justice. Readily applicable to the death of Jesus, these ideas exercise formative influence on the passion narratives, and are reflected with particular clarity in the Gospels' accounts of the crucifixion (Matt. 27:46-48; Mark 15:34-36; Luke 23:46-47; John 19:28-30).

**An Atoning, Redemptive Death.** The chief Old Testament background for the understanding of Jesus' death as redemptive is the fourth servant song of Second Isaiah (Isa. 52:13—53:12): "He was wounded for our transgressions, he was bruised for our iniquities; upon him was the chastisement that made us whole, and with his stripes we are healed" (52:5). Here salvific effects are attributed to suffering, which benefits others and atones for sin. New Testament references to Jesus' death as ransom (Mark 10:45) and expiation (Rom. 3:25), as death for our sins (1 Cor. 15:3), and as death "for many" (Matt. 26:28; Mark 14:24) or "for you" (Luke 22:20; 1 Cor. 11:24) reflect this strand of thought, which centuries later gave rise to Anselm's theory of satisfaction. While the first two types may maintain simply that Jesus is salvific despite his death, the third approach explicitly recognizes salvific value in the crucifixion.[95]

Whether all or any of these interpretations of the crucifixion can be retraced to Jesus is disputed. Schillebeeckx speaks of Jesus' death as a prophetic sign left for others to interpret in the light of Jesus' life, and Rahner seems content to leave open the issue of explicit

---

95. For Schillebeeckx's treatment of these issues see *Jesus*, 274–94. Marie-Louise Gubler (*Die frühesten Deutungen des Todes Jesu* [Fribourg: Universitätsverlag, 1977]), Günter Bader (*Symbolik des Todes Jesu* [Tübingen: Mohr, 1988]), and Martin Hengel (*The Atonement*) provide further information.

Schillebeeckx (*Jesus*, 35, 274–75, 411, 414) holds that some early Christians (the community behind Q) paid little or no attention to the crucifixion. Piet Schoonenberg ("Schillebeeckx en de exegese," *Tijdschrift voor Theologie* 15 [1975]: 256–59) finds this argument from silence unconvincing.

interpretation by Jesus. In contrast, Schürmann judges that Jesus expressed the salvific character of his death, at least unthematically, and Rudolf Pesch traces all three types of interpretation to the period shortly before the crucifixion.[96] There are telling arguments on both sides (in addition to exegeting individual texts, each has to provide a plausible account of christology's early development), and it is not likely that consensus will be reached. In any case, the validity of theological interpretations of the crucifixion depends on their corresponding to the way Jesus lived and died, not on their explicit origin with Jesus.

Attention to these divergent strands of early interpretation of the crucifixion gives rise to the question of the immediate theological implications of Jesus' death. The position most commonly held by contemporary theologians (e.g., Pannenberg, Kasper, O'Collins) is that Jesus' disgraceful execution called into question the validity of his preaching and his claim to speak on behalf of God—a state of affairs overcome only by his resurrection and its manifestation. Other authors (Pesch, Rahner in some texts), however, appeal to the traditions of the prophet-martyr and the righteous sufferer to argue that Jesus' death did not imply that his claims were illegitimate, either historically, in the eyes of the disciples, or factually, as far as later theological assessment is concerned.

At stake in this discussion is the relationship among Jesus' public life, death, and resurrection. While it seems inconsistent to recognize that his public life led to his crucifixion and yet assess his life in positive terms and his death negatively, the issue cannot be pursued until we look more closely at the resurrection.

## RESURRECTION

While factual data concerning Jesus' public life and death have important theological ramifications, they often neither presuppose nor entail Christian faith. Nonbelievers may note that Jesus preached the coming of God's kingdom and that he was crucified, yet judge that he was mistaken in his message and that his death lacks the significance that Christians attribute to it. The resurrection falls into a different category. It is hard to imagine anyone agreeing that Jesus is risen, in the sense that Christians affirm, yet not being or becoming

---

96. See Schillebeeckx, *Jesus*, 318–19; Rahner, *Foundations of Christian Faith*, 248–49; Schürmann, *Gottes Reich*, 198–223; Rudolf Pesch, *Das Abendmahl und Jesu Todesverstandnis* (Freiburg: Herder, 1978). For further consideration see Galvin, "Jesus' Approach to Death."

Christian.[97] Here event and meaning are so intimately linked that distanced historical description is scarcely possible.

The importance of the resurrection, classically expressed in Paul's dictum that "if Christ has not been raised, then our preaching is in vain and your faith is in vain" (1 Cor. 15:14), is acknowledged by all Christians. Nonetheless, theologians differ significantly in specifying what is meant by the confession that Jesus is risen, and especially in conceiving the relationship of the resurrection to the crucifixion. Indeed, as C. F. Evans has observed, "the principal difficulty here is not to believe, but to know what it is which offers itself for belief."[98] In order to examine the various aspects of the topic, the following section will consider both biblical material and major modern theologies of the resurrection.

*Biblical Data*

"Resurrection narratives" differ in kind from crucifixion narratives. While crucifixion narratives, though always permeated with theological interpretation, are in fact accounts of the crucifixion, no canonical resurrection narrative purports to describe the resurrection directly.[99] Instead, the chief New Testament texts fall into two categories: stories of the discovery of the empty grave and of appearances of the risen Lord, and brief formulas that proclaim Jesus' resurrection.[100]

---

97. Pinchas Lapide (*The Resurrection of Jesus: A Jewish Perspective* [Minneapolis: Augsburg, 1983]), an apparent exception, conceives of the resurrection as a resuscitation; see John P. Galvin, "A Recent Jewish View of the Resurrection," *Expository Times* 91 (1979–80): 277–79.

98. C. F. Evans, *Resurrection and the New Testament* (London: SCM, 1970), 130.

99. The Gospel of Peter, an apocryphal second-century text, portrays the resurrection directly (IX.35–X.42): "In the night whereon the Lord's day dawned, as the soldiers were keeping guard two by two in every watch, there came a great sound in the heaven, and they saw the heavens opened and two men descend thence, shining with a great light, and drawing near unto the sepulchre. And that stone which had been set on the door rolled away of itself and went back to the side, and the sepulchre was opened and both of the young men entered in. When therefore those soldiers saw that, they waked up the centurion and the elders (for they also were there keeping watch); and while they were yet telling them the things which they had seen, they saw again three men come out of the sepulchre, and two of them sustaining the other, and a cross following after them. And of the two they saw that their heads reached unto heaven, but of him that was led by them that it overpassed the heavens. And they heard a voice out of the heavens saying: Hast thou preached unto them that sleep? And an answer was heard from the cross, saying: Yea" (cited, with slight modifications, from M. R. James, *The Apocryphal New Testament* [Oxford: Oxford University Press, 1953], 52–53).

100. Reginald H. Fuller (*The Formation of the Resurrection Narratives* [New York: Macmillan, 1971]) offers a thorough account of the relevant texts. For a helpful chart

Each of the Gospels includes an account of Jesus' burial[101] and of discovery of the empty tomb (Mark 15:42—16:8; Matt. 27:57—28:15; Luke 23:50—24:11; John 19:38—20:18). While unanimous in reporting that women found Jesus' grave empty two days after his crucifixion, the accounts differ in several respects: The number and names of the women, their motivation in visiting the tomb, the events that occur in their presence, the number of heavenly figures whom they encounter, the message they receive, and their reaction to these events all vary considerably from text to text. Matthew alone includes mention of a Roman guard, and John alone (but see Luke 24:12, 24) mentions a story of two disciples racing to the grave. Matthew and John include divergent accounts, not paralleled in Mark and Luke, of an appearance of the risen Jesus at the tomb. These differences, which reflect the evangelists' theological perspectives, cannot be completely harmonized on a historical level.

The narratives of appearances of the risen Lord exhibit even greater variations. The stories vary in location (Jerusalem [Luke 24; John 20; Acts 1]; Galilee [Matt. 28; John 21]), in the circumstances of the appearances, and in the words ascribed to the risen Lord. Like the accounts of the empty grave, the appearance narratives are of considerable theological import. The texts weigh the nature and divine origin of faith, the identity and the transformation of the risen Jesus, and several sacramental (baptism; eucharist; forgiveness of sins) and ecclesiological (mission; apostleship; role of Peter) themes. But on a historical level, they resist amalgamation into a coherent unified account.

In addition to these narratives, the New Testament also contains numerous brief formulas that profess faith in Jesus' glorification. Such passages, most common in Paul's letters but also found in the Gospels, may embody hymns (Phil. 2:5-11), catechetical instruction (1 Cor. 15:3-8), or liturgical acclamations (Luke 24:34). They vary in vocabulary, sometimes speaking of resurrection (e.g., 1 Thess. 4:14; Rom. 10:9) and sometimes of exaltation (e.g., Phil. 2:9). Older than the writings into which they have been incorporated, these formulas have sometimes been modified or expanded for use in their current context.

In recent years, pre-Pauline formulas have assumed a central role in discussions of the resurrection. Because of its content and age, 1 Corinthians 15:3-8 is particularly significant in this respect:

---

illustrating the similarities and differences of the gospel narratives see Raymond E. Brown, "The Resurrection of Jesus," in *The New Jerome Biblical Commentary*, 1376.

101. On the burial see Raymond E. Brown, "The Burial of Jesus (Mark 15:42–47)," *Catholic Biblical Quarterly* 50 (1988): 233–45.

For I delivered to you as of first importance what I also received, that
Christ died for our sins according to the scriptures, that he was buried,
that he was raised on the third day according to the scriptures, and that
he appeared to Cephas, then to the twelve. Then he appeared to more
than five hundred brethren at one time, most of whom are still alive,
though some have fallen asleep. Then he appeared to James, then to all
the apostles. Last of all, as to one untimely born, he appeared also to
me.

The core of this passage, fixed in wording when Paul received
it, may be retraced to within a few years of the crucifixion. Neither
its original language (Aramaic or Greek) nor its geographical origin
(Damascus, Antioch, and Jerusalem are the chief possibilities) can be
determined with certitude. Nonetheless, the antiquity of the formula
is beyond question. Its importance for historical questioning is enhanced by v. 8, where Paul numbers himself among the recipients of
"appearances" of the risen Christ. Here he applies to his own experience the same verb (*ophthe*) used three times in the preceding verses
to designate appearances to prior witnesses to the resurrection. The
text contains no reference to the empty grave and no narrative of
a resurrection appearance. Unlike the gospel stories, however, it is
the direct expression of one who claims to have been an eyewitness
to an event of this sort (see also Gal. 1:16 and 1 Cor. 9:1, though
each of these texts uses different vocabulary).

In the following pages I shall note varying assessments of this text
on the part of contemporary theologians. Three points, however,
should be noted at this stage. First, the phrase "on the third day" in
the third clause of the formula is applied to the resurrection itself,
not to the discovery of the empty tomb or to the initial appearances.
Recent authors have argued on the basis of biblical (see Hos. 6:1-2;
Ps. 16:10) and intertestamental material that the phrase is not meant
chronologically, but rather refers to a moment of decisive divine
action.[102] (Modern references to rescue coming at the eleventh hour
can serve as a remote analogy.) If this analysis is correct, the verse is
an interpretation of the resurrection's theological significance, not
a specification of its date.

Second, the formula emphasizes the sequence in which appearances took place, and reflects a certain interest in the ecclesial status
of their recipients. At the same time, in the judgment of many, the
appearances are noted precisely as confirmation of the reality of the
resurrection.

---

102. See especially Karl Lehmann, *Auferweckt am dritten Tag nach der Schrift*
(Freiburg: Herder, 1968).

Third, the verb *ophthe*, "he was seen by" or "he appeared to," is of great significance. Paul does not use this precise form elsewhere. Its emphasis is on the active role of Christ, who lets himself be seen by chosen witnesses. In the Septuagint, the Greek translation of the Old Testament, *ophthe* is used frequently in narrating theophanies, where it serves as technical vocabulary for "appearing from heaven" (see e.g., Gen. 12:7; 17:1; 18:1; Exod. 3:2; 4:1; 6:3). All uses of *ophthe* in the New Testament reflect similar contexts,[103] a fact that raises questions about interpreting the "seeing" literally.

Divergent assessments of this background are reflected in two distinct interpretations of the fourth clause of the pre-Pauline formula. Most authors maintain that the text refers to a real seeing, though of a distinctive sort, that established faith in Jesus' resurrection and simultaneously established or confirmed the ecclesial position of the appearances' recipients.[104] Other theologians find that the ancient formula simply asserts the revelation of the resurrection and the ecclesial status of its witnesses, without providing information as to how such revelation occurred. To pursue this matter further, we shall have to consider recent treatments of the resurrection.

### Modern Theological Discussion

Contemporary discussion of the resurrection entails both exegetical and systematic issues, and the positions of theologians on this subject are deeply entwined with their overall theological methods and convictions. While the resurrection has not been a traditional source of division along confessional lines, foundational differences among Catholics and Protestants on the nature of faith and on the relationship of divine grace to human activity often influence approaches to this topic. Despite overlapping concerns, it will be best to keep the presentations of Protestant and Catholic theologians distinct. Since intense modern debate about the resurrection developed first among Protestants, and only later emerged in Catholic circles, the following survey will begin with a look at three major modern

---

103. The term occurs seventeen times in the New Testament: Matt. 17:3; Mark 9:4; Luke 1:11; 22:43; Acts 7:2, 26, 30; 13:31; 16:9; 1 Cor. 15:5, 6, 7, 8; 1 Tim. 3:16; Rev. 11:19; 12:1; 13:1. In each case, the reference is to an appearance from heaven. For an informative analysis of biblical terminology related to the resurrection, see Anton Vögtle, "Wie kam es zum Osterglauben?" in Anton Vögtle and Rudolf Pesch, *Wie kam es zum Osterglauben?* (Düsseldorf: Patmos, 1975), 9–131.

104. The difficulty here lies in specifying what was seen; see William P. Loewe, "The Appearances of the Risen Lord: Faith, Fact, and Objectivity," *Horizons* 6 (1979): 177–92.

Protestant authors: Rudolf Bultmann, Willi Marxsen, and Wolfhart Pannenberg.

**Rudolf Bultmann.** Bultmann's thought on the resurrection, a standard reference point for later treatments, reflects his basic theological program of demythologization through existential interpretation. In Bultmann's judgment, the New Testament expresses its theological convictions in largely mythological form. While acceptable and even inevitable at the time the biblical texts were composed, mythological expressions pose unnecessary obstacles to modern believers. In addition, they entail the risk of a false objectification that subjects matters of faith to human control. Drawing on the early philosophy of Martin Heidegger, Bultmann advocates overcoming these problems by means of existential interpretation, a process that seeks to wrest from the ancient texts their underlying understanding of human existence as confronted by God and called to decision before God. The purpose of the texts is to awaken faith, not to provide objective historical information.

Applying these principles to the theology of the resurrection, Bultmann dismisses historical issues as irrelevant: "Christian faith... is not interested in the historical question." Far from being concerned with such data, Bultmann maintains that "faith in the resurrection is nothing other than faith in the cross as the salvation event" and that "to believe in the cross of Christ means to accept the cross as one's own and to allow oneself to be crucified with Christ." Contrary to all outward appearances, it is in the Word of the cross (see 1 Cor. 1:18-24) and nowhere else that Christ crucified and risen encounters us. To seek demonstration of the truth of this preaching or a historical basis for believing in it is an illegitimate effort to circumvent the demands of faith.[105]

Bultmann's position recognizes that discussion of the resurrection cannot proceed in isolation, but requires reference to something else. Given his separation of Jesus' public life from his death, the resurrection could in principle be connected with either of these realities, but not both. But, as we have seen, Bultmann denies theological significance to the life of Jesus, and conceives of theology as essentially a theology of the cross. In addition, his interest lies in the awakening of faith in the present moment, not in detecting significance inherent

---

105. Rudolf Bultmann, "New Testament and Mythology: The Problem of Demythologizing the New Testament Proclamation," in Schubert M. Ogden, ed., *New Testament and Mythology and Other Basic Writings* (Philadelphia: Fortress Press, 1984), 1–43; the citations are taken from pp. 40, 39, and 34. This much-debated essay was originally published in 1941.

in past events. The result is a conception of the resurrection linked to the cross's paradoxical salvific character. The resurrection seems identified more with the rise of faith on the part of the disciples than with anything affecting Jesus personally.

Various interrelated elements of Bultmann's thought may well be challenged: the notion of faith as unsupported risk and consequent separation of faith from history; the denial of intrinsic significance to factual events; the option for existential interpretation and the resulting restriction of theological interest to the individual person and to the present time; the denial of theological significance to the historical Jesus; the false alternatives posed by separation of his death from his public life; the conception of the kerygma as immune from scrutiny. Nonetheless, Bultmann's insistence that the resurrection be subjected to critical interpretation has become an important reference point in subsequent discussion, even on the part of those who judge Bultmann's own position seriously flawed.[106]

**Willi Marxsen.** A stance similar in some respects to Bultmann's figures prominently in current discussion through the writings of Willi Marxsen, a German Lutheran exegete who shares Bultmann's notion of faith, interest in demythologization, and disjunction between Jesus' public life and crucifixion. Marxsen differs from Bultmann by insisting that nothing be permitted to detract from the Jesus of history. The result is a distinctive conception of the Easter faith and its origin: for Marxsen, "the question of the resurrection of Jesus is not that of an event which occurred after Good Friday, but that of the earthly Jesus."[107]

Arguing that the resurrection narratives, with their wealth of detail, are products of the early church, expressions of the Easter faith rather than reliable records of its origin, Marxsen identifies 1 Corinthians 15:3-8 as the most significant historical testimony to the resurrection. Since even this ancient formulation is suffused with theological interpretation, historical investigation is unable to detail the events that lie behind the claims of the witnesses. From analysis of the biblical data, Marxsen concludes that occurrences after Jesus' death, above all a foundational experience on the part of Peter, en-

---

106. For detailed presentation of Bultmann's position and his exchange with Karl Barth on this subject see Hans-Georg Geyer, "The Resurrection of Jesus Christ: A Survey of the Debate in Present Day Theology," in C. F. D. Moule, ed., *The Significance of the Message of the Resurrection for Faith in Jesus Christ* (London: SCM, 1968), 106–21.

107. Willi Marxsen, "The Resurrection of Jesus as a Historical and Theological Problem," in *The Significance of the Message of the Resurrection for Faith in Jesus Christ*, 50; see, in addition to this entire essay (pp. 15–50), Marxsen's *The Resurrection of Jesus of Nazareth* (Philadelphia: Fortress Press, 1970).

abled the church to proclaim that Jesus lives, that Jesus' cause (*die Sache Jesu*, a characteristic phrase) goes on despite his death. Drawing on the nondualistic anthropology and apocalyptic vocabulary of contemporary Judaism, early Christians adopted resurrection language to express their faith. This vehicle of interpretation implied in turn that Jesus' grave was empty and thus led to legendary accounts of the women's discovery of the empty tomb. But resurrection terminology, inevitable under the cultural conditions of the New Testament, is neither intrinsic to Christian faith nor viable in the modern world. Nor is the anthropology of the biblical period the same as ours. Alternative confessions—that Jesus' cause goes on, that Jesus is the living one, that he still comes today—are more suitable for contemporary believers.

Many of the objections registered against Bultmann's treatment of the resurrection also apply to Marxsen's position. The vague account of the foundational experiences of Peter and the other disciples is a further weakness, and it is doubtful that all anthropologies are equally suitable for expressing Christian faith. Marxsen's interpretation of the resurrection is thus in many respects unsatisfactory. Nonetheless, his concern that events after the crucifixion not detract from the importance of Jesus is worth bearing in mind.

**Wolfhart Pannenberg.** A conception of faith and theology diametrically opposed to those of Bultmann and Marxsen is operative in the work of Wolfhart Pannenberg, one of the chief critics of their thought on the resurrection. Pannenberg's treatment of the resurrection is part of an ambitious theological program, a context that accounts for many of his specific emphases and interests.

In Pannenberg's judgment, the central theological question posed by and since the Enlightenment is whether Christian faith is genuine faith or superstition:[108] whether, in other words, the Christian message is true. Theologians who dismiss this question as an act of unbelief fail to address the challenges posed by modernity. But the truth of the message can be judged only by reference to its content, for the authority of its sources is itself subject to dispute. Similarly, since Christians confess God as the all-determining reality, creator of heaven and earth, no retreat from the realm of public history to the interior decision of the individual is legitimate. On the contrary, it

108. Wolfhart Pannenberg, "Insight and Faith," in *Basic Questions in Theology* (Philadelphia: Fortress Press, 1971), 2:41–42. It is consistent with this conviction that Pannenberg's *Systematische Theologie*, vol. 1 (Göttingen: Vandenhoeck and Ruprecht, 1988) begins with a chapter on the truth of Christian doctrine as the theme of systematic theology (pp. 11–72).

is precisely in public history that revelation occurs, and the function of Christian preaching is to articulate the meaning inherent in the revelatory event when seen in its appropriate context. The validity of the Word is not exempt from critical scrutiny; and the point of reference for examining it is accessible to all.

Seen from this perspective, the resurrection of Jesus acquires central importance. First, the resurrection is decisive for christology due to the inadequacy of the historical Jesus. Jesus' implicit claim to speak and act on behalf of God is not self-justifying, but requires divine legitimation. Such confirmation was not given during Jesus' lifetime; and Jesus' death, especially when its specific circumstances are taken into account, seems to constitute a final refutation of his claim to represent God.[109] The resurrection, and public revelation of the resurrection, are indispensable if Jesus is to be believed; without supporting historical evidence Christian faith would be indefensibly rash.

But the resurrection is also decisive from a second perspective. Any interpretation of world history must place events in context, for the context affects the interpretation. While the immediate context of past events can be determined to a greater or lesser extent, the overall outcome of history still lies ahead; we cannot position ourselves at the end of history and pass judgment on its outcome. Finding meaning in history as a whole thus seems impossible. Jesus' resurrection, however, is an anticipation of the end of history, an advance occurrence of what is expected one day for all. It thus provides an escape from this dilemma, a vantage point from which the whole of history can be assessed. Nothing else, not even Jesus' own life-history, can do this. The resurrection is the key to interpreting both Jesus himself and human history as a whole.

The success of this theological program hinges on establishing the factuality of the resurrection as an event after Jesus' death. Strong historical warrant was needed for the first Christians to modify apocalyptic hope from envisioning general resurrection at the end of the world to confessing the resurrection of a single individual as already accomplished. Pannenberg's points of reference are the appearances and the empty grave. Appealing to 1 Corinthians 15:3-8 as ancient material that includes eyewitness testimony, he argues that the appearance tradition is historically reliable. The emptiness of

---

109. For Pannenberg, cross and resurrection constitute Jesus' double fate (*Jesus–God and Man*, 33, 210–11, 245–46); in both, Jesus has ceased to be active and a response is given to his life. Yet the two are not on the same level of importance. Pannenberg holds that the resurrection could be understood without the cross but that the cross could not be understood without the resurrection (p. 246).

Jesus' grave is also historically demonstrable, since otherwise the early Christian preaching of the resurrection in Jerusalem would have been exposed as false by reference to the presence of his body in the tomb. (In each case, Pannenberg classifies the detailed stories of the Gospels as later articulations of the theological meaning inherent in the resurrection, not as sources of further historical information.)

These historical facts require explanation, and the only plausible explanation is that Jesus is risen. While adopted from apocalyptic sources, resurrection language is the only vocabulary appropriate to the data; more general substitutes (e.g., of the sort proposed by Marxsen) fail to do justice to the historical facts. In Pannenberg's judgment, the core of apocalyptic hope for continued or renewed existence after death is a universal anthropological reality, not limited to the cultural conditions of the past. Far from rejecting this longing as evidence of non-Christian influence, he finds in it a reference point for Christianity's universal interests. Thus the resurrection of Jesus, a historically demonstrable event, provides both the needed divine confirmation of the personal claims raised by Jesus' public life and a suitable vantage point from which to assess the meaning of history as a whole.[110]

Pannenberg's treatment of the resurrection, like other aspects of his work, is characterized by careful reasoning and thorough pursuit of foundational issues. The insistence on truth and the detailed examination of historical questions are particularly valuable. Nonetheless, questions remain. Does Pannenberg's conception of the need for subsequent legitimation of the historical Jesus require too much by way of extrinsic demonstration and unintentionally undercut Jesus' significance? Do references to Jesus' double fate (death and resurrection) imply a dichotomy between Jesus' public life (active) and his fate (passive)? Is the resurrection of Jesus historically demonstrable to an open-minded but neutral observer? Is apocalyptic expectation of general resurrection at the end of the world the most significant background of early Christian preaching that Jesus is risen? These issues are worth bearing in mind as we look at three major Catholic figures in the recent discussion of the resurrection.

As noted in the introduction to this chapter, Catholic theologians in the past few centuries typically relegated the resurrection to the

---

110. Pannenberg, *Jesus—God and Man*, 53–114, and "The Revelation of God in Jesus of Nazareth," in James M. Robinson and John B. Cobb, eds., *Theology as History* (New York: Harper and Row, 1967), 101–33. Pannenberg also attributes to the resurrection a type of retroactive effect, the possibility of which remains obscure; on this issue see Brian O. McDermott, "Pannenberg's Resurrection Christology: A Critique," *Theological Studies* 35 (1974): 711–21.

domain of fundamental theology, where it was considered almost exclusively from an apologetic perspective; dogmatic christologies of this period accorded the resurrection little attention.[111] As the biblical and liturgical movements awakened appreciation of the significance of the resurrection in the New Testament and renewed awareness of the paschal mystery's centrality in the life of the church, Catholic theologians of the 1950s and 1960s sought to enhance the position of the resurrection in dogmatic theology.[112] Extended treatment of the subject is now standard in Catholic textbooks on christology.[113]

Such increased attention to the resurrection has been accompanied by the development of diverse theological positions on its nature and on the manner of its revelation. In addition, the salvific significance of the resurrection has been specified in different ways. The major systematic alternatives in recent Catholic thought are represented by Karl Rahner and Edward Schillebeeckx. In addition to considering these two authors, I shall also examine an innovative proposal advanced, with appeal to Rahner, by the exegete Rudolf Pesch.

**Karl Rahner.** While attentive to the issues involved in exegetical discussion, Karl Rahner directed his thought on the resurrection primarily to systematic aspects of the question. Here as elsewhere, Rahner saw the content of Christian faith as a confirmation and fulfillment of human hope. His starting point in approaching the resurrection was therefore theological anthropology, more specifically his understanding of human freedom and death.

Rahner's theology of freedom focused on personal self-disposal before God, not on the choice of individual objects. Freedom is not only a power to select one thing over another, but, on a deeper level, an ability to make something of oneself. Of its very nature, it seeks permanence, not reversibility, for constant change would be equivalent to indecision. For this reason, freedom must be limited temporally: The exercise of human freedom ends and culminates in death.

From this perspective, death is seen to contain both passive and active dimensions: It is at once the endured end of life, beyond one's

---

111. For a representative example, see Ludwig Ott, *Fundamentals of Catholic Dogma* (Cork, Ire.: Mercier, 1962). This work of 544 pages devotes pp. 192–95 to the resurrection and ascension.

112. The most influential work in this regard was F. X. Durrwell, *The Resurrection: A Biblical Study* (New York: Sheed and Ward, 1960).

113. See, e.g., Kasper, *Jesus the Christ,* 124–60, and O'Collins, *Interpreting Jesus,* 108–32.

control, and the completion of one's personal history of freedom. Human death is not extinction; rather, the freedom exercised over the course of a lifetime now bears eternal fruit in attaining a final state that includes all the constitutive dimensions of human existence. While the way in which this occurs is beyond our ability to envision, the result is neither perpetuation of life in its current form nor substitution of a new mode of existence entirely unrelated to what has preceded it. Death leads rather to the permanent personal validity of an individual's life. "Death . . . is not the nullifying end of history, but the event in which history elevates itself, by God's own act, into the infinite freedom of God."[114]

Jesus' resurrection, while unique because of his uniqueness, incorporates the basic characteristics of resurrection in general. Divine causality and human causality are joined here, just as they are linked elsewhere. Jesus' death is the culmination of his free self-disposal before God, and his resurrection is the permanent personal outcome of his life. Far from being an extrinsically imposed sign of divine approval, it is the perfected and perfecting end of his specific death: "The resurrection of Christ is not *another* event *after* his suffering and after his death, but . . . the appearance of what took place in Christ's death: the performed and undergone handing over of the entire reality of the one corporal man to the mystery of the mercifully loving God through Christ's collected freedom, which disposes over his entire life and his entire existence."[115]

From these considerations on the unity of death and resurrection, Rahner concludes that the meaning of the resurrection is inseparable from the meaning of the crucifixion. The resurrection is the definitive stage of Jesus' salvific life; without it, nothing would be complete. But the resurrection is the only possible result of his salvific life and death, not a new event, separable from what precedes it. Therefore: "If the fate of Jesus has any soteriological significance at all, this significance can be situated neither in the death nor in the resurrection taken separately, but can only be illuminated now from the one and now from the other aspect of this single event."[116]

---

114. Karl Rahner, "The Death of Jesus and the Closure of Revelation," in *Theological Investigations* (New York: Crossroad, 1984), 18:142 (corrected translation).

115. Karl Rahner, "Dogmatic Questions on Easter," in *Theological Investigations* (Baltimore: Helicon, 1966), 4:128 (corrected translation); see also idem, *Foundations of Christian Faith*, 266. The impact of Rahner's thought may be seen in the paraphrases of Kasper (*Jesus the Christ*, 150 [the similarity is far greater than the English translation suggests]) and Küng (*On Being a Christian*, 359).

116. Rahner, *Foundations of Christian Faith*, 266. Kasper and Küng do not draw this conclusion, which seems to be entailed in the positions that they do adopt.

With regard to manifestation of the resurrection in events after Jesus' death, Rahner's position has varied. Generally accenting the appearances more than the empty grave, he emphasizes that the appearances involve a transposition of the risen Jesus into the range of the disciples' possible perception, and allow us to draw no conclusions about the specific characteristics of a risen body. In several writings, Rahner holds that such experiences were limited to the early church, so that we are dependent on the first witnesses not only for the statement of fact but also for our knowledge of the possibility; yet in some later texts he tends to assimilate the appearances to the overall experience of grace and to argue that the indispensability of the apostolic message lies in its historical identification of Jesus.[117] While much of Rahner's later writing sees the resurrection as a confirmation of Jesus' implicit claims, he remains unalterably opposed to understanding the resurrection as an extrinsically conferred sign of divine approval.

Rahner's conception of the resurrection as completion rather than correction is more akin to Johannine thought than to the Synoptic Gospels. While similar to Bultmann in associating the resurrection closely with the crucifixion, Rahner nonetheless insists that the resurrection affects Jesus personally and cannot be reduced to the first disciples' coming to faith. His position constitutes one pole of the contemporary Catholic theological spectrum.[118]

**Edward Schillebeeckx.** The next figure to be examined in our look at contemporary theologies of the resurrection is Edward Schillebeeckx, whose thought on the nature of the resurrection diverges sharply from Rahner's and forms the major contemporary Catholic alternative to Rahner's position. While a general overview of Schillebeeckx's christology will be deferred until the next section of this chapter, some comments on his thought on death are needed to provide the background for his theology of the resurrection.

In contrast to Rahner, Schillebeeckx's theology of death pursues a phenomenological approach and identifies death as the extreme moment of human weakness and helplessness. In addition, he sees

---

117. For the first type see Rahner, "Resurrection," in *Sacramentum Mundi*, 5: 329–31, and "The Position of Christology in the Church between Exegesis and Dogmatics," in *Theological Investigations* (New York: Seabury, 1974), 11:210–14; for the second see idem, "Hope and Easter," in *Christian at the Crossroads* (New York: Seabury, 1975), 87–93; "Jesus' Resurrection," in *Theological Investigations* (London: Darton, Longman and Todd, 1981), 17:16–23; and *Foundations of Christian Faith*, 274–78.

118. For more thorough presentation of Rahner's thought see John P. Galvin, "The Resurrection of Jesus in Contemporary Catholic Systematics," *Heythrop Journal* 20 (1979): 125–30.

the crucifixion first and foremost as an act of cruelty and injustice. Given this background, the resurrection and death are not and cannot be seen as one event; the resurrection is not death's "other," salvific aspect. To Schillebeeckx, the resurrection is more than the revelation of what happened in Jesus' death. It is a new and distinct event, a divine correcting victory over the negativity of suffering and death, a divine act that confers on Jesus' death new meaning. While the resurrection affects Jesus personally and cannot be reduced to changes within his disciples, it remains metaempirical and metahistorical and must not be confused with a return to the conditions of Jesus' prior life. It is a confirmation that Jesus belongs to God, and thus of Jesus' person and message; yet it is not legitimation or confirmation in the normal sense of those words: One statement of faith cannot legitimate another, and in any case true legitimation of Christian faith remains a future, eschatological reality.

In addition to developing this interpretation of the resurrection's nature, Schillebeeckx has also presented a distinctive conception of its revelation. In his judgment, discovery of Jesus' empty grave is not a factor in the origin of faith in Jesus' resurrection.[119] Yet something is needed to account for the disciples' change of heart after the crucifixion. This "something" is tentatively identified as the disciples' grace-filled experiences of God's renewed offer of salvation in Jesus. Their essential component is not visual seeing, but the personal experience, possible only through grace, of reorienting one's entire life on the basis of recognition of Jesus as the Christ. In keeping with this interpretation, Schillebeeckx stresses similarities between the original disciples' coming to faith and the development of the faith of later Christians.

To specify matters further, Schillebeeckx undertakes a rather daring comparison of the tradition behind the appearance stories with the threefold account of Paul's experience on the road to Damascus in the Acts of the Apostles (Acts 9; 22; 26). The passages in Acts include a version that stresses conversion (Acts 9), an account that emphasizes mission (Acts 26), and a stage that incorporates both themes (Acts 22). Drawing on the work of Gerhard Lohfink, Schillebeeckx suggests that these three texts reflect different stages of a tradition in which the theme of conversion gradually yielded to that of mission. Noting the prominence of Peter in the resurrection

---

119. In *Jesus* (pp. 331–46), Schillebeeckx favors the view that the stories of finding the empty tomb derive from later liturgical celebrations at the place of Jesus' burial; he later grants that the tomb may have been found empty, but insists that this discovery did not in itself lead to faith (*Interim Report on the Books "Jesus" and "Christ"* [London: SCM, 1980], 86–88]).

tradition, and observing that the canonical stories of Jesus' appearances stress the theme of mission, Schillebeeckx tentatively suggests that the appearance narratives may be a later form of a tradition that originally concerned conversion experiences, but which has not been preserved in that earlier form. He therefore specifies the historical core of the appearance tradition as renewed experiences of forgiveness through Jesus, even after his death, which led to a reassembling of his followers at the initiative of Peter.[120]

Schillebeeckx's position has been misconstrued by some critics, as if he had reduced the resurrection itself, rather than the appearance tradition, to a conversion experience on the part of Jesus' disciples. Even apart from this misunderstanding, however, his historical reconstruction has been challenged as lacking textual foundation. Under the impact of such critique, Schillebeeckx has modified his position to some extent. While constant in insisting on the divine origin of faith in the resurrection and on the need for new experiences on the part of the disciples after Jesus' death, he no longer concentrates on the theme of conversion in his references to these experiences. Room is left for a possible visual component in the appearances, but explanations considered supranaturalistic remain excluded.[121]

**Rudolf Pesch.** Drawing on Rahner's conception of the nature of the resurrection, Rudolf Pesch has proposed a novel exegetical interpretation of the background and origin of Christian faith in the risen Christ. Apart from its interest as a historical reconstruction, his hypothesis raises significant questions about the treatment of foundational christological issues.

As noted in earlier sections of this chapter, Pesch is optimistic in assessing the extent of critically assured historical knowledge of Jesus. Among other points, he is convinced of the disciples' pre-Easter faith in Jesus as prophetic Messiah, of Jesus' preparation of his disciples for his approaching death, and of Jesus' interpretation of his death, during the Last Supper, as salvific. It is against this background that he analyzes the New Testament texts concerning the resurrection.

Dissatisfied with the standard accounts of the origin of Easter faith, Pesch finds that the tradition concerning the discovery of the empty tomb is historically inconclusive, and that attempted explanations of the nature of the appearances often lack concrete information. In his judgment, the *ophthe*-formula in 1 Corinthians

---

120. See Schillebeeckx, *Jesus*, 329–97, 516–44.

121. In addition to Schillebeeckx, *Jesus*, 644–50 (a section added to the third Dutch edition), see *Interim Report*, 74–93.

15:5-8 expresses the ecclesial status of those listed as recipients of the appearances, but does not provide factual data about the origin of their status. Drawing on the work of Klaus Berger on Jewish belief in the resurrection or exaltation of individual figures (prophet; Son of man) while history continued its course, Pesch proposes that faith in the resurrection originated with the historical Jesus: Given the events of Jesus' life and the way in which he died, the faith he elicited from his disciples was sufficient to survive his crucifixion and provide a basis for the (valid) conviction that God had raised him from the dead. The resurrection of Jesus is an object of faith, not a basis of faith that can be established historically. Later inquiry into the grounds of Christian faith is therefore pointed to the historical Jesus, not to stories of events after his crucifixion.[122]

Pesch's hypothesis generated considerable controversy, and a number of serious criticisms were registered against his position. As far as exegetical issues are concerned, Pesch's account of the historical Jesus is disputed, as is his argument that the *ophthe*-formula merely indicates the visionaries' ecclesial status. That conceptions of the resurrection or exaltation of individual figures were widespread in Jewish circles at the time of Jesus' death has also been questioned. In christological terms, some critics find excessive Pesch's emphasis on the historical Jesus, and fear that a low christology denying Christ's divinity will result. Significant christological issues are thus at stake in the discussion.[123]

*Conclusion*

As this survey of major recent interpretations of the resurrection shows, contemporary theologies of the resurrection vary widely in

---

122. See Rudolf Pesch, "Zur Entstehung des Glaubens an die Auferstehung Jesu," *Theologische Quartalschrift* 153 (1973): 201–28; for a summary of his position and the ensuing debate see John P. Galvin, "Resurrection as *Theologia crucis Jesu*: The Foundational Christology of Rudolf Pesch," *Theological Studies* 38 (1977): 513–25.

123. For further reaction to Pesch's thought see Francis Schüssler Fiorenza, *Foundational Theology: Jesus and the Church* (New York: Crossroad, 1984), 18–28, and Johannes Nützel, "Zum Schicksal des eschatologischen Propheten," *Biblische Zeitschrift* 20 (1976): 59–94. Pesch has subsequently altered his position (see "Zur Entstehung des Glaubens an die Auferstehung Jesu: Ein neuer Versuch," *Freiburger Zeitschrift für Theologie und Philosophie* 30 [1983]: 73–98). He continues to find the empty grave tradition unreliable, and to hold that in principle sufficient grounds for belief in Jesus' resurrection were available by the time of his death. Now, however, he argues that in fact the disciples' breakthrough to faith in the risen Lord was mediated by ecstatic visions of Jesus as the exalted Son of man. On Pesch's current views and the reaction of other authors to his shift to a more traditional position, see John P. Galvin, "The Origin of Faith in the Resurrection of Jesus: Two Recent Perspectives," *Theological Studies* 49 (1988): 25–44.

interest and content. Each conception is deeply embedded in its author's approach to christology and theology as a whole, and can be fairly evaluated only with reference to these wider contexts. The following section of this chapter will examine the overall christologies of Karl Rahner and Edward Schillebeeckx, in my judgment the most significant contemporary Roman Catholic christological projects. However, before taking up those matters this section will conclude with some principles concerning the interpretation of the resurrection.

First, it is clear from the above reflections that specifying the meaning of the resurrection is not an easy task. Given the unity of Jesus' person and message, I would argue that, as a minimum, the resurrection must be understood to affect Jesus personally; it is not reducible to changes within and among his disciples. In addition, it is necessary to avoid conceiving Jesus' resurrection as a resuscitation that brings about a return to his previous conditions of life (as, e.g., in the stories of the raisings of Jairus's daughter [Matt. 9:18-26; Mark 5:21-43; Luke 8:40-56], the widow's son [Luke 7:11-17], and Lazarus [John 11:1-44]). Paul's reflections (1 Cor. 15:35-57) on elements of continuity and transformation in the resurrection for which we hope may provide some useful guidelines for speaking of the resurrection of Jesus as well.

Second, the oft-neglected distinction between the resurrection and its revelation must be carefully preserved. Failure to do so results inevitably in confusion and misrepresentation of theological positions. The views of theologians on the historicity of the empty grave and of the appearances must be distinguished from their conclusions concerning the resurrection itself.

Third, while the initial position of Pesch may be exaggerated, examination of the grounds for faith in the resurrection should not be restricted to consideration of events after the crucifixion. The context established by Jesus' life and death is an indispensable factor in weighing the foundation of Christian faith that Jesus is risen.

Fourth, conceptions of the resurrection that undermine the significance of all that preceded it are open to telling objections on the grounds of escapism.[124] This consideration gives strong support to understanding the resurrection as confirmation rather than reversal.

Finally, the relationship of crucifixion and resurrection is the central point in any theology of the resurrection. Because of the influence of Bultmann's thought, a close association of death and

---

124. See Dietrich Bonhoeffer, *Letters and Papers from Prison*, rev. ed. (New York: Macmillan, 1967), 142, 176; Franz Schupp, *Vermittlung im Fragment* (Innsbruck: ÖH, 1975), 34–35.

resurrection is often identified with denial that the resurrection affects Jesus personally; yet in fact the two issues are quite distinct. Analyses of this relationship are strongly influenced by varying theologies of death and corresponding theological interpretations of the crucifixion. While debate on this subject is likely to continue, a completely negative theology of the crucifixion seems in the long run incompatible with a positive theological assessment of a public life that led inexorably to its violent end.

## TWO CONTEMPORARY CHRISTOLOGIES

The previous section of this chapter examined a number of items important in christological discussion. A plethora of issues emerged from a look at the contemporary literature, and it became clear that these themes are so tightly interwoven that none can be thoroughly weighed and adjudicated without reference to others. Against the background of what has been considered up to this point, this section of the chapter will outline in more systematic form the overall christological positions of two major contemporary Catholic theologians: Karl Rahner and Edward Schillebeeckx. Their positions on several individual topics have already been discussed; the goal now is to see the contours of their distinct interpretations of Jesus as the Christ.

Before considering the distinctive characteristics of either author, it will be well to note some interests that are common to both. While variations exist in the further specification of the issues and in the choice of means to pursue them, the following four concerns are so widespread that they can be considered, in broad terms, characteristic elements of recent Catholic christology.[125]

First, Rahner and Schillebeeckx share with many other theologians a desire to address in their christologies questions of urgent contemporary significance. In major theologians, this interest implies attention to the serious underlying questions of modernity, not preoccupation with fleeting or superficial issues. Increasingly characteristic of Catholic thought since World War II, though always in danger of deteriorating into a frantic quest for relevance, a legitimate and properly pastoral concern for current problems prevents most modern christology from pursuing a goal of timeless formulations.

---

125. In addition to Rahner and Schillebeeckx, these traits are reflected in the works of Walter Kasper, Hans Küng, Dermot Lane, and Gerald O'Collins.

Second, recent christology reflects a widespread desire to receive the results and to address the problems posed by modern biblical research. Both Rahner and Schillebeeckx studied theology at a time when Catholic dogmatic theology was more attuned to speculative, philosophical issues, and much less interested in biblical matters than it is today. Yet each author, like colleagues from a younger generation, has sought in his own way to become aware of pertinent biblical questions and has made efforts to address them a substantial factor in his thought.[126]

Third, both authors, again accompanied by many others,[127] wish to unify christology and soteriology, and to link them with other branches of theology. This is not merely a pedagogical matter; it expresses an awareness that Christian faith is a unified whole whose various aspects cannot be grasped accurately when divorced from one another. In this connection, both authors accord a certain primacy to soteriology: Our access to the person of Christ is mediated by his salvific deeds. Yet Rahner and Schillebeeckx also insist that Christ's work itself directs attention to his person.

Finally, both authors combine acceptance of the classical christology of the early councils with heightened recognition of its limitations. On the one hand, this twofold judgment implies a willingness to measure alternative christological formulations against the Chalcedonian dogma and to insist that proposed christologies not fall short of that council's affirmations; on the other hand, it entails freedom to depart from the conciliar terminology and framework of questioning.

## Karl Rahner

Karl Rahner's writings on christology span a half-century and pursue innumerable questions from a variety of perspectives. The closest approximation to a comprehensive summary of his christology is found in *Foundations of Christian Faith*,[128] but even this presentation differs in intent and scope from an integrated christological synthesis. Without attempting to retrace the genesis of Rahner's thinking, the following pages will recapitulate the main elements of his christology against the background of the chief concerns motivating his thought.

---

126. Biblical matters are treated in much greater detail and with much greater attention to specific exegetical works in Schillebeeckx than they are in Rahner, but such differences should not obscure the extent to which both authors are anxious to address, as systematic theologians, those biblical questions that have direct impact on doctrinal issues.

127. Wolfhart Pannenberg is a notable and distinguished exception.

128. Rahner, *Foundations of Christian Faith*, 176–321.

At the root of Rahner's christology lie three theological concerns, each of which comes to bear in the elaboration of his christological conception: God's universal salvific will; Jesus' indispensable role in the mediation of salvation; and the completeness of Jesus' humanity. While none of these themes is new to the history of theology, each assumes in Rahner's thought a prominence that it has not always enjoyed in the past.

As is evidenced in his early writing on membership in the church,[129] Rahner has been preoccupied from the start of his theological career with the universality of God's salvific will. This theme received its classical biblical articulation in 1 Timothy 2:4 ("God wills that all men be saved and come to a knowledge of the truth"), and has been reiterated in the Second Vatican Council's reference to the "universal design of God for the salvation of the human race" (*Ad Gentes* 3). While pursuit of this issue is not limited to christology, Rahner is anxious that christological formulations express the conviction that the divine offer of salvation extends to all, including those who lived before the time of Christ and others who, through no fault of their own, have never been exposed to the Christian message.

Juxtaposed to this foundational affirmation of the divine salvific will is an equally basic insistence on the indispensability of Jesus. The classical biblical texts on this score depict Jesus as saying, "I am the way, the truth and the life; no one comes to the Father except by me" (John 14:6), and proclaim that "there is salvation in no one else, for there is no other name under heaven given among men by which we must be saved" (Acts 4:12). The Second Vatican Council also speaks of Christ as the "sole mediator" (e.g., *Lumen Gentium* 8) between God and the human race. While aware that such biblical and conciliar texts require careful interpretation, Rahner is convinced that the indispensability of Jesus is no less essential to Christianity than the universality of God's salvific will. The difficulty lies in reconciling the two principles, which at first sight seem to contradict each other.

In reference to the third of his root theological concerns, Rahner argues that widespread misunderstanding of classical christological doctrine causes major pastoral problems. In his judgment, the conciliar teaching is often misconceived in a crypto-monophysite manner. While verbally orthodox in their profession of faith, those infected by this tendency unconsciously abbreviate Jesus' human nature, especially his human intellect and human freedom. The result is a mythological notion of Jesus as part divine, part human. While some

129. See, e.g., Rahner, "Membership of the Church according to the Encyclical of Pius XII 'Mystici Corporis Christi,'" in *Theological Investigations* (Baltimore: Helicon, 1963), 2:1–88. This article was originally published in 1947.

accept this conception of Jesus, wrongly imagining it to be orthodox doctrine, others reject it, also mistaking it for the church's teaching but finding it incredible. Common to both positions, in Rahner's judgment, is a misunderstanding of what the church actually teaches.

To address these issues, Rahner developed a conception of Jesus as the definitive Savior, or the eschatological (final) Mediator of salvation. While the origins of his christology lie in reflection on the church's teaching about Jesus, his thought is best grasped against the background of his theological anthropology. Rahner understands the human being as spirit-in-world, finite openness toward the infinite mystery of God. For a human being, salvation consists fundamentally in participation in divine life—over and above all that human nature, of itself, might demand or achieve. It is a free gift of God, freely offered to all.

To constitute salvation for human beings, the operation of grace must address every facet of human existence. Thus, while an intensely personal appeal to the human freedom of each individual, grace also has a public, historical dimension. Here the figure of Christ is, in Rahner's judgment, essential. Located at the "fullness of time" (Gal. 4:4), the climax of the history of salvation, the incarnation is the definitive divine assumption of a portion of creation into the inner life of God. As such, the incarnation is salvific: It is not merely the establishment of a figure who will subsequently perform salvific deeds. (This aspect of Rahner's theology is a contemporary retrieval of themes common in Eastern patristic thought.) Rahner argues that the offer of grace intrinsically requires, at some point, such public, historical expression. Jesus not only makes known God's universal salvific will; his existence is a constitutive element of the divine offer of salvation, without which an essential component would be lacking.

Yet the incarnation is the assumption not only of a complete human nature, but of a human life-history as well. This too is part of Jesus' being "like us in all things but sin" (DS 301; see Heb. 4:15). It is only with his death, when the life-long exercise of his individual human freedom is complete, that the definitive human acceptance of the offer of salvation takes place. As discussed earlier, this death leads of itself to resurrection, the permanent state of Jesus' existence before God. His multidimensional work as the definitive Savior is accomplished.

How does this conception enable Rahner to address the three concerns that underlie his christology? First, his interpretation of the salvific significance of Jesus, and especially his interpretation of Jesus' death as the definitive public expression and acceptance of the divine gift of salvation, accent from the start God's universal salvific will and eschew any suggestion of a God somehow hostile to the world prior to Jesus' death. The Johannine insistence that the sending of the Son is an effect of God's love for the world (see John 3:16-17) receives full force. At the same time, the indispensable salvific role of Jesus is also safeguarded. Jesus is not a religious leader on the same level as other important figures in the religious history of the human race. He is *the* Savior, *the* Christ, not only unsurpassed but unsurpassable, since he has definitively mediated participation in God's inner life. Finally, Rahner's picture of Jesus, especially his stress on the presence and exercise of Jesus' human freedom, accents without abbreviation the integrity of Jesus' humanity. Thus the concerns that motivate his christological reflection are adequately, if not exhaustively, addressed.

But does Rahner's notion of Jesus as the definitive Savior incorporate the early councils' teaching on Christ's divinity? The charge has been raised in some quarters that in fact (though not in intention) Rahner's christology falls short of the dogmas of Nicaea and Chalcedon.[130] While a full discussion of these issues is not possible here, the basic outline of Rahner's response may be noted. To Rahner, profession that Jesus is divine (in the nonmythological sense of the church's teaching) is not an addition to the confession that he is the Christ, but an explicitation of the latter statement's inherent meaning. Much as Anselm argued that only a divine figure can save by offering acceptable satisfaction for sin, Rahner argues that only a divine figure can save by definitively mediating participation in God's own life. In his judgment, at least, his understanding of Jesus as the definitive Savior includes the full content of Chalcedon's doctrine.[131]

### Edward Schillebeeckx

In sharp contrast to Rahner's emphasis on salvation as perfection of the good, Edward Schillebeeckx finds the starting point and permanent context of his christology in the universal human experience of evil. To Schillebeeckx, human history is an extended search for

---

130. For criticism of Rahner on this score see Heinz-Jürgen Vogels, "Erreicht Karl Rahners Theologie den kirchlichen Glauben?: Kritik der Christologie und Trinitätslehre Karl Rahners," *Wissenschaft und Weisheit* 52 (1989): 21–62. For a defense of the orthodoxy of Rahner's thought see Joseph H. P. Wong, *Logos-Symbol in the Christology of Karl Rahner* (Rome: LAS, 1984), and idem, "Karl Rahner's Christology of Symbol and Three Models of Christology," *Heythrop Journal* 27 (1986): 1–25.

131. For brief articulations of Rahner's position see his "Jesus Christ," in *Sacramentum Mundi*, 3:204–5, and *The Love of Jesus and the Love of Neighbor* (New York: Crossroad, 1983), 26–30.

meaning and liberation in the midst of suffering. No purely theoretical account of evil is of value; what is needed is action to overcome what ought not be.

Yet action requires foundation and support: a source of inspiration and of hope, and a memory of past injustice and suffering. In these respects, narrative holds more promise than theory: "People do not *argue* against suffering, but tell a *story*.... Christianity does not give any explanation for suffering, but demonstrates a way of life."[132] The primary form of christology, set from the start in a soteriological context, is to retell "the life-story of the man Jesus as a story of God."[133]

Aware that our access to Jesus is mediated through the church's response to his person and life, Schillebeeckx engages in detailed study of Jesus' preaching and conduct and evaluates them as an offer of definitive salvation from God. Since the general course of events offers no basis for this conviction on Jesus' part, Schillebeeckx posits a unifying source of Jesus' activity in his unique experience of God as unsurpassably close and as the committed opponent of all that is inhuman. (Alluding to Mark 14:36, Romans 8:15, and Galatians 4:6, though not relying on these texts in isolation, Schillebeeckx designates this reality as Jesus' "abba-experience," a term that has become identified with his theology.) In both historical analysis and systematic reflection, Schillebeeckx favors the category of eschatological prophet, the long-awaited prophet-like-Moses with whom God speaks face to face (see Deut. 18:15-18), as a vehicle for articulating Jesus' status and significance. The eschatological prophet is not simply an apocalyptic preacher of a message about the approaching end of the world. Rather, the eschatological prophet is a unique figure, God's definitive salvific representative in human history.

Since Jesus' person and message are inseparable, it is not surprising that the conflict engendered by popular rejection of his message culminated in his execution. Long aware of the possibility of a violent end, Jesus gradually became certain of death's approach. Retaining assurance of personal salvation and somehow integrating his approaching fate into his understanding of his mission, he left his death, as a kind of final prophetic sign, for his followers to interpret. In principle his death is a triumph of evil, an assault on the offer of salvation that Jesus embodied, though the manner in which he confronted and endured death imbued the entire event with a certain salvific significance. (In a sense, Schillebeeckx argues, we are

---

132. Schillebeeckx, *Christ*, 698–99.
133. Schillebeeckx, *Jesus*, 80.

redeemed more despite the death of Jesus than because of it.) In any case, death was not the last word. Renewed experiences of grace and of forgiveness of sin through Jesus soon led to a reassembling of the disciples, scattered at the time of the crucifixion, at the initiative of Peter. Thus the church experienced anew Jesus' salvific presence and recognized in faith that he had been raised from the dead.

Yet, for Schillebeeckx, the story does not end here. From the start the narrative has concerned an encounter: "The starting point of the Christian movement was an indissoluble whole consisting on the one hand of the offer of salvation through Jesus and on the other of the Christian response in faith."[134] This structure is retained in later periods as well, from the New Testament to the present day.

While interpretive categories have varied widely, underlying the entire history is a common experience of definitive salvation from God in Jesus. Schillebeeckx is unwilling to flesh this formula out more fully with individual biblical categories, for he is convinced that "New Testament Christianity can only be a model indirectly, and not directly,"[135] for later believers. Instead he distills from an analysis of the disparate New Testament material four structural principles, present throughout Christian history and normative for any Christian soteriology: (1) Salvation is offered in and through God's history with humanity. (2) Salvation has a christological nucleus, for the true countenance of God is shown in Jesus of Nazareth. (3) The history of Jesus is inseparable from our own history as his followers. (4) The conclusion of the story is eschatological, for it cannot be completed within the confines of world history. Without these four ingredients (God; Jesus; church; future) a story ceases to be Christian.[136]

Against this background, Schillebeeckx outlines a provisional sketch of soteriology. Axiomatic is the principle that God does not will human suffering. Salvation includes both earthly and eschatological dimensions. During the course of history, the divine promise of salvation is present in efficacious but fragmentary acts of reconciliation, anticipatory of future salvation.[137]

Schillebeeckx's christological project has generated intense discussion. Critics have questioned especially the adequacy of his classification of Jesus as the eschatological prophet and of his reconstruction

---

134. Schillebeeckx, *Christ*, 66.

135. Ibid., 561.

136. For the four structural principles, whose systematic importance is greater than the brevity of their presentation suggests, see *Christ*, 629–44, and *Interim Report*, 37, 51–55, 122–24.

137. For a brief summary of Schillebeeckx's christological project, work on which is not yet complete, see "Jesus the Prophet," in *God among Us* (New York: Crossroad, 1983), 33–44.

of the revelation of the resurrection. Further clarification of his views and explanation of their relationship to more traditional expressions of christology may be found in his published correspondence with the Congregation for the Doctrine of the Faith.[138]

The differences between the conceptions of Schillebeeckx and Rahner, especially evident in their theological assessments of the crucifixion and resurrection, should not blur recognition of common themes in their analyses of the historical Jesus and other important christological issues. Nor should it be imagined that their works exhaust recent thought on Jesus; among other studies, Raymund Schwager's rethinking of soteriology on the basis of René Girard's anthropological theory and Jon Sobrino's pursuit of christology from the perspective of a theology of liberation deserve special mention.[139] But Rahner and Schillebeeckx do stand as the most prominent contemporary models of two traditional approaches to christological reasoning: reflection on Jesus as the perfection of God's good creation, and reflection on Jesus as the divine remedy for the problem of evil.

# CONCLUSION

The bulk of this chapter has sought to identify central issues in the field of christology and to examine Christian thought on its various facets from its origins to the present. After examining various strands of christological thinking contained in the canonical New Testament, I traced the development of the church's normative doctrine on the person of Christ and the articulation of the classical interpretations of his redemptive activity. Turning from the themes of the patristic and medieval periods to the critical historical questioning characteristic of modernity, I first surveyed the development and implications of research into the public life of Jesus, his crucifixion, and his resurrection, and then considered in outline form the christological conceptions of two major contemporary theologians, Karl Rahner and Edward Schillebeeckx. In each of these areas, basic christological data have been presented, though none of the topics has been treated exhaustively. Now this compact reflection on Jesus

---

138. See Ted Schoof, ed., *The Schillebeeckx Case* (New York: Paulist, 1984).

139. See Raymund Schwager, *Must There Be Scapegoats? Violence and Redemption in the Bible* (San Francisco: Harper and Row, 1987); idem, *Der wunderbare Tausch*; idem, *Jesus im Heilsdrama: Entwurf einer biblischen Erlösungslehre* (Innsbruck: Tyrolia, 1990); Jon Sobrino, *Christology at the Crossroads* (Maryknoll, N.Y.: Orbis Books, 1976), and *Jesus in Latin America* (Maryknoll, N.Y.: Orbis Books, 1987).

Christ as the object and foundation of Christian faith will conclude with a few principles that may serve as reference points in developing and assessing christologies.

First, despite the passage of time, the christologies of the New Testament and the dogmatic definitions of the early councils retain their significance as norms against which later theological formulations must be measured. Contemporary christologies need not, and presumably in many instances will not, make use of the terminologies and modes of inquiry of the biblical and patristic periods. But modern thought about Jesus can be assessed by reference to these standards, to determine if new formulations fall short of fundamental Christian affirmations.

Second, both Jesus' own preaching of the kingdom of God and the church's subsequent proclamation of the Christian message presuppose an intrinsic link between the person of Jesus and the content of the gospel. To sever that connection is to deprive christology of its necessary foundation. In the past, this issue seemed easily resolved by appeal to Jesus' self-referential preaching in the Fourth Gospel, but in view of modern exegetical research it now requires more nuanced examination. An important task of christology is therefore to ascertain the relationship of Jesus' person and message and to elaborate its implications for understanding Jesus.

Third, as noted above, Christians have at various times related Jesus' salvific character to the incarnation, to his public life, to his death on the cross, or to his resurrection. Because each of these four reference points is intimately intertwined with the other three, it seems ultimately inconsistent to ascribe salvific value to one element of Jesus' existence in isolation from others. To speak, for example, of Jesus' public life as salvific without recognizing salvific value in his death (or vice versa) is to ignore the fact that Jesus' manner of life is what brought him to the cross. Christologies can therefore be tested by asking if their theological interpretations of the various reference points are consistent with the interrelationships inherent in their subject matter.

This third principle suggests a final consideration. To attribute salvific significance to the incarnation, public life, crucifixion, and resurrection taken severally is to dissolve christology into a series of disparate assertions without a unifying core. To prevent this from happening, one or another element will tend to be selected as the integrative factor. There is inevitably an element of decision in this choice, though the decision ought not be arbitrary. Over the course of the history of Christian thought, each of the four reference points has at times been accorded pride of place: the incarnation in much patristic thought; the incarnation and the crucifixion in medieval reflection; Jesus' public life in modern liberal theology; the resurrection in many christologies of recent vintage. That the public life of Jesus and the resurrection now receive such attention is in part a justified reaction against past neglect of these themes. Nonetheless, it may be doubted that they, alone or in tandem, are capable of sustaining the burden thus placed upon them. It is the crucifixion in which the public life of Jesus is epitomized and to which the resurrection is indissolubly linked. It is here that the focal point of christology—and of a life lived in discipleship—is to be found.

# FOR FURTHER READING

Grillmeier, Alois. *Christ in Christian Tradition*. Vol. 1. 2d ed. Atlanta: John Knox, 1975; vol. 2, pt. 1. Atlanta: John Knox, 1987.

Classic studies of christological thought in the patristic period.

Kasper, Walter. *Jesus the Christ*. New York: Paulist, 1976.

An informative textbook on christology, written by a well-known contemporary theologian.

Küng, Hans. *On Being a Christian*. Garden City, N.Y.: Doubleday, 1976.

A provocative presentation of the basics of Christian faith, with particular focus on christological issues.

Lane, Dermot. *The Reality of Jesus*. New York: Paulist, 1975.

A succinct introduction to christology.

Macquarrie, John. *Jesus Christ in Modern Thought*. London: SCM, 1990.

A thoughtful recent study of traditional themes and contemporary reflection on Christ.

Meier, John P. "Jesus." In *The New Jerome Biblical Commentary*. Ed. Raymond Brown et al. Englewood Cliffs, N.J.: Prentice Hall, 1990, pp. 1316–28.

A compressed but informative exegetical account of the historical Jesus.

Meyer, Ben F. *The Aims of Jesus*. London: SCM, 1979.

An overview of research on the historical Jesus and a thoughtful study, influenced by the work of Bernard Lonergan, on Jesus' goals.

O'Collins, Gerald. *Interpreting Jesus*. New York: Paulist, 1983.

An introductory textbook that attractively surveys the major issues.

Pannenberg, Wolfhart. *Jesus—God and Man*. Philadelphia: Westminster Press, 1968.

An influential modern examination of the grounds of Christian faith in Jesus Christ.

Pokorny, Petr. *The Genesis of Christology: Foundations for a Theology of the New Testament*. Edinburgh: T and T Clark, 1987.

Reflections by a Czech exegete on the origins of christological thought.

Rahner, Karl. *Foundations of Christian Faith*. New York: Seabury, 1978.

A summary of many major aspects of Rahner's theology, with particular focus on christology.

Schillebeeckx, Edward. *Jesus: An Experiment in Christology*. New York: Seabury, 1979. Idem. *Christ: The Experience of Jesus as Lord*. New York: Seabury, 1980.

The first two parts of a contemporary christological synthesis, by an eminent Dominican theologian.

Schwager, Raymund. *Must There Be Scapegoats? Violence and Redemption in the Bible*. San Francisco: Harper and Row, 1987.

A new interpretation, much influenced by the anthropological thought of René Girard, of the soteriological significance of Jesus' death.

Sobrino, Jon. *Jesus in Latin America*. Maryknoll, N.Y.: Orbis Books, 1987.

A presentation of christology from the perspective of the theology of liberation.

Witherington, Ben. *The Christology of Jesus*. Minneapolis: Fortress Press, 1990.

A thorough recent study of Jesus' self-understanding.

# INDEX

Page numbers following a Roman numeral I are in volume 1.
Those following a Roman numeral II are in volume 2.